THE NATIONAL TRUST
HANDBOOK

A GUIDE FOR MEMBERS AND VISITORS
MARCH 1994 TO MARCH 1995

HAM HOUSE

THE NATIONAL TRUST
36 Queen Anne's Gate, London SW1H 9AS
Tel. 071-222 9251

Registered Charity No.205846

IMPORTANT NOTES FOR NATIONAL TRUST MEMBERS

CRAGSIDE

Illustrations by: Norman Charlton, F. N. Colwell, Brian Delf, John Dyke, Brin Edwards, John Finnie, Lillias, Claude Page, Ian Penney, Eric Thomas, Soun Vannithone, Geoffrey Wood

Front cover: The entrance front of Springhill, County Londonderry, Northern Ireland (see p.299)
Photo: National Trust Photographic Library/Matthew Antrobus

Back cover: Children enjoying a visit to Charlecote Park, Wellesbourne, Warwickshire (see p.241)
Photo: National Trust Photographic Library/Mike Caldwell

© The National Trust 1994

ISBN 0 7078 0178 8
Designed by Pardoe Blacker Ltd, Lingfield, Surrey
Phototypeset in Monotype Lasercomp Photina Series 747
by Southern Positives and Negatives (SPAN), Lingfield, Surrey
Printed by Cox & Wyman Ltd, Reading

IMPORTANT NOTES FOR NATIONAL TRUST MEMBERS

Contents

About the National Trust	4
From the Director-General	5
How to use this Handbook	6
Information for all visitors	8
Opening arrangements and admission fees	8
Children 8; School parties 8; Group visits 8	
Visitors with Disabilities	9
Pensioners	9
Free Entry Day	9
Special information for members	10
Publications	11
Visitor Constraints, Comfort and Safety	12
Feedback	17
Associations and Centres	22
National Trust Enterprises	18
Who to contact in the National Trust	19
Regional Offices	final page
Key to symbols	22
Properties open to the public	23
Index	301

How you can support the National Trust
DONATIONS 7   VOLUNTEERS 11   MEMBERSHIP 15
ROYAL OAK FOUNDATION U.S.A. 17   LEGACIES 23

IMPORTANT NOTES FOR NATIONAL TRUST MEMBERS

About the National Trust

The National Trust

- is a charity
- is completely independent of the Government
- owns and protects over 580,000 acres of the most beautiful countryside in Britain, and 541 miles of outstanding coast
- protects and opens to the public over 300 historic houses, great and small, and over 150 of the finest gardens
- spends all its income on the care and maintenance of the land and buildings under its protection
- The National Trust can fulfil its purposes only because of the generosity of its supporters, through membership subscriptions, gifts of money and of time as volunteers, legacies and income produced by visitors to its properties, restaurants and shops
- was founded in 1895 and is approaching its centenary
- is governed by an Act of Parliament and has the unique power to declare its properties inalienable. This means that although they may be leased with the approval of the Charity Commission, they cannot be sold or mortgaged or compulsorily purchased against the wishes of the National Trust without the approval of Parliament. Nearly all Trust properties are held inalienably, in perpetuity, for the benefit of the nation. This special power enables the National Trust to ensure preservation forever
- looks after forests, woods, fens, farmland, downs, moorland, islands, archaeological remains, nature reserves and even villages. Wherever you go you will be close to land protected by the National Trust which is open to the public at all times subject only to the needs of farming, forestry and the protection of wildlife

LACOCK ABBEY

IMPORTANT NOTES FOR NATIONAL TRUST MEMBERS

Dear Supporter,

It gives me great pleasure to introduce the National Trust Handbook for 1994, and the early months of 1995 during which our Centenary celebrations will be gathering momentum.

As we make ready for the Centenary it has been decided not to promote a special theme for 1994. We do, however, intend to emphasise the beauty and variety of the many gardens in the Trust's care in England, Wales and Northern Ireland.

I should also like to draw attention to the re-opening to the public of Ham House, on the Thames at Richmond. Ham is one of the best and most complete examples in England of Stuart architecture and decoration, and contains fine furniture and pictures. During the past two years it has been closed for extensive restoration, the installation of new wiring and fire & security systems, and the creation of a new restaurant in the Orangery. Formerly in the care of the Victoria and Albert Museum, who continue to own its contents, Ham now re-opens under the Trust's management, and I hope readers of this Handbook may find an opportunity to visit it in 1994.

This year for the first time we welcome Frizzell Insurers as sponsors of this Handbook: we are most grateful to them. I also wish to express once again the Trust's deep appreciation and thanks to all its members, whose loyal support enables us to carry out our important conservation work.

Angus Stirling

Angus Stirling
Director-General

IMPORTANT NOTES FOR NATIONAL TRUST MEMBERS

How to use this Handbook

The National Trust Handbook gives details of how to visit National Trust properties open to the public. The properties are listed alphabetically within each county, and each entry gives a brief description of the property, the postal address and telephone number (wherever possible). Symbols are used to show facilities available on site. Please check the symbols at the top of each entry before visiting a property – a key is given on p.22.

County entries usually begin with a description of the Trust's coast and countryside properties. An outline map shows the locations of these, as well as the buildings and gardens. More detailed information about the Trust's landholdings is given in Properties of the National Trust, available free from the **Membership Department P.O. Box 39, Bromley, Kent BR1 1NH.**

HOW TO GET THERE ➔

At the end of each property entry is a brief description of location together with a grid reference. Car parking is usually available within 100 yards of the property.

Wherever possible, details of access by public transport are given. Please note that no indication of frequency of transport services is given, so check the times of services before setting out. 'Passing BR' (NIR in Northern Ireland) indicates the bus service passes the station entrance or approach road and 'Passing close BR' indicates that a walk is necessary. Unless otherwise stated bus services pass the property, and the railway station name is followed by the distance from the property.

Wheelchair users travelling by train should note that some stations are unstaffed. These are followed by a (U).

The National Trust is grateful to Barry Doe, a life member, for this travel information. If you experience difficulties following this information or have suggestions to make, he will be glad to reply to your comments. Please contact him at: Travadvice, 25 Newmorton Road, Moordown, Bournemouth, Dorset BH9 3NU. Tel. (0202) 528707.

COTEHELE

IMPORTANT NOTES FOR NATIONAL TRUST MEMBERS

How you can support the National Trust
MAKING A GIFT TO THE NATIONAL TRUST

Whether or not you are a member of the National Trust, you can contribute directly to the funding of vital conservation work. Millions of pounds are needed to continue this invaluable work at properties – houses, gardens, coast and countryside – throughout the country.

Please become one of the National Trust's much-valued supporters, funding specific, long-term conservation projects such as the restoration of the medieval moated manor house at Ightham Mote in Kent, Lake District countryside, or coastline acquisition under the Enterprise Neptune campaign.

For details of how to make a gift, contact the **National Trust's Membership Department, P.O. Box 39, Bromley, Kent, BR1 1NH.**

IGHTHAM MOTE

IMPORTANT POINTS ABOUT THE HANDBOOK

- Information in this Handbook is valid from 30 March 1994 to 31 March 1995
- Details are correct at the time of going to press, but are subject to revision
- Opening times and arrangements vary from property to property, and from year to year
- Last admissions are usually half an hour before the stated closing time
- Properties open during the winter months are usually closed on Christmas Day, Boxing Day and New Year's Day
- Please call the property in advance if you have any queries about your visit, but note that properties can provide a better service if calls are made on weekday mornings on days when the property is open

IMPORTANT NOTES FOR NATIONAL TRUST MEMBERS

Information for all visitors

Please read these notes carefully as they apply to all National Trust properties.

OPENING ARRANGEMENTS AND ADMISSION FEES

Members of the National Trust are admitted free to most properties (see Special Information for National Trust members, p.10).

Each property entry shows the normal adult admission fee. These include VAT and are liable to change if the VAT rate is altered.

Children: under 5s are free. Children under 17 are half the adult price, unless stated. Children not accompanied by an adult are admitted at the Trust's discretion.

School parties: many properties offer educational facilities and programmes. Teachers are urged to make a free preliminary visit by prior arrangement with the property. Reductions are usually available for groups of 15 or more schoolchildren aged under 19. Education Group Membership is recommended.

Group visits: Reductions are usually available for pre-booked groups of 15 or more. Group organisers are urged to book visits and arrange meals with the property in advance – it may not always be possible to admit groups which have not booked.

THE NATIONAL GARDENS SCHEME

Each year many of the National Trust's gardens are open specially in support of the National Gardens Scheme. Money raised on these days is donated by NGS to the MacMillan Nurses Fund and to projects in National Trust Gardens. The National Trust is pleased to ackowledge with gratitude the generous, continuing support of the National Gardens Scheme.

BELTON HOUSE

IMPORTANT NOTES FOR NATIONAL TRUST MEMBERS

VISITORS WITH DISABILITIES

The National Trust warmly welcomes to its properties visitors with physical, sensory and learning disabilities; also guide dogs for the blind and hearing dogs for the deaf. Most properties have a good degree of access, and manual wheelchairs are provided at the majority of houses and gardens. An increasing number of self-drive and volunteer-driven powered buggies are available at larger gardens and parks.

The necessary companion of a disabled visitor is admitted free of charge, while the normal charge applies to the disabled visitor.

For each property the paragraph signed with the wheelchair symbol indicates the facilities available for wheelchair users. The Sympathetic Hearing Scheme operates at many properties, and Braille guides are available at a large number of houses. General information and a free 48-page colour booklet on access are available from Mrs Valerie Wenham, Adviser, Facilities for Disabled Visitors (see p.19 for London Head Office address). Please enclose stamped addressed adhesive label, minimum postage.

Large-print copies of both the access booklet and information on individual counties from this Handbook are also available on request from Mrs Wenham.

PENSIONERS

As an independent registered charity, with no regular support from the Government, the National Trust regrets it cannot afford to offer pensioners a reduction in admission fees.

FREE ENTRY DAY

Each year the National Trust organises a day when all visitors are admitted free to many properties. It provides an opportunity to visit a Trust property for those who may not otherwise be able to do so. The Trust is grateful to the Rotary and Lions Clubs, and many others, who in 1993 provided transport and assistance to elderly, disabled and disadvantaged visitors on this day. Because Free Entry Day is generally very busy, National Trust members may prefer to plan their visits on quieter days. For the same reason we request that coach operators bringing groups must book their visits on Free Entry Day in advance with the property.

This year's Free Entry Day will be on Wednesday 14 September (1994).

IMPORTANT NOTES FOR NATIONAL TRUST MEMBERS

Special Information for National Trust members

- Membership of the National Trust allows you free entry to most properties open to the public, during normal opening times and under normal opening arrangements, **on presentation of a valid membership card.**
- Please check that you have your card with you before you set out on your journey as you cannot be admitted free of charge without it, and the Trust cannot refund members' entrance charges subsequently.
- If your card is lost or stolen, please contact the Membership Department (address on p.19) Tel. 081-464 1111 Monday to Friday, 9am to 5pm.
- A replacement card can be sent to a temporary address if you are on holiday. Voluntary donations to cover the administrative costs of replacement are always welcome.
- Membership cards are not transferable.
- Free entry is not guaranteed; additional charges may be made for the following:
  - When a special event is in progress at a property
  - When a property is opened specially for a National Gardens Scheme open day
  - Where the management of a property is not under the National Trust's direct control eg. Lyme Park, Cheshire, managed by Stockport MBC
  - Where special attractions are not an integral part of the property eg. Steam Yacht Gondola in Cumbria
- Entry to properties owned by the Trust but maintained and administered by English Heritage or Cadw (Welsh Historic Monuments) is free to members of the Trust, English Heritage and Cadw.
- Members of the National Trust are also admitted free to properties of the National Trust for Scotland. The National Trust for Scotland Guide to over 100 properties can be obtained by sending a self-addressed adhesive label and £1.50 to the National Trust for Scotland (see address on p.19).
- Reciprocal visiting arrangements also exist with certain overseas trusts including Australia, New Zealand, Barbados, Bermuda, Canada, Jersey, Guernsey and the Manx Museum on the Isle of Man. For a full list please send a s.a.e. to the National Trust Membership Department.
- National Trust members visiting properties owned by the National Trust for Scotland or overseas Trusts are only eligible for free entry on presentation of a valid membership card.

IMPORTANT NOTES FOR NATIONAL TRUST MEMBERS

How you can support the National Trust
WORKING FOR THE NATIONAL TRUST AS A VOLUNTEER

The National Trust invites the practical involvement of members through its developing volunteer programme. Some 26,000 volunteers, both members and non-members of all ages and backgrounds, support the Trust's permanent staff as active partners. In over 140 different ways they work in tasks ranging from the highly skilled and professional to those requiring only a gift of time and enthusiasm.

More room stewards are required at many houses. There are plenty of opportunities including inexpensive working holidays for outdoor conservation tasks. Offers of help for the Trust's fundraising activities are particularly welcome. Appropriate training is given.

To learn more about

- becoming an individual volunteer
- joining one of our 80 NTV, Friends or property-based groups
- taking part in one of our 400 environmental working holidays for people of all ages

send an s.a.e. to the **National Trust's Membership Department, P.O. Box 39, Bromley, Kent, BR1 1NH.**

Publications

The Trust produces a wide range of books. Most of these are available in National Trust shops and good bookshops, but you can also order them from the Mail Order Department, P.O. Box 101, Melksham, Wiltshire SN12 8EA. Copies of guidebooks to Trust properties, which include the souvenir Book of the House series, can be obtained from the London office (see address on p.19). If you would like a full list of publications, please write to the Trust's London address (enclosing s.a.e.).

NATIONAL TRUST HANDBOOKS

The Trust also publishes a series of supplementary Handbooks, which provide visitors with more specific information about the Trust's properties.

The Historic Houses Handbook gives details of the architectural history and important collections to be found in the historic houses of the National Trust

IMPORTANT NOTES FOR NATIONAL TRUST MEMBERS

The Family Handbook this new edition provides hundreds of ideas for a day out to a National Trust property for the whole family

The Gardens Handbook is a comprehensive guide to more than 130 National Trust gardens – new edition

The Countryside Handbook a selection of the most accessible and outstanding areas of National Trust countryside

Visitor constraints, comfort and safety

Visitors will recognise that the contents and fabric of many of the Trust's houses are fragile and valuable. After many years of thought and research into methods of improving preventive conservation and security, certain restrictive measures have been introduced. These constraints on visitors are essential to the safekeeping of houses in the Trust's care – by respecting them you will be helping the Trust to ensure that its houses and contents are preserved for future generations to enjoy. Symbols indicating restrictions are positioned to the right-hand side on the line following the property name.

FAMILIES

The Trust is committed to providing a welcoming, worthwhile and enjoyable visit for families with children. Many properties – and the number increases every year – provide baby feeding areas, nappy changing facilities (often combined in a purpose-designed parent and baby room), high chairs in restaurants together with children's menus and even occasionally play areas within restaurants. The range of children's guides to properties is expanding rapidly.

There is still much to do to improve facilities for families with children at National Trust properties, but equally we need to ask parents to observe a few important restrictions: prams, pushchairs and back carriers are not allowed inside historic houses, for the convenience of other visitors and to prevent damage to contents and floors.

For visitors with babies, front slings are usually available on loan, and occasionally reins for toddlers. The Trust recognises that the restriction on back-carriers causes particular difficulties for parents with older and/or heavier babies. We ask parents to recognise and understand the difficulties which the Trust faces in preserving historic properties and their contents in perpetuity. Please ask property staff for help and advice.

IMPORTANT NOTES FOR NATIONAL TRUST MEMBERS

PHOTOGRAPHY

The National Trust welcomes amateur photography out-of-doors at its properties. The Trust regrets, however, that such photography is not permitted indoors when houses are open to visitors.

For 1994, the Trust is happy to make special arrangements for interested amateurs (including voluntary National Trust lecturers, research students and academics) to take interior photographs by appointment outside normal opening hours. **Applications must be made in writing to the property concerned, for a mutually convenient appointment.**

All requests for commercial photography must be channelled through the appropriate Regional Office for permission.

SHOES

Any heel which covers an area smaller than a postage stamp can cause irreparable damage to all floors, carpets and rush matting. We regret, therefore, that sharp-heeled shoes are not permitted. When necessary, plastic slippers are provided for visitors with unsuitable or muddy footwear. Alternative slippers are available for purchase.

LARGE BAGS

At some properties visitors will be asked to leave behind large items of hand luggage while they make their visit. This is to protect furniture and contents from accidental damage and to improve security. This restriction includes rucksacks, large handbags, carrier bags, bulky shoulder bags and camera/camcorder bags. These bags can be safely left at the entrance to any house where the restriction applies (principally historic houses with vulnerable contents, fragile decorative surfaces or narrow visitor routes).

SMOKING

Smoking is not permitted inside National Trust houses, restaurants or shops. It is also discouraged in gardens, since the scent of flowers is such an important part of visitors' enjoyment in a garden.

DOGS

Dogs (except guide dogs) are not allowed inside National Trust houses and restaurants and seldom in gardens. Properties with no suitable areas for dogs are indicated by the no dogs symbol.

The symbol showing a dog on a lead indicates properties which welcome dogs on

IMPORTANT NOTES FOR NATIONAL TRUST MEMBERS

leads in their grounds (not gardens). In these cases dogs must be kept on the lead at all times to protect deer and grazing livestock.

Dogs are welcome at most countryside properties providing they are kept under control. However the Trust has introduced a restriction on dogs at some family beaches during the summer (contact the London office for details, address on p.19).

Conscious of the dangers associated with leaving dogs in cars, the Trust endeavours to provide a shady parking space in its car parks, water for drinking bowls, hitching posts where dogs may be safely left and advice on suitable areas where dogs may be exercised. These facilities will vary from property to property, and according to how busy it may be on a particular day. The primary responsibility for the welfare of their dogs remains of course with their owner.

SEATING

Seats for visitors' use are provided at various points in all the Trust's historic houses and gardens. Those visitors who wish to sit down – whether elderly, infirm, pregnant or simply tired – should feel free to use the seats available, or ask a room steward if seating is not immediately obvious.

HEAVILY VISITED PROPERTIES

Many properties are extremely popular on Bank Holidays and summer weekends. At some houses timed tickets may be issued to smooth the flow of people entering the property (not to limit the duration of a visit), and all visitors (including NT members) are required to use these tickets. This system is designed to create better viewing conditions for visitors and to minimise wear-and-tear on the historic interiors. On rare occasions entry to the property may not be possible on that day.

ENVIRONMENTAL CONTROL

Blinds are wholly or partly drawn in most rooms to protect contents from fading and decay caused by daylight. Light levels are carefully monitored to ensure reasonable viewing conditions and good preventive conservation.

HEALTH AND SAFETY

The National Trust endeavours to provide a safe and healthy environment for visitors at its properties as far as is reasonably practicable, and to ensure that the activities of its staff and contractors working on Trust properties do not in any way jeopardise the health and safety of visitors. You can help the Trust by observing all notices and signs relating to this subject during your visit, by following any instructions given by Trust staff, by ensuring that children are properly supervised and by wearing appropriate clothing and footwear at outdoor properties.

How you can support The National Trust
MEMBERSHIP

As a member of the National Trust you can enjoy free admission to the very best of the nation's heritage. As the National Trust is an independent charity, members make a direct contribution to the upkeep of well-loved landscapes as well as the historic houses and gardens in our care.

Members receive a membership card giving free entry to most Trust properties and three mailings a year which include the National Trust Handbook, *The National Trust Magazine*, a gift catalogue and regional newsletters.

A wide range of annual and life membership categories is available and are shown on the form overleaf. If you are already a member yourself, membership makes an excellent birthday or Christmas gift, and lasts all year round.

For immediate membership, you can join at a National Trust property or shop. Alternatively complete the form overleaf and send it to: **The National Trust, Freepost, Bromley, Kent, BR1 1UG**

You can obtain further details of categories, including Education Group membership, or join by credit card, by calling the Membership Department on 081-464 1111 (lines are open Monday to Friday, 9am to 5pm).

Pre-1968 Individual Life Members
Life members who took out their membership before 1968 have cards which admit one person only. These members wishing to exchange 'admit one' for 'admit two' cards, or those wishing to change from one category of Life membership to another, should contact the Membership Department at the above address.

IMPORTANT NOTES FOR NATIONAL TRUST MEMBERS

Application for membership
TO: THE NATIONAL TRUST, FREEPOST, BROMLEY, KENT BR1 1UG

Twelve-month membership

☐	**Individual:**	**£24**	and, for each additional member residing at the same address, £15. One card for each member.
☐	**Family group:**	**£44**	**one** card for two parents or partners and all their children under 18, living at the same address. One card covers the family.
☐	**Under 23:**	**£11**	please give date of birth

Life membership

☐	**Individual:**	**£575**	(£375 if aged 60 or over and retired). The card admits the member and a guest.
☐	**Joint:**	**£680**	for lifetime partners (£450 if either partner is aged 60 or over and retired). Separate card, each admitting one person.
☐	**Family joint:**	**£780**	Two cards, each admitting one partner and their children under 18 living at the same address. Please give date of birth.

PLEASE COMPLETE THE FORM IN CAPITALS

SOURCE 0069	DATE	
FULL ADDRESS		
		POSTCODE

TITLE	INITIALS	SURNAME	DATE OF BIRTH

AMOUNT ATTACHED:
CHEQUE/POSTAL ORDER   £
Delete as appropriate

Please allow 28 days for receipt of your membership card

Credit card payments can be made by telephoning 081-464 1111 (office hours)

Immediate membership can be obtained by joining at a National Trust property or shop

We promise that any information you give will be used for National Trust purposes only. We will write to you about our work and will occasionally include details of products developed in association with the Trust. We would also like to send you separate details of products but should you prefer not to receive these separate mailings please tick this box.
Registered charity no. 205846

☐

IMPORTANT NOTES FOR NATIONAL TRUST MEMBERS

Feedback

The National Trust would welcome feedback from its members and visitors on occasions when they have encountered especially good service as well as when some element of a visit has proved less than satisfactory. Such feedback will be most appropriately directed to the manager of the property concerned. Alternatively, contact the relevant Regional Office or the Trust's London Head Office. Many properties provide their own suggestion forms and boxes which visitors are encouraged to use. All comments will be noted, and action taken where necessary, but it is not possible to answer every comment or suggestion individually.

The National Trust adheres to the English Tourist Board's Code of Conduct for Visitor Attractions, and supports the Wales Tourist Board's 'Welcome Host' campaign.

Supporting the National Trust in the U.S.A.
THE ROYAL OAK FOUNDATION

Please join the group of more than 30,000 Americans who help the National Trust by supporting the Royal Oak Foundation, the Trust's U.S. membership affiliate.

Royal Oak member benefits include the National Trust Handbook, Magazine and gift catalogue, the quarterly Royal Oak Newsletter, and free admission to properties of the National Trust and those of the National Trust for Scotland.

Royal Oak also awards scholarships to U.S. residents for study in Britain and sponsors lectures, tours and events in the U.S., designed to inform Americans of the Trust's work.

Royal Oak is a U.S. not-for-profit organisation which helps the National Trust through the generous tax-deductible support of members and friends by making grants for its conservation and preservation work.

For further information please write, call or fax **The Royal Oak Foundation, 285 West Broadway, New York, NY 10013, USA. Tel. 010 1 212 966 6565. Fax. 010 1 212 966 6619.**

IMPORTANT NOTES FOR NATIONAL TRUST MEMBERS

National Trust Enterprises

The National Trust's shops, restaurants, tea-rooms and holiday cottages are all managed by National Trust Enterprises. The profit they generate goes to support the work of the National Trust, and in 1992 contributed £5 million to the Trust's funds.

SHOPS

Most National Trust properties have shops offering a wide range of merchandise – much of which is exclusive to the National Trust. These shops and their opening times are indicated in relevant property entries by the X symbol. Many of these shops are also open for Christmas shopping and dates are given in the appropriate entries. In addition the Trust now operates a number of shops in towns which are open during normal trading hours (contact the National Trust Membership Department for a full list of locations).

RESTAURANTS AND TEA-ROOMS

The National Trust operates over 100 restaurants and tea-rooms at its properties. Many specialise in serving local specialities, some are licensed and all concentrate on home cooking.

HOLIDAYS WITH THE NATIONAL TRUST

The National Trust has around 200 holiday cottages in some of the most beautiful parts of England, Wales and Northern Ireland. Some have been specially adapted for disabled visitors.

These cottages are especially popular during the main holiday period and it is wise to book as far in advance as possible. Out of the main season short breaks are available. Further details of prices and bookings are given in a colour brochure National Trust Holiday Cottages 1994. For a copy of the brochure or enquiries about bookings please contact the National Trust Holiday Booking Office, PO Box 536, Melksham, Wiltshire SN12 8SX (tel. (0225) 791199 for bookings or (0225) 791133 for brochure orders). Please include a cheque/postal order for 75p made payable to The National Trust (Enterprises) Ltd to cover post and packing.

For details of the many National Trust tenants who offer B&B accommodation please write to the London address (enclosing s.a.e.) for a leaflet. If you are interested in self-catering holidays in Scotland please contact the National Trust for Scotland (see page 19) enclosing s.a.e.

The Landmark Trust also offers self-catering holiday accommodation in unusual historic buildings. (tel. (0628) 825925).

IMPORTANT NOTES FOR NATIONAL TRUST MEMBERS

Who to contact in the National Trust

The National Trust is very willing to answer questions and receive comments from its members and visitors. The following list indicates who to contact within the Trust for particular enquiries.

PROPERTIES

Telephone the property for queries about a particular place (see property entry for address and tel. number)

Telephone the regional office for queries relating to several properties in a region, or about other regional matters (see list of addresses on p.304)

USEFUL ADDRESSES

1. **National Trust Membership Department**, P.O. Box 39, Bromley, Kent BR1 1NH (tel. 081-464 1111) for membership queries
2. **London Head Office**, 36 Queen Anne's Gate, London, SW1H 9AS (tel. 071-222 9251) for queries of a national nature
3. **The National Trust London Information Centre**, Blewcoat School, 23 Caxton Street, Westminster, SW1H 0PY (tel. 071-222 2877) for queries about visiting properties in Greater London
4. **Volunteers Office**, 33 Sheep St, Cirencester, Glos GL7 1QW (tel. (0285) 651818), or contact the Regional Volunteer Co-ordinator in each region (see list of regional addresses, p.304) for offers of volunteer help
5. **National Trust Enterprises**, The Stable Block, Heywood House, Westbury, Wilts BA13 4NA (tel. (0373) 858787) for matters relating to shops, restaurants, holidays and the catalogue. For **Mail Order**, write to P.O. Box 101, Melksham, Wiltshire SN12 8EA (tel. (0225) 705676).
6. **National Trust for Scotland**, 5 Charlotte Square, Edinburgh, EH2 4DU (tel. (031) 226 5922)

IMPORTANT NOTES FOR NATIONAL TRUST MEMBERS

How you can support the National Trust
ASSOCIATIONS AND CENTRES

Make the most of your membership – join your nearest National Trust Association or Centre: 100,000 people already have.

What are National Trust Associations?
They are supporters' clubs which are run locally for National Trust members. With 187 associations in England, Wales and Northern Ireland there is bound to be one nearby to help you enjoy your membership and take an active part in the National Trust's work. Founded first in 1948, they were originally known as Centres.

What do they offer?
A varied programme of coach outings, lectures, parties, rambles, tours and holidays in Britain and abroad throughout the year. They also offer opportunities for practical support through fundraising and promotion of the National Trust locally and voluntary work at nearby Trust properties and offices.

How can you join?
Association membership is open to all current members of the National Trust in return for a small annual subscription to cover the cost of administration, newsletters and events.

To obtain the new free National Trust Associations leaflet, contact the National Trust Membership Department, P.O. Box 39, Bromley, Kent, BR1 1NH, or Tom Burr, Associations' Liaison Manager, Eastleigh Court, Bishopstrow, Warminster, Wiltshire, BA12 9HW.

IMPORTANT NOTES FOR NATIONAL TRUST MEMBERS

How you can support the National Trust
YOUR WILL CAN PROTECT THE PLACES YOU LOVE

Whatever their size, legacies are vital to the National Trust. They are used to fund major restoration projects or to acquire and endow new properties around the country. Legacies are not spent covering administration costs.

Including a legacy to the National Trust in your will could prevent your estate paying inheritance tax and would certainly help maintain Britain's heritage for future generations.

We appreciate the concern you take in our work to preserve the country's heritage. We have now written a free booklet for our members, giving you all the information you need about making your will or adding a codicil to an existing one.

Help us protect the places you love – send for our will booklet today.

For more information, fill in the coupon and send it to: The Head of the Legacies Unit, 36 Queen Anne's Gate, London SW1H 9AS.

Or telephone 071-222 9251

Yes, I would like to receive the free Will Advice Booklet ☐

Title and initials..

Surname (capitals please)..

Address ....

....

.... Postcode ....

Membership number..

IMPORTANT NOTES FOR NATIONAL TRUST MEMBERS

Key to Symbols

- Castle
- Historic house
- Other buildings
- Mill
- Church, chapel etc
- Garden
- Park
- Countryside
- Coast
- Prehistoric/Roman site
- Industrial archaeology
- Farm/farm animals
- Nature reserve
- Country walk*
- Open
- Guided tours**
- Heavily-visited property

- No sharp heels in building
- No bulky bags
- Admission details
- Wheelchair access
- For visually handicapped visitor
- Parent & baby facilities
- Education
- Dogs admitted on leads
- No dogs please
- Refreshments
- How to find the property
- Shop
- Events
- No photography

Map symbols:

- ▲ Buildings & gardens
- ■ Coast & country

*Waymarked routes or specially recommended walks are indicated by [symbol]. Leaflets describing many of these walks are available from Regional Offices.

**The symbol [symbol] on the top line of an entry indicates that guided tours are the rule: in the left hand margin it indicates that guided tours are available at certain times or by arrangement.

Avon

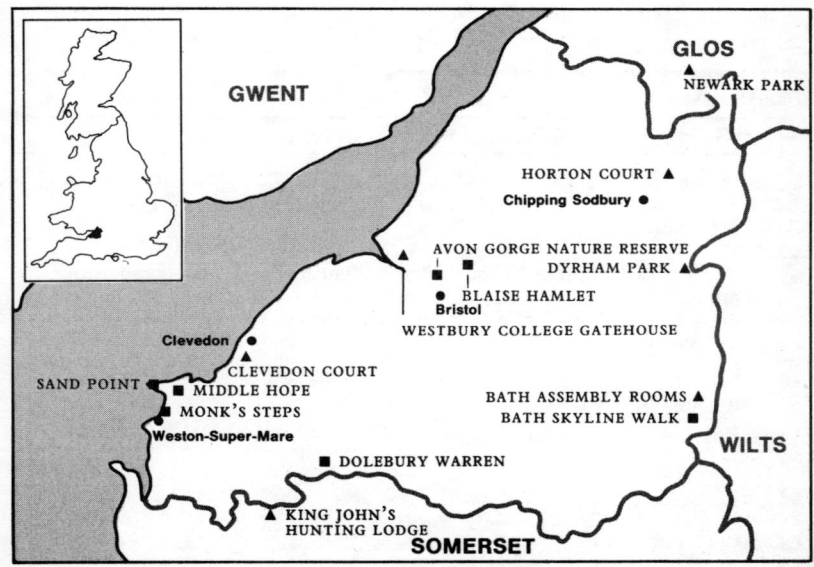

COUNTRYSIDE

At **Rainbow Wood** [172: ST777630] on Claverton Down, and **Smallcombe Wood** and fields [172: ST764640], at Bathwick, 560 acres of wood and farmland are part of the **Bath Skyline Walk**. A leaflet describes an 8-mile (or shorter) walk, past Iron Age field enclosures, ancient woodland and remains of the 18th-century expansion of Bath under Ralph Allen with breathtaking views across the city. Leaflet from NT Shop, Abbey Churchyard, Bath.

The **Avon Gorge Nature Reserve** on the west bank of the River Avon is approached from Bristol across the Clifton Suspension Bridge [172: ST560734]. Leigh Woods has flowers and fungi peculiar to the gorge, and an Iron Age hill-fort.

Blaise Hamlet, 4m N of central Bristol, W of Henbury village, just N of B4057 [172: ST559789], is a hamlet of nine different cottages designed in 1809 for John Harford by John Nash for Blaise Estate pensioners. Free access to the Green, cottages not open.

Dolebury Warren, 12m S of Bristol [182: ST450590] at Churchill is a wild and barren hilltop with one of the finest viewpoints in the Mendips dominated by an impressive Iron Age fort. The site is managed by the Avon Wildlife Trust.

COAST

A coastal path traverses the Trust properties of **Sand Point** at Kewstoke, north of Weston-super-Mare [182: ST325660] and the adjoining two miles of coastline at

23

AVON

Middle Hope. The limestone headland of **Sand Point** includes 'Castle Batch', thought to be a Norman motte. NT car park and WC's. The **Monk's Steps** at Kewstoke give views over the Severn estuary [182: ST336632]. Views from Middle Hope over the Bristol Channel to the Welsh mountains and to the Mendip Hills.

BATH ASSEMBLY ROOMS
Bennett Street, Bath BA1 2QH (0225) 461111 ext 2789

Designed by John Wood the Younger in 1769. The Rooms were bombed in 1942, re-opened 1963 and were restored and redecorated in 1979 and 1990. The Museum of Costume (not NT) housed in basement

- ◎ The Rooms are open to the public throughout Aug and when not in use for pre-booked functions. Visitors are advised to check in advance if Rooms are open. March to end Oct: Mon to Sat 9.30-6, Sun 10-6; also Nov to end Feb 1995: Mon to Sat 10-5, Sun 11-5. Closed 25 & 26 Dec
- £ No admission charge to Rooms; admission charge to Museum of Costume (incl. NT members)
- 𝑘 Hourly, when rooms not in use for pre-booked functions
- 🛈 Open daily
- ♿ Level access; WCs
- 🦮 Guide dogs only
- → N of Milsom Street, E of the Circus [156: ST749653] *Bus:* frequent from BR Bath Spa and surrounding areas (tel. (0225) 464446) *Station:* Bath Spa ¾m

CLEVEDON COURT
Twickenham Rd, Clevedon BS21 6QU (0275) 872257

Home of the Elton family, this 14th-century manor house, once partly fortified, has a 12th-century tower and 13th-century hall. The house contains a collection of Nailsea glass and Eltonware. There is a beautiful terraced garden

- ◎ 27 March to 29 Sept: Wed, Thur, Sun & BH Mon 2.30-5.30. Last admissions 5
- £ £3.30, children £1.60. Children under 17 must be accompanied by an adult. Parties of 20 or more and guided evening tours by prior arrangement; no reduction. Coaches by appointment. Unsuitable for trailer caravans or motor caravans
- 𝑘 Evening tours by prior arrangement. Pre-booked afternoon tours available for groups
- ♿ No wheelchairs; 4 steps to gain access to ground floor
- ☕ Tea-room in Old Great Hall 2.30-5 (not NT)
- 👶 Children's trail

AVON

School parties in the mornings by prior arrangement

1½m E of Clevedon, on Bristol road (B3130), signposted from exit 20 M5 [172: ST423716] *Bus:* Badgerline X7, 360-3, 662/3 from Bristol; X23/4, 823 from Weston-super-Mare, 360, 822/3 from Yatton (pass close BR Yatton). On all alight Clevedon Triangle (tel. (0272) 553231) *Station:* Yatton 3m

DYRHAM PARK
Dyrham Park, nr Chippenham SN14 8ER House (0272) 372501
Deer Park (0225) 891364

The mansion was built for William Blathwayt, Secretary at War and Secretary of State to William III, between 1691 and 1710. The rooms have been little changed since they were furnished by Blathwayt and their contents are recorded in his housekeeper's inventory. Surrounding the house, the 263-acre ancient parkland, with herd of fallow deer, overlooks the Severn Valley

Park: all year: daily 12-5.30 or dusk if earlier. Closed Christmas Day. Last admissions 5. **House & garden:** 26 March to 30 Oct: daily except Thur & Fri 12-5.30. Last admissions 5 or dusk if earlier

House, garden & park £4.80. Children £2.40. Deer Park only £1.50, children 80p. One coach per day by written appointment only *continued*

AVON

- Shop open same days as house, 12-5.30 (tel. (0272) 374300)
- Access to ground floor, Orangery and terrace only; parking by house. WC. Wheelchairs available
- Taped guide to house; Braille guide
- Refreshments in Orangery same days as house, 12-5.30; last orders 5; (tel. (0272) 374293). Picnics welcome in park, but parties over 20 please advise
- Children's Guide. Activity Trail Guides for house, park & garden, church
- School parties by appointment only; below stairs activities may be arranged
- Jazz concerts 8-9 July; Folk concert 9 July. For details contact the Events Organiser (tel. (0985) 847777)/(0225) 891364
- Dog walking area provided. No dogs in deer park
- 8m N of Bath, 12m E of Bristol; approached from Bath–Stroud road (A46), 2m S of Tormarton interchange with M4, exit 18 [172: ST743757] *Station:* Bath Spa 8m

HORTON COURT

Horton, nr Chipping Sodbury, Bristol BS17 6QR (0985) 847777

A Cotswold manor house with 12th-century Norman hall and early Renaissance features. Of particular interest is the late perpendicular ambulatory, detached from the house. Norman hall and ambulatory only shown

- 26 March to 29 Oct: Wed & Sat 2-6 or dusk if earlier. Other times by written appointment with tenant
- £1.50, children 80p. Unsuitable for coaches. No WCs
- Ambulatory only accessible; special parking facilities on application to tenant
- 3m NE of Chipping Sodbury, ¼m N of Horton, 1m W of the Bath–Stroud road (A46) [172: ST766851] *Station:* Yate 5m

WESTBURY COLLEGE GATEHOUSE

College Road, Westbury-on-Trym (0985) 847777

The 15th-century gatehouse of the College of Priests (founded in the 13th century) of which John Wyclif was a prebend

- Visitors to collect the key by prior written arrangement with the Rev. G. M. Collins, 44 Eastfield Road, Westbury-on-Trym, Bristol
- £1, children 50p
- 3m N of the centre of Bristol [172: ST572775] *Bus:* frequent from surrounding areas (tel. (0272) 553231) *Station:* Clifton Down 2m

Bedfordshire

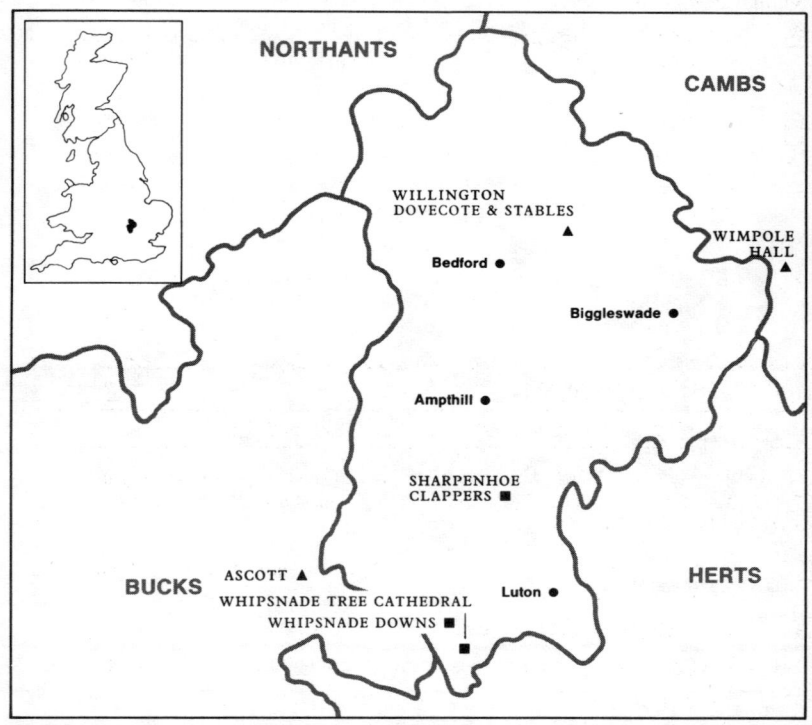

COUNTRYSIDE

At **Whipsnade Downs**, near Dunstable [166 & 165: TL000190], the Trust owns a 250-acre farm on the plateau and 50 acres of the chalk grassland on the scarp slope. There are views north towards Dunstable and west towards Ivinghoe Beacon (see Pitstone Windmill, p.36). On this stretch of unimproved downland, the Trust has re-introduced sheep grazing, the traditional form of management of these slopes. The effect has been to conserve the open grassland habitat which supports a rich variety of plants and insects. There is unrestricted access to the chalk downland; but only by footpaths across farmland. A car park is signposted off the B4540.

Whipsnade Tree Cathedral [166: TL008182] is one of the Trust's most unusual countryside properties. Many species of trees have been planted out in the traditional pattern of a cathedral, with grassy avenues for nave and transepts. This quiet, peaceful area may be reached from Whipsnade village green, beside which there is a car park. (An annual service is held at the cathedral; for details tel. the Regional Office.)

27

BEDFORDSHIRE

At the eastern end of the Chilterns, south-west of Barton-le-Clay, are the steep slopes of **Sharpenhoe Clappers** [166: TL067300]. The hilltop was the site of an Iron Age hill-fort. This stretch of the Chiltern scarp contains a wide variety of habitats, ranging from unimproved chalk grassland with its richly varied flora and fauna, through incipient and mature hawthorn scrub, to beech and ash woodland. Access to the viewpoint is from the car park beside the Streatley road, half a mile to the south.

MALLARD AND MOORHEN

WILLINGTON DOVECOTE & STABLES

Willington, nr Bedford

A 16th-century stables and stone dovecote, lined internally with nesting boxes for 1,500 pigeons

Note: the dovecote may be closed during May

- April to end Sept: by appointment with Mrs J. Endersby, 21 Chapel Lane, Willington MK44 3QG (tel. (0234) 838278)
- £1. No reduction for parties. Car park 30yds. No WCs
- Accessible, but floors uneven
- Guide dogs admitted by arrangement
- 4m E of Bedford, just N of the Sandy road (A603) [153: TL107499] *Bus:* United Counties 176–8 Bedford–Biggleswade (passing BR Bedford St John's & Biggleswade and close BR Sandy), alight Willington crossroads, ½m (tel. (0234) 262151) *Station:* Bedford St John's (U), not Sun, 4m; Sandy 4½m; Bedford 5m

Berkshire

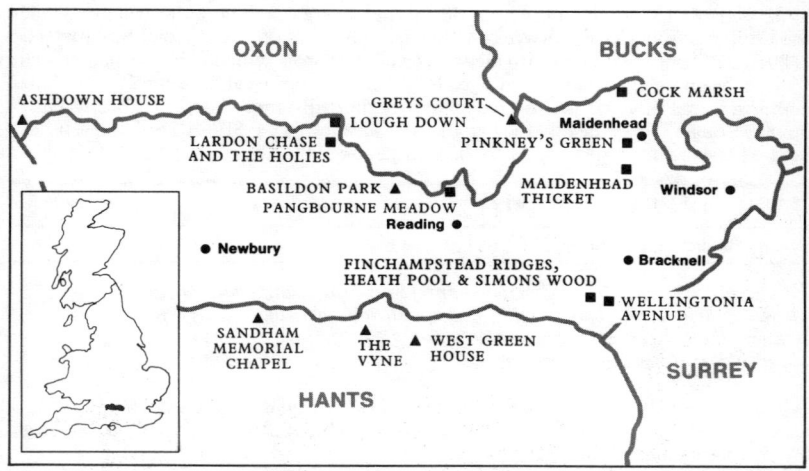

COUNTRYSIDE

Glimpses of Berkshire, Hampshire and Surrey may be seen from the steep, heather-clad ridge of **Finchampstead Ridges** [175: SU808634], 4 miles south of Wokingham, south of the B3348. The ridge overlooks the valley of the River Blackwater. North of the Ridges is **Simons Wood** [175: SU814637], a heathland and woodland area with a rich variety of tree species, including clumps of Scots pine over a century old. A popular walk is to **Heath Pool**, not far from a Roman ride known as 'The Devil's Highway'. The course of the London to Silchester Roman road also crosses the wood. The area has many attractions for naturalists and bird watchers, with siskins and spotted fly catchers among the species which may be sighted. You may park beside the B3348 at the Ridges, and further east along the same road there is a signposted car park in Simons Wood. Nearby is the impressive **Wellingtonia Avenue**, which forms part of the B3348. As its name suggests, it is lined by mature species of what is one of the world's tallest trees.

Common land on the south bank of the Thames at Maidenhead and Cookham provides a range of pleasant country walks. One of the features of **Maidenhead Thicket** [175: SU855810] is a prehistoric Belgic farm enclosure known for some reason as 'Robin Hood's Arbour'. The Thicket is perhaps at its most attractive in springtime, when a mass of primroses bloom here. Visitors may be fortunate enough to hear a nightingale.

Parts of **Cock Marsh** [175: SU890869], on the south bank of the Thames facing Bourne End, provide a fine example of a lowland marsh, a habitat which is increasingly at risk in Britain today. A group of burial barrows remains as evidence of Cock Marsh's ancient history. Adjoining Maidenhead Thicket to the north is **Pinkney's Green**, and in the same area the Trust also owns **Cookham Dean** village green, **Cookham Moor, Widbrook (or Whitebrook) Common, Bigfrith** and **Tugwood Commons**, and **North Town Moor**, half a mile north of Maidenhead and Winter Hill. Residents of the area bought and gave all these pleasant open spaces to the Trust in 1934. Today they con-

29

BERKSHIRE

tinue to be enjoyed by local people and visitors alike. There are several small car parks in the area, some of which are signposted.

The Holies [174: SU594797], **Lardon Chase** [174: SU588809] and **Lough Down** [174: SU588813] all lie on the west side of the Goring Gap where the Thames divides the Chilterns from the North Wessex Downs. The car park at the top of Streatley Hill [174: SU583806] gives access to all these properties, from which there are magnificent views. The chalk grassland is managed for its nature conservation interest. The Holies comprises grassland, scrub and woodland. A short distance away, just below Pangbourne Bridge, east of the B471 is Pangbourne Meadow [175: SU640768], a seven-acre area with some interesting flora, on the south bank of the Thames.

BASILDON PARK

Lower Basildon, Reading RG8 9NR (0734) 843040

A classical 18th-century house by John Carr of York, in a beautiful setting overlooking the Thames Valley. The focal point of the interior is an unusual Octagon room. The house also contains fine plasterwork, important pictures and furniture and a decorative shell room. There is a small formal garden and woodland walks

- **House:** 30 March to end Oct: Wed to Sat 2-6; Sun & BH Mon 12-6 (closed Good Fri & Wed following BH). **Grounds:** as house, but open 12-6 on Sat. Last admissions 5.30

- House and grounds £3.50. Family ticket £9. Grounds only £2.50. Family ticket £6. Party rates on application to Administrator: parties must book (no parties on Sun or BH Mon). Parking in grounds, 400yds from house

- Shop open 30 March to end Oct: Wed to Sat 2-5.30; Sun 1.30-5.30, BH Mon 12.30-5.30; Nov to 18 Dec: Fri 12-4; Sat & Sun 11-5 (tel. (0491) 671738)

- Access to garden via compacted gravel paths; tea-room accessible via ramps. Volunteer-driven buggy and stair-climber for house. Shop in stable yard; level access. Parking facilities for disabled drivers; please collect pass at ticket office; disabled passengers may be set down at house. WC in car park

- Braille guide

- Tea-room same months as house: teas Wed to Sun, also light lunches Sat, Sun & BH Mon; Wed to Fri 2-5.30; Sat, Sun & BH Mon 12-5.30. Also Nov to 18 Dec: Sat & Sun 12-4. Tel. (0734) 844080. Picnic area by car park

- High chair available in tea-room

- For details of summer events please send s.a.e. marked 'Events' to Administrator

- In grounds only, on leads. Not on main lawns near house

- Between Pangbourne and Streatley, 7m NW of Reading, on W side of A329; leave M4 at Jn 12 [175: SU611782] *Bus:* Oxford/Reading Bus 105; Reading-Oxford (passing BR Pangbourne) (tel. (0865) 711312). Also from Reading using Ridgeway X47 on summer Sundays. Tel. (0345) 090899 *Station:* Pangborne 2½m; Goring & Streatley 3m

REFER TO OPENING PAGES FOR GENERAL INFORMATION

Buckinghamshire

COUNTRYSIDE

The charming village of **Bradenham** [165: SU823970] to the north-west of High Wycombe belongs almost entirely to the Trust. There are over 1,000 acres of Chiltern beech woodland, hills and farmland to be explored. A network of paths provides easy access for the rambler. The church and 17th-century manor house provide an impressive backdrop to the sloping village green. The manor house, which is let and not open to the public, was once the home of Isaac Disraeli, whose Prime Minister son Benjamin lived at Hughenden Manor nearby (see p.35). Car parking is available at the village green.

Coombe Hill [165: SP849066], 3½ miles north-east of Princes Risborough, is the highest viewpoint in the Chilterns, rising to 852 feet. There are extensive views over the

BUCKINGHAMSHIRE

Vale of Aylesbury, towards the Berkshire Downs, to the Cotswolds north of Oxford and the woodland in which is set Chequers, the official country house of the Prime Minister. (The monument on Coombe Hill is not NT property.) During winter, sheep graze the chalk downland turf. In 1906, the then owner of Coombe Hill put fences on his property to keep the public out. However, the outraged people of nearby Wendover tore down the barriers and eventually public rights of way were legally established.

Adjoining Coombe Hill is **Low Scrubs**, bought by the National Trust in 1985. It includes an area of ancient beech coppice which was used for centuries by local poor people to provide fuel. There is a car park for both properties off the Dunsmore road [165: SP852063].

Pulpit Wood [165: SP832048], south of Coombe Hill, is a typical Chiltern beechwood, on which a hill-fort may be seen. This recent acquisition gives fine views over the Vale of Aylesbury. There is a small car park by the roadside [165: SP834045].

West Wycombe Hill and Village (see p.39) [175: SU829947] is situated 2 miles west of High Wycombe with fine views over West Wycombe Park (see p.39) and the surrounding countryside. The hill, on which is an Iron Age defended settlement, was given to the National Trust in 1935 just after the acquisition of most of the village a year earlier.

ASCOTT

Wing, nr Leighton Buzzard LU7 0PS (0296) 688242

Anthony de Rothschild collection of fine pictures, French and English furniture and exceptional Oriental porcelain. The garden contains unusual trees, flower borders, naturalised bulbs, water-lilies and a topiary sundial

- **O**   **House & garden:** 12 April to 15 May & 1–30 Sept: Tues to Sun 2–6. **Garden only:** 6 April & 18 May to 31 Aug: every Wed & last Sun in each month 2–6. Last admissions to House 5
- **£**   House & garden £5. Grounds only £3. No reduction for parties which must book. Parking 220yds
-     Access to ground floor only; limited access to garden; special parking by prior arrangement. WC
-     In car park only
- →   ½m E of Wing, 2m SW of Leighton Buzzard, on S side of A418 [165:SP891230] *Bus:* Aylesbury Bus/Wycombe Bus X14/15, 65, 325, Routemaster 5 Aylesbury–Leighton Buzzard (passing close BR Aylesbury & Leighton Buzzard) (tel. (0296) 382000) *Station:* Leighton Buzzard 2m

BOARSTALL DUCK DECOY

Boarstall, nr Aylesbury (0844) 237488

An 18th-century duck decoy in working order, in 13 acres of natural woodland; nature trail

- **O**   30 March to end Aug: Wed 4–7; Sat, Sun & BH Mon 10–5. School parties by arrangement. Talk/demonstration when Warden is available, Sat, Sun & BH Mon at 11 & 3. Exhibition Hall

BUCKINGHAMSHIRE

- [£] £2. Family ticket £5. Parties of six or more, which must book in advance, £1
- [♿] Nature trail, bird hide and decoy accessible in dry weather; ramps
- [🐕] In car park only
- [→] Midway between Bicester and Thame, 2m W of Brill [164 or 165: SP624151] *Station:* Bicester Town, (U), not Sun, 6½m; Bicester North, 7½m

BOARSTALL TOWER

Boarstall, nr Aylesbury HP18 9OX

The stone gatehouse of a fortified house long since demolished. It dates from the 14th century, and was altered in the 16th and 17th centuries, but retains its crossloops for bows. The tower is almost surrounded by a moat

- [O] By written appointment with tenant. May to end Sept: Wed 2–6
- [£] £1. No reduction for parties. No WCs
- [♿] Access to garden and ground floor of house (1 step); car park near house
- [🐕] In car park only
- [→] Midway between Bicester and Thame, 2m W of Brill [164 or 165: SP624141] *Station:* as for Boarstall Duck Decoy above

BUCKINGHAM CHANTRY CHAPEL

Market Hill, Buckingham

Rebuilt in 1475 and retaining a fine Norman doorway. The chapel was restored by Gilbert Scott in 1875, at which time it was used as a Latin or Grammar School

- [O] April to end Oct: by written appointment with the Buckingham Heritage Trust c/o The Book Barn, Church Way, Whittlebury, Northants NN12 8SX
- [£] Free. No WC
- [♿] Wheelchair access
- [→] On Market Hill [152 or 165: SP693340] *Bus:* Paynes 32, Road Car 51/A from Milton Keynes (passing close BR Milton Keynes Central); Aylesbury Bus/Road Car 66 from Aylesbury (passing close BR Aylesbury) (tel. (0296) 382000) *Station:* Wolverton 10m

CLAYDON HOUSE

Middle Claydon, nr Buckingham MK18 2EY (0296) 730349/730693

The most perfect expression of Rococo decoration in England, in a series of great rooms with wood carvings in the Chinese and Gothick styles. Relics of the Civil War and a museum with mementos of Florence Nightingale and the Verney Family

Note: All Saints Church in the grounds is open to the public (not NT) *continued*

BUCKINGHAMSHIRE

- April to end Oct: Mon, Wed, Fri, Sat & Sun 1-5. Last admissions 4.30
- £3.50. Family ticket £9. Parties must book; rates on application to Custodian
- Wheelchairs available. Car park close to front door; 3 steps to front door; ramps; then all ground floor rooms accessible. Access to garden via 2 steps; ramps. Half price admission to ground floor only; WC. Tea-room accessible
- Braille guide. Guided tours for groups of visually impaired people by arrangement
- Teas open 2-5
- Nappy-changing facilities
- Tel. (0296) 730349/730693
- In park on leads only
- In Middle Claydon 13m NW of Aylesbury, 3½m SW of Winslow; signposted from A413, A421 & A41; entrance by N drive only [165: SP720253] *Bus:* Aylesbury Bus 15, 17 from Aylesbury (passing close BR Aylesbury) (tel. (0296) 84919)

CLIVEDEN (BUCKS & BERKS)

Taplow, Maidenhead Berkshire SL6 0JA (0628) 605069

Set on cliffs 200 feet above the Thames. The present house, the 3rd on the site, built in 1851 by Sir Charles Barry, and once the home of Nancy, Lady Astor, is now let as an hotel. The 375 acres of garden and woodland include a magnificent parterre, a water garden and miles of woodland walks with spectacular views of the Thames

- **Grounds:** March to end Oct: daily 11-6; Nov & Dec: daily 11-4. **House (three rooms open):** April to Oct: Thur & Sun 3-6. Last admissions 5.30. Entry by timed ticket from information kiosk
- Grounds £3.80. Family ticket £9.50. House £1 extra. Party rates on application to Administrator; parties must book (no parties on Sun or BH Mon). Car parking 400yds from house

  Note: Mooring charge on Cliveden Reach £6 per 24hrs (up to 4hrs £2) (incl. NT members) but excl. admission fee to Cliveden. Tickets available from River Warden. Moorings for more than ½m downstream from Cliveden boathouse
- Shop in Old Grape House adjacent to main car park. Open 30 March to end Oct: Wed to Sun & BH Mon (incl. Good Fri) 1-5.30; Nov to 18 Dec: Wed to Sun 12-4. Tel. (0628) 665946
- Garden & Grounds largely accessible; maps with suggested routes available; powered vehicle available. Wheelchair access to open rooms in house, but some steps. Restaurant and shop accessible. WC. Car park 200yds from house but other arrangements available, please enquire
- Morning coffee, light lunches, teas and vegetarian dishes, open same days as shop 11-5 in Conservatory restaurant, but Nov to 18 Dec: Sat & Sun only 12-2. High chairs available. Parties of more than 20 must book. Tel. (0628) 661406

BUCKINGHAMSHIRE

- **E** 22 June to 3 July, Open Air Theatre Festival; s.a.e. please, for details.
- 🐾 In specified woodlands only; not in garden
- ➔ 3m upstream from Maidenhead, 2m N of Taplow; leave M4 at Jn 7 onto A4 or M40 at Jn 4 onto A404 to Marlow and follow signs. Entrance by main gates opposite Feathers Inn [175: SU915851] *Station:* Taplow, not Sun, 2½m; Burnham 3m

DORNEYWOOD GARDEN ✤
Dorneywood, Burnham SL1 8PY

The house was given to the Trust as an official residence for either a Secretary of State or Minister of the Crown; only the garden is open

- **O** Garden open by **written apointment only** on Wed 6 & 13 July, and Sat 6 & 13 Aug: 2-6. Application to the Secretary, Dorneywood Trust, at above address
- **£** £2.50. No reduction for parties
- ♿ Access to part of garden only
- ➔ SW of Burnham Beeches, 1½m N of Burnham village, 2m E of Cliveden. On Dorneywood road from Burnham village, take Beaconsfield road, 1st rt outside village; or from M40, Jn 2, take A355 to Slough, 1st rt to Burnham, 2m, then 2nd left after Jolly Woodman PH [175: SU938848] *Bus:* Chiltern Bus/Bee line 704 High Wycombe–Heathrow Airport (passing close BR Slough & Beaconsfield), alight Farnham Common, 1½m walk through Burnham Beeches (tel. (0494) 464647) *Station:* Burnham 2½m

HUGHENDEN MANOR 🏛 ✤ ♣
High Wycombe, HP14 4LA (0494) 532580

Bought in 1847 by Disraeli, who refashioned the house and grounds and lived here until his death in 1881. The house contains much of his furniture, pictures, books and other relics. Hanging and Flagmore Woods contain remnants of Disraeli's tree planting schemes, while Great and Little Tinkers Woods form a backdrop to Disraeli's monument. Access to woodland on Hughenden Manor Estate

- **O** 5-27 March: Sat & Sun only 2-6. 30 March to end Oct: Wed to Sat 2-6; Sun & BH Mon 12-6. Closed Good Fri. Last admissions 5.30
- **£** £3.50. Family ticket £9. Parties must book – rates on application to the House Steward; no parties Sat, Sun or BH Mon. Coach parking: space for only one coach at a time; car park 200yds from house
- 🏠 Open as house (closes 5.30). Also Nov to 18 Dec: Wed to Sun 11-3. Tel. (0494) 440718
- ♿ Access to ground floor only; car parking arrangements; WC
- 🔊 Braille and taped guides
- 🚫 No refreshments available at this property

continued

35

BUCKINGHAMSHIRE

> In Park and car park only

> 1½m N of High Wycombe; on W side of the Great Missenden road (A4128) [165: SU866955] *Bus:* Wycombe Bus 323/4 High Wycombe–Aylesbury (passing close BR High Wycombe) (tel. (0494) 520941) *Station:* High Wycombe 2m

KING'S HEAD

The Market Square, Aylesbury HP20 1TA (0296) 415158

An hotel, partly mid-15th-century. The large contemporary window in the parlour contains fragments of figures of angels holding shields, some of which bear the arms of Henry VI and his wife, Margaret of Anjou

Note: Currently closed for refurbishment and re-letting; tel. (as above) for information about opening

> At NW corner of Market Square *Bus:* from surrounding areas (tel. (0296) 84919) *Station:* Aylesbury 400yds

LONG CRENDON COURTHOUSE

Long Crendon, Aylesbury HP18 9AN

A 14th-century building of two storeys, partly half-timbered, probably first used as a wool store. The manorial courts were held here from the reign of Henry V until recent times. The ground floor, re-arranged as a flat, is let

> Upper floor only April to end Sept: Wed 2–6; Sat, Sun & BH Mon 11–6

> £1. No reduction for parties. No WCs

> 2m N of Thame, via B4011, close to the church [165: SP698091] *Bus:* Aylesbury Bus/Oxford 260/1, Aylesbury–Thame (passing BR Haddenham & Thame Parkway) (tel: (0296) 84919) *Station:* Haddenham & Thame Parkway 2m by footpath, 4m by road

PITSTONE WINDMILL

Ivinghoe

One of the oldest post mills in Britain; in view from Ivinghoe Beacon

> May to end Sept: Sun & BH Mon 2.30–6. Last admissions 5.30

> 70p. For details of arrangements for parties, contact I. A. Horn, 1 Wellcroft, Ivinghoe, Leighton Buzzard, Beds (tel. (0296) 668227). Parking 200yds (by B488). Not suitable for disabled or visually handicapped visitors. No WCs

> ½m S of Ivinghoe, 3m NE of Tring, just W of B488 [165: SP946158] *Bus:* Aylesbury Bus/Luton & District 61 Aylesbury–Luton (passing close BR Aylesbury & Luton) (tel. (0296) 84919) *Station:* Tring 2½m; Cheddington 2½m

BUCKINGHAMSHIRE

PRINCES RISBOROUGH MANOR HOUSE

Princes Risborough HP17 9AW

A 17th-century red brick house with Jacobean oak staircase

- House & garden by written arrangement only with tenant, Wed 2.30-4.30. Last admissions 4. Principal rooms and staircase shown. Garden by appointment at weekends April to Sept. Tel. (0844) 343168
- £1. No reduction for parties. Public car park 50yds
- Admitted by arrangement with tenant
- Opposite church, off market square [165: SP806035] *Bus:* Wycombe Bus 323/4 High Wycombe–Aylesbury (passing close BR Aylesbury) (tel. (0494) 520941) *Station:* Princes Risborough 1m

STOWE LANDSCAPE GARDENS

Buckingham MK18 5EH (0280) 822850

One of the supreme creations of the Georgian era. The first, formal layout was adorned with many buildings by Vanbrugh, Kent and Gibbs: in the 1730s Kent designed the Elysian Fields in a more naturalistic style, one of the earliest examples of the reaction against formality leading to the evolution of the landscape garden. Miraculously, this beautiful garden survives; its sheer scale must make it Britain's largest work of art

Note: The creators of the Gardens were Lord Cobham and Earl Temple whose home was Stowe. The House has been owned and occupied by Stowe School since 1923. The State Rooms and Marble Hall may be visited and the view of the Gardens from the South Portico should not be missed.

- 26 March to 17 April daily; 18 April to 1 July–Mon, Wed, Fri, Sun; 3 July to 4 Sept daily; 5 Sept to 21 Oct–Mon, Wed, Fri, Sun; 22 Oct to 30 Oct daily; 17 Dec to 23 Dec daily. Closed Christmas Eve, Christmas Day & Boxing Day. 27 Dec to 8 Jan daily, 1995. 10-5 or dusk if earlier. Last admissions 1 hour before closing. **House:** (not NT) 26-29 March; 5-17 April; 5 July-25 Aug, 30 Aug-2 Sept, daily except Sat 2-5. House occasionally closed for private functions; please check before visiting (tel. (0280) 813650). During school term time, groups on Sun by prior arrangement

  Note: visitors are advised to allow plenty of time as complete route takes 2hrs to walk

- Grounds: £3.60; family ticket £9. House: (incl. NT members) £2. Party visitors by prior arrangement with Administrator (tel. (0280) 822850)
- NT gift shop in Menagerie, open as grounds: Mon to Fri 9-5; Sat & Sun 11-5. For other times of opening tel. (0280) 813164/822850
- Unsuitable for manual wheelchairs; powered self-drive cars (one 2 seater) available free (please pre-book if possible); details from Administrator. Access to tea-room. WC *continued*

BUCKINGHAMSHIRE

- 👁 Braille and audio-cassette guides available
- 🍽 Morning coffee, light lunches and teas. Same days as gardens 11-5 (Dec & Jan 11-4)
- 🪑 High chairs available
- 🅔 For details of Music & Fireworks (6 & 7 Aug) & Opera, please send s.a.e. to 'Box Office', Stowe Landscape Gardens (or tel. (0280) 823334/822850)
- 🐕 On leads only
- ➡ 3 miles NW of Buckingham via Stowe Avenue, off A422 Buckingham/Banbury road [152: SP665366] *Bus:* Paynes 32, Road Car 51/A from Milton Keynes (passing BR Milton Keynes Central) Aylesbury Bus/Road Car 66 from Aylesbury (passing close BR Aylesbury) (tel. (0296) 382000). On all, alight Buckingham, thence 3m

WADDESDON MANOR 🏠 ✿ ♣   🚫 🐕

Waddesdon, nr Aylesbury HP18 0JH (0296) 651211

Waddesden was designed by the French architect Destailleur in the 1870s for Baron Ferdinand de Rothschild. The Renaissance style château was conceived as a showcase for the Baron's prodigious collection and as a work of art in its own right. It includes French Royal furniture, Savonneric carpets and Sèvres porcelain, important portraits by Gainsborough and Reynolds and works by Dutch and Flemish masters of the 17th century.

The Manor is open again after 3 years of restoration & conservation undertaken by Lord Rothschild in association with the National Trust. The remodelled wine cellars, containing an exceptional collection of Château Lafite-Rothschild and other interesting vintages, are now open to the public for the first time. New museum rooms on the 1st floor will open in 1995. The restoration has included work in the gardens where many original features were reinstated. The aviary houses a large collection of exotic birds

- 🅞 **House, Bachelor's Wing and Wine Cellars:** 31 March to 16 Oct: Thur to Sat 1-6; Sun & BH Mon 11-6; also open Wed 1-6 in July & Aug. **Grounds, Aviary, shop and tea-room:** 31 March to 24 Dec: Wed to Sun and BH Mon 11-6; shop & tea-room close at 5 when house closed
- 💷 Grounds aviary and parking: £3, children £1.50. Family ticket (2 adults, 2 children) £7.50. Grounds season ticket: £10; family £15. House, Wine Cellars & Bachelor's Wing: adults & children £4. Additional charge to House, Wine Cellars & Bachelor's wing on Sun and BH Mon: adults and children £1. Timed ticket system in operation; all groups are advised to book to guarantee entry to house
- 🚶 Private tours by arrangement on Wed & Thur mornings during house open season; £12 per person
- 📷 Open as grounds
- ♿ Gift shop and tea-room easily accessible. Most of garden and grounds easy; some gravel
- 👁 Braille guide; guide dogs in grounds only

BUCKINGHAMSHIRE

- Light lunches and teas in tea-room, open as grounds. Enquiries to (0296) 651211. Picnics welcome except on lawns in front of house
- Play area for young children
- 6m NW of Aylesbury, on A41, accessible from M40 (Junction 7), via Thame & Long Crendon; 11m SE of Bicester, entrance in Waddesdon village [165: SP740169] *Bus:* Aylesbury Bus 14-18 from Aylesbury (passing close BR Aylesbury) (tel. (0296) 84919) *Station:* Aylesbury 6m

WEST WYCOMBE PARK
West Wycombe HP14 3AJ (0494) 524411

A Palladian house with frescoes and painted ceilings, fashioned for Sir Francis Dashwood in the mid 18th century. The landscape garden and lake were laid out at the same time as the house, with various classical temples, including some by Nicholas Revett

Note: The West Wycombe Caves and adjacent café are privately owned, and National Trust membership cards are therefore not accepted for entry to these

- **Grounds only:** April & May: Sun & Wed 2-6; Easter, May & Spring BH Sun & Mon 2-6. **House and grounds:** June, July & Aug: Sun to Thur 2-6. Weekday entry by timed ticket. Last admissions 5.15. Guided tours, depending on visitor numbers
- House & grounds £4. Grounds only £2.50. No reduction for pre-booked parties which must book. Parking 250yds. Pushchairs and wheelchairs not admitted to house
- Grounds only; special parking
- Guide dogs in car park only
- In car park only
- At W end of West Wycombe, S of the Oxford road (A40) [175: SU828947] *Bus:* from surrounding areas (tel. (0494) 520941). Also Green Line 290 London-Oxford (tel. (0494) 464647) *Station:* High Wycombe 2½m

WEST WYCOMBE VILLAGE AND HILL

This Chilterns village is made up of buildings representing six centuries, including fine examples from 16th-18th centuries. The hill is part of the 18th-century landscape of West Wycombe Park; it is surmounted by an Iron Age hill-fort, in which stands the church and Dashwood mausoleum, and commands fine views

Note: The church, mausoleum and caves do not belong to the National Trust

- All year. Parking available at top of hill and in village. Village architectural trail leaflet available in village store
- George and Dragon, Plough, and Swan public houses. Also Bread Oven tea-room in village store
- 2m W of High Wycombe, on both sides of A40. *Bus/Rail:* as above

Cambridgeshire

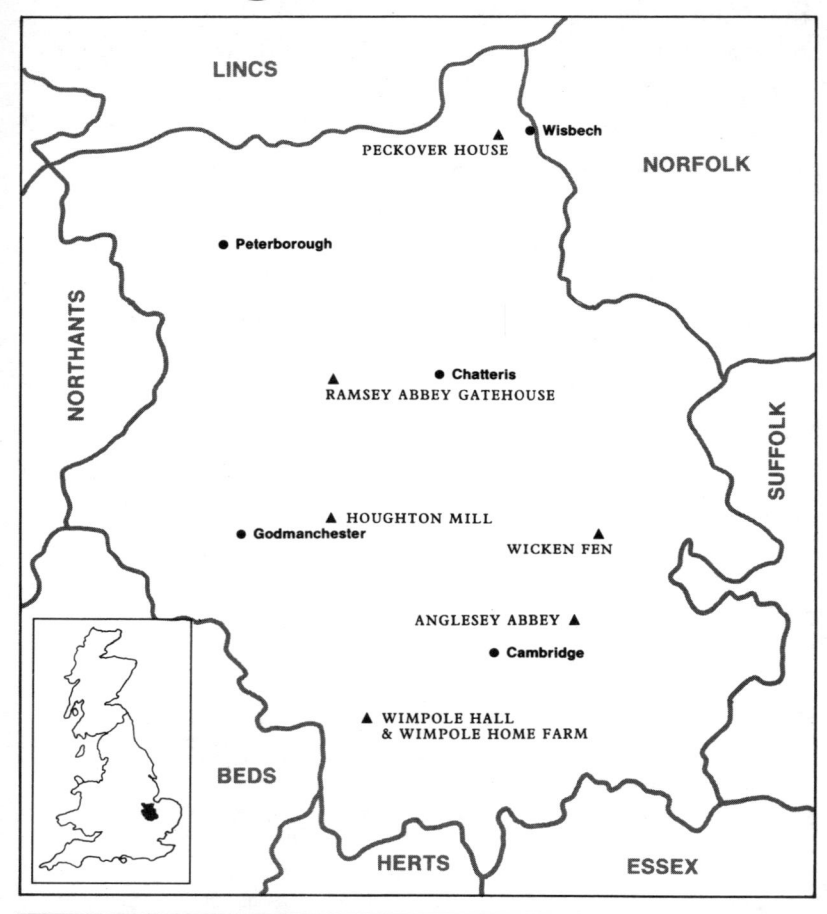

ANGLESEY ABBEY AND GARDEN
Lode, Cambridge CB5 9EJ (0223) 811200

The house, dating from 1600, is built on the site of an Augustinian abbey, and contains the famous Fairhaven collection of paintings and furniture. It is surrounded by an outstanding 100-acre garden and arboretum with a wonderful display of hyacinths in spring and magnificent herbaceous borders and a dahlia garden in summer. A watermill in the grounds is in full working order and the machinery is demonstrated on the first Sunday in each month. The Visitors' Centre includes a restaurant, shop and plant centre

CAMBRIDGESHIRE

- **House:** 26 March to 16 Oct: Wed to Sun & BH Mon 1.00–5.00. **Garden:** 26 March to 10 July: Wed to Sun & BH Mon 11–5.30; 11 July to 6 Sept: daily 10–5.30; 7 Sept to 16 Oct: Wed to Sun 11–5.30. Last admission to House & Garden 4.30. Property closed Good Fri. **Lode Mill:** 26 March to 16 Oct: Wed to Sun & BH Mon 1.30–5.15

- House & garden £4.75; Sun & BH Mon £5.75. Parties £3.80. Garden only £3.00; Sun & BH Mon £3.50. Lode Mill free. Parties please book with s.a.e. to Administrator (no reductions Sun & BH Mon)

  Note: Timed tickets to the house are issued Sun & BH Mon to overcome problems of overcrowding

- Shop & Plant Centre open 26 March to 16 Oct: Wed to Sun & BH Mon (daily 11 July to 6 Sept) 11–5.30. 20 Oct to 18 Dec: Thur to Sun 11–4. Jan to March 1995: Sat & Sun 11–4

- Special entrance arrangements: please contact Administrator at least 24hrs in advance. Access to garden and restaurant; house difficult (only 3 rooms accessible to wheelchair users via 3 stone steps). WC; self-drive vehicle

- Braille guide to house only. Hyacinth garden in spring

- Lunches and teas (table licence) in restaurant by car park, 26 March to 16 Oct: Wed to Sun & BH Mon 11–5.30; Christmas & New Year opening times as shop. Refreshments open 11 July to 6 Sept: Mon & Tues. Picnic area. Seating: 120 in restaurant, 60 in covered open air area

- Children's guide to house. Baby slings available. Restaurant: children's menu, baby food, high chairs, scribble sheets

- Details of garden walks and other events from Administrator

- In village of Lode, 6m NE of Cambridge on B1102 [154: TL533622] *Bus:* Cambus 111/122 from Cambridge (frequent services link BR Cambridge and bus station) (tel. (0223) 423554); also Neals 14 from Cambridge (Sun only) (tel. (0223) 317740) *Station:* Cambridge 6m

HOUGHTON MILL

Houghton, nr Huntingdon PE17 2AZ (0480) 301494

A large timber-built watermill on an island on the River Great Ouse, two miles downstream from Huntingdon. Much of the 19th-century machinery is intact and is operational on milling days, every Sun from April to end Aug, when corn is ground and the flour sold. An art gallery displays local artists' work   *continued*

41

CAMBRIDGESHIRE

- ⭕ **Mill:** 26 March to 16 Oct: Sat, Sun & BH Mon 2–5.30; also 27 June to 7 Sept: Mon to Wed 2–5.30. Last admissions 5.15. Parties and school groups at other times by arrangement with Custodian. **Art Gallery:** June to end Sept: Sat & Sun 2.30–5
- 💷 £1.80. Children 90p, £2.20 on milling days. No reduction for parties. Car park on adjacent private land (no street parking); charge £1 (NT members 30p on days when the mill is open). Coaches must park 300yds away in village
- 🚶 By prior arrangement
- ♿ Access to ground floor only; steep wooden stairs
- 👶 Children's guide
- 🏫 Guided tours for pre-booked school parties
- ➡️ In village of Houghton, signposted off A1123 to Huntingdon, to St Ives [153: TL282720] *Bus:* United Counties 74, Whippet 1A, 4 from Huntingdon (passing close BR Huntingdon) (tel. (0223) 317740) *Station:* Huntingdon 3½m

PECKOVER HOUSE 🏠 🏠 ✿   🚫 🚫 🚫
North Brink, Wisbech PE13 1JR (0945) 583463

A town house, built c.1722, with fine plaster and wood rococo decoration, and a collection of the Cornwallis family portraits. The notable 2-acre Victorian garden includes an orangery and the recently restored Reed Barn

- ⭕ **House & garden:** 26 March to 30 Oct: Sun, Wed & BH Mon 2–5.30. **Garden only:** as house, but also open Sat, Mon & Tues. Parties on House open days by arrangement with tenant
- 💷 £2.40 (£1 on garden only days). Parties £1.80. *Note:* Members may, by written appointment with the tenants, view Nos. 14 and 19 North Brink
- ♿ Access to garden only, on prior application to tenant
- 🌸 Scented flowers and plants
- ☕ Teas in House from mid-June to mid-September on Sun, Wed & BH Mon. Booking essential for parties
- **E** For details of art exhibitions and musical events send s.a.e. to tenant
- 🚫 No dogs
- ➡️ On N bank of River Nene, in Wisbech (B1441) [143: TF458097] *Bus:* Eastern counties 794, Viscount 336 from Peterborough (some from BR Peterborough); Eastern Counties 46, 794 from King's Lynn (passing close BR King's Lynn) (tel. (0223) 317740) *Station:* March 9½m

REFER TO OPENING PAGES FOR GENERAL INFORMATION

CAMBRIDGESHIRE

RAMSEY ABBEY GATEHOUSE
Abbey School, Ramsey, Huntingdon (Regional Office (0263) 733471)

Remains of a 15th-century gatehouse of the Benedictine Abbey

- **O** 2 April to end Oct: daily 10–5. Other times by written application to Curator
- **£** Free (but collection box for contributions). No WCs
- **→** At SE edge of Ramsey, at point where Chatteris road leaves B1096, 10m SE of Peterborough [142: TL291851] *Bus:* Enterprise 429 Huntingdon–Ramsey (passing close BR Huntingdon) (tel. (0354) 692504) *Station:* Huntingdon 10m

WICKEN FEN
Lode Lane, Wicken Ely CB7 5XP (0353) 720274

This undrained remnant of East Anglia's Great Fens is the oldest nature reserve in the country. The 600-acre wetland reserve is particularly rich in plant and insect life, with a wide variety of habitats for birds of scrub, marsh, reeds and water. A display in the William Thorpe Building explains the history of the Fen's evolution. Stout footwear is essential in winter and spring but ¾m board walk gives easy access. The traditional Fen Cottage was built using natural materials from the fen, and is furnished as it might have been in 1930s

- **O** **Fen:** all year: daily except Christmas Day. The nature of the property means that parts of the Fen can be waterlogged and to minimise damage visitors are advised that some areas may be temporarily closed. However, the ¾m boardwalk trail together with access to the Tower Hide will be open at all times. **Fen Cottage:** April to Oct: Sun & BH Mon 2–5. Other times by appointment
- **£** Fen & Cottage £2.50. Cottage only 50p. Pre-booked parties £1.90, school/educational groups 90p by arrangement with the Education Officer (tel. (0353) 723095 or write enclosing s.a.e.). Special facilities available. Simple self-catering accommodation available for parties of up to 30
- ♿ Raised ¾m boardwalk for disabled visitors; special parking by previous arrangement. Ramp into William Thorpe building. Limited access to Fen Cottage. WC (closed Dec to end March, but alternative unadapted WCs available)
- Full-time Education Warden available to help with planning of visits by schools and colleges
- Admitted only if kept under very strict control. Not allowed in Fen Cottage
- **→** S of A1123, 3m W of Soham (A142), 9m S of Ely, 17m NE of Cambridge via A10 [154: TL563705] *Bus:* Neals 19 Cambridge–Ely (Sun only) Greys 117 from Ely, (Thurs, Sat only); Cambus 122 Cambridge–Ely (Wed, Fri, Sat only); otherwise Cambus 116/122 from Cambridge, Ely & Newmarket, alight Soham Downfields, 3m; 109 Cambridge–Ely, alight Stretham 3½m (tel. (0223) 317740). All pass BR Ely *Station:* Ely 9m

CAMBRIDGESHIRE

WIMPOLE HALL 🏠 🏛 ✝ ✽ 🍴 🚹   📷 ❌ 🐕

Arrington, Royston, Hertfordshire SG8 0BW (0223) 207257

The most spectacular mansion in Cambridgeshire, built in a restrained 18th-century style. The fine interior is both intimate and formal, with work by Gibbs, Flitcroft and Soane. Servants' quarters include the housekeeper's room, butler's pantry and basement corridor. A 350-acre park, landscaped by Bridgeman, Brown and Repton, includes a grand folly, Chinese bridge and pleasant walks (leaflet). Heavy horses operate from the Victorian stableblock

🅞	26 March to 30 Oct: Tues, Wed, Thur, Sat & Sun 1-5 (BH Sun & BH Mon 11-5); also 22 July to 26 Aug 1-5
£	Hall & Garden £4.50. Parties £3.50 (parties of 40 or more £3.20), please send s.a.e. to Property Manager. Joint ticket with Home Farm £6. Car park 200yds
🚶	By special arrangement outside normal opening hours
🛍	Shop open same days as house 11-5.30. Also 1 Nov to 18 Dec & Jan to end March 1995: Tues, Wed, Thur, Sat & Sun 11-4
♿	Apply to Reception for special access. Staff may be available to lift wheelchairs up steps to ground floor of house, which is then level and fully accessible. Wheelchair access to Great Dining Room by arrangement. WC open 10.30-5.30 at stable block; 12-5.30 at Hall. 2 battery operated vehicles available. Please book in advance
👁	Braille guide
🍴	Full lunches and teas in Great Dining Room same days as house 12-5. Also 1 Nov to 18 Dec and Jan to end March 1995: Tues to Thur, Sat & Sun 11-3.30. Table licence for wines. Light refreshments in stables same days as house 10.30-5.30. Restaurant capacity 95. Picnic area

CAMBRIDGESHIRE

Children's guide. Parents' and babies' room in stable block; baby slings available. Restaurant: children's menu, baby food, high chairs, scribble sheets

Full education programme; details from Education Officer. Tel. (0223) 207801

For details of musical and other events send s.a.e. to Property Manager. Open air Music Festival with Fireworks 8, 9, 10 July; 8 July Pasadena Roof Orchestra; 9 July Humphrey Lyttelton; 10 July Cambridge Philarmonic Society. Pimlico Opera 4 June; 'I Pagliacci' and 'Gianni Schicci'. 10% discount on all tickets booked before end April

In park only, on leads

8m SW of Cambridge (A603), 6m N of Royston (A1198) [154: TL336510] *Bus:* Whippet 175, Neals 14 Cambridge–Biggleswade (passing close BR Biggleswade & Cambridge) (tel. (0223) 317740) *Station:* Shepreth 5m

WIMPOLE HOME FARM

As Wimpole Hall (0223) 207257

Wimpole Home Farm was built in 1794 as a model farm. The Great Barn, designed by Sir John Soane, houses a collection of farm machinery of the kind used here over 200 years. Rare breeds of animals, including sheep, goats, cattle, pigs and horses, can be viewed in paddocks and the thatched buildings. There is an adventure woodland and horse and cart rides are available

12 March to 30 Oct: Tues, Wed, Thur, Fri, Sat & Sun (but open BH Mon) 10.30–5; also open Mons; 8 July–29 Aug. 1 Nov to 5 March 1995 Sat & Sun 11–4 (closed Christmas & New Year). 11 March 1995 to 29 Oct 1995 as 1994

NT members £1.80. Non-members £3.50. Children over 3 £1.75. Parties £2.50, please book with s.a.e. to Property Manager, Wimpole Hall. Joint ticket for Hall & Farm £6. School parties especially welcome (£1.25 per child, school corporate members 90p per child). Part of a building is reserved for their use. Parking 400yds, at Hall

By special arrangement

Shop open same times as Farm; sells leaflets about the Farm

Level access throughout Farm and ramps to all farm buildings; klaxon at Farm gate to summon assistance. WC at stable block. Wheelchairs available. Battery operated vehicles available at Stable Block; please book in advance

Braille guide

Simple refreshments only; or see Hall entry, above

Special area set aside as a children's corner; woodland adventure playground; children's publications. Special events for children, April, May, Aug

Full education programme; details from Education Officer tel. (0223) 207801

Special lambing weekends March 1995; 11/12, 18/19 March 11–4. Heavy horse show 4 Sept 1994. Flower garden show 28–30 May 1994

No dogs allowed

Bus/Rail: as Wimpole Hall, above

Cheshire

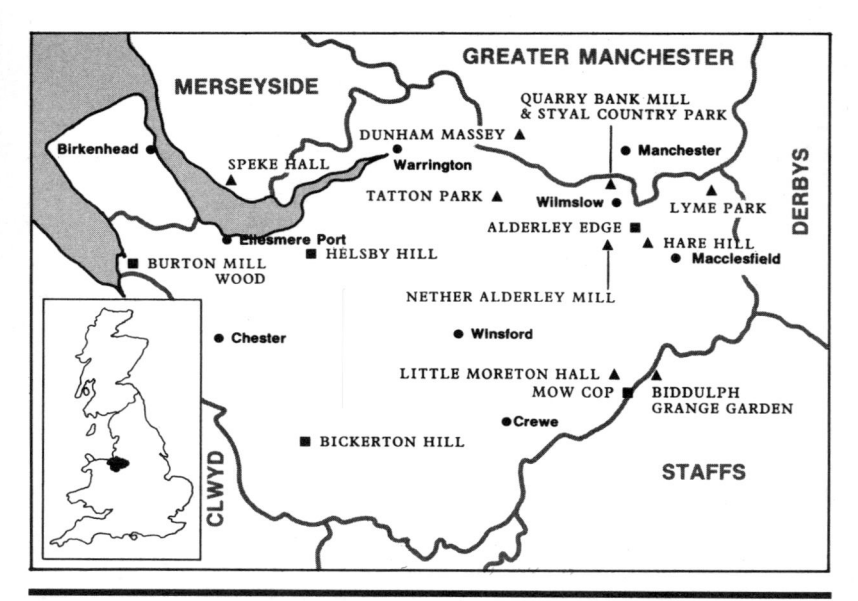

COUNTRYSIDE

Several of the Trust's beauty spots in this county are very near the great industrial conurbations that fringe its northern and eastern boundaries. **Alderley Edge** [118: SS860775] is within easy reach of Manchester and Macclesfield and gives splendid views of the Cheshire Plain. It is 600ft high and its wooded sandstone escarpment once harboured a large Neolithic settlement. Bronze Age pottery and tools have been found here. A footpath has been created which is linked to the Trust's nearby Hare Hill Estate; walkers are asked to return by the same route and not along the highway. There is a signed path from the car park suitable for wheelchairs (but a strong pusher is needed) along the Edge, giving fine views. WC. A mile away is **Nether Alderley Mill** (see p.50).

About 20 miles due west of Alderley Edge is **Helsby Hill** [117: SJ491752], a sandstone outcrop overlooking the Mersey, and giving views of the mountains of North Wales. The climb to the summit takes about fifteen minutes and you will pass an Iron Age hill-fort near the top.

On the Staffordshire border, a hill rises to nearly 1100ft above sea level. It is topped by a Gothic folly in the shape of a castle, now ruined. **Mow Cop** [118: SJ857573] marks the beginning of the Staffordshire Way footpath and gives views towards Alderley Edge and beyond to Manchester to the north, north-east to the Peak District, south to Cannock Chase and Shropshire and west to Wales and the Berwyn Mountains. From Mow Cop you can walk 3 miles to the timber-framed **Little Moreton Hall**, Congleton (see p.48).

CHESHIRE

Bickerton Hill [117: SJ497526] lies at the southern tip of the Peckforton Hills – over 260 acres of mixed woodland, heathland and fields accessible by public footpath. The Peckforton Hills are a wooded red sandstone ridge running from Maiden Castle, an Iron Age fort in the south, to the 13th-century Beeston Castle in the north. The Sandstone Trail, a 30-mile long-distance footpath, traverses the length of the hills from Grindley Brook to Frodsham, passing a variety of dwellings from black and white cottages to prehistoric hill-forts.

Burton Mill Wood – 20 acres of woodland adjacent to the village of Burton, 8 miles north west of Chester. Easy walking with views across the Dee estuary to the Welsh hills beyond [117:SJ315745].

DUNHAM MASSEY

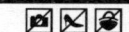

Altrincham WA14 4SJ 061-941 1025

A Georgian house with Edwardian additions, and set in a 250-acre wooded deer park. Until 1976 this was the home of the 10th and last Earl of Stamford. Over 30 rooms are open, with outstanding collections of furniture, paintings and silver; also a fine library, kitchen, laundry and stables. The house is built on the site of a Tudor building whose moat provides power for a working Jacobean mill. There is a large garden with shrubs, herbaceous borders, mature trees and waterside plants

- 2 April to 30 Oct: **House:** Sat to Wed 12-5. Last admissions 4.15. **Garden:** 1 April to 30 Oct: daily 11-5.30; also 25 Feb to 26 March 1995: Sat & Sun 12-4. The mill machinery will normally operate on Wed & Sun. Park open until 7.30 or dusk if earlier

- House & garden £4.50 incl. free audio tour, children £2. Family ticket £11. House only £3 incl. free audio tour, children £1.50. Garden only £2.50. Reduced rate for booked parties. Park only: £2 per car; coaches free (NT members free). Car park & picnic area 250yds from house

- Outside normal hours, guided tours of house for booked parties £5 per person (min. charge £200). Rest room for coach drivers

- Shop open 1 April to 30 Oct: daily 12-5. Also open 3 Nov to 18 Dec: Thurs to Sun 12-4; 7 Jan to 26 Mar 1995: Sat & Sun 12-4

- Some steps to ground floor and throughout house; garden, park, outbuildings and shop via cobbled area; car parking by prior arrangement; 2 wheelchairs & self-drive buggy available; wheelchair path to canal; WC

- Braille guide; large print guide

- Licensed self-service restaurant on first floor of stable block, April to Oct daily 11-5; lunches 12-2 (limited lunch menu Thur & Fri); Nov to March open as shop. Children's portions available. Functions & booked parties by arrangement (tel. Catering Manager 061-941 2815). Seating for 150; also coach party room (must be pre-booked)

- Baby slings available; nappy changing unit; high chairs in restaurant; children's guide and quiz

- Victorian living history programme & environmental studies in deer park for schools by arrangement with Education Co-ordinator (tel. 061-941 4986).

continued

CHESHIRE

- **E** Edwardian Extravaganza 8/9 July; ticket line 061-954 1600. For details of musical and other events please send s.a.e. to Administrator
- In park only, on leads
- 3m SW of Altrincham off A56; junction 19 off M6; junction 7/8 off M56 [109: SJ735874] *Bus:* North Western/Warrington Transport 38 BR Altrincham Interchange–Warrington (tel. (0244) 602666) *Station:* Altrincham 3m; Hale 3m

HARE HILL
Over Alderley, Macclesfield SK10 4QB

A woodland garden surrounding a walled garden with pergola, rhododendrons and azaleas; parkland; link path to Alderley Edge (2m)

- 30 March to 30 Oct: Wed, Thur, Sat, Sun & BH Mon 10–5.30. Special opening to see rhododendrons and azaleas: 13 May to 3 June: daily 10–5.30. Closed Nov to March
- £2.50. Entrance per car £1.50 refundable on entry to garden. Parties by written appointment c/o Garden Lodge, Oak Road, Over Alderley, Macclesfield, SK10 4QB; not suitable for school parties
- Gravel paths, some help needed. Wheelchair available
- Scents & sounds of wooded parkland; scented plants in walled garden
- No dogs in garden, elsewhere on leads
- Between Alderley Edge and Prestbury, turn off north at B5087 at Greyhound Road [118: SJ875765] *Bus:* Star Line/Stevensons 287 BR Wilmslow–Macclesfield (passing BR Prestbury), to within ¾m (tel. (0244) 602666) *Station:* Alderley Edge 2½m; Prestbury 2½m

LITTLE MORETON HALL
Congleton CW12 4SD (0260) 272018

Begun in the 15th century, it is regarded as the most perfect example of a timber-framed moated manor house in the country. A long wainscoted gallery, chapel, great hall and knot garden are of particular interest. The South Range was extensively restored in 1991

- 26 March to 30 Sept: Wed to Sun 12–5.30 (closed Good Fri); BH Mon 11–5.30; Oct: Sat & Sun 12–5.30 or dusk if earlier. Last admissions 5. Special morning openings by arrangement with Administrator
- £2.80. Family ticket £7. Weekends & Bank Holidays £3.60; family ticket £9. Pre-booked parties by arrangement. Parking 150yds, £2, refundable on entry to Hall (NT members free); car park open from 11
- Optional free guided tours most afternoons
- Shop as house, but closes 5.15

CHESHIRE

    Access to ground floor; includes Great Hall, Parlour, Chapel, tea-room, shop, exhibition room. Cars may be driven to entrance, but then must park in car park. Garden accessible. Electric scooter and wheelchairs available by arrangement. WC

    Braille guide; large print guide

    Light lunches and home made teas (waitress service); children's portions available; licensed; limited seating – no reservations. Last admissions 5. Picnic area adjacent to car park

    Nappy-changing unit; high chair available; children's guide

    School parties April to end Sept: Wed to Fri, mornings only, by prior arrangement with Administrator. Schoolroom available; education resource pack

    Service in Chapel each Sun 3.45. Open-air theatre in July

    In car park only

    4m SW of Congleton, on E side of A34 [118: SJ832589] *Bus:* PMT 77 Congleton–Hanley (passing close BR Kidsgrove & Congleton), alight Brownlow Heath 1½m (tel. (0244) 602666) *Station:* Kidsgrove 3m; Congleton 4½m

LYME PARK

Disley, Stockport SK12 2NX (0663) 762023/766492

Home of the Legh family for 600 years – the largest house in Cheshire. Part of the original Elizabethan house survives with 18th- and 19th-century additions by Giacomo Leoni and Lewis Wyatt. Four centuries of period interiors – Mortlake tapestries, Grinling Gibbons

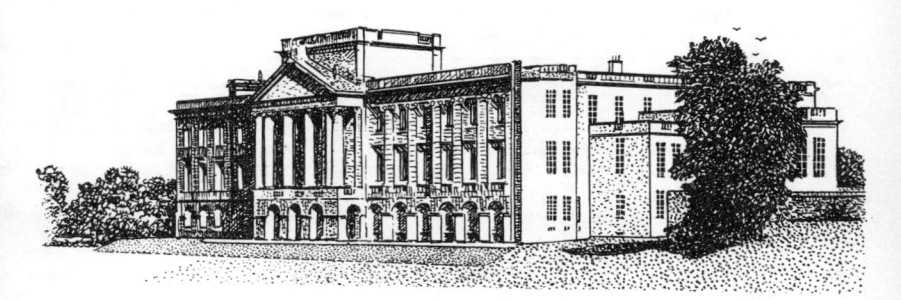

carvings, unique collection of English clocks. Set in extensive historic gardens with orangery by Wyatt, a lake and the 'Dutch' garden. 1,377 acre park, home to red and fallow deer. Magnificent views of Pennine Hills and Cheshire Plain

    Hall: From 1 April; for details of times and days, ring information line (0663) 766492. **Gardens:** April to Sept inclusive; open daily 10.30–5; Oct to March inclusive; Tues to Sun 10.30–4. Closed Mondays & 25/26 Dec. **Estate:** open every day of year; 8 to dusk   *continued*

CHESHIRE

£ Charges under review; ring (0663) 766492

NT members please note: Lyme Park is financed and managed by Stockport M.B.C. Members are required to pay Estate admission and are also charged for entrance to specific events. Hall admission is free during normal opening hours to NT members

K Hall: on days, other than Sundays and BHs when free-flow operates, or by arrangement, anytime, for pre-booked parties. Garden: by arrangement. Estate: dates and details (0663) 762023 (Ranger Service), or by arrangement, anytime, for pre-booked parties

O April to Sept: 12–5. Oct to Dec (Sundays only): 1–4. Closed Jan to March

& Tea-room and shop accessible; parts of hall, gardens and park; WC hall and lakeside; Booster Scooter (free) for park, gardens, special trail and picnic area; advanced notice ensures help will be available when necessary

🍽 Light lunches & teas in Servants Hall tea-room: April to Sept, daily 11.30–5; Oct to Dec, (Sun only) 12–4. Closed Jan to March

👶 High chairs available in Servants Hall tea-room. Adventure playground

▮ Extensive education opportunities, tailored to suit National Curriculum in term time with trained staff. Various activities during holidays

E Many & various throughout year in Hall and park. Tel. for details (0663) 762023

🐕 In park under control, and on leads in garden

→ Entrance on A6, 6½m SE of Stockport, 9m NW of Buxton *Bus:* Glossopdale 361 from Stockport to Hall entrance (Sun: May–Sept only); otherwise frequent from surrounding areas to Park entrance (tel. (061) 228 7811) *Station:* Disley ½m from Park entrance

NETHER ALDERLEY MILL

Congleton Road, Nether Alderley, Macclesfield SK10 4TW (0625) 523012

A fascinating overshot tandem wheel watermill, originally 15th century, with a stone-tiled low pitched roof. The machinery was derelict for 30 years, but has now been restored to full working order, and grinds flour occasionally for demonstrations

O 29 March to end May & Oct: Wed, Sun & BH Mon 1–4.30. Also June to Sept: Tues to Sun & BH Mon 1–5

£ £1.80. Parties (max. 20) by prior arrangement (tel. (0625) 523012). Parking space for one coach at a time; must book. No WCs

K As required

& Ladder stairs. Unsuitable for wheelchairs

▮ Visits by arrangement

→ 1½m S of Alderley Edge, on E side of A34 [118: SJ844763] *Bus:* C-Line/Timeline 127/9, 130 Manchester Macclesfield (passing BR Alderley Edge) (tel. (0244) 602666) *Station:* Alderley Edge 2m

CHESHIRE

QUARRY BANK MILL & STYAL COUNTRY PARK
QUARRY BANK MILL
Wilmslow SK9 4LA (0625) 527468

A major Georgian cotton mill restored as a working museum of the cotton industry, now running under waterpower. There are demonstrations of weaving and spinning, and galleries illustrate the millworkers' world, textile finishing processes, the Gregs as pioneers of the factory system and water as a source of energy. The original Apprentice House, as lived in by mill apprentices in 1830, is fully restored

The Mill is managed for the National Trust by the tenant, Quarry Bank Mill Trust Ltd

Summer opening: April to Sept. **Mill:** daily 11-6. Last admissions 4.30. Also specified evenings in May, June & Sept. **Apprentice House & Garden:** (closed Mon except BH Mon) Tues to Fri 2-5.30. Weekends & 28 March-10 April and Aug, as Mill. Tickets for interpretive tours limited; to avoid disappointment please reserve timed ticket at Reception on arrival.

Winter opening: Oct to March. **Mill:** daily 11-5 except Mon. Last admissions 3.30. Pre-booked groups from 9.30 except weekends & BH Mon. Visitors wishing to avoid crowds are advised not to visit on BH and Sun afternoons in spring and summer. **Apprentice House and Garden:** Tues to Fri 2-4.30; weekends & 26 Dec to 8 Jan 1995: as Mill

Mill & Apprentice House £4.25, children/concessionaries £3. Family ticket £12.50. Mill only £3.30, children/concessionaries £2.40. Apprentice House & Garden only £2.50, children/concessionaries £2 (may change). Advance booking essential for groups of 10 or more (please apply for booking form at least 3 weeks in advance; guides may be booked at same time). Groups of 20 or more admitted at concessionary rate. *Note:* NT members expected to pay charges for special events

Mill shop sells goods made from cloth woven in the Mill and wide range of gifts & souvenirs. Mail Order catalogue for Styal Calico, send A4 s.a.e

Exterior and accessible route through part of interior, using step lift. Wheelchair available on request; cars may set down passengers in Mill yard. Please tel. for special access leaflet. WCs. Mill unsuitable for guide dogs

continued

CHESHIRE

- Braille guide & large print guides
- The Mill Kitchen: (licensed). Mill Pantry for snacks, drinks and ice cream. Conference and banqueting facilities available; weddings, meetings, meals for booked groups etc.
- Parent & baby room; baby slings and backpacks available
- School groups should tel. for separate opening times and information. Education office and school party base
- No dogs
- 1½m N of Wilmslow off B5166, 2½m from M56, exit 5, 10m S of Manchester [109: SJ835835] *Bus:* Bee Line 100 BR Manchester Piccadilly–Styal Sunday only (tel. (061) 288 7811) *Station:* Styal, ½m. (not Sun)

STYAL COUNTRY PARK

Estate Office, 7 Oak Cottages, Styal, Wilmslow SK9 4JQ (0625) 523012

Part of the valley of the river Bollin, combining natural beauty with historic interest. There are pleasant riverside walks in fine woodlands; the Country Park includes Quarry Bank Cotton Mill, the factory colony village of Styal and associated farmland

- All year during daylight hours
- Admission charge per car to country park, £1.50
- Guided tours of woodlands and village from main car park on 2nd Sun in each month at 2.30
- Shop at mill
- A circular woodland route is available from the Twinnies Bridge end of the country park. (Not from the main car park).
- Braille and large print guides
- Available from Mill
- *Bus/Rail:* as for Quarry Bank Mill, above

TATTON PARK

Knutsford WA16 6QN (0565) 654822 – Infoline (0565) 750250

One of the most complete historic estates open to visitors in England. The 19th-century Wyatt house, set in more than 1,000 acres of deer park, contains the Egerton family collection of pictures, books, china, glass, silver and specially commissioned Gillow furniture; servants' rooms and cellars depict life downstairs. The 50-acre garden contains an authentic Japanese garden, Italian garden, orangery, fernery, rose garden and pinetum. Also, a medieval old hall, an 18th-century farm working as in 1930s and many varieties of wildfowl. There is a new outdoor and sailing centre for pre-booked groups. A walk round the Landscape History Trail begins the interpretive theme A Story for Every Age

CHESHIRE

Members please note: Tatton Park is financed, administered and maintained by Cheshire County Council. All NT members are subject to car park charges and are also charged for entrance to events (listed below) where it is impossible to separate access arrangements.

> [O] Summer opening: 1 April to 30 Sept. **Mansion, Old Hall** (enquire before visiting May to end July). **Farm:** daily except Mon (but open BH Mon) 12–5; Oct: Sat & Sun. **Gardens:** daily except Mon (but open BH Mon) 10.30–6. **Park:** daily 10.30–7. Last admissions 1hr before closing
>
> Winter opening: all sites open weekends in Oct. Nov to end March 1995: **Garden:** daily except Mon 11–4. **Farm:** Sun only 12–4. **Park:** daily except Mon 11–5. **Mansion and Farm:** open for 'Tatton at Christmas' (see E). All attractions open school holidays, Oct (NT members charged)

> [£] All sites (incl. admission to Park) £6, children £4.20. Mansion £2.50, children £2. Garden £2.50, children £2. Old Hall £2, children £1.30. Farm £1.80, children £1.30. NT Annual Members must pay full charge for Old Hall & Farm. Free admission to the gardens is at the kind discretion of Cheshire County Council. Admission to Park £2 per car (incl. all NT members), coaches, bicycles and pedestrians free. Pre-booked parties may visit all attractions with a guide outside normal opening times on payment of an additional charge

> Old Hall only during normal opening hours

> Shop open April to Oct 12–5.30; Nov to end March 1995 Sun only 11.30–4.30. Garden sales open same days as Gardens

> Parking in stableyard, at Old Hall and at Home Farm. Easy access to Mansion and ground floor, garden, park, farm tea-room & shop. WC. Leaflet available on request.

> Braille guide available in Gardens entrance

> All meals catered for in Stableblock; bookings Knutsford (0565) 632914. Open same days as Mansion 10.30–5.30. Also Oct to March: Sun 11–4

> Adventure playground. Nursing mothers invited to use emergency rest room

> Study programmes, role playing, living history days, self-guided tours, special projects. All guided tours and booked groups are charged. New outdoor schools and youth programme

> [E] All NT members will be expected to pay the special charges which apply to all events. Additional park charge 18–19 June for Carriage Driving Trials. Special Christmas opening days Mansion, the Tenants Hall family museum will often be closed for maintenance work and functions. Infoline tel. (0565) 750250. Please send s.a.e. for calendar of events

> On leads at Home Farm and in park under close control. No dogs in garden

> 3½m N of Knutsford, 4m S of Altrincham, 5m from M6, junction 19; 3m from M56, junction 7, well signposted on A556; entrance on Ashley Road, 1½m NE of jn. A5034 with A50 [109 & 118: SJ745815] *Bus:* Tonys X2 BR Altrincham Interchange–Chester, Sun only otherwise from surrounding areas to Knutsford, thence 2m (tel. (0244) 602666) *Station:* Knutsford 2m

Cleveland

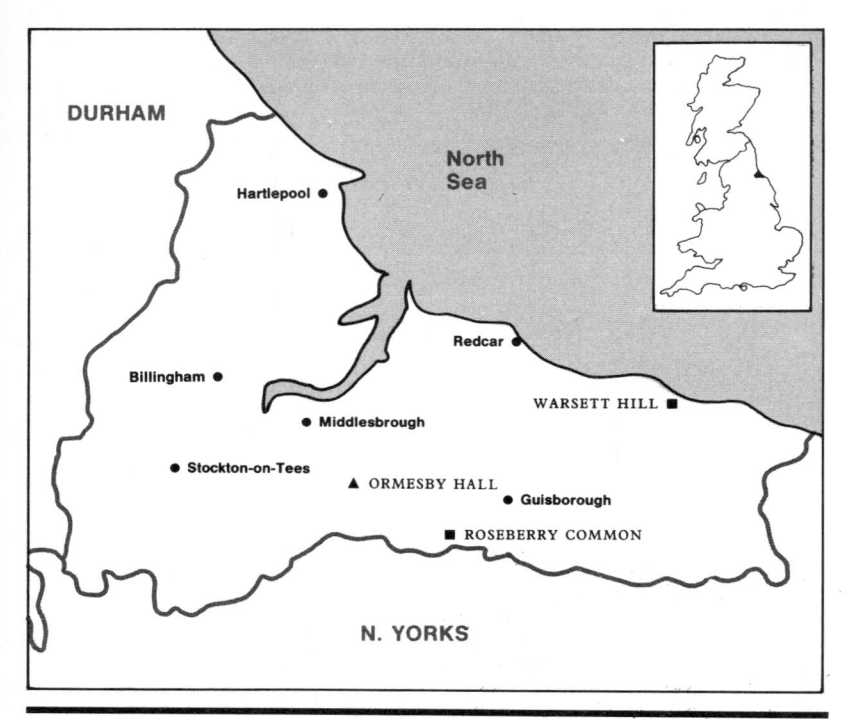

COAST

The first acquisition on Cleveland's Heritage Coast has now been completed adjacent to Hunt Cliff, south of Saltburn; 150 acres of cliff and farmland are capped by Warsett Hill – a popular local viewpoint.

COUNTRYSIDE

The bent pinnacle of Roseberry Topping [93: NZ575126] has been described as a miniature Matterhorn. The summit rises to 1,057 feet and provides panoramic views over the Cleveland Hills and across Teesside to the North Sea.

Roseberry Topping has a long and romantic history. Prehistoric herdsmen and hunters occupied the site and to the Vikings it was a sacred hill. The Topping was used as a beacon station at the time of the Spanish Armada and during the Napoleonic Wars. Captain James Cook, one of the world's great navigators, worked with his father at Aireyholme Farm on the Topping's southern slopes. The Topping lies on the northern

CLEVELAND

edge of the North York Moors National Park, south-west of Guisborough, and about 8 miles south-east of Middlesbrough. Access is from the car park on the A173, 1 mile north-east of Great Ayton [93: NZ571128]. The Trust's purchase of **Roseberry Common** and part of Roseberry Topping in 1985 included the northern and eastern slopes of the hill, as well as a stretch of heather moorland and an oak wood on its western flank; a total of some 300 acres.

Some 5 miles to the north-west is **Ormesby Hall** (see entry below).

ORMESBY HALL
Church Lane, Ormesby, Middlesbrough TS7 9AS (0642) 324188

A mid 18th-century house with opulent decoration inside, including fine plasterwork by contemporary craftsmen. A Jacobean doorway with a carved family crest survives from the earlier house on the site. The stable block, attributed to Carr of York, is a particularly fine mid 18th-century building with an attractive courtyard leased to the Mounted Police; also, a 5-acre garden

- 26 March to 30 Oct: Wed, Thur, Sat, Sun, BH Mon & Good Fri 2–5.30. Last admissions 5. Special parties on weekdays by arrangement with Administrator
- House & Garden: £2, children £1. Parties £1.70, children 90p. Garden: 90p, children 40p. Parking 100yds
- Special evening tours
- Shop as house. Also certain dates in Nov & Dec
- Access to ground floor of house, shop, tea-room & garden; cars may bring disabled visitors to front door; please notify Administrator in advance of visit; WC opposite car park
- Tea-room and tea garden serving home made teas open as house and certain dates in Nov & Dec
- Baby changing facilities. Pushchairs may be left at entrance. Children's menu in tea-room
- School groups on Wed, Thurs, Fri mornings during season
- For a detailed programme and inclusion on the mailing list, send s.a.e. to the Administrator
- In park only on leads
- 3m SE of Middlesbrough, W of A171 [93: NZ530167] *Bus:* From Middlesbrough (passing close BR Middlesbrough) (tel. (0642) 210131) *Station:* Marton (U), not Sun, except May to Sept, 1½m; Middlesbrough 3m

CORNWALL

Cornwall

COAST

The Trust's countryside holdings in Cornwall are mainly of truly spectacular coastline – more than 110 miles, including some of the most famous and beautiful holiday stretches.

On the north coast between the Devon border and Bude the Trust owns three blocks of coastline. The most northerly, centred on **Morwenstow** [190: SS2015], has associations with the celebrated 19th-century cleric and poet, Hawker of Morwenstow. The Trust property from north of **Duckpool** to south of **Sandy Mouth** [190: SS2011] extends inland up the **Coombe Valley**. There is a café, WCs and a car park at **Sandy Mouth** where, at low tide, the beach lives up to its name. A narrow strip at **Maer Cliff** [190: SS2008] runs between Northcott Mouth and Crooklets Beach.

Crackington Haven [190: SX1497] is flanked by **Dizzard Point** where there is a stunted oak wood; **Penkenna Point**; and **High Cliff**, the loftiest height on the Cornish coast at 731ft. **Trevigue Farm** has a shop, café and information point.

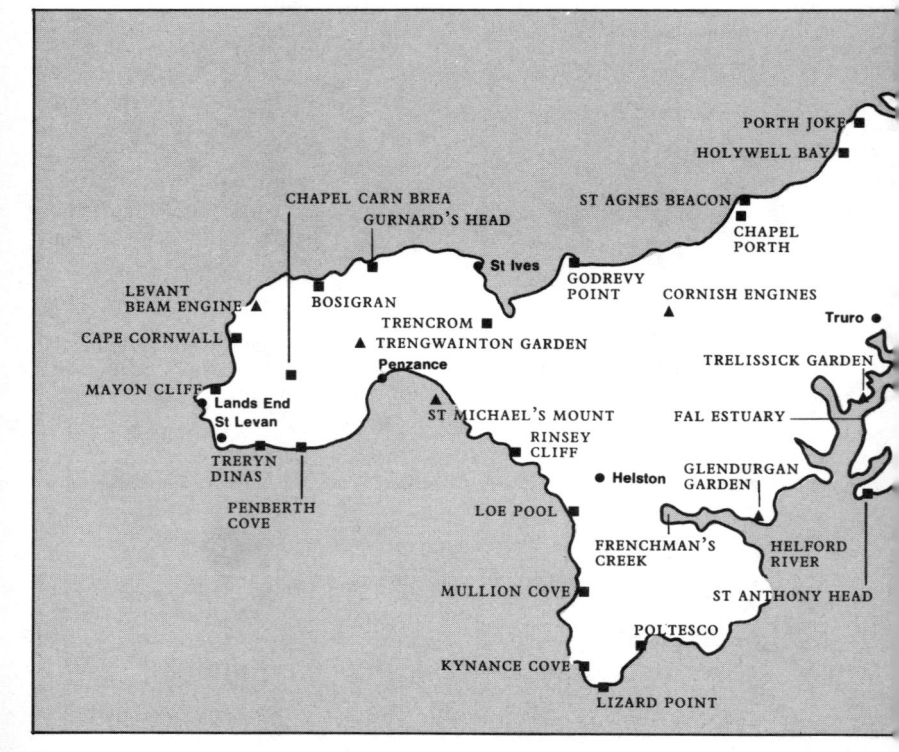

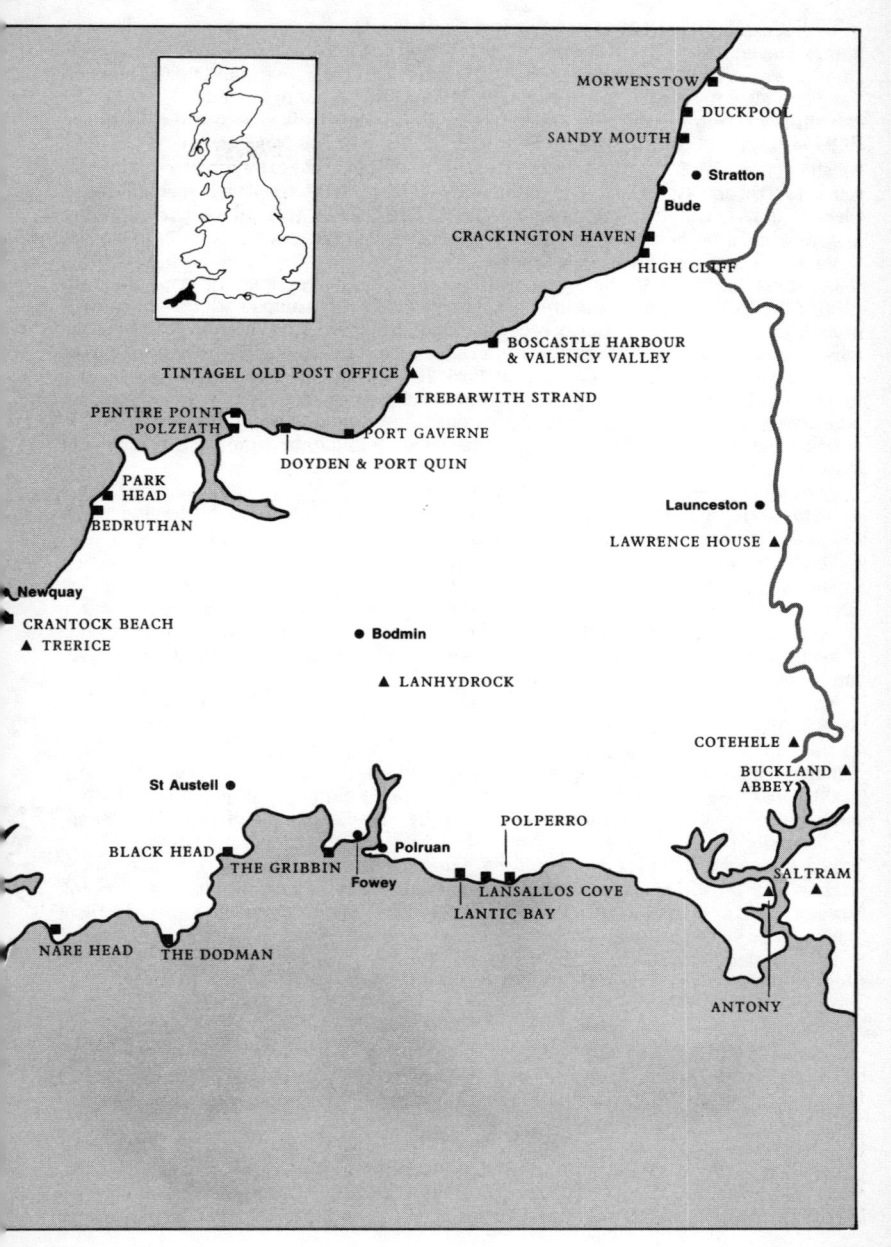

CORNWALL

CORNWALL

At **Boscastle** [190: S1091] the Trust owns both sides of the picturesque harbour, a natural haven still used by fishermen. The NT shop and information centre, with wheelchair access, is open in summer in the Old Smithy. The Trust owns land up the wooded **Valency Valley** towards St Juliot, rich with Thomas Hardy connections.

Visitors to **Tintagel Old Post Office** (see page 66) can walk out to the cliffs to see **Willapark** [200: SX0689], where there is a cliff castle; **Barras Nose**, the Trust's earliest coastal acquisition in England; or the lengthy stretch of coast extending from Tintagel south to **Trebarwith Strand**. The old cliffside slate quarries are worth seeing, and at **Glebe Cliff** a viewpoint has wheelchair access. The cliffs at **Tregardock** and adjoining **Dannonchapel** are best viewed from the coast path. The Trust owns a cluster of old fish 'cellars' and the foreshore at **Port Gaverne**.

The next highlight is the wonderful 6-mile stretch from **Port Quin** to **Polzeath** [200: SW9380]. The main features are **Pentire Point**; **the Rumps** with its cliff castle – probably the finest on the Cornish coast; **Lundy Bay**; **Doyden Castle**, a 19th-century folly; and **Port Quin** itself where there is a car park and a clutch of NT holiday cottages.

The remote, convoluted coastline at **Park Head** [200: SW8471], with its seabird breeding colonies, is the perfect foil for the more gregarious pleasures to be found at **Bedruthan** [200: SW8569]. The justly famous beauty spot of Bedruthan Steps (not NT) can be viewed from the Trust's clifftop land. NT shop and information centre, café and WCs in the car park.

Immediately west of Newquay the trio of sandy beaches, **Crantock Beach**, **Porth Joke** and **Holywell Bay**, are backed and separated by an extensive Trust hinterland [200: SW7760]. This is wonderful walking country.

The high ground of **St Agnes Beacon** (629ft) is Trust owned, and the whole area is rich in industrial relics from mining days. **Chapel Porth** [203: SW7050] is another fine beach, at low tide; the ruin of **Towanroath engine house** stands prominently above it.

Between **Gwithian** and **Portreath** the Trust owns over 6 miles of almost continuous coastline [203: SW6545 to 5842]. The awesome drop at **Hell's Mouth** and the headlands of **Godrevy** and **Navax Point** are the most dramatic features.

Not on the coast, but only 2 miles inland from Carbis Bay, is **Trencrom Hill** [203: SW5236], a 64-acre granite eminence which sits in its strategic position at the gateway to the Land's End peninsula. Two main rock piles are surrounded by lesser outcrops which are linked by an Iron Age wall, and the remains of stone dwellings can be seen.

Once west of St Ives the character of the landscape changes. This is West Penwith, a coastline of rocky headlands and coves backed by a flattish plateau of small fields where traditionally managed farms are overlooked by a serrated ridge of granite outcrops called carns; **Carn Galver** is the most prominent although adjoining **Watchcroft** is higher. The Trust owns a number of the headlands, as well as larger areas at **Treveal**, **Rosemergy** and **Bosigran** [203: SW4237]. A walk out to **Zennor** and **Gurnard's Head** will give the visitor a flavour of this very Celtic, unspoilt coast.

From **Cape Cornwall** [203: SW3532], England's only cape, there are good views up the coast and south to Land's End. The adjoining **Bollowall Common** (with its rocky pinnacle of Carn Gloose) was bought in 1993.

The three properties nearest to Land's End are the mile of **Boscregan** and **Nanjuliam** [203: SW3630], to the north of Whitesand Bay; the ¾mile of **Mayon Cliff** [203: SW3526] between Sennen Cove and Land's End; and **Chapel Carn Brea** [203: SW3828], a 53-acre hilltop reaching 657ft, 2 miles inland from Whitesand Bay, which claims the widest sea view from the British mainland.

Once round Land's End the south coast of Cornwall begins, and the first Trust property encountered is the point called **Pedn-men-an-mere** [203: SW3821] which protects the open-air Minack Theatre (not NT) from south-westerly gales. Beyond **Porthcurno** the Trust owns 2 miles, passing the little fishing cove of **Penberth**, perhaps

CORNWALL

Cornwall's most perfect fishing cove [203: SW4023]. Between the two is the thrusting cock's comb peninsula of **Treryn Dinas**, the famous 66-ton Logan Rock perched on its rocky crest.

St Michael's Mount (see p.65) is the first Trust property east of Penzance, followed by three detached sites at **Cudden Point**, **Lesceave Cliff** and **Rinsey Cliff**, the last-named having a restored 19th-century mine engine house on the cliff slope.

Once east of Porthleven the extensive **Penrose Estate** [203: SW6425] spreads inland to the outskirts of Helston and south to **Gunwalloe Church Cove**. It contains the remarkable and beautiful **Loe Pool**, Cornwall's largest natural freshwater lake, separated from the sea by the shingle barrier of Loe Bar. A 5-mile footpath follows the edge of the lake, and a bird hide looks out onto the reed bed. **Gunwalloe Towans** is a fine sweep of sand dunes now used by Mullion Golf Club.

Trust ownership along the west-facing Lizard coast is fragmented into a number of properties. South of Poldhu the **Marconi Memorial** site marks Guglielmo Marconi's first trans-Atlantic wireless message. **Mullion Cove** and **Island** [203: SW6617] are owned by the Trust. About a mile to the south, at **Predannack Head**, the 674-acre Predannack holding spreads inland almost to the A3083. Biologically, this is one of the Trust's most interesting sites. **Kynance Cove** [203: SW6913] which is accesible to wheelchair users, offers good bathing at low tide, and the Trust has just landscaped and improved the clifftop car park. The ½mile of rugged coast to the east of **Lizard Head** includes **Pistil Meadow** where the bodies of 200 people are buried – drowned in one of the worst wrecks off this most treacherous point. Britain's most southerly outpost, **Lizard Point**, together with nearly a mile of coastline to the head of Housel Bay, was acquired by the Trust in 1991. Parking is available in Lizard village, whence a footpath leads down to the Point, or in the NT car park adjacent to the lighthouse.

On the east-facing Lizard coast, on either side of the stone and thatch village of **Cadgwith** [203: SW7214], where fishermen still winch their brightly-coloured craft up the beach, the Trust owns several miles of cliff land. Of particular interest are the remains of the 19th-century serpentine works – serpentine is the local stone – at **Poltesco**. Three detached properties at **Beagles Point**, **Black Head** and **Lowland Point** flank the next village along the coast, Coverack [204: SW7818].

The shores of the **Helford River** [204: SW7626], probably Cornwall's most beautiful estuary, together with its subsidiary **Gillan Creek**, are protected by the Trust along several miles of its length, and at the northern approach, **Rosemullion Head** [204: SW8028]. One of these safeguarded areas is the enchanting **Frenchman's Creek**, the location of Daphne du Maurier's novel. **Glendurgan Garden** (see p.64) fronts the mouth of the estuary. Between the Helford River and Falmouth is a mile of open cliff on either side of the popular beach of **Maenporth**.

Trelissick Garden (see p.67) and estate straddles the western approach to the King Harry Ferry on the B3289, and **Turnaware Point** [204: SW8338] on the east side marks the end of Carrick Roads and the beginning of the Fal Estuary. The Trust owns 2 miles of farmland between **St Just** [204: SW8434] and **St Mawes**, the footpath through which provides wide views over Carrick Roads and the town of Falmouth.

St Anthony Head and **Zone Point** [204: SW8631] form the once-fortified eastern approach to Falmouth harbour. The old defences are largely cleared away, but some of the accommodation is available as holiday lets (see p.18), with wheelchair access and facilities in the cottages. A viewfinder on the highest point, approached by a path suitable for wheelchair users, identifies the features in the wide-ranging panorama.

East of here, Trust ownership extends from the sea on both sides of **Porthmellin Head** [204: SW8732] across the waist of the St Anthony peninsula to the creek and estuary waterfronts facing St Mawes. This is largely farmland, but paths give good access to the main places of interest. Another property fronts the **Percuil River** further up.

CORNWALL

Nare Head [204: SW9137] with its off-lying Gull Rock, is the focus for a concentration of Trust properties, with a 4½ mile coastline, and extending to about 900 acres. A Trust car park at Penare was part of a major tidying-up scheme. A wheelchair ramp and picnic area overlook Kiberick Cove.

The Dodman [204: SX0039] is the grandest headland on the south Cornish coast. The remains of an Iron Age promontory fort can be seen across its broad back and there are Bronze Age barrows. To the west and east are the detached properties of Lambsowden Cove and Maenease Point and, further on, Turbot Point and Bodrugan's Leap, where Sir Henry Trenowth of nearby Bodrugan is said to have jumped into the sea to make his escape by boat to France. Within St Austell Bay is Black Head, where yet another Iron Age earthwork can be seen, together with a rifle range from more recent times.

Much of the coastline to the east and west of Fowey is owned by the Trust. Gribbin Head [200: SX1050] with its boldly striped navigational daymark begins the sequence of properties. There is a gap at Polridmouth Cove (always called Pridm'th) where the Trust owns only the east side of the cove, then a wide strip of mostly Trust land to the outskirts of Fowey. Upstream, overlooking the china clay loading quays, the Trust safeguards the 31 acres of woods and meadow at Station Wood [200: SW1252]. Across Fowey harbour is the tree-fringed creek of Pont Pill [200: SX1451] where the lovely Hall Walk passes through the woods. Much of the farmland encircling Polruan was acquired, with the help of a local appeal, in 1991. Thereafter, Trust ownership follows the coast for several miles to beyond the village of Lansallos [201: SX1751], and extends some distance inland. There are attractive beaches at Lantic Bay and Lansallos Cove.

On each side of Polperro [201: SX2151] the Trust has one mile of coastline. The eastern strip was willed to the Trust by Miss Angela Brazil, the author of school stories for girls, and another mile of Trust land projects into the Channel at Hore Point [201: SX2451].

Trust ownership east of Looe consists of smallish properties at Bodigga, Trethill Cliff, Higher Tregantle Cliffs and Sharrow Point, where there is a cliffside folly called Sharrow Grot [201: SX3952].

A series of detailed leaflets, with maps, has been produced about the Trust's coastal properties. They are available from NT shops in Cornwall or from the Regional Trading Manager (see regional address on final page).

No. 1	Bude to Morwenstow	60p
No. 2	Crackington Haven	40p
No. 3	Boscastle	60p
No. 4	Tintagel	60p
No. 5	Polzeath to Port Quin	50p
No. 6	Bedruthan and Park Head	50p
No. 7	Crantock to Holywell Bay	50p
No. 8	St Agnes and Chapel Porth	40p

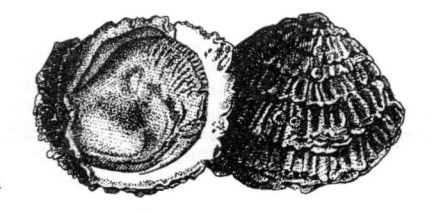

OYSTER

CORNWALL

No. 9	Godrevy to Portreath	50p
No. 10	West Penwith: St Ives to Pendeen	80p
No. 11	West Penwith: Cape Cornwall to Logan Rock	60p
No. 12	Loe Pool and Gunwalloe	60p
No. 13	The Lizard, West Coast: Gunwalloe Church Cove to Kynance	60p
No. 14	Kynance Cove	50p
No. 15	The Lizard, East Coast: Landewednack to St Keverne	60p
No. 16	Helford River	60p
No. 17	Trelissick	60p
No. 18	The Roseland Peninsula	50p
No. 19	St Anthony Battery	50p
No. 20	Nare Head and the Dodman	60p
No. 21	Fowey	80p
No. 22	East Cornwall: Lantic Bay to Sharrow Point	60p

ANTONY

Torpoint, Plymouth PL11 2QA (0752) 812191

One of Cornwall's finest early 18th-century houses, built of silvery-grey Pentewan stone, offset by colonnaded wings of red brick and set within extensive grounds. The fine garden contains a national collection of day lilies, magnolias and summer borders. Also of note is an 18th-century dovecot and the 1789 Bath Pond House

30 March to 31 Oct: Tues, Wed, Thur & BH Mon 1.30–5.30; also Sun in June, July & Aug 1.30–5.30. Last guided tour of house 4.45. Bath Pond House can be seen on prior written application to Administrator and only when house is open

£3.40. Pre-arranged parties £2.60

Available

Shop open as house

House not suitable for wheelchair users. Garden largely accessible. Shop, tea-room & family history exhibition accessible. WC

Braille guide

Tea room open as house

No dogs allowed

5m W of Plymouth via Torpoint car ferry, 2m NW of Torpoint, N of A374, 16m SE of Liskeard, 15m E of Looe [201: SX418564] *Bus:* Western National 80/1, 180 from Plymouth (passing close BR Plymouth), alight Great Park Estate, ¼m, (tel. (0752) 222666) *Station:* Plymouth 6m via vehicle ferry. *Ferry:* Torpoint 2m

continued

CORNWALL

CORNISH ENGINES
Pool, nr Redruth (0209) 216657

Two great beam engines (one with a cylinder $7\frac{1}{2}$ ft in diameter), used for pumping water from over 2,000ft deep and for winding men and ore. They impressively evoke the days when the tin and copper mining industry dominated Cornish life. $\frac{1}{4}$ mile to the west is the Geological Museum of the Camborne School of Mines, where the Trust's Norris collection of minerals can be seen. The engines exemplify the use of high pressure steam patented by the Cornish engineer Richard Trevithick in 1802. The winding engine is rotated today by electricity

- 30 March to 31 Oct: daily 11–5.30 or sunset if earlier (11–5 in Oct). Last admissions $\frac{1}{2}$hr before closing. (Geological Museum Mon to Fri, 9–5, free entry)
- £2. No reduction for parties.

Note: A further engine (Robinson's) is preserved at a mine which is still working and can only be seen when visits can be arranged to fit in with normal mine routine; arrangements must be sought beforehand from the Manager. South Crofty (tel. (0209) 714821)

- Available
- Shop open same times
- Unsuitable for disabled visitors, many flights of stairs. No WCs
- Braille guide
- Refreshments available nearby
- Schools resource pack available. Mining diagrams and working models in both properties
- No dogs allowed
- At Pool, 2m W of Redruth on either side of A3047 [203: SW672415] *Bus:* From surrounding areas (some passing BR Redruth) (tel. (0209) 719988) *Station:* Redruth 2m; Camborne 2m

THE LEVANT STEAM ENGINE
Trewellard, Pendeen, nr St Just (0209) 216657

The oldest working beam engine in Cornwall, sited dramatically in its house on the cliff edge. The engine has recently been restored to steam power after lying motionless for fifty years. Half a mile along the cliff is Geevor mine which closed in 1991, where the surface workings and a mining museum can be viewed

- Open Easter, May & Spring BH Sun & Mon; June: Wed, Thurs, Fri & Sun; July to end Sept: daily except Sat 11–4

CORNWALL

£ £2. Stewarded by volunteer members of the Trevithick Society. Members are invited to contribute to the cost of the project

👶 Available

🏫 Suitable for small groups only (max 40) by prior arrangement

➡ 1m W of Pendeen, on B3306 St Just–Zennor road [203: SW368346]
Bus: Western National 10A from BR Penzance (tel. (0209) 719988)
Station: Penzance 7m

COTEHELE

St Dominick, nr Saltash PL12 6TA (0579) 50434; information (0579) 51222

Built 1485–1627, and home of the Edgcumbe family for centuries, the house contains original furniture, armour and a remarkable set of tapestries and other textiles. The gardens are on several levels, and contain a medieval dovecote. Cotehele Mill has been restored to working condition, with an adjoining cider press. Also of interest is Cotehele Quay, on the Tamar, with 18th- and 19th-century buildings, an outstation of the National Maritime Museum, and the restored Tamar sailing barge Shamrock

Note: The number of visitors to this small and fragile house has to be limited to no more than 600 per day. Please arrive in good time and be prepared to wait to gain entry. There is no electric light in the rooms; visitors should avoid dull days early and late in the season. There are eleven holiday cottages on the estate

O **House & Mill:** 30 March to 31 Oct: daily except Fri (open Good Fri). **House:** 12-5.30 (12-5 in Oct). **Mill:** 11-5.30 (11-5 in Oct). Last admissions ½hr before closing or dusk if earlier. **Garden:** daily 11-5.30 or dusk if earlier. A timed ticket system may be operated on BH weekends which may lead to delays in admission to the house. Nov to end March 1995: garden only, open daily during daylight hours

£ House, garden & mill £5. Garden & mill only £2.50. Parties £4 by prior written arrangement only with the Administrator. Coach party organisers are advised to obtain a copy of the route from Administrator. No parties Sun or BH Mon

🛍 Shop open daily 30 March to 31 Oct 11-5.30 (11-5 in Oct). Also 11-4 Wed to Sun, Nov to Christmas. Tel. (0579) 50072. Cotehele Quay Art & Craft Gallery: open daily 12-5; 11-4 Wed to Sun, Nov to Christmas

♿ Hall and kitchen only. Ramps available at house and restaurant (please enquire); most of garden unsuitable as very steep. Special parking and entrance arrangements; mostly loose gravel. WC

👁 Braille guides for house, garden & mill; scented plants

☕ Coffee, lunches and teas in the Barn Restaurant 30 March to 31 Oct (closed Fri) 11-5.30 (11-5 in Oct) and on Cotehele Quay (open daily) during season, 11-5.30 (11-5 in Oct) and limited opening Nov to Christmas. Tel. (0579) 50652

👶 Parent & baby room

🏫 Schools resource pack available. Environmental Education facilities available. National Maritime Museum outstation on Quay

continued

CORNWALL

- [E] Programme of events – details from Administrator
- 🐕 No dogs allowed
- → On W bank of the Tamar, 1m W of Calstock by footpath (6m by road), 8m SW of Tavistock, 14m from Plymouth via Saltash Bridge; 2m E of St Dominick, 4m from Gunnislake (turn at St Ann's Chapel); can be reached from Plymouth by water (contact Plymouth Boat Cruises Ltd – tel. (0752) 822202) [201: SX422685] *Bus:* Fords 622 Tavistock–Calstock Quay (tel. (0822) 832264) *Station:* Calstock (U), not Sun (except July Aug), 1¼m, Cotehele is signposted on the station

GLENDURGAN GARDEN

Mawnan Smith, nr Falmouth TR11 5JZ
Enquiries (0208) 74281 or (0326) 250906 (opening hours only)

A valley garden of great beauty with fine trees and shrubs, a laurel maze and water gardens. A wooded valley runs down to the tiny village of Durgan on the river. The house is tenanted and not open

- [O] 1 March to 31 Oct: Tues to Sat & BH Mon (closed Good Fri) 10.30–5.30. Last admissions 4.30
- [£] £2.60. No reduction for parties
- Shop and plant sales open as garden
- The lower valley paths are too steep for wheelchairs
- Braille guide
- Giant's Stride (a pole with ropes to swing from). The Maze will re-open on 1 July after restoration
- → 4m SW of Falmouth, ½m SW of Mawnan Smith, on road to Helford Passage [204: SW772277] *Bus:* Trurorian 324 from Falmouth (passing close BR Penmere) (tel. (0872) 73453) *Station:* Penmere (U) 4m

LANHYDROCK

Bodmin PL30 5AD (0208) 73320

Superbly positioned above the River Fowey, this 17th-century house is a blend of Victorian splendour and some elements from the original house, before the disastrous fire which almost destroyed it in 1881. The gatehouse (1651) and the north wing, including a 116-ft gallery with fine plaster ceiling, are unaltered. A total of 42 rooms are open. Formal and shrub gardens are of interest and beauty in all seasons

- [O] 30 March to 31 Oct: garden daily; house daily except Mon, but open BH Mon, 11–5.30 (closes 5 in Oct). Last admissions to house ½hr before closing. Nov to end March 1995: garden only, open daily during daylight hours
- [£] House, garden & grounds £5. Garden & grounds only £2.50. Pre-arranged parties £4. Car park at end of long drive, 600yds.

CORNWALL

🛍	Shop and plant sales open daily 30 March to 31 Oct. Daily 11–4 in Nov & Dec. Tel. (0208) 74099
♿	Disabled visitors may be driven to house; close parking, for assistance consult car park attendant. Access to house via loose gravel and shallow steps, or via ramp to restaurant; most ground floor rooms accessible; small lift to first floor; WC. Shop has some steps. Garden has some steps and sloping gravel paths, steep in places – access via steps; ramp available. Powered self-drive buggy
👁	Braille guides for house & garden. Aromatic plants; water sounds
🍽	Coffee, lunches and snacks. 30 March to 31 Oct: daily. Limited opening in Nov & Dec. Tel. (0208) 74331
👶	Parent and baby room
🎒	Schools resource book. Schools base; children's guide; handling collection
E	Programme of events; details available from Administrator
🐕	In park only, on leads
→	2½m SE of Bodmin, overlooking valley of River Fowey; follow signposts from either A30, Launceston–Bodmin, A38, Bodmin–Liskeard, or B3268, Bodmin–Lostwithiel roads [200: SX085636] *Bus:* (tel. (0209) 719988) *Station:* Bodmin Parkway 1¾m by original carriage-drive to house, signposted in station car park; 3m by road

LAWRENCE HOUSE 🏛

9 Castle Street, Launceston PL15 8BA (0566) 773277 or 773047

The house was given to the Trust to help preserve the character of the street, and is now leased to Launceston Town Council as a museum and civic centre

O	April to early Oct: Mon to Fri 10.30–4.30. Open BH Mon. Other times by appointment
£	Free, but visitors are invited to contribute towards museum expenses
→	[201: SX330848] *Bus:* Western National 76 from Plymouth; Tilleys from Exeter (tel. (0392) 382800)

ST MICHAEL'S MOUNT 🏛 🏠 ✝ 🏰   🚫 ✉ 🏢

Marazion, nr Penzance TR17 0HT (0736) 710507

Originally the site of a Benedictine chapel established by Edward the Confessor. The spectacular castle on its rocky island dates from the 14th century. Approached by a causeway at low tide, the castle presents fine views towards Land's End and The Lizard, fascinating early rooms and an outstanding armoury

Note: Owing to narrow passages within the castle it may be necessary to restrict numbers; visitors are warned that some delays may occur at the height of the season. On Sun from June to Sept a short non-denominational service is held in the Castle Chapel at 11; seating is limited   *continued*

CORNWALL

- 🅾 30 March to 31 Oct: Mon to Fri 10.30–5.30. Last admissions 4.45. Nov to end March: Mon, Wed & Fri guided tours or free flow, as tide, weather and circumstances permit (no regular ferry service during this period; ferries may only operate in favourable boating conditions at any time of year). The times stated above apply from the visitors' entrance on the island, therefore ample time should be allowed for travel to the island

  Note: **The Mount is also open most weekends during the season; these are special charity open days, when NT members are asked to pay for admission**

- £ £3.20. Family ticket £8. Pre-arranged parties £2.80
- 🛍 Shop open 30 March to 31 Oct daily. Tel. (0736) 711067
- ♿ The causeway and paths are cobbled, and therefore unsuitable for wheelchairs, prams or pushchairs
- 👁 Braille guide
- 🍴 Island café (not NT), 30 March to end Sept: Mon to Fri. Coffee, lunches and teas in 'The Sail Loft' restaurant, 30 March to 31 Oct: daily; limited out of season service. Tel. (0736) 710748
- 🏫 Special educational visits for schools and organisations on Tues from March to end May, weather permitting, by prior arrangement with Mr O. Bartle, Manor Office, Marazion. Schools resource pack available
- 🐕 No dogs allowed
- ➡ ½m S of A394 at Marazion, whence there is access on foot over the causeway at low tide or, during summer months only, by ferry at high tide (return ferry tickets should not be taken). Tide and ferry information only: tel. (0736) 710265 [203: SW515298] *Bus:* Western National 2, 2A Penzance Falmouth (passing BR Penzance) (tel. (0209) 719988) *Station:* Penzance 3m

TINTAGEL OLD POST OFFICE 🏫

Tintagel PL34 0DB (0840) 770024 during opening hours only

Small and fascinating 14th-century stone house built to the plan of a medieval manor house, with a large hall. It was used in the 19th century for nearly fifty years as the letter-receiving office for the district and is now restored as such

- 🅾 30 March to 31 Oct: daily 11–5.30 (closes 5 in Oct)
- £ £1.90. No reduction for parties
- 🛍 Shop open as property
- ♿ Ground floor & garden accessible
- 👁 Braille guide
- ➡ In centre of village [200: SX056884] *Bus:* Western National 52 from Wadebridge (with some from BR Bodmin Parkway) (tel. (0209) 719988) Fry's service from Plymouth (tel. (0840) 770256)

REFER TO OPENING PAGES FOR GENERAL INFORMATION

CORNWALL

TRELISSICK GARDEN 🌸 🌿 🦋 🏛 🚶

Feock, nr Truro TR3 6Q (0872) 862090; information 865808

The rare shrubs and plants make this large garden attractive at all seasons. There is also an extensive park, woodland walks beside the river and farmland, with beautiful views over the Fal Estuary and Falmouth harbour. The house is not open, but there is an Art and Craft Gallery by the Home Farm courtyard. 4 holiday cottages available

- **O**   1 March to 31 Oct: Mon to Sat 10.30–5.30; Sun 12.30–5.30; (closes 5 in March & Oct). Last admissions ½hr before closing. Woodland walk also open Nov to end Feb
- **£**   £3. No reduction for parties. £1 car park fee refundable on admission
- 🛍   Shop and plant sales, open as garden. Tel. (0872) 865515. Trelissick Art & Craft Gallery, open as garden, tel. (0872) 864084. Shop & gallery open daily 1 Nov to Christmas
- ♿   Upper parts of garden reasonably flat with loose gravel paths; parking near shop & restaurant; powered self-drive buggy. WC near shop & car park
- 👁   Braille guide. Small walled garden specially planted with aromatic plants
- ☕   Coffee, lunches and teas in Trelissick Garden Barn, and light refreshments in the Courtyard Room, on garden open days, Mon to Sat 11–5.30; Sun 12–5.30 (closes 5 in March & Oct); additional limited daily opening in Nov & Dec. Tel. (0872) 863486
- 🎒   Schools resource pack
- **E**   Programme of theatrical and musical events; details from Administrator
- 🐕   In woodland walk and park only, on leads
- ➡   4m S of Truro, on both sides of B3289 above King Harry Ferry [204: SW837396] *Bus:* Truronian 311 from Truro, (passing close BR Truro) (tel. (0872) 73453) *Station:* Truro 5m; Perranwell (U), not Sun, except July & Aug, 4m

TRENGWAINTON GARDEN 🌸

nr Penzance TR20 8RZ (0736) 63021 or 68410 (during opening hours)

This large shrub garden, with views over Mount's Bay, is particularly colourful in spring and early summer. The walled garden has many tender plants which cannot be grown in the open anywhere else in England

- **O**   1 March to end Oct: Wed to Sat, BH Mon & Good Fri 10.30–5.30 (closes 5 in March & Oct). Last admissions ½hr before closing
- **£**   £2.50. No reduction for parties
- 🛍   Plant sales
- ♿   Car parking on request. WC

continued

67

CORNWALL

- 👁 Braille guide; fragrant plants; stream; pools; water sounds
- ☕ Light refreshments (not NT) available in the farmhouse garden
- ➡ 2m NW of Penzance, ½m W of Heamoor on Penzance Morvah road (B3312), ¼m off St Just road (A3071) [203: SW445315] *Bus:* Western National 10/A Penzance–St Just (tel. (0209) 719988) *Station:* Penzance 2m

TRERICE

nr Newquay TR8 4PG (0637) 875404

A delightful, small, secluded Elizabethan manor house, built in 1571, containing fine fireplaces, good plaster ceilings, oak and walnut furniture, and clocks. A small museum in the barn traces the development of the lawn mower. The summer garden has some unusual plants and there is also an orchard of old varieties of fruit trees

- ⊙ 30 March to 31 Oct: daily except Tues 11–5.30 (closes 5 in Oct). Last admissions ½hr before closing
- £ £3.60. Pre-arranged parties £3
- 🛍 Shop open as house. Plant sales
- ♿ Ground & upper (via grass slope) floors of house, restaurant & shop accessible; some loose gravel and cobbles. Garden more difficult. Close parking by prior arrangement with Administrator. WC
- 👁 Braille guide and Braille disabled access leaflet
- ☕ Coffee, lunches and teas in the Barn. Organisers of parties should arrange for meals beforehand tel. (0637) 879434
- 👶 Parent and baby room
- 🏫 Schools may visit the House from 10 by prior arrangement with the Administrator. Schools are welcome to picnic in the Orchard
- E Programme of events – details available from the Administrator
- 🐕 No dogs allowed
- ➡ 3m SE of Newquay via A392 and A3058 (turn right at Kestle Mill) [200: SW841585] *Bus:* Western National 90 Newquay–Truro, alight Kestle Mill, ¾m (tel. (0209) 719988) *Station:* Quintrell Downs (U), not Sun, except July–Aug, 1½m

Cumbria

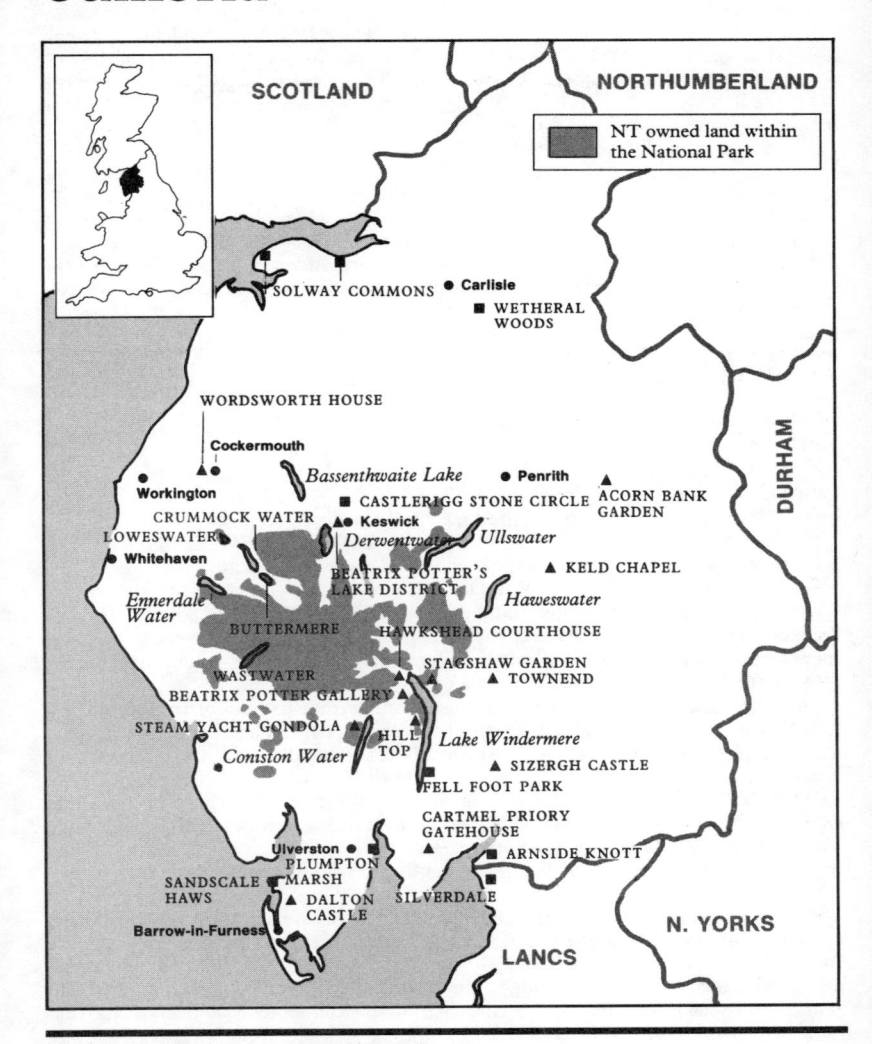

LAKE DISTRICT LANDSCAPE

The Trust's most important work in Cumbria is the conservation of more than one quarter of the Lake District National Park. Almost all the central fell area and the major valley heads are owned or held on lease by the Trust, and six of the main lakes and much

CUMBRIA

of their shoreline are also fully protected. These 140,000 acres are about a quarter of the Trust's entire holding throughout the country and by far the largest portion of any National Park protected by the Trust.

The Trust bought its first property in the Lake District, **Brandelhow Woods** [89: NY250200], in 1902 to guarantee public access to the shore of Derwentwater. Some of the most important of the Trust's 7,000 acres of woodland in the National Park are in the Borrowdale Valley: **Great Wood** [89: NY2721], with a well-screened car park (charge for non-members) and lake access, **Manesty Wood** [89: NY251191] with its caravan site run by the Caravan Club, and **Johnny Wood** [89: NY252142] a Site of Special Scientific Interest. Ruskin called the view from **Friar's Crag** [89: NY264223], on the north shore of Derwentwater, one of the finest in Europe: his memorial stands upon the crag which itself is a memorial to Canon Hardwicke Rawnsley whose inspiration and energy began the great work of the Trust. Nearby at the Keswick boatlandings is a National Trust information centre and shop. To the east of Keswick on a magnificent site is **Castlerigg Stone Circle** [89: NY293236], a free-standing megalithic circle of 40 stones.

In **Keswick**, The Trust has created a Visitor Centre to tell the fascinating story of how the Lake District's landscape developed, how, early this century, Beatrix Potter identified and countered the growing threats to its continuance, and how the Trust is carrying on her great work (see p.74).

Loweswater [89: NY1221], **Crummock Water** [89: NY1518] and **Buttermere** [89: NY1815] (car park charge for non-members) are all under Trust protection; a boat can be hired on all three lakes for fishing. Around these lakes the Trust is increasing the native hardwoods, planting predominantly oak. Scale Force [89: NY150171] south-west of Crummock Water, is the highest waterfall in a district renowned for its falls.

Much of the northern and all of the southern shore of **Ennerdale Water** [89: NY1015], is protected by the Trust, as are all the high fells to the west and south.

Further south still is dramatic **Wasdale**, arguably the wildest of all the valleys [89: NY1606], almost entirely protected by the Trust: from **Scafell Pike** [89: NY215071], England's highest mountain, and **Great Gable** [89: NY215106] at its head, to the awesome screes sliding down into **Wastwater**, England's deepest lake. Even the bed of the lake is in the Trust's care. There is a Trust campsite here.

There are dramatic views of the lakeless Eskdale from the top of **Hardknott Pass** [89: NY230015]. In this valley alone the Trust protects 3,750 acres of land, including the summit of **Bowfell** [89: NY247064] and all the surrounding fells. One of the Trust's isolated holiday cottages, Bird How, is situated in this quiet and beautiful valley.

Dunnerdale [96: SD2093], beloved of the poet Wordsworth (whose birthplace in Cockermouth is under Trust care and open to the public, see p.79), with the tumbling River Duddon, scattered woods and steep side-valleys, leads up to **Wrynose Bottom** [89: NY260020], where much work has recently been done in repairing dilapidated dry stone walls.

Wrynose Pass leads down to the Langdale Valleys. **Great Langdale** [89: NY3006] is climbing country: here there is a permanent campsite. For those less hardy the Old Dungeon Ghyll Hotel [89: NY286060] provides much more comfortable accommodation. Evidence of some of the huge amount of footpath repair undertaken in recent years can be seen just a short walk up the fell from the well-screened and landscaped car park beneath **Stickle Ghyll** (car park charage for non-members) [89: NY295064]. 16,842 acres of land in this area are held on lease from the 7th Earl of Lonsdale. This large area includes the famous **Langdale Pikes**, together with all the high land from **Seat Sandal** on the slopes of Helvellyn to the head of Great Langdale, the bed of **Grasmere Lake**, and part of **Rydal Water**, **White Moss and Elterwater Commons**.

Moving to the softer hills of the south, Trust ownership around Coniston is centred on

CUMBRIA

the vast Monk Coniston Estate which includes **Tarn Hows** [89: NY3300]; (car park charge for non-members). Here the Trust has created a new section of the path round the tarns to enable those with walking difficulties to enjoy this beautiful place to the full. But there are unavoidably some steep inclines: strong helpers and great care are needed by those attempting a circumnavigation in wheelchairs. Tarn Hows was bought by Beatrix Potter, better known locally as Mrs William Heelis. She sold half at cost to the Trust (the purchase of Tarn Hows being funded by Sir Samuel Scott), and then bequeathed to it the other half. Restored and relaunched by the National Trust in 1980 the Victorian steam yacht **Gondola**, first launched in 1859, gently plies the length of Coniston Water (see p.78). In **Hawkshead village** there is a National Trust shop [96: SD352982] and the **Beatrix Potter Gallery**, with a selection of her original watercolours on display (see p.73). **Hill Top** [89: SD370956], Beatrix Potter's first acquisition in the Lake District, in Near Sawrey, is best visited at off-peak times (see p.76).

It was through money raised by Beatrix Potter that the Trust was able to purchase **Cockshott Point** [96: SD396965] on the shore of Windermere. On this lake, the most popular of all, the Trust protects some 90% of the land from which the public has free access to the shore. On the west side is **Low Wray Campsite** [89: NY372011] and **Claife Woods**, along some 3 miles of shore stretching from near Ferry Nab to Wray Castle [96: SD3898]. At the southern tip of the lake, near Newby Bridge, is **Fell Foot Park** [96: SD382870], with picnic areas, boats for hire and a boathouse café (see p.75).

Bridge House, perched over Stock Ghyll in Ambleside, once home to a family of six, is now the Trust's oldest Information Centre and smallest shop [89: NY375045]. Between Ambleside and Grasmere lies **White Moss Common** (car park charge for non-members) [89: NY348065] where the Trust has provided a wheelchair path leading from the car park to the river. **Church Stile** houses a Trust shop and Information Centre [89: NY336074] in Grasmere village, while at the head of the valley the Trust has pitched a totally new footpath up Helm Crag to overcome the massive erosion problems and provide a more attractive route to the summit of this family favourite.

Aira Force [89: NY399205]; (car park charge for non-members); provides a glimpse of a landscaped Victorian park with dramatic waterfalls, arboretum and rock scenery. There is also a café. After a walk along this shore of Ullswater Wordsworth wrote 'I wandered lonely as a cloud'. Trust purchase in 1913 ensured that this area would not be developed into a housing estate.

In the small area of the Lake District are tranquil lakes, quiet valleys, gently rolling vales and awesome mountains, each individual and with its own special character. Today it is still a working community of farmers and sheep where the Trust's protection of so much of this glorious landscape is aimed at maintaining the delicate balance between man and nature. In one three year period alone, the Trust has planted 135,000 trees in the Lake District, the majority native hardwoods, predominantly sessile oak. In the past eleven years 40 major footpath rebuilding projects have been completed as well as many smaller projects right across the Lake District. Since 1985 major works have been completed on well over three quarters of the Trust's 81 Lake District farms, and less extensive repairs and improvements have been carried out to nearly every farm the Trust owns. Many miles of walls have also been repaired by Trust gangs, although with an estimated 2,000 miles of wall on Trust land alone, there is still a lot to do.

THE REMAINDER OF CUMBRIA

While most of the countryside under the Trust's protection lies within the National Park, there are some outstanding areas in other parts of Cumbria. Near Carlisle **Wetheral Woods** [86: NY470533] provides riverside walks by the River Eden, while at

CUMBRIA

the other end of the county the limestone escarpment of **Arnside** Knott [89: SD456774] and **Heathwaite** offers wonderful views over Morecambe Bay. Only two miles from Barrow is **Sandscale Haws** (car parking [96: SD200756] signed Roanhead off A595, just north of Dalton-in-Furness) an internationally renowned nature reserve, with beach, flora-rich dunes and marshes, the breeding site of the rare Natterjack toad and with a strong population of the Coral Root orchid; Braille guide available. Nearby stands **Dalton Castle**, a 14th-century pele tower in the main street of Dalton-in-Furness (see p.75). Three miles from Kendal is the **Sizergh Castle Estate** [89: SD498878] with not only the castle and its extensive garden (see p.77), but also long walks through surrounding woods and hills. On a smaller scale is **Keld Chapel** [90: NY554145] (see p.76), a charming pre-Reformation building near Shap. **Cartmel Priory Gatehouse** (see p.74) also dates from before the Reformation and is the only building, other than the church, which remains of the Augustinian Priory. Plumpton Marsh [96/97:3198] is a small but intriguing coastal saltmarsh 1m east of Ulverston with views of the Leven estuary and adjacent to the mouth of the Ulverston Canal (not NT). At the opposite end of the county is **Acorn Bank Garden** [91: NY612281] (see XX), a fascinating contrast of well established herb garden and newly opened-up woodland. The furthermost north-west of the Trust's properties are the **Solway Commons** [85: NY3156], 170 acres of common land and 1½ miles of coastline with a solitary beauty and magnificent views of the estuary and of the mountains of Galloway.

Holiday Cottages. The National Trust's holiday cottages in the Lake District do not attempt to be anything but homely and reasonably comfortable bases from which to explore. The cottages can be conveniently categorised as either fell or waterside. The waterside cottages stand within yards of lakeshores and river banks. They tend to be of easier access and slightly more modern in their facilities than the fell cottages. As their name implies the fell cottages are at a higher level, often at the end of rough tracks; some are quite isolated.

Restharrow Cottage, on the quiet western shore of Windermere, has been adapted for disabled visitors, who will be given booking preference. For a leaflet or bookings for all cottages, contact the Regional Office.

Boating and Fishing. A leaflet detailing the boating and fishing available on National Trust waters in the Lake District is available from NT Information Centres or from the Bookings Secretary, Fell Foot Park, Newby Bridge, nr Ulverston, Cumbria LA22 8NN (please send s.a.e.). NT rowing boats are available for hire on Buttermere, Crummock Water, Loweswater and Windermere.

Tarn Hows, White Moss Common, Fell Foot Park, Castlerigg Stone Circle, Aira Force and Friar's Crag and Sizergh Castle have special provision for disabled visitors: details are given in a special leaflet.

Campsites. Leaflets detailing the campsites run by the Trust can be obtained from Fell Foot Park.

CUMBRIA

ACORN BANK GARDEN ✵
Temple Sowerby, nr Penrith CA10 1SP (07683) 61893

A 2½-acre garden protected by fine oaks under which grow a vast display of daffodils. Inside the walls there are two orchards containing a variety of fruit trees. Surrounding the orchards are mixed borders with shrubs, herbaceous plants and roses, while the impressive herb garden has the largest collection of culinary and medicinal plants in the north. A circular woodland walk runs beside the Crowdundle Beck; the mill is under restoration, but not yet open to visitors. The house is let to the Sue Ryder Foundation

- ⓞ 1 April to 31 Oct: daily 10–5.30. Last admissions 5. The house is not open to the public
- £ £1.60, children 80p. Pre-arranged parties £1.10. Car parking within grounds
- 🛍 Small shop and plants for sale, open same times as garden
- ♿ Access to herb garden, herbaceous borders, greenhouse & shop. WC
- 👶 Baby-changing facilities
- 🐕 Admitted on leads to woodland walk, but not to walled garden
- → Just N of Temple Sowerby, 6m E of Penrith on A66 [91: NY612281]
  Station: Langwathby (U) 5m; Penrith 6m

BEATRIX POTTER GALLERY 🏠
Main Street, Hawkshead LA22 0NS (05394) 36355

An annually changing exhibition of Beatrix Potter's original illustrations from her children's story books. The building was once the office of her husband, the solicitor William Heelis, and the interior remains largely unaltered since his day

- ⓞ 1 April to 31 Oct: Mon to Fri (& BH Sun) 10.30–4.30. Last admissions 4. Admission is by timed ticket incl NT members
- £ £2.50, children £1.30. No reduction for parties. Car and coach parking in town car park 200yds
- 🛍 Shop 30yds open daily 9.30–5.30, except Tues out of season (tel. (05394) 36471)
- ♿ We regret Gallery unsuitable for wheelchairs
- 👁 Braille guide
- ☕ Available in Hawkshead
- 👶 We regret the Gallery is not suitable for baby backpacks or pushchairs
- → In The Square [96: SD352982] *Bus:* CMS 50516 Ambleside to Coniston (connections from BR Windermere) tel. (0946) 63222 *Station:* Windermere 6½m via vehicle ferry

REFER TO OPENING PAGES FOR GENERAL INFORMATION

CUMBRIA

BEATRIX POTTER'S LAKE DISTRICT
Packhorse Court, Keswick CA12 5JB (07687) 75173

The National Trust Visitor Centre for the Lake District. 16 min. dramatic slide and video presentations bring to life Beatrix Potter's most important achievement; her 'saving' of 6,000 acres of the Lake District and her careful and sensitive conservation of this magnificent area on behalf of the nation which is continued by the National Trust. Japanese commentary available

- 1 April to 31 Oct: daily 10.30–5.30; Nov to March: weekends 12–4
- £2.50, children £1.30. Discount for NT members. This is an enterprise, not held for preservation, to raise funds towards conservation of the Trust's Lake District properties. Pre-arranged parties £2.15, children £1; family ticket £7 for 2 adults and up to 4 children. Further details from Beatrix Potter's Lake District. Shows every half hour. Parking in Keswick
- Open same times as show & exhibition. Also 4 Nov to 24 Dec; Fri, Sat, Sun & Mon 10-4 and Jan to March 1995, weekends 10-4. Accessible from Visitor Centre or from Standish Street entrance
- Accessible to wheelchairs. WC nearby
- Induction loop for impaired hearing. Guide dogs admitted
- Refreshments and WC available nearby
- Contact Exhibition Manager
- In the centre of Keswick, signed within Packhorse Court, a pedestrian precinct; access from Main Street, from Station Road and from Standish Street *Bus:* CMS X5, 34, Wrights 888 BR Penrith–Workington; CMS 555 Lancaster–Keswick (passes close BR Lancaster, Kendal & Workington) (tel. (0228) 812812) *Station:* Penrith 17m, Aspatria 16m

LOW YEWDALE FARM

CARTMEL PRIORY GATEHOUSE
Cavendish Street, Cartmel, Grange-over-Sands LA11 6QA (05395) 36522

All that is left, apart from the church, of the Augustinian priory, dating from about 1330. A picturesque building which served as a grammar school from 1624–1790. Leased as a picture gallery

- 1 April to 30 Oct: Tues to Sun 11–5. If closed on stated opening days tel. (05395) 36522 for accompanied visit
- Free. Parking in the village
- [96: SD378788] Cavendish Street, Cartmel, Grange-over-Sands *Bus:* CMS 530/1, Kendal–Cartmel (passing BR Grange-over-Sands) (tel. (0946) 63222) *Station:* Cark (U) 2m

CUMBRIA

DALTON CASTLE

Market Place, Dalton-in-Furness, Cumbria LA15 8AX (05394) 35599

A 14th-century tower in the main street of Dalton-in-Furness. Local exhibition by Friends of Dalton Castle

- **O** Easter to end Sept: Sat 2–5
- **£** Free but donation welcome
- **→** In main street of Dalton [96: SD226739] *Bus:* from surrounding areas (tel. (0946) 63222) *Station:* Dalton ¼m

FELL FOOT PARK

Newby Bridge, Ulverston LA12 8NN (05395) 31273

An 18-acre park and garden in the process of being restored, with lakeshore access and magnificent views of the Lakeland fells. Good shows of daffodils and rhododendrons. Boat launching, rowing boats for hire, picnics; ideal for a day's outing

Note: No launching or landing of speedboats or jet skis

- **O** **Park:** all year 10–8 or dusk if sooner. Rowing boat hire 1 April to 31 Oct, daily incl. Good Fri. 11–5 (buoyancy aids available)
- **£** Car park £2.50. Coaches £10 by arrangement
- 🛍 11–5
- ♿ Accessible but please be careful; slopes and unfenced water. Access to café; WC beside café; special parking for 4 cars
- 🍽 Coffee, light lunches, teas and ice creams in boathouse café, 1 April to 31 Oct 11–5.
- 🐕 Admitted on leads
- **→** At the extreme S end of Lake Windermere on E shore, entrance from A592 [96/97: SD381869] *Bus:* CMS 518 Ulverston–Ambleside (passing BR Windermere) (tel. (0946) 63222) *Station:* Grange-over-Sands 6m

HAWKSHEAD COURTHOUSE

Hawkshead, nr Ambleside (Cumbria Regional Office (05394) 35599)

Dating from the 15th century, the Courthouse is all that is left of the manorial buildings of Hawkshead, once held by Furness Abbey

- **O** 1 April to 31 Oct: daily 10–5, by key from NT shop, The Square, Hawkshead. May occasionally be in use by the local community
- **£** Free. No WCs. No parking facilities

continued

75

CUMBRIA

→ At junction of Ambleside and Coniston roads, ½m N of Hawkshead on B5286 [96/97: SD349987] *Bus:* CMS 505/6 Ambleside–Coniston (connections from BR Windermere) (tel. (0946) 63222) *Station:* Windermere 6½m via vehicle ferry

HILL TOP

At Near Sawrey, Ambleside LA22 0LF (05394) 36269

Beatrix Potter wrote many Peter Rabbit books in this little 17th-century house, which contains her furniture and china. A selection of her original illustrations is displayed at the Beatrix Potter Gallery, Hawkshead (see p.73)

Note: Hill Top is a very small house and only a limited number of visitors can be admitted at any one time. During the busiest periods this may give rise to long delays and some visitors may not gain admission at all. Please help to preserve Hill Top by avoiding peak times, particularly wet mornings in school holidays (closed Thur & Fri except Good Fri)

○ 1 April to 31 Oct: Mon to Wed, Sat & Sun 11–5 (closed Thur & Fri except Good Fri). Last admissions 4.30

£ £3.30. Children £1.70. No reduction for parties. Parking 200yds; no parking for coaches

⌂ Shop daily 10–5 during season

♿ Unsuitable for wheelchairs

👁 Accompanied visually impaired people welcome, but are advised to visit outside peak times as house is so small and approach paths are narrow; Braille guide

🍽 Bar lunch and evening bar meal at the Tower Bank Arms (NT owned, and let to tenant) next door, during licensing hours (tel. (05394) 36334)

🚸 Unsuitable for back-packs or push chairs

→ 2m S of Hawkshead, in hamlet of Near Sawrey, behind the Tower Bank Arms [96/97: SD370955] *Bus:* tel. (0946) 63222. Frequent from BR Windermere to Bowness Pier, thence ferry & 2m walk *Station:* Windermere 4½m via vehicle ferry

KELD CHAPEL ✠

Shap, nr Kendal

Small pre-Reformation building, still used for occasional services

○ At all reasonable hours; key available in village; notice on chapel door

£ Free. Unsuitable for coaches. No WCs

→ 1m SW of Shap village, close to River Lowther [90: NY554145] *Bus:* CMS 107 Penrith–Shap (passing close BR Penrith), thence 1m (tel. (0946) 63222) *Station:* Penrith 10m

CUMBRIA

SIZERGH CASTLE 🏰 ✥

Sizergh, nr Kendal LA8 8AE (05395) 60070

The Strickland family still lives here after more than 750 years. This impressive 14th-century pele tower was extended in Tudor times, with some of the finest Elizabethan carved overmantels in the country. Contents include good English and French furniture and family portraits. The castle is surrounded by gardens (including the Trust's largest limestone rock garden) of beauty and interest; good autumn colour. Large estate; walks leaflet available in shop

- **Castle:** 3 April to 31 Oct: Sun to Thur 1.30–5.30. **Garden:** as Castle from 12.30. Last admissions 5
- £3.30, children £1.70. Garden only £1.70. Parties of 15 or more £2.50 by arrangement (not BH). Car park 100yds
- Shop open as garden
- Access to most of garden mainly via gravel paths; wheelchair available. Lower Hall & tea-room accessible. WC
- Garden & first floor suitable for accompanied visually impaired visitors; Braille guide
- Tea-room in basement of pele tower open 1.30. Picnic tables in car park
- Young Explorers Questionnaire. Castle unsuitable for baby back-packs and pushchairs
- No dogs
- 3½m S of Kendal NW of interchange A590/A591 [97: SD498878] *Bus:* CMS 555 Keswick–Lancaster (passing close BR Lancaster & Kendal) (tel. (0946) 63222) *Station:* Oxenholme 3m; Kendal (U) 3½m

STAGSHAW GARDEN ✥

Ambleside LA22 0HE (05394) 35599

This woodland garden was created by the late C. H. D. Acland, Regional Agent for the Trust. It contains a fine collection of azaleas and rhododendrons, planted to give good blends of colour under the thinned oaks on the hillside; also many trees and shrubs, including magnolias, camellias and embothriums

- 1 April to end June: daily 10–6.30. July to end Oct: by appointment with NT North West Regional Office (see final page). Please send s.a.e.
- £1. No reduction for parties. Parking very limited; access dangerous; visitors may park at Waterhead car park and walk to Stagshaw. No access for coaches park in Waterhead car park, Ambleside. No WCs
- Difficult for pushcairs
- ½m S of Ambleside on A591 [90: NY380030] *Bus:* CMS (tel. (0946) 63222); 518, 555, W1 from BR Windermere *Station:* Windermere, 4m

CUMBRIA

STEAM YACHT GONDOLA

The National Trust (Enterprises) Ltd, Gondola Bookings, Pier Cottage, Coniston LA21 8AJ (05394) 41288

The steam yacht Gondola, *first launched in 1859, and now completely renovated by the Trust, provides a steam powered passenger service, carrying 86 passengers in opulently upholstered saloons. Travel aboard* Gondola *is an experience in its own right, and a superb way to see Coniston's scenery*

- **Sailings:** Steam Yacht *Gondola* sails to a scheduled daily timetable during the season, weather permitting, starting at 11, except Sat, when sailings start at 12.05. 1994 sailings begin on 30 March and continue to 31 Oct. The Trust reserves the right to cancel sailings in the event of high winds or lack of demand. Piers at Coniston, Park-a-Moor at SE end of the lake and Brantwood (not NT). Parties from Coniston Pier only. Free parking & WCs at Coniston Pier

- Ticket prices and timetable on application and published locally. No reduction for NT members as *Gondola* is an enterprise and not held solely for preservation. Parties & private charters: by prior arrangement. Contact may be made direct between 9.00am & 10.30am; answerphone in operation at other times

- Guidebook and some souvenirs available on board

- Visually impaired people may travel on *Gondola* but not suitable for wheelchairs; guide dogs admitted

- Coniston ($\frac{1}{2}$m to Coniston Pier) *Bus:* CMS (tel. (0946) 63222) 505/6 from Ambleside, (connections from BR Windermere) *Station:* Foxfield (U), not Sun, 10m; Windermere 10m via vehicle ferry

TOWNEND

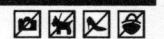

Troutbeck, Windermere LA23 1LB (05394) 32628

An exceptional relic of Lake District life of past centuries. Originally a 'statesman' (wealthy yeoman) farmer's house, built about 1626, Townend contains carved woodwork, books, papers, furniture and fascinating domestic implements of the past, accumulated by the Browne family who lived here from that date until 1943

- 1 April to 30 Oct: Tues to Fri, Sun & BH Mon, 1–5 or dusk if earlier. Last admissions 4.30
- £2.50, children £1.30. No reduction for parties which must be pre-booked. Townend and the village are unsuitable for coaches; 12 & 15 seater minibuses are acceptable; permission to take coaches to Townend must be obtained from the Highways Dept, Cumbria CC, Carlisle, Cumbria. Car park (no coaches)
- Unsuitable for wheelchairs
- Refreshments available in the village
- Unsuitable for baby back-packs or pushchairs
- 3m SE of Ambleside at S end of Troutbeck village [90: NY407020] *Bus:* tel. (0946) 63222) From surrounding areas (many passing BR Windermere) to within 1m *Station:* Windermere 3m

WORDSWORTH HOUSE

Main Street, Cockermouth CA13 9RX (0900) 824805

The house where William Wordsworth was born in 1770. This north-country Georgian town house was built in 1745. Seven rooms are furnished in 18th-century style, with some personal effects of the poet; his childhood garden, with terraced walk, leads down to the Derwent. Video display in the old stables

- 1 April to 31 Oct: weekdays 11–5. Also Sat 2 & 30 April, 28 May and all Sats 9 July to 3 Sept. Closed remaining Sats and all Suns. Last admissions 4.30
- £2.40, children £1.20. Pre-booked parties £1.80. Parking in the town
- Shop same months as house: Mon to Sat 10–5. Also 1 Nov to end March 1995 11–4 (closed Thur, Sun & week after Christmas)
- Unsuitable for severely disabled people
- Suitable for escorted visually impaired visitors; Braille guide
- Morning coffee, light lunches & refreshments (licensed for beer and wine); teas in the old kitchen
- We regret the house is not suitable for baby back-packs, pushchairs or wheelchairs. Baby sling available (up to 2 yrs)
- [89: NY118307] *Bus:* CMS X5, 34 BR Penrith–Workington (passing close BR Workington); 58 from Maryport (passing close BR Maryport) (tel. (0946) 63222) *Station:* Maryport 6½m

Derbyshire & Peak District

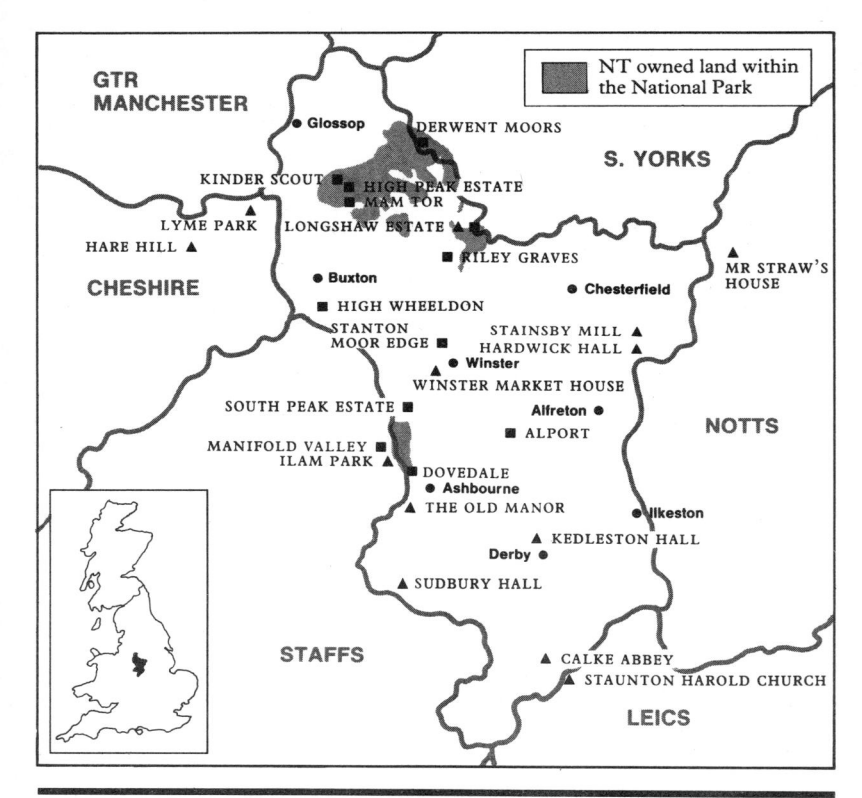

COUNTRYSIDE

Derbyshire is a county of contrasts – gentle river valleys, pastures, woodland and the high peat moorlands and towering limestone crags of the Peaks.

The Trust's holdings here, primarily in Derbyshire, Staffordshire and South Yorkshire, amount to some 12 per cent of the Peak District National Park, the first of ten to be designated in England and Wales by Government in the 1950s and '60s. While the Trust and the National Park Authorities work closely together they are entirely separate bodies; the National Parks are statutory authorities, and the Trust is an independent charity. The Trust's extensive ownership in the Peak District is managed in two estates.

High Peak & Longshaw Estates (tel. Estate Office: Hope Valley (0433) 670368).
High Peak Estate: An important part of the Trust's High Peak Estate is in South Yorkshire; the Derwent Moors extend to some 5,000 acres, with an extra 1,400 acres

DERBYSHIRE & PEAK DISTRICT

which spill over into Derbyshire [110: SK1944]. This vast stretch of moorland on the east bank of the River Derwent rises to 1,775ft and overlooks the three main reservoirs in the Peak District, created at the turn of the century by flooding the dales – the Ladybower, the Derwent and the Howden.

By far the largest single holding of the Trust's 36,500 acres in Derbyshire is the **Hope Woodlands**, 16,500 acres, 12 miles west of Sheffield [110: SK135935]. This has less woodland than its name suggests; it is largely wild and dramatic Pennine moorland adjoining Kinder Scout and giving superb views over the Peak District. The moors are open except on published grouse-shooting days. The property is crossed by the Pennine Way.

Kinder Scout [110: SK0888] came to the Trust in 1982. Probably the most famous landmark in the Peak District at 2,000ft high, known not only for its magnificence, but because of the mass trespass here in 1932 when ramblers campaigned, eventually with some success, for the right of access to uplands in England.

[🏃] The Kinder estate marches with the Trust's holdings in Edale, where several hill farms are owned with viewpoints such as **Lord's Seat** and **Lose Hill Pike** [110: SK153853]. But perhaps the most fascinating landmark here is **Mam Tor** – the 'shivering mountain' of which Celia Fiennes said in 1697 '... a high hill that looks exactly round but on the side next Castleton ... it's all broken but it looks just in resemblance as a great Hayricke thats cut down one halfe ... and on that broken side the sand keeps trickling down all wayes ...' This description fits today, and there are views from its 1,700-ft summit towards Kinder and the High Peak [110: SK1383].

Next to Mam Tor is the spectacular limestone gorge of **Winnats Pass** close to the Blue John mines of Treak Cliff (not NT) which yield an amethyst-coloured stone from which ornaments have been made since the 18th century.

Longshaw Estate (tel. Hope Valley (0433) 631708 Visitor Centre/631757 Warden's Office). (See also entry on p.85–6).

At **Longshaw** near Hathersage the Trust owns nearly 1,600 acres of moor, pasture and woodland by the Burbage Brook which varies from a raging torrent in wet weather to a babbling brook in summer. In a disused quarry are half-finished millstones – a reminder of the end of the millstone-making industry centred here about a hundred years ago.

In 1665 the Plague came to Eyam near Tideswell, carried there from London in some clothing. When it was discovered, the villagers – led by their rector – took a terrible decision: they isolated the village and no-one was allowed in or out until the infection had burnt itself out. Three-quarters of the inhabitants died and seven members of one family, the Hancocks, are buried in the **Riley Graves** in a meadow called the Righ Lea. The Trust owns the graves and protects the meadow [110: SK229766].

South Peak Estate (tel. Estate Office: Thorpe Cloud (033 529) 503).

This area of outstanding natural beauty in the southern limestone region of the Peak District extends to 3,200 acres and consists of **Ilam Hall** (now a Youth Hostel) its grounds and parkland [♿] (see p.199); **Dovedale**, internationally famous for its ashwoods and geological features [♿]; the former Manifold and Hamps Light Railway is now a well-surfaced tarmac track, providing easy access into dramatic limestone scenery. There is an Information Shelter at Milldale.

Ilam Hall is at the centre of **Ilam Country Park**, where there are very pleasant walks (leaflet available; address on p.199), also an Information Centre/Shop and the Manifold Restaurant and tea-room (tel. Thorpe Cloud (033 529) 245); also a Day Visit Room, bookable for use by visiting groups; book in advance via the National Park Study Centre, Losehill Hall, Castleton, Derbyshire (tel. Hope Valley (0433) 20373).

PLEASE REFER TO PAGES 5–9

DERBYSHIRE & PEAK DISTRICT

CALKE ABBEY
Ticknall, Derby DE73 1LE (0332) 863822

The house that time forgot; this Baroque mansion, built 1701–3 for Sir John Harpur, is virtually unaltered since the death of the last baronet in 1924. Within the house there is a unique Caricature Room, gold and white drawing room, Sir Vauncey's childhood bedroom, the Gardner Wilkinson Library and beer cellar. Fascinating natural history collections. Magnificent early 18th-century state bed. A carriage display in the stable block; walled gardens & pleasure grounds; Portland sheep in the park; an early 19th-century church. 'Story of Calke' films in the Chop House (near car park). Staunton Harold Church nearby

Note: One way system operates in the Park; access only via Ticknall entrance. Entry to the house is by timed ticket (incl. NT members). Waiting time may be spent in the park, garden, church, stables, restaurant or shop; visitors are advised that at BH periods the delay in gaining admission to the house may be considerable, and very occasionally admission may not be possible

- Summer opening: 30 March to end October: Sat to Wed incl. BH Mon (closed Good Friday). **House and church:** 1–5.30. **Garden:** 11–5.30. **Ticket office:** 11–5. **Park:** during daylight hours. Last admissions 5. Admission to house for all visitors (incl NT members) is by timed ticket, obtained on arrival. This gives the time of entry to the house, but does not restrict the time visitors may spend on their tour. Winter opening: **Park:** open during daylight hours all year

- All sites: £4.50, children £2.20. Garden only: £2.00. Discount for parties. Vehicle charge £2.00 payable throughout the year (refundable on entry to the house when open)

- Guided tours for parties outside normal open hours may be arranged, Sat, Mon, Tues, Wed mornings (not BH weekends). Tours last approx. 1hr 20 min; (extra charge incl. NT members); evening meals are also available with house tours. Parties must book through Calke office (tel. (0332) 863822)

- Shop and Information Room open same days as house 11–5.30. Also Nov to 18 Dec: Sat & Sun 12–4

- Access above ground floor difficult. Moderate access to garden, park and church (some steps), good access to stables and all visitor facilities. 4-seater volunteer driven buggy (ask at ticket office)

- Braille guide

- Licensed restaurant open as shop serving wide variety of home-cooked hot and cold lunches 12–2 and teas 2–5 (12–4 Nov & Dec). Seats 126 (children's portions on selected dishes)

DERBYSHIRE & PEAK DISTRICT

- Parent and baby facilities; high chairs available
- Concerts in summer; occasional events; details from Administrator (s.a.e. please)
- In park only, on leads (not in garden, house or church, except guide dogs)
- 10m S of Derby, on A514 at Ticknall between Swadlincote and Melbourne [128: SK356239] *Bus:* Trent 68 from Derby (passing close BR Derby), alight Ticknall, thence 1½m walk along drive to house (tel. (0332) 292200) *Station:* Derby 10m; Burton-on-Trent 9m

HARDWICK ESTATE: STAINSBY MILL
Stainsby, Chesterfield (0246) 850430

An 18th-century water-powered corn mill, repaired and restored in 1991

- As Hardwick Hall (but closes 4.30). Last admissions 4. Parties by prior arrangement only (no reduction) with Administrator, Hardwick Hall
- £1.50, children 70p. Children under 15 must be accompanied by an adult

  Note: No WC at Mill, but available in Hall car park
- Limited access to ground floor only; no wheelchairs available
- Refreshments available at Hardwick Hall
- From junction 29 M1 take A6175 signed to Clay Cross then first left and left again to Stainsby Mill *Bus:* as for Hardwick Hall, but alight Heath, thence 1m (1½m on X2) *Station:* Chesterfield 7m

HARDWICK HALL
Doe Lea, Chesterfield S44 5QJ (0246) 850430

A late 16th-century 'prodigy house' designed by Robert Smythson for Bess of Hardwick. The house contains outstanding contemporary furniture, tapestries and needlework, many pieces identified in an inventory of 1601; a needlework exhibition is on permanent display. Walled courtyards enclose fine gardens, orchards and a herb garden. The Country Park contains Whiteface Woodland sheep and Longhorn cattle. Information Point in Country Park

Note: Due to limited light in the Hall's ancient rooms, visitors wishing to make a close study of tapestries and textiles should avoid dull days early and late in the season. To avoid congestion, access to the house may be limited at peak periods. The remains of Hardwick Old Hall in the grounds are in the guardianship of English Heritage

- **Hall:** 30 March to end Oct: Wed, Thur, Sat, Sun & BH Mon 12.30–5, or sunset if earlier (closed Good Fri). Last admissions 4.30. **Garden:** 30 March to end Oct: daily 12–5.30. No picnics in gardens; only in car park & country park. Car park gates close 6. Country park open daily throughout the year, dawn to dusk

  Note: Old Hall (EH) open as Hall   *continued*

DERBYSHIRE & PEAK DISTRICT

£ Hall & garden £5.50, children £2.70. Garden only £2. No reduction for parties; parties of 10 or more only by written arrangement with Administrator; please send s.a.e. Vehicle charge £2.00 (refundable on purchase of house or garden ticket; members free). Car park charge for Country Park to non members 20p. Joint ticket available for Hall (NT) and Old Hall (EH). Children under 15 must be accompanied by an adult

Shop open as Hall

Access to garden and some parts of park. Great Kitchen accessible (several steps). Access to house limited to ground floor via steps to main entrance. WC. No wheelchairs available

Herb, flower garden particularly recommended to visually impaired visitors; Braille guide to the Hall

Lunches 12–1.45 & teas 2.15–4.45 in licensed restaurant in the Great Kitchen, on days Hall is open. Party bookings by written application only; s.a.e. please. Seats 60; children's portions available

Mother & baby facilities, accessible from car park

School parties Wed and Thur only; please send s.a.e.

In Country Park only, on leads, not in garden

Note: All visitors please note that a one way traffic system operates in the Park; access only via Stainsby Mill entrance (leave M1, exit 29, follow brown signs), exit only via Hardwick Inn. Park gates closed at night (7 in summer, 5.30 in winter)

6½m W of Mansfield, 9½m SE of Chesterfield; approach from M1 (exit 29) via A6175 [120: SK463638]. *Bus:* E Midland X2, 63 Sheffield–Nottingham, 48 Chesterfield–Bolsover (local buses link with Chesterfield BR station), alight Glapwell 'Young Vanish' 1½m and follow signs to Rowthorne, tel. (0332) 292200 *Station:* Chesterfield 8m

ILAM HALL & COUNTRY PARK see STAFFORDSHIRE

KEDLESTON HALL
Derby DE22 5JH (0332) 842191

Palladian mansion set in a classical park landscape, built 1759–65 for Nathaniel Curzon, 1st Baron Scarsdale, whose family has lived at Kedleston since the 12th century. The house has the most complete and least altered sequence of Robert Adam interiors in England, and the rooms still contain their original great collection of family portraits, old masters, and their original furniture and other contents. Indian Museum exhibition of Robert Adam architectural drawings, an Adam bridge and fishing pavilion in the park, and a garden and pleasure grounds

House: 30 March to end Oct (closed Good Fri): Sat to Wed 1–5.30 (last admissions to house 5). **Garden:** same days as house 11–6. **Park:** April to end Oct: daily 11–6; Nov to 18 Dec: Sat & Sun only 12–4 (vehicle entry charge £2, on Thur & Fri and during Nov & Dec)

84

DERBYSHIRE & PEAK DISTRICT

£ £4.20, children £2.10. Reduced rate for booked parties on application

🛍 Shop open as house. Also Nov to 18 Dec: Sat & Sun only 12-4

♿ Difficult steps for wheelchairs; please telephone Administrator in advance. WC. Access to restaurant

🍴 Licensed restaurant same days as house serving wide variety of home cooked hot and cold lunches 12-2, teas 2-5. Also Nov to 18 Dec, Sat & Sun 12-4. Party bookings by written application (s.a.e. please). Seats 70; children's portions available

👶 WC with nappy changing facility; children's guide

🏫 Schoolroom & teacher's pack available

E Concerts and special events; contact Administrator (s.a.e. please)

🐕 In park only, on leads

➡ 5m NW of Derby, signposted from roundabout where A38 crosses A52 close to Markeaton Park *Bus:* Dunn-Line 109 Derby–Ashbourne, alight Keddleston Village, thence 1m; Trent 1/2 from Derby to Askerfield Ave, thence 2m; Trent 154, Sun, from Derby to Allestree Lane End, thence 2½m (all pass close BR Derby) (tel. (0332) 292200) *Station:* Duffield (U) 3½m; Derby 5½m

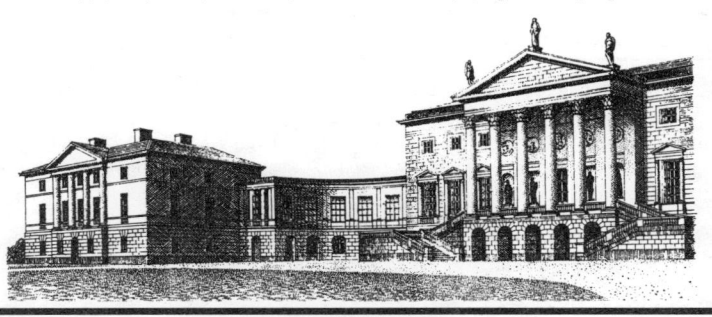

LONGSHAW ESTATE
Sheffield S11 7TZ (0433) 631708

1,700 acres of open moorland, woodland and farms in the Peak National Park, with dramatic views and varied walking. Stone for the Derwent and Howden Dams was quarried from Bolehill, and millstones may be seen in quarries on the estate. There is a quarry winding house above Grindleford station

O **Estate:** open at all times. Lodge is converted into flats and is not open. **Visitor Centre (café, shop and information centre):** weekends throughout year incl. BH Mon 11-5 or sunset if earlier. Also open Wed & Thur from 23 March to 24 Dec 11-5; re-opens 7 Jan 1995. Booked parties at other times by arrangement

£ Car park 200yds from Visitor Centre [SK266800]; access difficult for coaches; no coaches at weekends or BH. Car parks for Estate at Haywood [110/119: SK256778] and Wooden Pole [110/119: SK267790]. Riding permits available. Longshaw Walks & Family leaflets from Visitor Centre *continued*

DERBYSHIRE & PEAK DISTRICT

⚑ Guided walks around the estate may be booked by groups: contact Warden's Office (tel. (0433) 631757)

▣ Weekends throughout year incl. BH Mon 11–5 or sunset if earlier. Also open Wed and Thur from 23 March to 24 Dec 11–5; re-opens 7 Jan 1995

♿ Access to Visitor Centre. Carriage drives only suitable; disabled visitors may be driven to Visitor Centre and WC; drivers must, however, return and park in main car park, unless only visiting WC. No car parking at Centre or at adjacent lodge. No wheelchairs available

☕ Selection of home made light lunches and teas at Visitor Centre. Seats 32; children's portions available

E 1–3 Sept, Longshaw Sheepdog Trials

🐕 On leads only; no dogs in Visitor Centre

→ 7½m from Sheffield, next to A625 Sheffield–Hathersage Road; Woodcroft car park is off B6055, 200yds S of junction with A625 [110/119: SK266802] *Bus:* Mainline 240 Sheffield–Bakewell (passing BR Grindleford); Mainline/Hulley's 272 Sheffield–Castleton (passing BR Hathersage). All pass close BR Sheffield (tel. (0322) 292200) *Station:* Grindleford (U) 2m

THE OLD MANOR 🏛 🏠 ✝ ✻
Norbury, Ashbourne DE6 2ED

A stone built 13th- to 15th-century hall with a rare king post roof, undercroft and cellars; the hall is of specialist architectural interest only. Also, a late 17th-century red brick manor house, incorporating fragments of an earlier Tudor house, tenanted (and not open). The church (not NT) is well worth a visit

O Medieval Hall by written appointment only with the tenant Mr C. Wright. 30 March to end Sept: Tues, Wed & Sat afternoons

£ £1.50

→ *Bus:* Stevensons 409 Uttoxeter–Ashbourne (passing close BR Uttoxeter), alight Ellastone, ¾m (tel. (0332) 292200) *Station:* Uttoxeter (U) 7½m

SUDBURY HALL 🏛 ✻
Sudbury, Ashbourne DE6 5HT (0283) 585305

One of the most individual of late 17th-century houses, begun by George Vernon c.1661. The rich decoration includes wood carvings by Gibbons and Pierce, superb plasterwork, mythological decorative paintings by Laguerre, and the great staircase is one of the finest of its kind in an English house

Note: Owing to low light levels, visitors wishing to study the Hall's plasterwork or paintings in detail should avoid dull days and late afternoons towards end Sept

O 30 March to 30 Sept: Wed to Sun & BH Mon (closed Good Fri) 1–5.30 or sunset if earlier. Last admissions 5. Grounds open 12–6

DERBYSHIRE & PEAK DISTRICT

Note: the Hall will close at end Sept in 1994 because of essential repair work

£   Hall £3.20, children £1.60. Joint ticket for Hall & Museum (recommended) £4.40. All party bookings by prior arrangement with the Booking Secretary

Guided and specialist tours available; contact Administrator

Shop open as Hall. Also Nov to 18 Dec: Sat & Sun only 12–4

Hall difficult. Grounds & tea-room accessible; for special arrangements, please contact Administrator. WC in Museum. No wheelchairs available

Licensed Coach House tea-room serving light lunches and teas. Open same days as house 12.30–5.30 (last orders 5); also Nov to 18 Dec Sat & Sun 12–4. Coaches by appointment only, booking form by written application (s.a.e. please). Seats 72

Nappy changing facilities in Museum of Childhood; children's portions available in tea-room

Special facilities linked to National Curriculum for pre-booked school parties, by arrangement with Education Officer (tel. (0283) 585022)

E   Concerts & special events; details from Administrator; please send s.a.e.

In car park only

→   6m E of Uttoxeter at the crossing point of A50 Derby Stoke and A515 Lichfield–Ashbourne roads [128: SK160323] *Bus:* Stevensons 401 Burton on Trent Uttoxeter (passing BR Tutbury & Hatton and close BR Burton on Trent (tel. (0332) 292200) *Station:* Tutbury & Hatton (U) 5m

THE NATIONAL TRUST MUSEUM OF CHILDHOOD, SUDBURY

Sudbury Hall, Sudbury, Ashbourne DE6 5HT (0283) 585305

Situated in the 19th-century service wing of Sudbury Hall, the Museum of Childhood contains fascinating and innovative displays about children from the 18th century onwards, but with particular emphasis on life in Victorian and Edwardian periods. There are chimney climbs for the adventurous 'sweep sized' youngster. Betty Cadbury's fine collection of toys and dolls is displayed in the specially designed Toybox Gallery   *continued*

DERBYSHIRE & PEAK DISTRICT

- **O** 30 March to 30 Sept: Wed to Sun & BH Mon (closed Good Fri) 1-5.30. Last admissions 5

    Note: the property will close at end Sept in 1994 because of essential repair work

- **£** Museum & Garden £2.20, children £1.10. Joint ticket for Hall & Museum (recommended) £4.40. Party bookings by arrangement with the Bookings Secretary

- **♿** Most of Museum accessible. WC. Wheelchairs not available

- Licenced Coach House tea-room serving light lunches and teas. Open same days as Museum 12.30-5.30 (last orders 5); also Nov-18 Dec Sat & Sun 12-4. Coaches by appointment only, by written application (s.a.e. please)

- Nappy changing facilities; back-pack baby carriers accepted; pushchairs difficult

- Educational materials available. Special facilities for pre-booked school parties as for Sudbury Hall

- **E** Special events & activities for children. Details from Education Officer (please send s.a.e.)

- In car park only

- **→** 6m E of Uttoxeter at the crossing point of A50 Derby–Stoke and A515 Lichfield–Ashbourne roads [128:160323] *Bus:* Stevensons 401 Burton-on-Trent–Uttoxeter (passing BR Tutbury & Hatton and close BR Burton on Trent (tel. (0339) 292200) *Station:* Tutbury & Hatton (U) 5m

WINSTER MARKET HOUSE
nr Matlock (033 529) 245

A market house of the late 17th or early 18th century. The ground floor is of stone with the original five open arches filled in, while the upper storey is of brick with stone dressings. The building was bought in 1906 and restored; it is now a NT Information Room (no attendant)

- **O** 30 March to end Oct: open daily
- **£** Free. Public WC in side street near House
- **→** 4m W of Matlock on S side of B5057 in main street of Winster [119: SK241606] *Bus:* Hulley's 170/2 Matlock–Bakewell (passing close BR Matlock) (tel. (0322) 292200) *Station:* Matlock (U) 4m

BLACKBERRIES

Devon

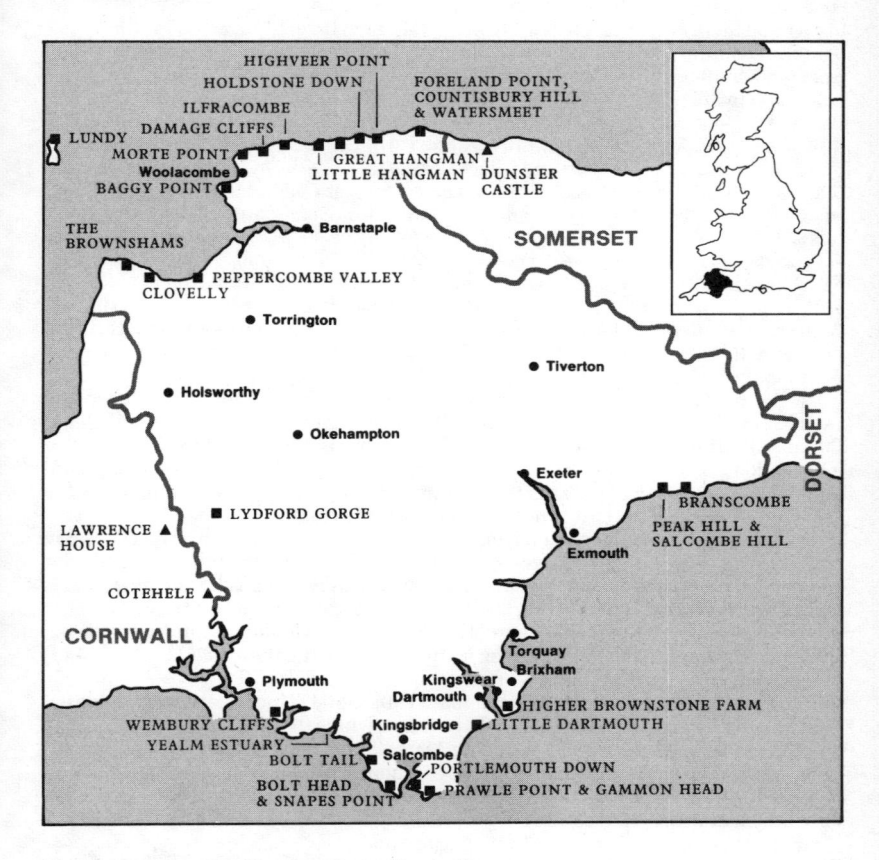

The Trust owns over 80 miles of coastline in Devon.

On the south coast, near Plymouth, $5\frac{1}{2}$ miles of cliff and woodland are owned, on both sides of the **Yealm Estuary**. **Wembury Cliffs** extend for $1\frac{1}{2}$ miles from Wembury Head (see also p.100) [201: SX530480]. A further 250 acres of spectacular countryside near Ringmore [202: SX645457] has recently been acquired, including Aymer Cove, the valley inland and 1 mile of coastline.

From **Bolt Tail** [202: SX6639] to **Overbecks** near Salcombe (see p.101) are 6 miles of rugged cliff land traversed by the coast path which dips to give access to safe bathing at **Soar Mill Cove**, **Starehole Bay** and at **Bolberry Down** car park a path leads to the west and is suitable for wheelchair users . **Bolt Head** and **Bolt Tail** are the best places from which to observe seabirds. The Trust's first property in the Kingsbridge Estuary, **Snapes Point** [202: SX745394] is the keystone to the conservation of the estuary landscape and has a footpath around the unspoilt headland, and a small car park .

DEVON

Another extensive holding lies between **Portlemouth Down** [202: SX740375] and **Prawle Point** [202: SX773350]. 330 acres of low cliffs with walks, views and sandy coves. The walker can choose whether to use higher or lower paths, and the cliffs grow higher and more craggy further east towards **Gammon Head** [202: SX765355].

In the beautiful estuary of the river Dart, the Trust protects, on the Dartmouth side, woodland, hilltop and 165 acres at **Little Dartmouth** [202: SX880490] – cliff and farmland forming the western approach to Dartmouth Harbour for $1\frac{1}{2}$ miles from the Dancing Beggars rocks off Warren Point to the harbour entrance. Across the estuary at Kingswear, 298 acres at **Higher Brownstone Farm** [202: SX901505] gives access to paths to the coast on the **Coleton Fishacre Estate** (see p.95). On 970 acres and nearly 5 miles of coast, the Trust has created a coastal footpath and several linking paths to small car parks. There are two popular beaches at Man Sands and Scabbacombe along this stretch of coast between Kingswear and Brixham.

In East Devon the Trust owns **Peak Hill** [192: SY109871] and **Salcombe Hill** [192: SY143882], buttresses to the town of Sidmouth. Following the acquisiton of **Coxes Cliff** at Weston, the Trust now protects the $3\frac{1}{2}$ miles of coastline between Salcombe Hill and Branscombe, including farmland and foreshore in places. Some cottages, farms, the forge and the bakery (now a tea-room and baking museum) are also owned by the Trust at Branscombe.

On the north coast the Trust's ownership begins near the Somerset border and extends to Countisbury where it protects about 1,500 acres of **Foreland Point, Countisbury Hill** and the wooded valleys of **Watersmeet** [180: SS744487]. There is an information point, shop and self-service restaurant at **Watersmeet House** (see p.103) and miles of signposted footpaths traverse the hanging oak woods clothing the steep sides of the valleys of the East Lyn River and Hoar Oak Water.

The Trust now protects over three miles of continuous coastline between Woody Bay and Trentishoe including **Highveer Point** [180: SS655498] where there is a circular walk and access to the Roman Signal Station at Martinhoe. More cliff and moorland is owned at **Holdstone Down** [180: SS620475] with car parking at Trentishoe. The dramatic cliffs of the **Great Hangman** [180: SS601480], the highest in North Devon, then fall westward to the more striking features of the **Little Hangman** [189: 584481] immediately to the east of Combe Martin.

Two hundred and sixty acres at **Ilfracombe** [180: SS5047] include most of the coastal land from the town's outskirts to the village of Lee, where the Trust owns 5 miles of fine coastline as far as **Woolacombe**, including **Morte Point** [180: SS554445] and **Damage Cliffs** [180: SS470465]. South-west to Croyde more coastal holdings include the viewpoint of **Baggy Point** where there is a path suitable for wheelchair users [180: SS4241].

Lundy's vessel, *Oldenburg*, sails from Bideford and Ilfracombe to the island in the Bristol Channel (see p.98). At Bideford Bay between **Abbotsham** and **Bucks Mills** the Trust owns 5 miles of remote coastline, acquired in 1988. Although footpaths are being upgraded, access by vehicle is limited, with small car parks only at each end, and very few linking footpaths back to the main coast road. Further west at **Clovelly** more than 600 acres of cliff, farm and woodland – with two ancient farmhouses at **The Brownshams** [190: SS285260] – are protected by the Trust.

Our properties can be enjoyed more fully with the aid of an OS map.

LYDFORD GORGE

DEVON

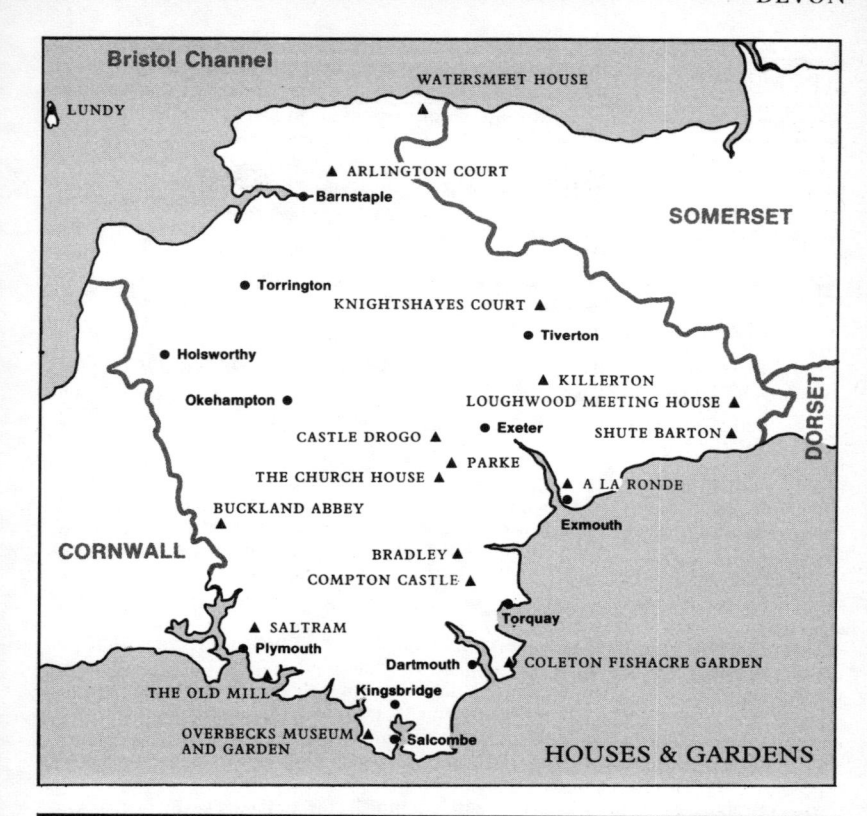

A LA RONDE 🏠

Summer Lane, Exmouth EX8 5BD (0395) 265514

A unique 16-sided house built in 1796 for two spinsters, Jane and Mary Parminter. The fascinating interior decoration includes a shell-encrusted room, a feather frieze, and many 18th-century contents and collections brought back by the two women from a European Grand Tour

- 30 March to 30 Oct: daily except Fri & Sat 11–5.30. Last admissions ½hr before closing. Timed tickets may be necessary on busy days
- £3. No party reduction; unsuitable for coaches
- Open as house
- Tea-room open as house
- 2m N of Exmouth on A376 [192SY:004834] *Bus:* Devon General X57 Exeter–Exmouth to within ¼m (tel. (0392) 56231) *Station:* Lympstone Village 1¼m

91

DEVON

ARLINGTON COURT
Arlington, nr Barnstaple EX31 4LP (0271) 850296

The house, built in 1822, contains fascinating collections for every taste, including model ships, shells, costumes, pewter and furniture of the last century. A large array of early horse-drawn vehicles is displayed in the stables and there are carriage rides from the front of the house. The park is grazed by Shetland ponies and Jacob sheep

- **House, Victorian Garden & Park:** 30 March to 30 Oct: daily except Sat but open Sat of BH weekends 11–5.30. Last admissions ½hr before closing. **Park:** footpaths across parkland open during daylight hours Nov to March
- £4.60. Garden only £2.40. Pre-arranged parties of 15 or more paying visitors £3.50. Parking 300yds
- Same days as house 11–5.30. Also 2 Nov to 18 Dec: Wed to Sun 11–5. Tel. (0271) 850348
- Garden (gravel paths), grounds & shop accessible. Ramped steps to front of house, help available; then ground floor accessible. Limited access to carriage museum. Special parking arrangements; disabled visitors may be driven to house by arrangement with Administrator. WC. Wheelchairs available; ask at visitor reception
- Braille guides for house and carriage collection
- Licensed restaurant and tea-room at house, open as house, but restaurant open 12–5.30, also Sun 12–4 in Nov & open for pre-booked Christmas lunches in Dec. Tel. (0271) 850629. Restaurant opening during Oct may vary from that printed, although light refreshments will always be available during opening hours. If in doubt, please telephone the property
- Table in ladies' WC available for nappy changing. Children's quiz
- Schools' room available; book with Administrator. Children's study book
- In park only, on short leads
- 7m NE of Barnstaple on A39 [180: SS611405] *Bus:* Red Bus 13 Ilfracombe–Barnstaple, Tue, Fri only; otherwise 310 Barnstaple–Lynmouth (passing close BR Barnstaple), alight Blackmoor Gate, 3m (tel. (0271) 45444) *Station:* Barnstaple 8m

BRADLEY
Newton Abbot TQ12 6BN (0626) 54513

A small medieval manor house set in woodland and meadows. Bradley is occupied by Mrs A. H. Woolner and family

- 30 March to end Sept: Wed 2–5; also Thur 7 & 14 April, 22 & 29 Sept. Last admissions ½hr before closing
- £2.60. No party reduction; parties over 15 by written appointment only with Secretary. Lodge gates are too narrow for coaches. No WCs.

DEVON

🐕 No dogs allowed in house or grounds

➔ Drive gate (with small lodge) is on outskirts of town, on Totnes road (A381) [202: SX848709] *Bus:* (tel. (0392) 382800) *Station:* Newton Abbot 1½m

BUCKLAND ABBEY
Yelverton PL20 6EY (0822) 853607

The spirit of Sir Francis Drake is rekindled at his home with new exhibitions of his courageous adventures and achievements throughout the world. Originally a 13th-century monastery, the Abbey was ingeniously transformed into a family residence by Sir Richard Grenville of Revenge fame before Drake bought it in 1581. Also of interest are monastic farm buildings, craft workshops and country walks

Buckland Abbey is jointly managed by the National Trust and Plymouth City Council

🅞 30 March to 30 Oct: daily except Thur 10.30–5.30; also Nov to end March 1995: Sat & Sun 2–5 (Wed for pre-arranged parties only). Last admissions ¾hr before closing. Closed 19 Dec to 30 Dec 1994

💷 £4. Grounds only £2. Pre-arranged parties £3.20. Workshops only free. NB There may be an increased charge on certain days (NT members incl.) when special events are in progress. See Events below. Car park 150yds, £1 refundable on admission

🛍 Shop open as house (tel. (0822) 853706), but Nov to end March 1995 Sat & Sun 12.30–5. Independent craft workshops throughout year, variable opening (not Thur) . Please check with individual workshops: Basket maker (0822) 852103, Shoe maker (0822) 852650, Bellows maker (0566) 784480, Wood turner (0822) 855250

♿ Disabled passengers may be set down at the Abbey after admission at main Reception. Car park area for disabled drivers near Reception; access via gravel paths from car park. Site steep with access to lower levels of house only; restaurant accessible. Motorised buggy may be available; please enquire. Two wheelchairs available at reception. Advice leaflet on request. WC

👁 Braille house guide and audio-guide; scented herbs and plants in garden. Advice leaflet on request

🍴 Licensed restaurant and tea-room (peak periods only) open 30 March to 18 Dec as shop. Tea-room only Jan to March 1995 as shop. Last servings ½hr before closing. Also open for pre-booked Christmas lunches and candlelit dinners in Dec. Tel. (0822) 855024. Picnics in car park only. Restaurant opening hours during Oct may vary from that printed, although light refreshments will always be available during opening hours. If in doubt, please telephone the property when you are planning a visit

🧒 Children's guide

🏫 Fully equipped school base; book with Administrator. GCSE pack available

E Please contact Administrator for details of evening concerts & other events. An additional entrance charge may be applied on certain days including 25 June, Summer Craft Fair (adult members £1) and for Living History Days *continued*

DEVON

🐕 In car park only, on leads; dog posts in shade

➡️ 6m S of Tavistock, 11m N of Plymouth: turn off A386 ¼m S of Yelverton [201: SX487667] *Bus:* Plymouth Citybus 55 from Yelverton (with connections from BR Plymouth) (tel. (0392) 382800) *Station:* Bere Alston (U) not Sun (except July–Aug), 4½m

CASTLE DROGO
Drewsteignton, nr Exeter EX6 6PB (0647) 433306

This granite castle, built between 1910 and 1930, is one of the most remarkable works of Sir Edwin Lutyens. It stands at over 900ft overlooking the wooded gorge of the River Teign with beautiful views of Dartmoor. Spectacular walks through surrounding 600 acre estate

🅾️ **Castle:** 30 March to 30 Oct: daily except Fri 11–5.30. (Open Good Fri.)
Garden: 30 March to 30 Oct: daily 10.30–5.30. Last admissions ½hr before closing

Note: The croquet lawn is open; equipment for hire. Please book through visitor reception

💷 Castle, garden & grounds £4.60. Garden & grounds only £2. Pre-arranged parties £3.60. Car park 400yds

🛍️ Shop and plant centre by car park open daily 30 March to end Oct from 10.30. Also 2 Nov to 18 Dec Wed to Sun 11–4.30. Tel. (0647) 433563

♿ Limited access to part of castle; garden accessible. Special parking and access by arrangement at visitor reception. WC near shop. Wheelchairs available

Braille guide; audio-guide to castle; scented plants

🍴 Licensed restaurant at castle, open 30 March to 30 Sept, same days as castle: 12–5.30. Tea-room in grounds, open 30 March to 31 Oct daily: 10.30–5.30; also limited opening Nov & Dec (tel. (0647) 432629)

👶 Children's guide

🐕 On leads in car park and surrounding public footpaths only

➡️ 4m S of A30 Exeter–Okehampton road via Crockernwell (car access only); coaches must turn off A382 Moretonhampstead–Whiddon Down road at Sandy Park [191: SX721900] *Bus:* Red Bus 359 from Exeter (passing close BR Exeter Central) (tel. (0392) 382800) *Station:* Yeoford (U) 8m

DEVON

THE CHURCH HOUSE 🏠
Widecombe in the Moor, Newton Abbot TQ13 7TA (03642) 321

Originally a brewhouse dating back to 1537, this former village school is now leased as a village hall and occasionally open to the public. The adjacent Sexton's Cottage is a NT and Dartmoor National Park Information Centre and gift shop

- 🅾 June to mid Sept: Tues & Thur 2-5
- 💷 Church House free (donation box)
- 🛍 Shop in Sexton's Cottage open daily mid Feb to 29 March 10-4.30; daily 30 March to end Oct 10-6; daily Nov to 24 Dec 10-5; Closed Jan to mid Feb 1995
- ➡ In centre of Dartmoor, N of Ashburton, W of Bovey Tracey [191: SX718768] *Bus:* DevonBus 171, 193, 671 from Newton Abbot (tel. (0392) 382800)

COLETON FISHACRE GARDEN 🌸 🏛 👤
Coleton, Kingswear, Dartmouth TQ6 0EQ (0803 752) 466

A 20-acre garden in a stream-fed valley set within the spectacular scenery of this Heritage Coast. The garden was created by Lady Dorothy D'Oyly Carte between 1925 and 1940, and is planted with a wide variety of uncommon trees and rare and exotic shrubs. Coleton Fishacre House can be viewed by written appointment with Mr B. Howe. 2 holiday cottages

- 🅾 March: Sundays only 2-5; also 30 March to 30 Oct: Wed, Thur, Fri & Sun 10.30-5.30 or dusk if earlier. Last admissions ½hr before closing
- 💷 £2.60. Pre-booked parties £2
- 🛍 No shop but small selection of plants for sale at reception
- ♿ Limited access to parts of garden, steep slopes (strong pusher essential)
- 👁 Scented herbs and plants
- 🍴 Refreshment kiosk open as garden, weather permitting
- 🚫🐕 No dogs allowed in garden
- ➡ 2m from Kingswear; take Lower Ferry road, turn off at toll house [202: SX910508] *Bus:* Bayline 22 Brixham–Kingswear (with connections from BR Paignton), alight ¾m SW of Hillhead, 1½m (tel. (0803) 613226) *Station:* Paignton 8m; Kingswear (Dart Valley Rly) 2¼m by footpath, 2¾m by road

COMPTON CASTLE 🏰 ✝
Marldon, Paignton TQ3 1TA (0803) 872112

A fortified manor house with curtain wall, built at three periods: 1340, 1450 and 1520, by the Gilbert family. It was the home of Sir Humphrey Gilbert (1539–1583), coloniser of Newfoundland and half-brother of Sir Walter Raleigh; the family still lives here. Compton Castle is occupied and administered by Mr & Mrs G. E. Gilbert

95

DEVON

◯ 30 March to 30 Oct: Mon, Wed & Thur 10-12.15 and 2-5, when the courtyard, restored great hall, solar, chapel, rose garden and old kitchen are shown. Last admissions ½hr before closing

£ £2.60. Pre-booked parties £2; organisers should notify Secretary. Additional parking and refreshments at Castle Barton opposite entrance

♿ Limited access for wheelchair users

🍴 Morning coffee, lunches and teas at Castle Barton (not NT) from 10 (tel. (0803) 873314)

🐕 On leads in car park only

➔ At Compton, 3m W of Torquay, 1m N of Marldon; from the Newton Abbot–Totnes road (A381) turn left at Ipplepen crossroads and W off Torbay ring road via Marldon [202: SX865648] *Bus:* Bayline 7 BR Paignton–Marldon, thence 1½m (tel. (0803) 613226) *Station:* Torquay 3m

KILLERTON 🏠 🏚 ✝ ❉ ♣ 🍴 🏛 🚶   📷 ✉
Broadclyst, Exeter EX5 3LE (0392) 881345

The house, home of the Aclands, was rebuilt in 1778 to the design of John Johnson. It is furnished as a comfortable family home and includes the Paulise de Bush costume collection, dating from the 18th century to the present day, set in period rooms, and a Victorian laundry. The 15-acre hillside garden is beautiful throughout the year, with rhododendrons, magnolias, herbaceous border and rare trees. The surrounding parkland and woods offer lovely walks. Also of interest is the 19th-century chapel, an estate exhibition, and the site of an Iron Age hill-fort

◯ **House:** 30 March to 30 Oct: daily except Tues 11-5.30. Last admissions ½hr before closing. **Park & garden:** open all year from 10.30 to dusk

£ £4.60. Garden only £2.80. Garden & Park winter rate (Nov to Feb) £1. Pre-booked parties £3.50

🛍 Shop and plant centre in Stable Courtyard. Open 30 March to end Oct daily 11-6; 2 Nov to 24 Dec Wed to Sun 11-5; Jan to end Feb 1995 Wed to Sun 11-4, and daily during March 11-5. Tel. (0392) 881912. Produce shop open 30 March to end Oct daily 11-6; Nov to 24 Dec Wed to Sun 11-5

96

DEVON

    3 steps to house (ramp available), accessible ground floor. Lower levels of garden accessible, but gravel paths and grass. Volunteer-driven buggies available for tour of gardens. WCs. Special parking for disabled drivers and transfer by buggy to house and garden. Wheelchair lift to upper level of shop. Wheelchairs available

    Braille guides for house and costume collection; scented plants

    Licensed restaurant open same days as house 12-5.30 and for pre-booked Mothering Sunday & Christmas lunches. Tel. (0392) 882081. Tea-room in Stable Courtyard open 30 March to end Oct daily 10.30-5.30; 2 Nov to 19 Dec Wed to Sun 10.30-4.30; Jan to end March 1995 Sat & Sun only 11-4. Restaurant opening hours during Oct may vary from that printed, although light refreshments will always be available during opening hours

    Table & chair in ladies' WCs near Stable Courtyard, and at house. Children's guide

    Education room for pre-booked parties; teachers resource guide (£2.50)

    10 April, Horse Trials; 16 & 17 July, Exeter Festival Open Air Concerts. Full programme from Administrator, please send s.a.e

    Note: only ticket holders to the Exeter Festival concerts will be admitted to the garden after 5; house will close at 5 on 16, 17 July

    In park only

    On W side of Exeter Cullompton road (B3181 formerly A38) entrance off B3185; from M5 northbound, exit 29 via Broadclyst and B3181 southbound, exit 28 [192: SX9700] *Bus:* DevonBus 375; Devon General 54/A, DevonBus 327, 374 from Exeter (all passing close BR Exeter Central), some pass the house, but on most alight Killerton Turn ¾m (tel.(0392) 382800) *Station:* Pinhoe (U), not Sun, 4½m; Whimpole (U), not Sun, 6m; Exeter Central & St David's, both 7m

KNIGHTSHAYES COURT

Bolham, Tiverton EX16 7RQ (0884) 254665

Begun in 1869, the house is a rare survival of the work of William Burges, with its richly decorated Victorian interior. It stands on the east side of the Exe valley and has one of the finest gardens in Devon, with rare shrubs, spring bulbs and summer flowering borders

    30 March to 30 Oct: **Garden:** daily 10.30-5.30; **House:** daily, except Fri (but open Good Fri) 1.30-5.30. Last admissions ½hr before closing. Nov & Dec: Sun 2-4 for pre-booked parties only; please note that some items normally on view may not be displayed due to conservation work

    £4.80. Garden & Grounds only £2.80. Pre-booked parties £3.80. Parking 450yds. Visitor reception: tel. (0884) 257381

    Shop and plant centre open 19 March to 29 March daily 11-4; 30 March to end Oct daily 10.30-5.30; 2 Nov to 18 Dec Wed to Sun 11-5; March 1995 Wed to Sun 11-4. Tel. (0884) 259010

continued

DEVON

House, garden, shop and restaurant accessible. Small lift to first floor suitable for ambulant disabled people only. Access to picnic area in car park. Disabled drivers may park near house, or disabled passengers may be set down by house entrance. NB All tickets must please be purchased initially at the visitor reception point in the Stables. WC

Scented plants. Braille house guide

Licensed restaurant for coffee, lunches and teas 19-29 March daily 11-4; 30 March to end Oct daily 10.30-5.30; Nov & Dec Wed to Sun 11-4.30; March 1995 Wed to Sun 11-4. High chair available. Also open for pre-booked Christmas lunches and candlelit dinners. Tel. (0884) 259416. Picnic area in car park. Restaurant opening hours during Oct may vary, although light refreshments will always be available during opening hours

Baby changing facilities in ladies' WC

In park only, on leads

2m N of Tiverton; turn right off Tiverton–Bampton road (A396) at Bolham [181: SS960151] *Bus:* Kingdoms 698 Tiverton–Dulverton, alight Bolham (¾m); otherwise Tiverton & District 373/4 from BR Tiverton Parkway; Devon General 55/A/B Exeter–Tiverton (passing close BR Exeter Central) (tel. (0392) 382800). On all alight Tiverton 1¼m *Station:* Tiverton Parkway 8m

LOUGHWOOD MEETING HOUSE
Dalwood, Axminster EX13 7DU (0392) 881691

Built c.1653 by the Baptist congregation of Kilmington. The interior was fitted in the early 18th century

All year

Free (donation box provided)

4m W of Axminster; turn right on Axminster/Honiton road (A35), 1m S of Dalwood, 1m NW of Kilmington [192 & 193: SY253993] *Bus:* Red Bus 380 Axminster–Ottery St Mary (passing close BR Axminster) (tel. (0392) 382800) *Station:* Axminster 2½m

LUNDY
Bristol Channel EX39 2LY (0237) 431831

This unspoilt island, with its rocky headlands and fascinating animal and bird life, is leased to the Landmark Trust. It is the ideal place to explore for a day trip, with no cars to disrupt the peace. The small island community includes a church, tavern and castle. There is a steep climb to the village from the landing beach

Lundy is financed, administered and maintained by the Landmark Trust

Always. Groups and passenger ships by prior arrangement

£3 entrance fee waived for passengers on MS *Oldenburg*, no reduction for NT members

DEVON

🏠	Shop selling the famous Lundy stamps, souvenirs and postcards, along with general supplies and groceries
♿	Disabled visitors are very welcome but should telephone in advance so that disembarkment arrangements may be made
🍴	Food and drink at The Marisco Tavern *Accommodation:* 23 holiday cottages; camping site for up to 40 people. For bookings, apply to The Landmark Trust, Shottesbrooke, Maidenhead, Berkshire SL6 3SW (tel. (0628) 825925)
👶	Facilities for nappy changing in ladies WC. Children are welcome on the island and particularly enjoy the farm animals
🐕	Dogs may accompany visitors staying overnight if prior written permission has been granted by the Island Agent only
➡️	11m N of Hartland Point, 25m from Ilfracombe, 30m S of Tenby [180: SS1345] *Bus:* Frequent Red Bus Services from BR Barnstaple to Bideford or Ilfracombe (tel. (0392) 382800) *Station:* Barnstaple: 8½m to Bideford, 12m to Ilfracombe

LYDFORD GORGE 🍴 👶   ✕ 🏨

The Stables, Lydford Gorge Lydford, nr Okehampton EX20 4BH
(082 282) 441/320

This famous gorge is 1½ miles long, providing an exciting riverside walk to the 90ft high White Lady waterfall. The walk then enters a steep-sided, oak-wooded ravine scooped out by the River Lyd into a succession of potholes, including the spectacular Devil's Cauldron

🕐	30 March to 30 Oct: daily 10-5.30; also Nov to March 1995: daily 10.30-3, but from waterfall entrance as far as waterfall only. Note: There are delays at the Devil's Cauldron during busy periods. The walk is arduous in places; visitors should wear stout footwear
£	£2.80. Pre-arranged parties £2.20
🏠	Shop at main entrance open as gorge. Small shop at far end of gorge 30 March to end Oct as gorge, but 5 Nov to 18 Dec Sat & Sun 11-5
♿	Gorge unsuitable for disabled visitors. Accessible picnic area; WC
🍴	Main entrance; light refreshments 30 March to end Sept daily (weather permitting) 10.30-5. Oct Sat & Sun 11-4.30
👶	Children's guide
📚	Teachers' resource pack
🐕	Must be kept on leads
➡️	At W end of Lydford village; halfway between Okehampton and Tavistock, 1m W off A386 opposite Dartmoor Inn; main entrance at W end of Lydford; second entrance near Manor Hotel [191 & 201: SX509846] *Bus:* Down's 118 Tavistock-Okehampton (with connections from Plymouth); Red Bus 86 Plymouth-Barnstaple; Devon Bus 187 BR Gunislake-Okehampton, summer Sun only (connects with trains) (tel. (0392) 382800)

DEVON

MARKER'S COTTAGE

Broadclyst, Exeter EX5 3HR (0392) 461546

Mediaeval cob house with cross-passage screen painting of St Andrew

- 30 March to 30 Oct: Sun, Mon, Tues 2-5. No WC
- £1. House unsuitable for coach parties
- Access difficult; 4 steps into house
- On W side of Exeter–Cullompton Road (B3181) in village of Broadclyst. Turn right opposite church (coming from Exeter direction) and then second right [192:SX985973] *Bus:* Devon General 54A from Exeter–Cullompton (passes close BR Exeter Central) *Station:* Exeter Central 5½m

THE OLD BAKERY, BRANSCOMBE

Branscombe, Seaton EX12 3DB (029 780) 333

A traditional stone built and partially rendered building beneath a slate roof which was, until 1987, the last traditional bakery in use in Devon. The baking room has been preserved and houses a large faggot fired oven, two large dough bins and other traditional baking equipment. The remainder of the building is used as tea-rooms. Information room

- **Baking Room and Tea-rooms:** daily Easter to Oct, weekends in winter 11-5
- Free. Car park on opposite side of road, donations in well
- WC
- Morning coffee, light lunches and teas
- Welcome
- Admitted, except to Baking Room and Tea-room
- In the village of Branscombe off A3052 [192: SY198887] *Bus:* (tel. (0392) 382800) Axe Valley 899 *Station:* Honiton 8m

THE OLD MILL

Wembury Beach, Wembury PL9 0HP (0752) 862314

Café and shop housed in a former mill house, standing on a small beach near the Yealm estuary

- **Shop:** 30 March to end Oct: daily 10.30-5. Limited opening Nov & Dec. Car park beside beach, parking charge to non members
- Drinks, refreshments, ice cream, etc; take-away service; open as shop, also Nov to 18 Dec Sat & Sun 10-5
- Admitted, except to cafe
- At Wembury, nr Plymouth [201: SX517484] *Bus:* Western National 48 from Plymouth, thence ½m (tel. (0752) 222666) *Station:* Plymouth 10m

DEVON

OVERBECKS MUSEUM AND GARDEN
Sharpitor, Salcombe TQ8 8LW (0548) 842893 or 843238

Spectacular views over Salcombe estuary can be enjoyed from the beautiful 6-acre garden, with its many rare plants, shrubs and trees. The elegant Edwardian house contains collections of local photographs taken at the end of the last century, local ship building tools, model boats, toys, shells, birds, animals and other collections, together with a secret room for children. Also of interest is an exhibition showing the natural history of Sharpitor

- **Museum:** 30 March to 30 Oct daily except Sat 11–5.30. Last admissions 5. **Garden:** daily throughout year 10–8 or sunset if earlier. WC open as Museum 11–4.45 due to joint use with YHA. No WC facilities during winter months

- Museum & garden £3.40; garden only £2. No party reduction. Small car park; charge refundable on admission. Roads leading to Overbecks are narrow (single track) and therefore unsuitable for coaches

- Shop open same days as museum 10.45–5.30

- Garden is steep but largely accessible with a strong pusher; details of parking available from Administrator. Ground floor of museum, shop and tea-room accessible via steps

- Tea-room for snacks and light refreshments same days as museum 12–4.15. Picnicking allowed in garden

- Secret room with dolls, toys and other collections; quiz guide; ghost hunt for children

- 1½m SW of Salcombe, signposted from Malborough and Salcombe [202: SX728374] *Bus:* Tally Ho! 606 from Kingsbridge (with connections from Plymouth, Dartmouth & BR Totnes), alight Salcombe, 1½m (tel. (0392) 382800)

PARKE
Haytor Road, Bovey Tracey TQ13 9JQ (0626) 833909

Over 200 acres of parkland in the wooded valley of the River Bovey, forming a beautiful approach to Dartmoor. There is a series of lovely walks through woodlands, beside the river and along the route of the old railway track. National Trust and Dartmoor Park Information Centre (tel. (0626) 832093)

Rare Breeds Farm: A private collection of farm animals, many of which have been used to provide our food for thousands of years. An interpretation centre and farm trails help people to discover yesterday's farm and bring it to life. Covered all-weather farmyard

- **Rare Breeds Farm:** 30 March to 30 Oct: daily 10–5, and 1 July to 5 Sept open until 6. Last admissions 1hr before closing. **Parkland:** open all year

  Note: It is advisable to tel. in advance to check opening times

- Parkland free. Rare Breeds Farm prices on application (NT members included)

- In farm buildings (coffee, light lunches and cream teas). Picnic site   *continued*

DEVON

- There are baby animals and a special Pets Corner for children, and a collection of model pigs
- In parkland only
- Just W of Bovey Tracey on N side of B3344 to Manaton, follow brown signs from A38 Drumbridges roundabout [191: SX805785] *Bus:* Devon General 72 from Newton Abbot (passing close BR Newton Abbot) (tel. (0392) 56231) *Station:* Newton Abbot 6m

SALTRAM

Plympton, Plymouth PL7 3UH (0752) 336546

A remarkable survival of a George II mansion and its original contents, in a landscaped park. Two of the most important rooms were designed by Robert Adam, with magnificent interior plasterwork and decoration. The house contains fine period furniture, china and pictures, including many portraits by Reynolds. Also of interest is the Great Kitchen, the stables, a gallery of West Country art in the chapel, and an orangery in the gardens

- **House:** 30 March to 30 Oct: daily except Fri & Sat 12.30–5.30. **Art gallery, Garden & Great Kitchen:** open as house but from 10.30. Last admissions ½hr before closing
- £5; garden only £2.20. Parking 500yds, £1
- Shop in stable block. Open same days as house 10.30–5.30; Nov to 18 Dec daily 11–5; Jan 1995 daily 11–4; Feb & March 1995 Sat & Sun 11–4. Tel. (0752) 330034
- House and garden accessible but house not suitable for powered chairs; disabled visitors may be set down at front door by prior arrangement; lift (2'2" wide × 2'10" deep) to first floor. Information available from ticket office in stable block. One wheelchair available at house and one at ticket office for use in garden
- Braille guide; scented plants
- Licensed restaurant open same days as house 12–5.30, last admissions 5 (entrance from garden at garden admission price); also open for pre-booked Christmas lunches (tel. (0752) 340635). High chair available. Drinks, light refreshments and ice cream at Coach House tea-room near car park at peak times; also 6 Nov to end March 1995 Sat & Sun 11–4. Restaurant opening hours during Oct may vary from that printed, although light refreshments will always be available during opening hours. If in doubt, please telephone the property when you are planning a visit
- Please ask Administrator for facilities
- In designated areas only
- 2m W of Plympton, 3½m E of Plymouth city centre, between Plymouth/Exeter road (A38) and Plymouth/Kingsbridge road (A379); take Plympton turn at Marsh Mills roundabout [201: SX520557] *Bus:* Plymouth Citybus 20/A, 21, 22/A, 51 from Plymouth, alight Plymouth Road/Plympton Bypass Jn, ¾m footpath (tel. (0752) 222221) *Station:* Plymouth 3½m

DEVON

SHUTE BARTON
Shute, nr Axminster EX13 7PT (0297) 34692

One of the most important surviving non-fortified manor houses of the Middle Ages. Commenced in 1380 and completed in the late 16th century, then partly demolished in the late 18th century, the house has battlemented turrets, late Gothic windows and a Tudor gatehouse

- The house is tenanted; there is access to most parts of interior for conducted tours: 30 March to 30 Oct: Wed & Sat 2-5.30. **Garden:** 25 June only, additional admission £1 (NT members included)

  Note: no WC

- £1.60. Pre-arranged parties £1.20
- Special opening of garden in aid of National Trust and local church on 25 June. Additional admission £1 (NT members included)
- 3m SW of Axminster, 2m N of Colyton on Honiton–Colyton road (B3161) [177(193): SY253974]. *Bus:* DevonBus 380 Axminster–Honiton (passes close BR Axminster and Honiton) alight Shute Cross, ¾m; Axe Valley 885/Red Bus 378 BR Axminster–Seaton, alight Whitford, thence 1½m (tel. (0392) 382800) *Station:* Axminster, 3m

WATERSMEET HOUSE
Watersmeet Road, Lynmouth EX35 6NT (0598) 53348

A fishing lodge c.1832 in a picturesque valley at the confluence of the East Lyn and Hoar Oak Water, used for information, recruiting, refreshments and a NT shop. The site has been a tea-garden since 1901, and is the focal point for several beautiful walks (steep in places)

- 30 March to 30 Oct: daily 10.30-6 (Oct: 10.30-5)
- Free. Pay-and-display car park, or free car parks at Combepark Wood, Hillsford Bridge and Countisbury
- 30 March to end Sept daily 11-6 (Oct: 11-5)
- Access arrangements for disabled visitors strictly by appointment
- Coffee, lunches and teas in tea-room and garden beside the river: 30 March to end Sept daily 10.30-5.30; (Oct: 10.30-4.30). Party catering by arrangement
- Baby changing facilities in both men's and ladies' WCs
- Admitted, but not to restaurant or shop
- 1½m E of Lynmouth, in valley on E side of Lynmouth/Barnstaple road (A39) [180: SS744487] *Bus:* Red Bus 310 Barnstaple–Lynmouth (passing close BR Barnstaple) thence walk through NT Gorge; Lyn Valley Bus from Lynmouth June to Sept only (tel. (0392) 382800)

REFER TO OPENING PAGES FOR GENERAL INFORMATION

Dorset

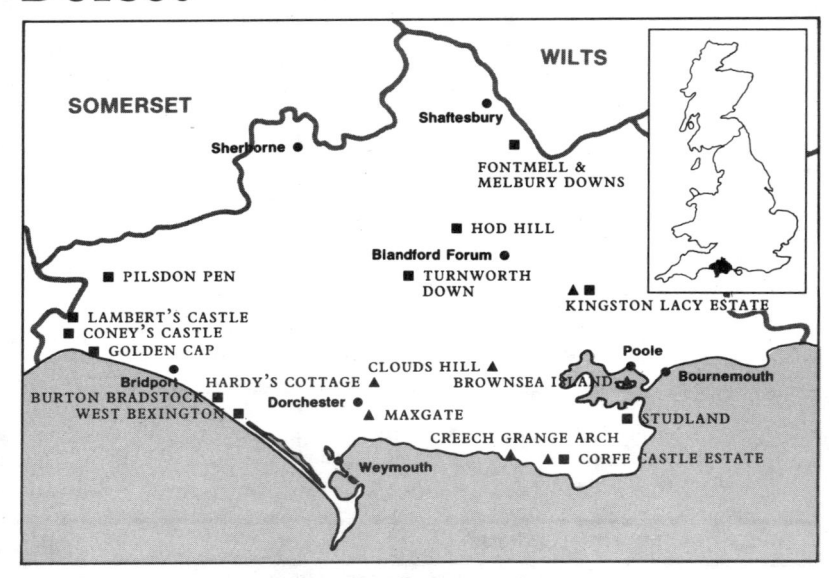

COUNTRYSIDE

The Trust's estate at **Fontmell Down**, between Shaftesbury and Blandford [183: ST884184] includes **Melbury Beacon** and **Melbury Down** [184: ST900193], a total of 730 acres; with magnificent walks across chalk downland overlooking, to the west, the Blackmore Vale. Fontmell Down was bought by public appeal to commemorate the Dorset of Thomas Hardy. Car park at the top of Spread Eagle Hill and at Compton Abbas airfield. Refreshments available (not NT). Limited access for disabled visitors.

Magnificent views from **Creech Grange Arch**, a folly near Corfe Castle (see p.106) [195: SY212818] may be enjoyed.

Dorset is dominated by Iron Age forts and many of these are now in the permanent care of the National Trust, including **Pilsdon Pen**, near Broadwindsor [193: ST414012], **Lambert's Castle**, north of Lyme Regis [193: SY370986] and the adjacent **Coney's Castle**. **Hod Hill** and **Turnworth Down**, north-west of Blandford, are equally rewarding as archaeological sites and for superlative views. The familiar ancient figure of the Cerne Giant is cut in the chalk of Giant's Hill near Cerne Abbas, 8m N of Dorchester. Re-chalking due 1995.

On the **Kingston Lacy Estate** (see p.108) the Trust has opened a number of walks (some of which are accessible to wheelchair users). The 7,000-acre agricultural estate is crossed by public footpaths, many still following Roman and Saxon tracks past medieval cottages. The estate is dominated by the Iron Age hill-fort of **Badbury Rings**. Leaflets on the Kingston Lacy Estate walks and on Badbury Rings is available from the shop at Kingston Lacy and from Badbury Rings at weekends, April to October. Audio guide to Badbury available for hire. Badbury Rings are regularly grazed to manage

DORSET

grassland. For the protection of livestock dogs are not permitted on the Rings. Point to point races are held at Badbury on three Saturdays early in the year. On these days a charge is made for car parking.

COAST

The Dorset coast is rich in variety; hills, coombes, cliffs, bays and islands. One such island in Poole Harbour, is **Brownsea** (see below), and immediately south is the Trust's **Studland** peninsula, part of the 7,000-acre **Corfe Castle** estate (see p.106). This includes the whole of Studland Bay with Old Harry Rocks and Shell Bay (see p.109). The heathland behind Studland beach is designated a National Nature Reserve, of particular interest to naturalists in winter because of its variety of overwintering birds. There are several public paths and two nature trails here. Spyway Farm, near Langton Matravers, supports important bird and butterfly habitats and many rare plants. There are several public paths. Restoration work and conservation grazing continues in 1994.

At **Golden Cap** [193: SY4092] the Trust owns more than 2,000 acres of hill, farmland, cliff, undercliff and beach (7½ miles of coastline from the Devon border to Eype). Here is the highest cliff in southern England – so named because of the yellow limestone forming a cap above the blue lias clay cliffs and clumps of golden gorse near its summit. This splendid viewpoint and the remainder of the estate have 20 miles of paths for walkers including a 7½-mile coastal footpath. There is a campsite at St Gabriel's on the estate; booking through the Warden tel. (0297) 89628. **Stonebarrow Hill** has an adapted WC for wheelchair users and paths here are accessible. Langdon woods also has a circular path (Rada Padlocks). Seasonal shop and information centre. Parking prohibited at St Gabriel's.

The shingle beach at **Burton Bradstock** is accessible to wheelchair users, from its grassy car park; no dogs on beach from June to Sept. There are riverside and cliff walks through this 93-acre Trust property which includes a stretch of the South-West Coastal Footpath [193/194: SY491889].

The Hardy Monument which overlooks the Dorset coast 6 miles south-west of Dorchester was erected in 1844 in memory of Vice-Admiral Sir Thomas Masterman Hardy, flag-captain of the Victory at the Battle of Trafalgar. This viewpoint is suitable for visitors in wheelchairs [194: SY613876]. Monument requires essential restoration work; no access to it at present.

BROWNSEA ISLAND

Poole Harbour BH15 1EE (0202) 707744

A 500-acre island of heath and woodland, with wide views of Dorset coast. The island includes a 200-acre nature reserve leased to the Dorset Trust for Nature Conservation

- **Access:** Boats run from Poole Quay and Sandbanks. Visitors may land on the beach with a dinghy

    26 March to 9 Oct: daily 10-8 or dusk if earlier; check time of last boat

- Landing fee: £2.10, children £1. Family ticket £5.20 (2 adults & 2 children) available April, May, June & Sept. Parties £1.90, children 90p, by written arrangement with Warden

- Guided tours of nature reserve please contact Dorset Trust for Nature Conservation Warden (tel.(0202) 709445   *continued*

DORSET

- 🛍 Shop open daily 26 March to 9 Oct 10-6 (tel. (0202) 700852)
- ♿ Island paths hilly and rough, but area around Quay accessible; powered chair may be available; mainland car parking near Poole Quay; all boats will accept and help wheelchairs; WC near Island Quay. Refreshments accessible
- 👁 Braille guide
- 🍴 Coffee, lunches and teas in the Restaurant near landing quay. Open daily 26 March to 9 Oct from 10.15; closes ½hr before last boat departs (tel. (0202) 700244). Tuck shop daily
- 🏛 Portman Study Centre. School groups welcome
- **E** Open air theatre, and other events in summer; contact Warden for details, tel. (0202) 707744
- → [195: SZ032878] *Bus:* From surrounding areas to Poole Quay. To Sandbanks: Wilts & Dorset 150 Bournemouth–Swanage (passing BR Branksome); 152 from Poole (passing close BR Parkstone) (tel. (0202) 673555); Yellow Buses 12 from Christchurch, summer only (tel. (0202) 557272) *Station:* Poole ½m to Quay; Branksome or Parkstone 3½m to Sandbanks

CLOUDS HILL 🏠

Wareham BH20 7NQ (0985) 847777

T. E. Lawrence (Lawrence of Arabia) bought this cottage in 1925 as a retreat; it contains his furniture

- **O** 27 March to 30 Oct: Wed, Thur, Fri, Sun & BH Mon 2-5 or dusk if earlier; no electric light
- **£** £2.20. No reduction for parties or children. Unsuitable for coaches or trailer caravans. No WCs
- 👁 Braille guide
- → 9m E of Dorchester, 1½m E of Waddock crossroads (B3390), 1m N of Bovington Camp [194: SY824909] *Bus:* Southern National 67, Bere Regis Coaches from BR Wool, alight Bovington, 1m (tel. (0305) 783645) *Station:* Wool 3½m; Moreton (U) 3½m

CORFE CASTLE 🏰

Corfe Castle, Wareham BH20 5EZ (0929) 481294

One of the most impressive ruins in England, this former royal castle was besieged and sleighted by Parliamentary forces in 1646

- **O** 7 Feb to end Oct: daily 10-5.30 or dusk if earlier. Open Good Fri and BH Mon. Nov to Feb 1995: Sat & Sun only 12-3.30
- **£** £2.90, children £1.40. Parties £2.40; children £1.20. Car & coach parking available at Castle View Cafe (NT) off A351, subject to a charge (NT members free)

DORSET

- 📷 By arrangement with Custodian
- 🛍 Shop daily: 28 March to 29 Oct 10–6; 30 Oct to 29 March 1995 10–4. Tel. (0929) 480921
- ♿ WC at ticket office. Wheelchair access very difficult
- 🍴 Licensed tea-room; coffee, lunch and cream teas (at castle entrance) open daily 1–27 March, 11–4; 28 March to 30 Oct 10.30–5.30; Nov to Feb 1995, weekends only, 11–4. Tel. (0929) 481332
- 🚸 Children's guidebook
- 🏫 Education pack available; contact Custodian for details
- **E** Contact the Events Organiser for details. Tel (0985) 847777
- 🐕 On leads only
- ➡ On A351 Wareham–Swanage road [195: SY959824] *Bus:* Wilts & Dorset 142/3/4 Poole–Swanage (passing BR Wareham) (tel. (0202) 673555) *Station:* Wareham 4½m

HARDY'S COTTAGE

Higher Bockhampton, nr Dorchester DT2 8QJ (0305) 262366

A small thatched cottage where the novelist and poet Thomas Hardy was born in 1840. It was built by his great grandfather and little altered; furnished by the Trust. (See Max Gate, p.109)

- ⭕ 26 April to 30 Oct: daily (except Thur) 11–6 or dusk if earlier. Open Good Fri. Approach only by 10 min. walk from car park through woods. Interior by appointment with Custodian. Exterior from end of garden
- £ Interior £2.50. No reduction for children or parties. Schools: 6th forms only. Coaches by prior arrangement only. No WCs. Hardy's works on sale
- 🛍 Shop in Dorchester (0305) 267535
- ♿ Access to garden only; special car parking arrangement with Custodian
- 🐕 No dogs in garden

continued

DORSET

➔ 3m NE of Dorchester, ½m S of A35 [194: SY728925] *Bus:* Wilts & Dorset X84, 184/6 Weymouth–Salisbury, 187/8 Poole–Dorchester (all pass BR Dorchester South & close Dorchester West), alight Bockhampton Lane, ½m (tel. (0202) 673555) *Station:* Dorchester South 4m; Dorchester West (U) 4m

KINGSTON LACY
Wimborne Minster BH21 4EA (0202) 883402

A 17th-century house, designed for Sir Ralph Bankes by Sir Roger Pratt, and altered by Sir Charles Barry in the 19th century. The house contains an outstanding collection of paintings, including works by Rubens, Titian, Van Dyke and Lely. The 'Spanish Room' is in gilded leather with a gilded ceiling brought from the Contarini Palace in Venice. Fine collection of Egyptian artefacts. The mansion is set in 250 acres of wooded park with a fine herd of Red Devon cattle

O 26 March to 30 Oct: daily except Thur & Fri. House & Garden 12–5.30; last admissions 4.30. Park 11.30–6

£ House, garden and park £5.20, children £2.60. Pre-booked parties (20 or more) £4.60, children £2.40. Garden and Park £2, children £1. Parking 100yds

📷 26 March to 30 Oct 11.30–5.30. Also open weekends only in Nov & Dec 12–4. Tel. (0202) 841424

♿ Access to garden only; some thick gravel; self-drive buggy. Restaurant accessible; WC. Special parking by arrangement with Administrator. Two special days for visitors in wheelchairs, May & Sept. For details contact the Administrator

👁 Visitors with guide dogs please contact Administrator in advance; Braille guide

🍴 Lunches & teas in licensed stable restaurant open 26 March to 30 Oct 11.30–5.30. Also open for Christmas lunches at weekends in Dec, and party bookings only weekdays & evenings; tel. (0202) 889242. Picnics in north park only

▮ Frizzell Study Centre & active education programme; children's guide

E Outdoor theatre & concerts with fireworks. For details contact the Administrator

🐕 On leads in north park only

➔ On B3082 Blandford–Wimborne road, 1½m W of Wimborne [19: SY980019] *Bus:* Wilts & Dorset X13, 132/3/9 from Bournemouth, Poole, Shaftesbury (passing close BR Bournemouth & Poole). On all alight Wimborne Square 1½m, but occasional service to house in peak summer period (tel. (0202) 673555) *Station:* Poole 8½m

DORSET

MAX GATE

Alington Avenue, Dorchester DT1 2AA (Regional Office (0985) 847777)

Poet and novelist Thomas Hardy designed and lived in the house from 1885 until his death in 1928. The house is leased to tenants and contains no Hardy memorabilia.

- Garden & Drawing Room open April to end Sept; please tel. to check opening times (office hours). Hardy scholars and literary societies by prior written appointment with the Thomas Hardy Society, PO Box 1438, Dorchester, Dorset DT1 1YH
- Garden & Drawing Room £2, children £1. No WCs
- 1m E of Dorchester *Bus:* Southern National D from town centre (tel. (0305) 783645) *Station:* Dorchester South 1m; Dorchester West (U) 1m

STUDLAND BEACH & NATURE RESERVE

1 Marine Terrace, Studland, Swanage BH19 3AX (0929) 44259

Three miles of fine sandy beaches backed by the Studland Heath National Nature Reserve, extending from the South Haven Point to the chalk cliffs of Handfast Point and Old Harry Rocks

- All year. Car parks 9–8
- Car parks (Shell Bay, The Knoll, Middle Beach and South Beach): April, Sept & Oct £1.70; May & June £2.50; July & Aug £3; rest of year £1. NT members free. Coaches £13. WCs. Boat launching: powered craft £13 per day. Others, incl. sail boards £4.50 per day (incl. NT members)

  Note: Boats – third party insurance cover must be shown

- Knoll Visitor Centre: shop open daily 1 March to 30 June 11–4*; 1 July to 31 August 10–5*; 1 Sept to 30 Oct 11–4*; 31 Oct to Feb 1995 11–4; Wed to Sun only, weather permitting *minimum opening hours; tel. (0929) 44500
- Knoll Car Park has good access. In summer, boardwalk for wheelchairs along part of Knoll beach. WCs
- Beach cafe in Visitor Centre open same days and times as shop. Tel. (0929) 44305
- Exhibitions and hands-on displays in Knoll Visitor Centre
- Must be kept on leads May to end Sept, and not allowed to foul the beach
- [195: SZ036835] *Bus:* Wilts & Dorset 150 Bournemouth–Swanage (passing BR Branksome) to Shell Bay and Studland; 152 Poole–Sandbanks (passing close BR Parkstone) (tel. (0202) 673555); Yellow Buses 12 Christchurch–Sandbanks, summer only (tel. (0202) 557272) (Vehicle ferry from Sandbanks to Shell Bay) *Station:* Branksome or Parkstone, both 3½m to Shell Bay or 6m to Studland via vehicle ferry

REFER TO OPENING PAGES FOR GENERAL INFORMATION

County Durham

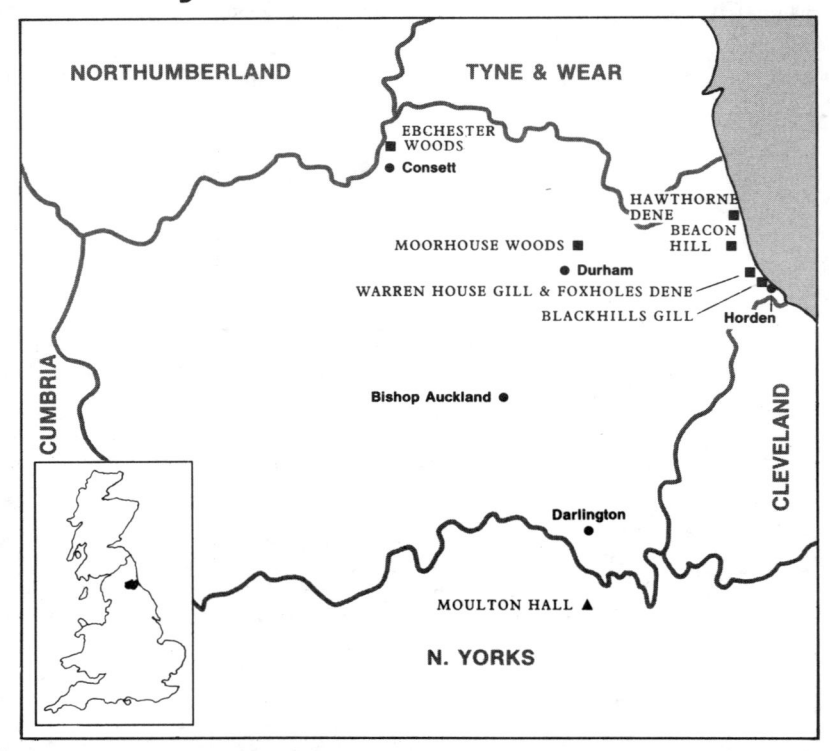

COAST AND COUNTRYSIDE

Just north of Easington, the Trust owns part of Hawthorne Dene and adjoining coastal strip, together with **Beacon Hill**, the highest point on the Durham Coast. It provides spectacular views; access on foot through Hawthorne Dene [88: NZ425460].

Further south, near Horden, are two denes, **Warren House Gill** and **Foxholes Dene** (the Trust owns only the southern half of this dene), connected by a narrow coastal strip; access from B1283 via footpaths [88: NZ444427]. This piece of coast marks the 500th mile acquired through the Trust's coastal appeal, Enterprise Neptune. South of Horden, the Trust owns around 110 acres of clifftop, including **Blackhills Gill**: access via A1086.

Inland, the Trust-owned **Moorhouse Woods** [88: NZ305460], are just to the north of Durham City; peaceful woodland walks are available on the banks of the River Wear. Access to Moorhouse Woods can be gained from Leamside across a footbridge over the A1(M). At the village of **Ebchester** [88: NZ100551] in north-west County Durham is a short woodland walk along the banks of the River Derwent.

Essex

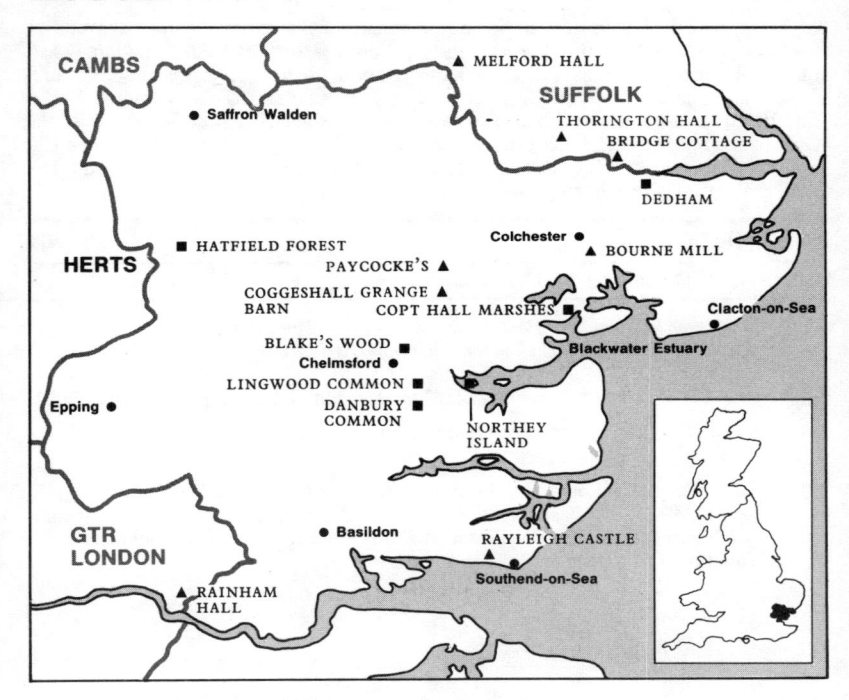

COUNTRYSIDE

Five miles east of Chelmsford, **Danbury & Lingwood Commons** [167: TL7805] are a survival of the medieval manors of St Clere and Herons, where commoners from the settlements roundabout grazed their animals on these heath and woodland areas. Danbury is more open with heather, bracken, broom and brambles, some oak and silver birch, and areas of hornbeam coppice and standard trees. One clearing on this common is one of the few known breeding grounds in this country for the Rosy Marbled moth. Lingwood Common has more woodland, with open glades and a fine viewpoint. Near Little Baddow, 2 miles to the north-west, the Trust owns **Blake's Wood** – more than 100 acres of hornbeam and chestnut coppice and renowned for bluebells [167: TL773067]. All these areas are Sites of Special Scientific Interest. **Hatfield Forest**, near Bishop's Stortford, on the Herts/Essex border offers well over 1,000 acres of undulating wooded country and open grassland for walkers and riders to explore (see p.113). **Rayleigh Castle** is a Domesday site in the centre of Rayleigh (see p.114). At Dedham the Essex Way passes through **Bridges Farm** and **Dalethorpe Park** (see also Flatford entry, Suffolk) [168: TM0533311].

ESSEX

COAST

The Trust owns the bird reserve of **Northey Island** in the Blackwater estuary. Permits to visit must be sought from the Warden, Northey Cottage, Northey Island, Maldon, Essex at least 24 hours in advance of a visit). It is a Grade 1 site for overwintering birds, and for saltmarsh plants. The island is cut off at high tide so access is limited [168: TL872058]. Eight miles south of Colchester is the **Copt Hall Marshes**, near Little Wigborough on the Blackwater estuary [168: TL981146]. The saltmarsh is extremely important for overwintering birds. 1½ mile waymarked circular route. Footpath suitable for balloon-tyred wheelchairs. Small car park.

BOURNE MILL

Bourne Road, Colchester (0206) 572422

Originally a fishing lodge built in 1591, it was later converted into a mill, with a 4-acre mill pond. Much of the machinery, including the waterwheel, is intact

- Only BH Mon & Sun preceding BH Mon. Also Sun & Tues in July & Aug 2–5.30
- £1.30. Children must be accompanied by an adult. No reduction for parties. No WCs
- 1m S of centre of Colchester, in Bourne Road, off the Mersea Road (B1025) [168: TM006238] *Bus:* Colchester Transport 7A, 8, Eastern National 67 from Colchester (passing BR Colchester) (tel. 0345 000333) *Station:* Colchester Town ¾m; Colchester 2m

ESSEX

COGGESHALL GRANGE BARN 🏠   ✗

Grange Hill, Coggeshall, Colchester CO6 1RE (0376) 562226

The oldest surviving timber framed barn in Europe, dating from around 1140, and originally part of the Cistercian Monastery of Coggeshall. It was restored in the 1980s by the Coggeshall Grange Barn Trust, Braintree District Council and Essex County Council. Features a small collection of farm carts and wagons

- 🕐 27 March to 9 Oct: Tues, Thur, Sun and BH Mon 1-5
- £ £1.10. Parties 90p. Joint ticket with Paycocke's £2
- ♿ Barn accessible
- 🐕 No dogs allowed in the barn
- ➡ Signposted off A120 Coggeshall bypass; ½m from centre of Coggeshall, on Grange Hill (signposted) [168: TQ848223] *Bus:* Eastern National 133, Freeman's 70 BR Bishop's Stortford & Stansted Airport–Colchester (passing close BR Marks Tey) (tel. 0345 000333) *Station:* Kelvedon 2½m

HATFIELD FOREST 🏞 🌳 🚶

Takeley, nr Bishop's Stortford, Hertfordshire
Head Warden: (0279) 870678

Over 1,000 acres of ancient woodland, once part of the royal forests of Essex. This historic landscape has been designated a Site of Special Scientific Interest, with an observation hide for bird-watching and a nature walk. The chases and rides afford excellent walks, and there is good coarse fishing on the two lakes

- 🕐 All year. Vehicle access restricted Nov to Easter
- £ Car park £2.40. Coaches £20; school coaches £10. Parties must book in advance with Head Warden. Riding for members of Hatfield Forest Riding Association only. Contact Head Warden
- ♿ Adapted WC and reserved car parking; accessible paths and grassland
- 🍴 Refreshments available near the lake
- 📖 Resource book available from Warden
- 🐕 Must be kept on leads where cattle are grazing and around lake
- ➡ [167: TL547208/546199] *Bus:* Eastern National 333 Epping–Stansted Airport (passing close BR Bishop's Stortford) (tel. 0345 000333) *Station:* Stansted Airport 3m

GREEN WOODPECKER

ESSEX

PAYCOCKE'S 🏠 ❁

West Street, Coggeshall, Colchester CO6 1NS (0376) 561305

A merchant's house, dating from about 1500, with unusually rich panelling and wood carving. A display of lace for which Coggeshall was famous is on show, and there is a pleasant garden

- **O** 27 March to 9 Oct: Tues, Thur, Sun & BH Mon 2–5.30
- **£** £1.40. Parties of 6 or more must book in advance with the tenant. No reduction for parties. Children must be accompanied by an adult. Joint ticket with Coggeshall Grange Barn £2
- **♿** Access to garden and ground floor; but one awkward step at front door. The house is small; please contact the tenant before a visit
- **🐕** No dogs
- **→** Signposted off A120, on S side of West Street, about 300yds from centre of Coggeshall, on road to Braintree next to the Fleece Inn, 5½m E of Braintree [168: TL848225] *Bus:* Eastern National 133, Freeman's 70 BR Bishop's Stortford & Stansted Airport–Colchester, (passing close BR Marks Tey) (tel. 0345 000333) *Station:* Kelvedon 2½m

RAINHAM HALL see London, page 156

RAYLEIGH CASTLE

Rayleigh (0263) 733471

A four-acre site in the middle of Rayleigh Town, on which once stood the Domesday castle, erected by Sweyn of Essex

- **O** All year 7am–7pm or dusk if earlier
- **£** Free
- **→** 6m NW of Southend, path from Rayleigh station (A129) [178: TQ805909] *Bus:* From surrounding areas (tel. 0345 000333) *Station:* Rayleigh 200yds

Gloucestershire

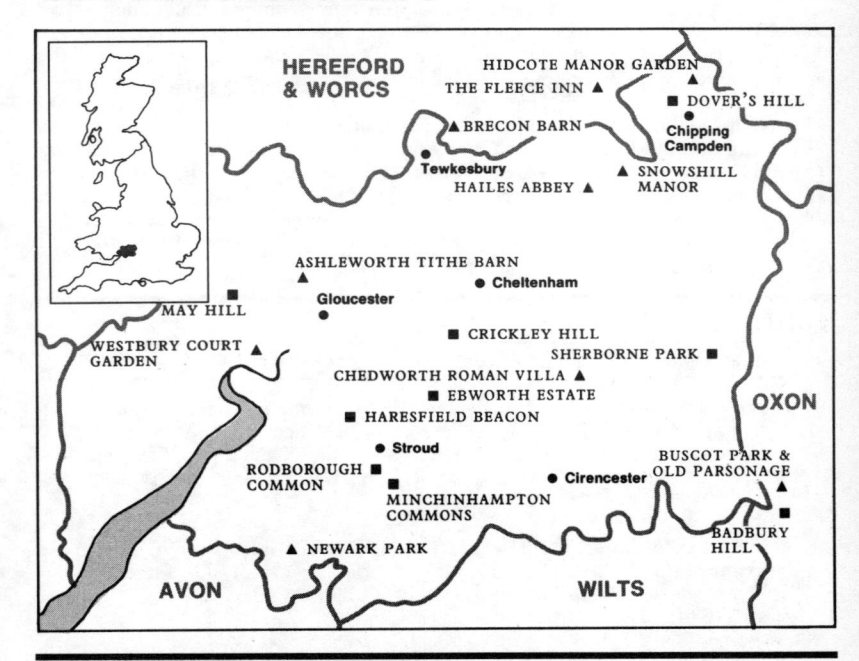

COUNTRYSIDE

Dover's Hill, 1 mile north of Chipping Campden, [151: SP135395] forms a natural amphitheatre on a spur of the Cotswolds, giving glorious views over the Vale of Evesham. The Cotswold 'Olympick Games' have been held here since 1612, and are re-enacted every year on the evening of the first Friday following Spring Bank Holiday. There is a way-marked woodland walk. Wheelchair access to viewpoint and topograph.

Six miles to the east of Gloucester is **Crickley Hill** [163: SO930163], on the Cotswold escarpment, commanding magnificent views over the Severn Vale to the Forest of Dean and Welsh hills beyond. It is run as a country park in conjunction with adjoining land owned by the County Council; leaflets of various guided walks are available at the information point. The promontory is the site of an Iron Age and Neolithic hill-fort.

Three miles north-west of Stroud is **Haresfield Beacon** [162: SO820089]. The site of a hill-fort, and several hundred acres of nearby woodland, provide spectacular views towards the Severn estuary and across to the Forest of Dean. A topograph (signposted from a small car park) is sited on the adjoining spur known as Shortwood; it displays the area in relief and indicates the views. There are many footpaths through the woodland and the Cotswold Way long distance footpath traverses the property.

The Ebworth Estate close to Sheepscombe, 2 miles north-east of Painswick, provides excellent woodland walking through magnificent beechwoods rich in wildlife. Access to Workmans Wood [163: SO897107] and Lord's and Lady's Woods [163: SO888110] is

115

GLOUCESTERSHIRE

by public rights of way only and there are no parking facilities. Blackstable Wood [163: SO894097] is also accessible by public rights of way with car parking available nearby.

Two miles south of Stroud, **Minchinhampton** and **Rodborough Commons** [162: SO855010/850038] together amount to nearly 1,000 acres of high open grassland and woods for walking and other quiet recreation. The commons form a steep-sided plateau, rich in wild flowers and other wildlife, with views across the Stroud valleys which contain former wool and cloth mills, to distant hills beyond. There are a number of interesting archaeological sites including the impressive Minchinhampton Bulwarks.

Three miles south-west of Newent and 9 miles west of Gloucester are **May Hill** and **May Hill Common** [162: SO694218]. Walks to the pine trees on the 969ft summit (not NT) are signposted from the minor road below the hill. This is a wild and romantic area of heath and grassland, from which there are spectacular views in every direction.

Sherborne Park Estate [163: SP157144] is off the A40, 3 miles east of Northleach. Attractive waymarked walks through woods and parkland, with fine views.

ASHLEWORTH TITHE BARN

Ashleworth, Gloucestershire (0684) 850051

A 15th-century tithe barn with two projecting porch bays and fine roof timbers

April to end Oct: daily 9–6 or sunset if earlier. Closed Good Fri. Other times by prior appointment only with Severn Regional Office, address on last page

60p

6m N of Gloucester, 1¼E of Hartpury (A417), on W bank of Severn, SE of Ashleworth [162: SO818252] *Bus:* Swanbrook Transport Gloucester–Tewkesbury (passing close BR Gloucester), alight Ashleworth ¼m (tel. (0242) 574444) *Station:* Gloucester 7m

CHEDWORTH ROMAN VILLA

Yanworth, nr Cheltenham GL54 3LJ (0242) 890256

The remains of a Romano-British villa, excavated 1864. The mosaics and two bath houses are well preserved, and a museum houses the smaller finds. There is a 9 min. introductory film

March to end Oct: Tues to Sun & BH Mon 10–5.30 (closed Good Fri). Last admissions 5. Also, 2 Nov to 4 Dec: Wed to Sun 11–4, also 10 & 11 Dec. Feb 1995: site open for pre-booked parties.

£2.60. Family ticket £7.15. School and other parties are given an introduction to the site, but must be booked in advance. No reduction for parties, which must be limited to one coach at a time. Free coach and car park. Picnic area in nearby woodland, open April to end Sept

Shop open as villa

Partly accessible but some steps & slopes. WC in Reception building

3m NW of Fossebridge on Cirencester–Northleach road (A429), approach from A429 via Yanworth or from Withington (coaches must avoid Withington) [163: SP053135] *Station:* Cheltenham Spa 9m

GLOUCESTERSHIRE

HAILES ABBEY ✠

nr Winchcombe, Cheltenham GL54 5PB (0242) 602398

Seventeen cloister arches and extensive excavated remains in lovely surroundings of an abbey founded by Richard, Earl of Cornwall, in 1246. There is a small museum and covered display area. Hailes Abbey is owned by the National Trust and managed and maintained by English Heritage

- Site & Museum: 1 April to 31 Oct: daily 10-6. Nov to end March 1995: Tues to Sun 10-4 (closed 24-26 Dec & New Year BH)

  Note: Access to site daily, but museum is closed on certain days from Oct to end March for staffing reasons. To avoid disappointment please tel. the property direct or EH Regional Office, 7/8 King St, Bristol BS1 4EQ (tel. (0272) 750700)

- £1.90, children 95p (OAPs, students & UB40 holders £1.40) incl. of tape guide; free admission to English Heritage members
- Small English Heritage shop in Museum
- Access to most of site and museum. WC
- Some touch prints available
- Teachers' handbook available. Free admission for pre-booked school parties; tel. for information
- On leads only, in Abbey grounds, but not in Museum
- 2m NE of Winchcombe, 1m E of Broadway road (B4632) [150: SP050300] *Bus:* Castleways from Cheltenham (passing close BR Cheltenham) alight Didbrook, 1½m, or more frequent to Greet, 1¾m by footpath (tel. (0242) 602949) *Station:* Cheltenham 10m

HIDCOTE MANOR GARDEN ❈

Hidcote Bartrim, nr Chipping Campden GL55 6LR (0386) 438333

One of the most delightful gardens in England, created this century by the great horticulturist Major Lawrence Johnston. A series of gardens within the whole, separated by walls and hedges of different species, Hidcote is famous for rare shrubs, trees, 'old' roses and borders

- April to end Oct: daily except Tues & Fri 11-7 (closed Good Fri). Last admissions 6 or 1hr before sunset if earlier
- £4.80. Family ticket £13.20. Parties by written appointment only. No picnicking in garden. Free car park 100yds
- Shop open as garden 11-6; also open 5 Nov to 18 Dec: Sat & Sun 12-4. Plant sales centre open as garden April-end Sept:10.30-5.45
- Access limited for wheelchair users due to the nature of some informal stone paved paths. Wheelchair users requiring restaurant facilities should contact Restaurant Manager as level access can be arranged (see p.118). Partially adapted WC in plant sales centre adjacent to car park

GLOUCESTERSHIRE

Licensed restaurant serving coffee & lunches 11-2, teas 2.15-5. Also open as shop in Nov & Dec. Parties to book in advance with Restaurant Manager (tel. (0386) 438703). Light refreshments available in plant centre April–Sept: 10.30-5.45

4m NE of Chipping Campden, 1m E of B4632 (originally A46), off B4081 [151: SP176429] *Station:* Honeybourne (U) 4½m

LITTLE FLEECE BOOKSHOP
Bisley Street, Painswick, Gloucestershire

17th-century building in heart of Painswick, originally part of Great Fleece Inn. An exemplary restoration carried out in 1935 with the advice of Sir George Oatley, enhancing the existing 17th-century features and character. Ground floor room now open as a bookshop

2 April-31 Oct: Tues to Sat 10-5. (Closed Good Fri) Nov & Dec: Sat only 10-5

3m N of Stroud A46, 6m SE of Gloucester B4073. Off main High Street, Painswick [162:SO868098] *Bus:* Stroud Valleys 46 Stroud–Cheltenham Spa (passes close BR Stroud) (tel. (0453) 763421) *Station:* Stroud 4m

NEWARK PARK
Ozleworth, Wotton-under-Edge GL12 7PZ (0453) 842644

Elizabethan 'standing' or hunting lodge built on the edge of a cliff by the Poyntz family, made into a four-square castellated country house by James Wyatt, 1790. The house is of specialist architectural interest, and is in the course of rehabilitation by present tenant, Mr R. L. Parsons, who is responsible for the showing arrangements

June to Sept: Wed & Thur afternoons by prior appointment only with tenant; guided tour

£1.50. No reduction for parties. Car park. Not suitable for coaches. No WCs

1½m E of Wotton-under-Edge, 1¾m S of junction of A4135 & B4058 [172: ST786934] *Bus:* Badgerline 309 Bristol–Dursley, alight Wotton-under-Edge, 1¾m. Frequent services link BR Bristol Temple Meads with the bus station (tel. (0272) 553231) *Station:* Stroud 10m

SNOWSHILL MANOR
Snowshilll, nr Broadway, Worcs WR12 7JU (0386) 852410

A Tudor house with a c.1700 façade, best known for Charles Paget Wade's eclectic collections of craftsmanship and design, including musical instruments, clocks, toys, bicycles, weavers' and spinners' tools, Japanese armour, which are displayed in 21 rooms of the house. A small cottage-style garden and Charles Wade's cottage are also on view

Note: There is no access to the Costume Collection at present

GLOUCESTERSHIRE

- 🅾 April & Oct: Sat & Sun 1-5 & Easter Sat, Sun, Mon 1-6. May to end Sept: daily (except Tues) 1-6. Last admissions to house ½hr before closing
- 💷 £4.20. Family ticket £11.60. School parties by prior written appointment . Free car park on N side of village. No coach parties. No picnicking. Student and specialist photography only by prior written arrangement with Administrator. Liable to serious overcrowding on Sun & BH Mon
- 🛍 Shop open as house
- Short guide available
- 🐕 No dogs
- ➡ 3m SW of Broadway, turning off the A44 [150: SP096339] *Bus:* Castleways BR Evesham–Broadway, thence 2½m (tel. (0242) 602949) *Station:* Moreton-in-Marsh 7m

WESTBURY COURT GARDEN

Westbury on Severn, Gloucestershire GL14 1PD (0452) 760461

A formal water garden with canals and yew hedges, laid out between 1696 and 1705. It is the earliest of its kind remaining in England, restored in 1971 and planted with species dating from pre-1700, including apple, pear and plum trees

- 🅾 April to end Oct: Wed to Sun & BH Mon 11-6. Closed Good Fri. Other months by appointment only
- 💷 £2.20. Free car park. Parties of 15 or more by written arrangement. Picnic area
- ♿ All parts of garden accessible. WC
- Scented plants
- 🐕 No dogs
- ➡ 9m SW of Gloucester on A48 [162: SO718138] *Bus:* Red & White 73 BR Gloucester–Newport (passing close BR Newport); 31 BR Gloucester–Coleford (tel. (0633) 266336) *Station:* Gloucester 9m

Hampshire

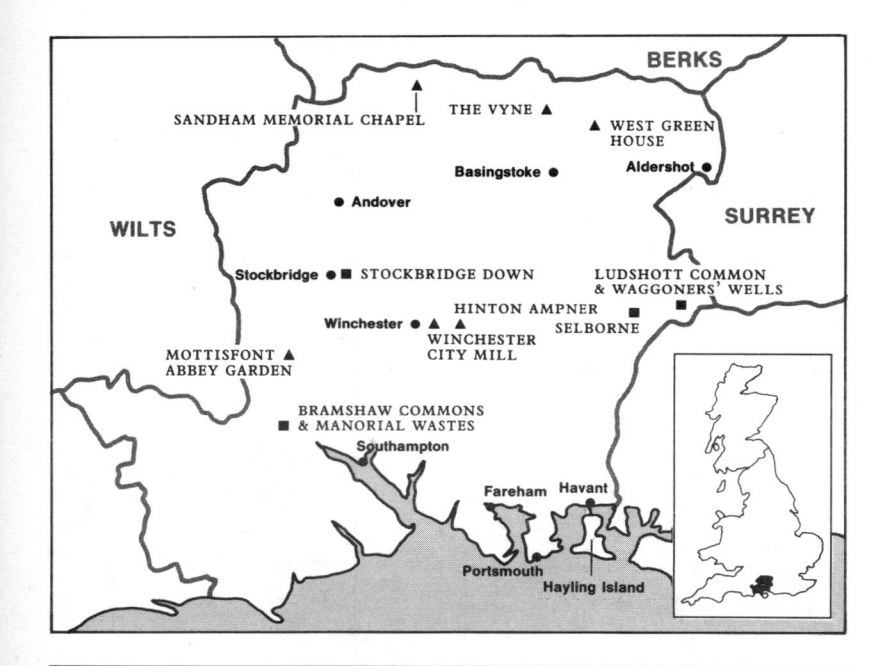

COUNTRYSIDE

On the northern edge of the New Forest between Bramshaw, Cadnam and Plaitford, the Trust owns 1,400 acres of **Bramshaw Commons and Manorial Wastes**, [184/185: SU2717]. They consist of Cadnam and Stocks Cross Greens; Cadnam, Furzley, Half Moon, Penn and Plaitford Commons; Hale Purlieu and Millersford Plantation; and Hightown Common. They abut onto the New Forest and local grazing animals may safely stray from one area to another.

At **Ludshott Common**, a fine example of lowland heath, and **Waggoners' Wells** on the Hampshire/Surrey border [186: SU855350], there is a string of man-made ponds which are a source of the River Wey (see p.223). There are many footpaths and rides and a number of nature walks. Wheelchair access. Gilbert White's walks on Selborne Hangar [186:SU735333] have now largely been cleared of storm damage.

Some 10 miles due north of **Mottisfont Abbey Garden** (see p.121) is **Stockbridge Down**, 1 mile east of Stockbridge [185: SU379349]. The chalk downland is rich in plant and insect life. Pleasant walks here are accessible from two car parks on the A272. Also at Stockbridge is the Common Marsh [185: SU354340] with attractive walks beside the River Test, and car park W of A3057, S of Stockbridge. Limited access.

HAMPSHIRE

HINTON AMPNER 🏠 ❊   ◨ ✗ ✉
Bramdean, nr Alresford SO24 0LA (0962) 771305

The house was remodelled by the late Ralph Dutton in 1936, but was gutted by a fire in 1960, destroying much of his collection. He re-built and re-furnished the house with fine Regency furniture, 17th-century Italian pictures and porcelain. Set in superb countryside, the garden combines formal design and informal planting, producing delightful walks with many unexpected vistas

- **◯** 1 April to end Sept: **Garden:** Sat, Sun, Tues, Wed, Good Fri & BH Mon 1.30–5.30; **House:** Tues & Wed only also Sat & Sun in Aug 1.30–5.30. Last admissions 5. Car park open at 1.15
- **£** House & garden £3.60; garden only £2.30. Reduction for parties. Special entrance for coaches; please book in advance. No group bookings in Aug
- **♿** House, tea-room & most of garden and tea-room accessible; map of wheelchair ramps available. Parking in front of house. WC by house
- **👁** Braille guides to house and garden available
- **☕** Tea-room open same days as garden 2–5. Picnics in car park only
- **➔** On A272, 1m W of Bramdean village, 8m E of Winchester, leave M3 at Jn 9 and follow signs to Petersfield [185: SU597275] *Bus:* Stagecoach Hampshire Bus 67 Winchester–Petersfield (passing close BR Winchester and passing BR Petersfield) (tel. (0962) 852352) *Station:* Alresford (Mid Hants Rly) 4m; Winchester 9m

MOTTISFONT ABBEY GARDEN ❊
Mottisfont, nr Romsey SO51 0LP (0794) 341220 during opening hours, otherwise 340757

A tributary of the River Test flows through the garden forming a superb and tranquil setting for a 12th-century Augustinian priory, which, after the Dissolution, became a house. It contains the spring or 'font' from which the place-name is derived. The magnificent trees, walled gardens and the national collection of old-fashioned roses combine to provide interest throughout the seasons

Notes on the house: The Abbey contains a drawing room decorated by Rex Whistler and the cellarium of the old priory. Management of the property is currently under review with the aim of improving access and visitor facilities at the Abbey. However, visitor access may be restricted at peak times so please check with the property before planning a visit to the Whistler Room

- **◯** **Garden:** 2 April to end Oct: Sat to Wed 12–6 (or dusk if earlier). June: Sat to Wed 12–8.30. Last admissions 1hr before closing. **House:** (Whistler room only) April to end Oct: Tues, Wed & Sun 1–5. In Oct closes at 4
- **£** Garden £2.50, £3.50 during rose season (varies according to weather; check with property in June); house 50p extra. No reduction for parties; coaches please book in advance

continued

HAMPSHIRE

Note: As the roses are renowned for their scent, please refrain from smoking in the walled gardens in June

- 12.30–5.30. June 12.30–8, Oct 12.30–4
- WCs partly adapted. Wheelchairs and powered buggy available; parking area for shop & rose garden only. Please ask at main car park kiosk on arrival.
- Braille guide; rose garden
- Light lunches and home-made teas at local Post Office nearby (separate car park), not NT (tel. (0794) 340243)
- Open-air events in summer; for details tel. (0794) 341930
- In car park only
- 4½m NW of Romsey, ¾m W of A3057 [185: SU327270] *Station:* Mottisfont Dunbridge (U) ¾m

SANDHAM MEMORIAL CHAPEL ✝

Burghclere, nr Newbury, Berkshire (0635) 278292

A First World War memorial built in the 1920s, and notable for the paintings by Stanley Spencer of war scenes in Salonica, which cover the chapel walls, 'The outstanding English monument to painting of the pioneering years of the 20th century' (Pevsner)

Note: As there is no lighting in the chapel, it is best to view the paintings on a bright day

HAMPSHIRE

- 🅾 30 March to end Oct: Wed to Sun & BH Mon, (closed Wed after BH Mon) 11.30–6. Nov 1994 and March 1995: Sat & Sun only, 11.30–4. Closed Dec to Feb
- 💷 £1.30, children 75p. No reduction for pre-booked parties. No WCs. Road verge parking. Picnics on front lawn
- ♿ Accessible via two small sets of steps
- ➡ 4m S of Newbury, ½m E of A34 [174: SU463608] *Bus:* Newbury Buses 123/4 from Newbury (passing close BR Newbury) (tel. (0635) 40743) *Station:* Newbury 4m

THE VYNE 🏛 ✥

Sherborne St John, Basingstoke RG26 5DX (0256) 881337

A house of diaper brickwork, dating back to the time of Henry VIII. It was built by William, 1st Lord Sandys in early 16th century, and extensively altered in mid 17th century, when John Webb added the earliest Classical portico to a country house in England. Within the house there is a fascinating Tudor chapel with Renaissance glass, a Palladian staircase and a wealth of old panelling & fine furniture. Grounds with herbaceous border, lawns and lake. Woodland walks

- 🅾 30 March to end Sept: daily, except Mon & Fri (open Good Fri & BH Mon but closed Tues following). **House:** 1.30–5.30, BH Mon 11–5.30. **Grounds:** 12.30–5.30. Grounds only weekends in March & Oct 12.30–4. Last admissions ½hr before closing
- 💷 House & grounds £4. Grounds only £2. Parties £3, Tues, Wed & Thur only. Parking 100yds
- 🛍 Shop open as grounds. Also open weekends in March & Oct 12.30–4 and for Christmas shopping (tel. (0256) 880039 for dates) *continued*

HAMPSHIRE

- ♿ Access to grounds & ground floor only (wheelchair ramp). Shop accessible. Disabled visitors may be driven to door by prior arrangement. WC
- 👁 Braille guide
- 🍴 Light refreshments and home-made teas in the Old Brew House (licensed) 30 March to end Sept 12.30-2 & 2.30-5.30 (last orders 5). Also open weekends in March 12.30-2 and 2.30-4 and at special times pre-Christmas. Coach parties by prior arrangement with Administrator. Picnics not allowed in grounds
- **E** Events held in garden & Stone Gallery; please send s.a.e. or telephone for information
- 🐕 In car park only
- ➔ 4m N of Basingstoke between Bramley and Sherborne St John [175 & 186: SU637566]. From Basingstoke Ring Road, follow Basingstoke District Hospital signs until property signs are picked up. Follow A340 Aldermaston Rd towards Tadley. Right turn into Morgaston Rd. Right turn into Vyne Rd *Bus:* Hampshire Bus 45 from Basingstoke (passing BR Basingstoke) (tel. (0256) 464501) *Station:* Bramley 2½m

WEST GREEN GARDEN 🏠 ✻
Hartley Wintney, Basingstoke RG27 8JB (0372) 453401

Small early 18th-century house of great charm in a delightful garden at its best before July

- 🅾 West Green Garden closed for restoration work during 1994. Future opening arrangements for garden currently under review
- ➔ *Bus:* Stagecoach Hampshire Bus Basingstoke–Camberley (passing BR Winchfield), alight Phoenix Green 1m (tel. (0256) 464501) *Station:* Winchfield 2m

WINCHESTER CITY MILL ✻ ✻ 🐕
Bridge Street, Winchester SO23 8EJ (0962) 870057

Built over the river in 1744, the mill has a delightful small island garden and an impressive millrace. Part of the property is used by the Youth Hostels Association

- 🅾 Open Sat & Sun in March 12-4. 28 March to end Sept daily 11-4.45. Sat & Sun in Oct 12-4. Last admission ¼ hr before closing
- £ 60p. No reduction for parties. Parking in public car park, 200yds. No WCs
- 🛍 Shop open 28 March to Christmas Eve 10-5. Open Sats & Suns in March
- ♿ Not suitable for wheelchair users; many steps
- 👁 Braille Guide; visually impaired visitors may enjoy the sound of rushing water
- ➔ At foot of High Street, beside City Bridge [185: SU487294] *Bus:* From surrounding areas (tel. (0962) 852352) *Station:* Winchester 1m

Hereford & Worcester

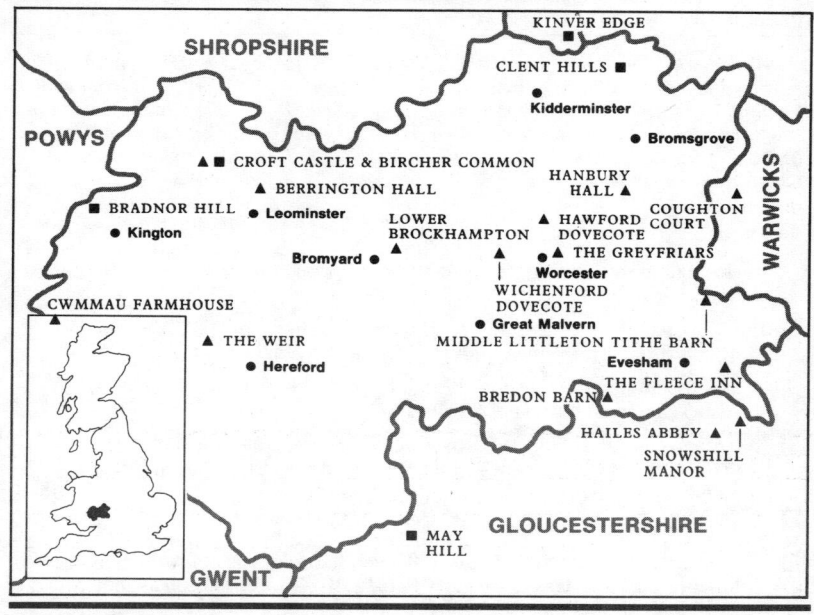

COUNTRYSIDE

Just south of Stourbridge at the south-western edge of Birmingham are the **Clent Hills**, now a Country Park and managed by the Hereford and Worcester County Council. The Trust owns over 400 acres of these hills which are covered with heathy grassland. This is ideal country for walkers and riders with superb views in every direction. There is an excellent wheelchair path to a toposcope which explains all the views, with perching points and seats for less able people to regain their breath and enjoy the surrounding countryside [139: SO9379].

At **Croft Castle** (see p.127), the Trust owns nearly 1,400 acres, including the high open grassland of **Bircher Common**, where local people still graze their animals. The Iron Age hill-fort of **Croft Ambrey** on a 1,000ft limestone ridge can give views over several counties. The estate is home to hares, squirrels, fallow deer, stoats, weasels and even polecats which have ventured here from across the Welsh border. Britain's largest finch, the hawfinch, is sometimes seen feeding on hornbeam seeds on Croft Ambrey. There are walks through the park to the hill-fort; butterflies and wild flowers abound on the estate.

At **Bradnor Hill** near Kington [148: SO282584] is 340 acres of common land rising to 1,284ft with the highest golf course in Britain on the summit.

At Brockhampton near Bromyard, the Trust owns nearly 1,700 acres which include wonderful woodlands and parkland which is open to the public. There are a number of waymarked footpaths to follow with magnificent views. Visitors may also like to visit **Lower Brockhampton** (see p.129) [149: 693548].

125

HEREFORD & WORCESTER

BERRINGTON HALL

nr Leominster HR6 0DW (0568) 615721

An elegant neo-Classical house of the late 18th century, designed by Henry Holland and set in a park landscaped by 'Capability' Brown. The formal exterior belies the delicate interior with beautifully decorated ceilings and fine furniture, including the Digby collection and a recently restored bedroom suite. Also, a nursery, Victorian laundry and pretty tiled Georgian dairy. There is an attractive garden with interesting plants and recently planted historic apple orchard in walled garden

- **O** 26 March to end Sept: daily except Mon & Tues (open BH Mon but closed Good Fri) 1.30–5.30; also Oct: Wed to Sun 1.30–4.30. Last admissions ½hr before closing. Grounds open from 12.30. Park walk open Jul, Aug, Sept & Oct same days as house
- **£** £3.50. Family ticket £9.60. Grounds only £1.60. Parties of 15 or more by prior written arrangement only. Free car and coach park
- Shop open same days as house 26 March to end Sept:1–5.30. Oct: 1–4.30. Also 5 Nov to 18 Dec: Sat & Sun 1–4.30
- Access to grounds only. WC. No wheelchair access to restaurant but arrangements will be made in good weather if requested. Parking; please enquire at ticket office
- Available upon request
- Licensed restaurant in Servants' Hall open same days as house: homemade lunches 12.30–2, teas 2.30–5.30; Oct: 12.30–4.30. Also open as shop Nov & Dec 12.30–4.30. Picnic tables in car park
- Children's quiz
- **E** Please contact the Administrator for details
- → 3m N of Leominster, 7m S of Ludlow on W side of A49 [137: SO510637] *Bus:* Midland Red West/Go Whittle192, 292 Birmingham–Hereford (passing close BR Ludlow & Leominster), alight Luston 2m (tel. (0905) 766880) *Station:* Leominster (U) 4m

BREDON BARN

Bredon, nr Tewkesbury, Gloucestershire (0684) 850051

A 14th-century barn, 132ft long, with fine porches, one of which has unusual stone chimney cowling. The barn was restored with traditional materials after a fire in 1980

- **O** April to end Nov: Wed, Thur, Sat & Sun 10–6 or sunset if earlier. Dec to Feb: by prior appointment only with Severn Regional Office (see final page)
- **£** 60p
- → 3m NE of Tewkesbury, just N of B4080 [150: SO919369] *Bus:* Spring & Son Evesham–Cheltenham (passing close BR Evesham); Boomerang from Tewkesbury (tel. (0905) 766800) *Station:* Pershore (U) 8½m

HEREFORD & WORCESTER

CROFT CASTLE 🏛️✝️❀️♿🏚️🚶

nr Leominster HR6 9PW (0568) 780246

Home of the Croft family since Domesday (with a break of 170 years from 1750). The walls and corner towers date from 14th and 15th centuries, while the interior is mainly 18th century, when the fine Georgian-Gothic staircase and plasterwork ceilings were added. A splendid avenue of 350 year old Spanish chestnuts runs through the park, and an Iron Age fort (Croft Ambrey) may be reached by footpath

- 🕐 April & Oct: Sat & Sun 2-5. Easter Sat, Sun & Mon (2-4 April) 2-6. May to end Sept: Wed to Sun & BH Mon 2-6. Last admissions to house ½hr before closing. Car park, parkland and Croft Ambrey open all year

- £ £3.00. Family ticket £8.25. Free car parking. Parties of 15 or more by prior written arrangement

- ♿ Access to ground floor, garden and part of grounds; parking near castle

- 2 copies available upon request

- Picnics in car park only

- In parkland only, on leads

- ➡️ 5m NW of Leominster, 9m SW of Ludlow; approach from B4362, turning N at Cock Gate between Bircher and Mortimer's Cross; signposted from Ludlow-Leominster road (A49) and from A4110 at Mortimer's Cross [137: SO455655] *Bus:* Midland Red West/Go Whittle 192, 292 Birmingham-Hereford (passing close BR Ludlow & Leominster), alight Gorbett Bank, 2¼m (tel. (0905) 766880) *Station:* Leominster (U) 7m

CWMMAU FARMHOUSE 🏚️

Brilley, Whitney on Wye HR3 6JP (0497) 831251

Early 17th-century timber-framed and stone-tiled farmhouse

- 🕐 Easter, May, Spring & Summer BH weekends only, (Sat, Sun & Mon 2-6). Other times by previous appointment only with tenant, Mr D. Joyce

- £ £2. Not suitable for coaches

- 🚶 Viewing by guided tours only

- No dogs

- ➡️ 4m SW of Kington between A4111 & A438; approach by long narrow lane leading S from Kington-Brilley road at Brilley Mountain [148: SO267514]

127

HEREFORD & WORCESTER

THE FLEECE INN

Bretforton, nr Evesham (0386) 831173

A medieval farmhouse in the centre of the village, containing family collection of furniture. It became a licensed house in 1848, and remains largely unaltered

- **O** Only during normal public house licensing hours
- **£** Car parking in village square. Coaches by written appointment only
- 🍴 Lunchtime snacks
- ➔ 4m E of Evesham, on B4035 [150: SP093437] *Bus:* Barry's/Creswell/Spring & Son/Midland Red West 554 from Evesham (tel. (0905) 766800) *Station:* Evesham 3m

THE GREYFRIARS

Friar Street, Worcester WR1 2LZ (0905) 23571

Built in 1480, with early 17th- and late 18th-century additions, this timber-framed house was rescued from demolition at the time of the Second World War and has been carefully restored and refurbished; interesting textiles and furnishings add character to the panelled rooms. An archway leads through to a delightful garden – a haven of peace in the centre of a busy city

- **O** April to end Oct: Wed, Thur & BH Mon 2–5.30. Last admissions ½hr before closing
- **£** £2.00. Family ticket £5.50. Parties of 15 or more by written appointment. No reductions. Not suitable for large parties of children. Public car park in Friar Street. No WCs
- ➔ [150: SO852546] *Bus:* From surrounding areas (tel. (0345) 212 555) *Station:* Worcester Foregate Street ½m

HANBURY HALL

Droitwich WR9 7EA (0527) 821214

William & Mary-style red brick house, completed in 1701. Hanbury is a typical example of an English country house built by a prosperous local family, with outstanding painted ceilings and staircase by Thornhill. The Watney Collection of porcelain is also on display in the house. There is a contemporary orangery in the garden, and an ice house. Reinstatement of formal 18th-century (in part) garden. Work commenced autumn 1993

- **O** 26 March to 31 Oct: Sat, Sun & Mon 2–6. Aug: Sat, Sun, Mon, Tues, Wed 2–6
- **£** £3.50. Family ticket £9.60. Garden only; £1. House is available for private and commercial functions, please contact Administrator. Free car and coach parking. Picnic area in car park

HEREFORD & WORCESTER

|🕅| Evening guided tours for pre-booked parties. May to Sept: Mon only (£3.50 incl. NT Members, minimum charge £70)

|🛍| Shop open as house

|♿| Wheelchair access to ground floor, tea-room; access to garden may be restricted due to reinstatement project; disabled visitors may be driven to front door; parking available near house. WC

|☕| Cream teas in tea-room in the house, open as house

|🐕| No dogs in garden, but allowed on leads in park on footpaths only

|➡| 4½m E of Droitwich, 1m N of B4090, 6m S of Bromsgrove, 1½m W of B4091 [150: SO943637] *Bus:* Midland Red West 142/4 Worcester–Birmingham (passing close BR Droitwich Spa), alight Wychbold, 2½m (tel. (0345) 212 555) *Station:* Droitwich Spa 4m

HAWFORD DOVECOTE 🏠
Hawford (0684) 850051

A 16th-century half-timbered dovecote. Access (on foot only) via the entrance drive to adjoining house

|🅾| April to end Oct: daily 9–6 or sunset if earlier. Closed Good Fri. Other times by prior appointment only with Severn Regional Office (see final page)

|£| 60p

|➡| 3m N of Worcester, ¼m E of A449 [150: SO846607] *Bus:* Midland Red West 303 Worcester–Kidderminster (passing BR Worcester Foregate Street & Kidderminster), alight Hawford Lodge, ¼m (tel. (0345) 212 555) *Station:* Worcester Foregate Street 3m; Worcester Shrub Hill 3½m

LOWER BROCKHAMPTON 🏠 🕅
Bringsty WR6 5UH (0885) 488099

A late 14th-century moated manor house, with an attractive detached half-timbered 15th-century gatehouse, a rare example of this type of structure. Also, the ruins of a 12th-century chapel

|🅾| Medieval Hall & Parlour only April to end Sept: Wed to Sun & BH Mon 10–5; closed Good Fri; Oct: Wed to Sun 10–4

|£| £1.50. Family ticket £4.10

|♿| Access to all parts

|➡| 2m E of Bromyard on Worcester road (A44); reached by a narrow road through 1½m of woods and farmland [149: SO682546] *Bus:* Midland Red West 419/20 Worcester–Hereford (passing BR Worcester Foregate Street & close BR Hereford) (tel. (0345) 212 555)

129

HEREFORD & WORCESTER

MIDDLE LITTLETON TITHE BARN 🏠
Middle Littleton, Evesham (0684) 850051

Magnificent 13th-century tithe barn, built of blue lias stone, and still in use as a farm building

🅾️ April to end Oct: daily 9–5. Closed Good Fri. Key available if closed (see notice). Other times by prior appointment only with Severn Regional Office

💷 60p

➡️ 3m NE of Evesham, E of B4085 [150: SP080471] *Bus:* Midland Red West 146, 176 Evesham–Redditch (passing close BR Evesham), alight Middle Littleton School Lane, ½m (tel. (0905) 766800) *Station:* Honeybourne (U) 3½m; Evesham 4½m

THE WEIR ✳️
Swainshill, nr Hereford (0684) 850051

A delightful riverside garden particularly spectacular in early spring, with fine views over the River Wye and Black Mountains

🅾️ 16 Feb to end Oct: Wed to Sun (incl. Good Fri) & BH Mon 11–6

💷 £1.50; free car park (unsuitable for coaches). No WCs

➡️ 5m W of Hereford on A438 [149: SO435421] *Bus:* Yeoman's Canyon 446 from Hereford; Midland Red West 101 Hereford–Credenhill (both passing close BR Hereford), thence 1½m (tel. (0905) 766800) *Station:* Hereford 5m

WICHENFORD DOVECOTE 🏠
Wichenford (0684) 850051

A 17th-century half-timbered dovecote

🅾️ April to end Oct: daily 9–6 or sunset if earlier. Closed Good Fri. Other times by prior appointment only with Severn Regional Office

💷 60p

➡️ 5½m NW of Worcester, N of B4204 [150: SO788598] *Bus:* Midland Red West 310/2/3 from Worcester (passing close BR Worcester Foregate Street), alight Wichenford, ½m (tel. (0345) 212 555) *Station:* Worcester Foregate Street 7m; Worcester Shrub Hill 7½m

SLOES

130

Hertfordshire

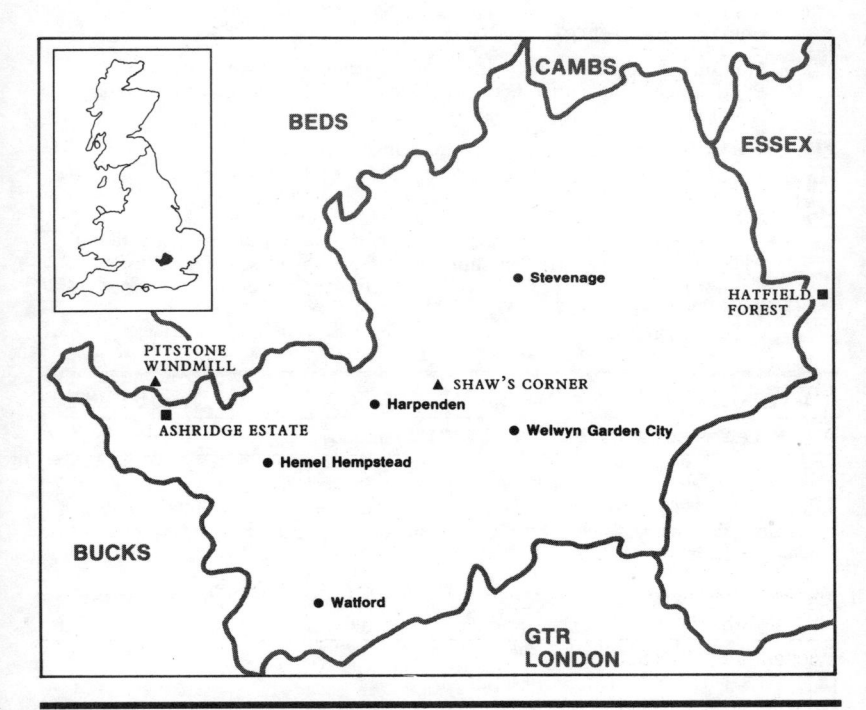

ASHRIDGE ESTATE

Ringshall, Berkhamsted (044 285) 227

The Ashridge Estate covers some 6 square miles in Hertfordshire and Buckinghamshire, running along the main ridge of the Chiltern Hills from Berkhamsted to Ivinghoe Beacon. It comprises over 4,000 acres of woodlands, commons and downland. At the northerly end of the Estate the Ivinghoe Hills are an outstanding area of chalk downland which supports a rich variety of plants and insects. The Ivinghoe Beacon itself offers splendid views from some 700ft above sea level. This area may be reached from a car park at Steps Hill. The rest of Ashridge is an almost level plateau with many fine walks through woods and open commons. Wildlife is well represented; a wide variety of birds is always in evidence, including the goldcrest and the lesser spotted woodpecker. Some 400 fallow deer roam freely; muntjac deer, badgers and foxes also abound and almost unique to the area, is the glis-glis, or edible dormouse. The main focal point of the Estate is the granite Monument erected 150 years ago to the 3rd Duke of Bridgewater, the canal Duke. An illustrated booklet about the Ashridge Estate is available at the Information Centre near the Monument

HERTFORDSHIRE

- ⊙ **Estate:** open all year. **Monument, Shop & Information Centre:** April to end Oct: Mon to Thur & Good Fri 2–5, Sat, Sun & BH Mon 2–5.30. Last admission to monument ½hr before closing
- £ Monument £1. Note: for further information, shop and party bookings tel. (044 285) 227; Estate Office tel. (0442) 842488. Riding permits available from riding warden tel. (0442) 842716
- ♿ Monument area, monument drive and Information Centre accessible. WC. Parking near Information Centre. Self-drive vehicles available free of charge from Information Centre; advance booking advisable
- ☕ Tea kiosk next to Information Centre, summer weekends
- 🐕 Admitted if kept under control
- ➡ Between Northchurch & Ringshall just off B4506, 3m N of A41 [165: SP970131] *Bus:* Monument: Aylesbury Bus 27 from BR Tring, alight Aldbury, ½m; Beacon: 61 Aylesbury–Luton (passing close BR Aylesbury & Luton); Seamarks 327 from Tring to Monument & Beacon, summer Suns (tel. (0992) 556765) *Station:* Monument: Tring, 1¾m. Beacon: Cheddington 3½m

SHAW'S CORNER

Ayot St Lawrence, nr Welwyn AL6 9BX (0438) 820307

An early 20th-century house, and the home of George Bernard Shaw from 1906 until his death in 1950. Many literary and personal relics are shown in the downstairs rooms, which remain as in his lifetime. Shaw's bedroom and bathroom are also on view, and there is a display room upstairs

- ⊙ 30 March to end Oct: Wed to Sat 2–6; Sun & BH Mon 2–6 (closed Good Fri). Parties by written appointment only, March to end Nov. Last admissions 5.30. On busy days admission will be by timed ticket
- £ £3. No reduction for parties. Car park 50yds
- ♿ Access to garden and house, but some steps. Please enquire about best times for visits; unsuitable for severely disabled visitors
- 👶 No back-packs in house, but front sling baby carrier available
- E For details of Shaw's Birthday Play and other events, please send s.a.e. to Administrator
- 🐕 In car park only
- ➡ At SW end of village, 2m NE of Wheathampstead; approx. 2m from B653 [166: TL194167] *Bus:* Sovereign 304 BR St Albans City–Hitchin, alight Gustardwood, 1¼m (tel. (0992) 556765) *Station:* Welwyn North 4m; Harpenden 5m

REFER TO OPENING PAGES FOR GENERAL INFORMATION

Humberside

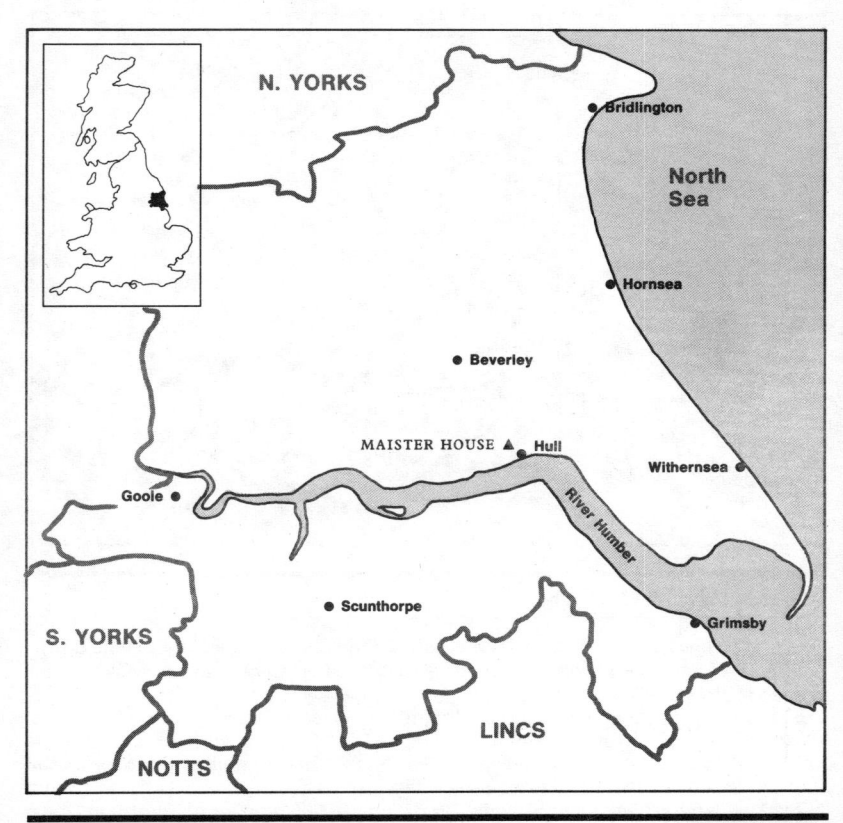

MAISTER HOUSE 🏠

160 High Street, Hull HU1 1NL (0482) 24114

Rebuilt in 1744, the house contains a superb staircase hall designed in the Palladian manner and ironwork by Robert Bakewell; let as offices

- **◉** Staircase and entrance hall only: all year: Mon to Fri 10-4; closed BH, Good Fri & 1 Jan

- **£** 80p, incl. guidebook. Indoor photography by permission only. Unsuitable for parties. No parking at property. No WCs

- **→** Hull city centre *Bus:* Local services to within 100yds (tel. (0482) 222222) services from surrounding areas (tel. (0482) 27146) *Station:* Hull ¾m

Isle of Wight

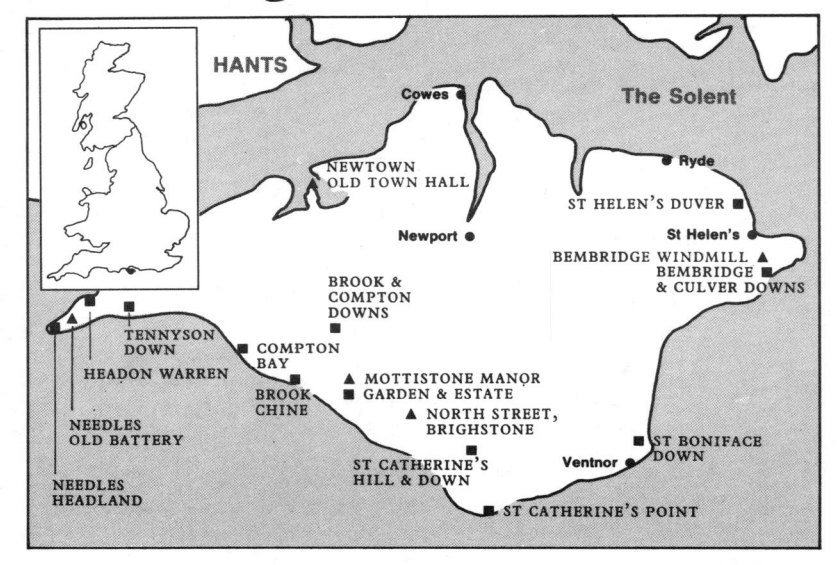

COAST AND COUNTRY

The Trust owns more than 3,500 acres of the Island, including beautiful chalk downland and 15 miles of spectacular coastline, and nearly all of it freely accessible for visitors to enjoy.

The best-known landmark on West Wight is the Needles, the sharp points of rock stretching into the sea at the extreme west of the Island. Overlooking the famous rocks the Trust owns the **Needles Headland** [196: SZ300848], as well as the Needles Old Battery (see p.136) and three coastguard cottages, let as holiday homes (see p.18). From here Trust land extends to Freshwater Bay, along the chalk cliffs of **Tennyson Down** [196: SZ330855], where the Poet Laureate walked every day when he lived at nearby Farringford.

South-east from Freshwater Bay the Trust also owns much land along the Back of the Wight. On the coast **Compton Bay** [196: SZ378840], one of the Island's most popular bathing beaches, is protected by the Trust (dogs not allowed on beach from July to mid Sept), as is **Brook Chine** [196: SZ385835]. Inland the Trust owns the Downs from Afton to **Brook Down** [196: SZ376850/SZ395891]. The Trust's **Mottistone Estate** [196: SZ405837] is further east and includes the Manor, the gardens (see p.135), farmland, woodland, Mottistone Down and most of Mottistone village. In Brighstone, the Trust has the attractive terrace of 18th-century thatched cottages built of chalk blocks, situated in North Street, including the gift shop and post office.

At the southernmost tip of the Island is **St Catherine's Point** [196: SZ495755], where there is another National Trust holiday cottage. Inland, **St Catherine's Hill** and **St Catherine's Down** [196: SZ494772/495785] give magnificent views over both the eastern and western ends of the Island. Also in the south, the Trust protects much of the Ventnor Downs, including the highest point on the Island, **St Boniface Down** [196: SZ565782] which rises steeply to 764ft and is renowned for its beautiful views and New Forest ponies grazing in the summer.

On the east of the Island the Trust owns **Bembridge & Culver Downs** [196: SZ624869], which overlook to the north the village of Bembridge and its windmill (see below). Stretching almost across Bembridge harbour mouth is **St Helen's Duver** [196: SZ637891], a wide sand and shingle spit which used to be a golf course. The Club House has been converted to a holiday cottage, also adapted for disabled visitors.

The Trust owns a spacious Edwardian holiday cottage next to the sea at Cowes on the north of the Island, with an apartment for disabled visitors. On the north-west coast the ancient borough of **Newtown** [196: SZ424906] is now reduced to a small village, although the outlines of the 13th-century town are still clearly visible. The Trust owns the Old Town Hall (see p.136) and protects much of the old borough and the entire river estuary, which is now a nature reserve.

The Trust publishes a free visitors' guide to all the coast and countryside it protects on the Isle of Wight. Copies are available from 35a St James' Street, Newport, PO30 1LB (tel. (0983) 526445).

BEMBRIDGE WINDMILL

Bookings and enquires to the Custodian, Mill Reach, Kings Road, Bembridge, Isle of Wight PO35 5NT (0983) 873945 during opening hours

Dating from around 1700. The only windmill to survive on the island. Much of the wooden machinery can still be seen

- **O** 30 March to 30 Oct: daily except Sat (but open Easter Sat & daily in July & Aug) 10-5. Last admissions 4.45. Conducted school parties and special visits March to end Oct (but not July or Aug) by written appointment. Small shop
- **£** £1.20. No reduction for parties. All school parties are conducted by a NT guide; special charge applies. Parking 100yds. No WCs. Picnic field
- **→** ½m S of Bembridge on B3395 [196: SZ639874] *Bus:* Southern Vectis 7/A, 8 BR Ryde Esplanade–Sandown (tel. (0983) 862264) *Station:* Brading (U) 2m by footpath. Ferry: Ryde (Wightlink Ltd) 6m; E. Cowes (Red Funnel), 13m

MOTTISTONE MANOR GARDEN

Bookings and enquiries to the Custodian, Moreys Lodge, Brook, Isle of Wight PO30 4EJ (0983) 740552

Colourful herbaceous borders, flowering fruit trees and delightful sea views combine to make a perfect setting for the Elizabethan Manor House. 2 holiday cottages on estate

- **O** **Garden:** 2 March to 28 Sept: Wed only & BH Mon 2-5.30. Last admissions 5. Parties by written appointment. House opening currently under review, please check with Custodian of IoW office for times & prices
- **£** Garden £1.80. No reduction for parties. Parking 50yds. No WCs
- **E** Please send s.a.e. to IoW office or telephone for information   *continued*

ISLE OF WIGHT

- On leads
- At Mottistone, 2m W of Brighstone on B3399 [196: SZ406838] *Bus:* Southern Vectis 1B Newport–Freshwater (tel. (0983) 523831). Ferry: Yarmouth (Wightlink Ltd) 6m; E Cowes (Red Funnel) 12m

THE NEEDLES OLD BATTERY

Bookings and enquiries to the Administrator, 3 Winkle Street, Calbourne, Newport PO30 4JF (0983) 754772 during opening hours

A Victorian coastal fort built in 1862, 77m above sea level. A 60m tunnel leads to spectacular views of Needles Rocks, lighthouse and Hampshire and Dorset coastline. Two original Rifled Muzzle Loader gun barrels are mounted on carriages in the parade ground, and the Laboratory, Searchlight Position and Position Finding Cells have been restored. The children's exhibition tells the story of 'The Needles at War' and there are new cartoon information boards

- 27 March to 30 Oct: Sun to Thur (but open Easter weekend and daily in July & August)10.30-5. Last admissions 4.30. School parties and special visits 27 March to end Oct (but not Aug) by written appointment
- £2.40. No reduction for parties; all parties are conducted by a NT guide; a special charge applies. No vehicular access to Battery. Parking 1m away at Alum Bay (not NT; charge £1.50). Bus hourly to Battery ($\frac{1}{2}$ hourly in peak season), see below. Children and dogs must be kept under strict control because of the cliffs. Not recommended to visitors with disabilities
- Shop open same days as Battery 11-4.30, but closed 2-13 Oct
- Tea-room open same days as Battery, 11-4.30
- At Needles Headland, W of Freshwater Bay and Alum Bay (B3322) [196: SZ300848] *Bus:* Southern Vectis 42 Yarmouth–Needles, May–Oct only, otherwise any service to Alum Bay, thence $\frac{3}{4}$m (tel. (0983) 523831)

OLD TOWN HALL, NEWTOWN

Bookings and enquiries to the Custodian, Ken Cottage, Upper Lane, Brighstone (0983) 741052

The small, now tranquil, village of Newtown once sent two members to Parliament, and the Town Hall was the setting for these often turbulent elections

- 30 March to 30 Oct: Mon, Wed & Sun (but open Good Fri, Easter Sat and Tues & Thur in July & Aug) 2-5. Last admissions 4.45. Guided tours by written appointment
- £1.10. No reduction for parties. No WCs
- Between Newport and Yarmouth, 1m N of A3054 [196: SZ424905] *Bus:* Southern Vectis 7 Newport–Freshwater (passing Yarmouth Ferry Terminal), alight Barton's Corner, 1m (tel. (0983) 523831) *Ferry:* Yarmouth (Wightlink Ltd) 5m; E Cowes (Red Funnel) 6m

Kent

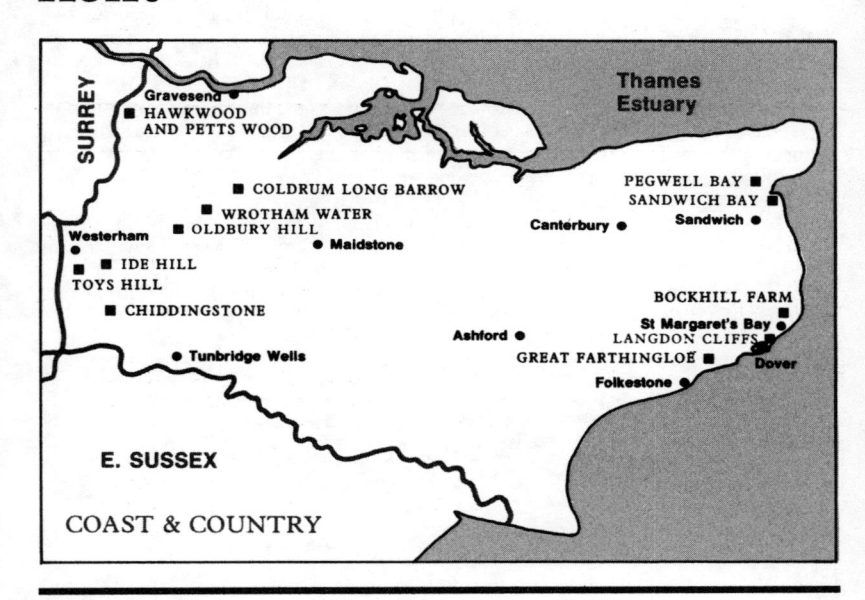

COAST

The Trust owns 560 acres of land on either side of Dover stretching to over 5¼ miles of the famous White Cliffs; 67 acres of cliff and farmland with fine walks to the south west at **Great Farthingloe** [179: TR2902393], 160 acres of clifftop grassland behind the port of Dover at Langdon Cliffs and Langdon Hole and the remainder at St Margaret's Bay to the north-east, including **Bockhill Farm**. Paths across Bockhill Farm are suitable for wheelchair users – (a strong pusher is needed) [179: TR372448].

Further north at **Sandwich Bay** [179: TR347620] and **Pegwell Bay** [179: TR343627] are 550 acres of coastal saltmarsh, sand dunes, mudflats and foreshore, managed for the Trust as a nature reserve by the Kent Trust for Nature Conservation and forming part of a Site of Special Scientific Interest (SSSI). Guided walks can be arranged from the Sandwich Bay Bird Observatory. Formed by the serpentine river Stour which finally reaches the sea at Pegwell Bay, the saltings, mudflats and freshwater marshes attract migrant waders as well as British sea and shore birds, including some rare species. One of the footpaths is suitable for wheelchairs and leads to an accessible birdhide. Access to this is from the Pegwell Bay side. Send an s.a.e. for a leaflet to the KTNC, Tyland Barn, Sandling, Maidstone, Kent ME14 3BD (tel. (0622) 662012).

COUNTRYSIDE

The Trust owns a row of 16th- and 17th-century houses in the lovely village of **Chiddingstone** near Edenbridge, including the Castle Inn, the post office and stores.

KENT

There is public footpath access to the **Chiding Stone** standing on half an acre of land given to the Trust by Lord Astor of Hever.

East of Trottiscliffe (now popularly spelt Troseley) is **Coldrum Long Barrow** [188: TQ654607], a megalithic burial chamber surrounded by standing stones. The tomb was opened in 1910 and 22 skeletons were found, dating from 3,000 BC – the New Stone Age. Not far away south-west of Wrotham at **Oldbury Hill** [188: TQ582561] is the southern half of an Iron Age hill-fort, where flint implements have been found, thought to date back to Neanderthal times. At **Wrotham Water** [188: TQ629597] are 400 acres of farmland with footpath access including part of the North Downs Way. Between Chiselhurst and Orpington are **Hawkwood** and **Petts Wood**, 333 acres of farmland, woodland and heath with footpaths [177: TQ441690] (see London).

At **Toys Hill**, south of Brasted [188: TQ465517] and on the neighbouring **Ide Hill** the Trust owns some 400 acres of heath and woodland including several viewpoints on Toys Hill where there is also a wheelchair route. The Trust's founder, Octavia Hill, knew this area well, and 100 acres of woodland given by the Sevenoaks District Council here bears her name. Part of the area is a Site of Special Scientific Interest.

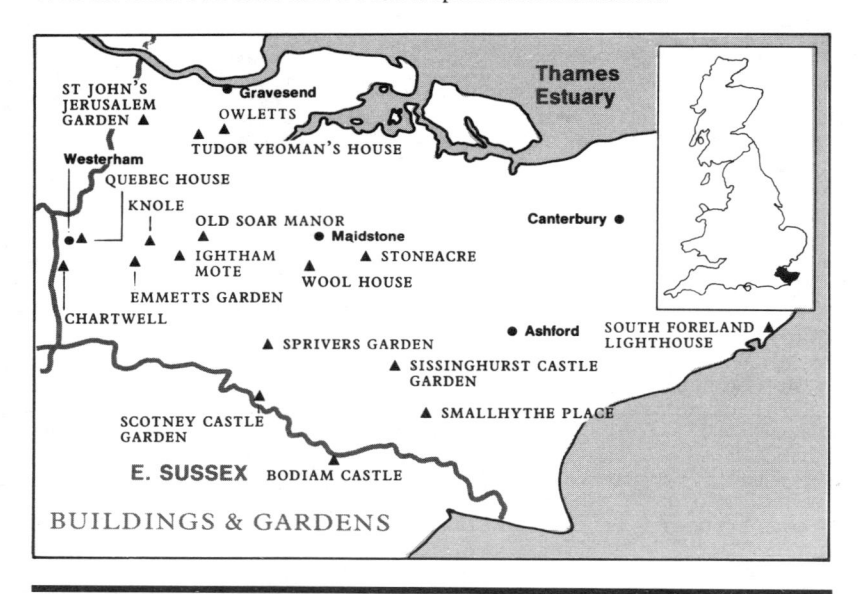

CHARTWELL 🏠 ❋ 🚶

Westerham TN16 1PS (0732) 866368

Home of Sir Winston Churchill from 1924 until the end of his life. The rooms, left as they were in his lifetime, evoke his career and interests, with pictures, maps, documents and personal mementoes. Two rooms are given over to a museum of his many gifts and uniforms. New exhibition 'The Chartwell Years' opens 1994. Terraced gardens descend towards the lake; the garden studio contains many of Sir Winston's paintings

Note: Owing to the large numbers visiting Chartwell, entry to the house is by timed

KENT

ticket; the waiting time may be spent in the garden, but visitors are warned that occasionally in summer the delay in gaining admission to the house is considerable

- 🅞 2 April to end Oct: Tues, Wed & Thur 12–5.30; Sat, Sun & BH Mon 11–5.30. Nov: house only, Sat, Sun and Wed 11–4.30. Last admissions ½hr before closing. Closed Good Fri and Tues following BH. Guided tours by prior arrangement with Administrator
- 💷 House and garden £4.20. Garden only £2. Studio 50p. House only (Nov) £2.50. No reduction for parties. Parking 500yds
- 🚶 Guided tours by arrangement, tel. Administrator
- 🛍 Shop open same days as house; April to end Oct: 10.30–5, Nov 10.30–4. Also Christmas shop, tel. Administrator for details
- ♿ Car park is hilly, with steps; tel. Administrator or enquire at information kiosk for special parking. Ground floor accessible; small lift to first floor; wheelchair available. Access to shop and restaurant. Garden difficult; WC in coach park.
- ☕ Coffee, lunches and teas; licensed self-service restaurant (no spirits). Open same days as house; April to end Oct: 10.30–5, Nov 10.30–4. Also Christmas opening, tel. Administrator for details
- 👶 Children's guide
- 🅴 June, '1940s Dance'; 29 July, Sheepdog trial; for details contact NT Regional Box Office (tel. (0892) 891001)
- 🐕 In grounds only, on leads
- ➡️ 2m S of Westerham, fork left off B2026 after 1½m [188: TQ455515] *Bus:* London & Country 320 BR Bromley N–Westerham (passing BR Bromley S); 410 Reigate–Westerham (passing BR Oxted); Kentish Bus 483 Sevenoaks–Westerham (passing BR Sevenoaks) (tel. (0800) 696996). On both, alight Westerham, 2m *Station:* Edenbridge (U) 4m; Edenbridge Town 4½m; Oxted 5½m; Sevenoaks 6½m

EMMETTS GARDEN 🍀 🚶

Ide Hill, Sevenoaks TN14 6AY (0732) 750367 or 750429

This friendly 5-acre garden boasts the highest treetop in Kent and is noted for its rare trees and shrubs, bluebells, rose and rock gardens. Perched on one of the highest spots in Kent, it has wonderful views across the Weald and Bough Beech Reservoir

- 🅞 April to end Oct: Wed to Sun & BH Mon: 1–6. Pre-booked parties welcome Thur 11–1. Last admissions 5
- 💷 £2.50, children £1.30. Pre-booked parties £2
- 🛍 Open in tea-room 2–5
- ♿ Most of garden accessible; golf buggy (seats 3) available from car park to ticket hut only; wheelchairs available for garden; WC. Access to shop and tea-room
- 🌀 Fountain and waterfall; scented azaleas in spring and roses in summer for visually impaired visitors. Beware sheer drop at end of shrub garden   *continued*

KENT

- 🥤 Tea-room, open 2-5 on same days as garden
- 👶 Baby changing facilities
- 📖 Teacher's resource book. Tree trail
- 🇪 20-21 Aug, Country Fair (tel. (0732) 750367/750429)
- 🐕 On leads only
- ➡️ 1½m S of A25 on Sundridge to Ide Hill road, 1½m N of Ide Hill off B2042, leave M25 at exit 5, then 4m [188: TQ477524] *Bus:* Nu Venture 404 from BR Sevenoaks, alight Ide Hill, 1½m (tel. (0800) 696996) *Station:* Sevenoaks 4½m; Penshurst (U) 5½m

IGHTHAM MOTE

Ivy Hatch, Sevenoaks TN15 0NT (0732) 810378

A beautiful medieval moated manor house with important later additions. Features include the Great Hall, Old Chapel and crypt c.1340, Chapel with painted ceiling c.1520, Drawing Room with Jacobean fireplace, frieze and an 18th-century Palladian window. The newly-restored North East quarter is now open, and an exhibition in the Billiards Room explains the largest building conservation programme ever undertaken by the Trust. Gardens, lake and woodland walk

Note: The house is very busy on Sun & BH between 2 & 4: a timed ticket system may be in operation. Large scale repairs in progress; an excellent opportunity to see conservation in action

- 🅾 April to end Oct: daily except Tues & Sat, weekdays 12-5.30; Sun & BH Mon 11-5.30. Last admissions 5. Shop & gardens open ½hr earlier
- £ £4. Pre-booked parties of over 20 weekday afternoons £3 (no reduction Sun & BH). Tel. for details
- 🇰 Pre-booked guided tours on open week-day mornings. Tel. for details
- 🛍 Shop open ½hr before house. Closes 5.30

KENT

    [♿] Access to most of ground floor, garden, courtyard, tea pavilion and ground floor of shop. Wheelchair available. Woodland walk accessible via steep slope. Special parking, apply to ticket kiosk; WC. Further woodland walk on estate close to house, apply at ticket kiosk when open for combination to lock

    [🍴] Tea pavilion (serving light refreshments only) open 12-5 weekdays, 11-5 Sun. May close early in Oct. Picnic area near coach park

    [👶] Baby feeding facilities available upon request. Changing facilities available. Children's guide

    [📚] Teacher's resource book. Special tours for schools, tel. for details

    [E] July, 'Music at the Mote' concert series; for details contact NT Regional Box Office (tel. (0892) 891001)

    [→] 6m E of Sevenoaks, off A25, and 2½m S of Ightham, off A227 [188: TQ584535] *Bus:* Maidstone & District 222 BR Borough Green–BR Tunbridge Wells; Nu-Venture 404 Sevenoaks–Plaxtol (passing BR Sevenoaks), on both alight Ivy Hatch, ¼m; Transcity Link 406 BR Sevenoaks–BR Borough Green, alight Ightham Common, 1½m (tel. (0800) 696996) *Station:* Borough Green & Wrotham 3½m; Hildenborough 4m

KNOLE 🏛 ✤ 🌳

Sevenoaks TN15 0RP (0732) 450608

Knole is the largest private house in England and it sits within a magnificent deer park owned by Lord Sackville. Dating from 1456, the house was enlarged in 1603 by Thomas Sackville, 1st Earl of Dorset, to whom it was granted by Elizabeth I. The 13 state rooms which are open to the public contain a collection of portraits, including works by Reynolds and Gainsborough, silver, tapestries and an important collection of 17th-century English furniture. This house is a must for the connoisseur

    [O] **House:** April to end Oct: Wed, Fri, Sat, Sun & BH Mon 11-5; Thur 2-5. Last admissions 4. Pre-booked groups accepted on Wed, Fri & Sat 11-4, Thur 2-4. **Park:** open daily to pedestrians by courtesy of Lord Sackville. **Garden:** May to Sept: first Wed in each month only

    [£] £4. Pre-booked parties £3. Parking (NT members free) £2.50. Park free to pedestrians. Only vehicles carrying visitors to the house are allowed in the park

    [👤] Guided tours for pre-booked parties on Thur 10-1 throughout season; no reduction

    [🛍] Shop open as house. Christmas shop, tel. Administrator for details

    [♿] Access to Great Hall, Stone Court, Green Court, shop, restaurant and park; WC

    [🍴] Tea-room open as house. Light lunches available. Thur – open from 12

    [🐕] In park only, on lead

    [→] At S end of Sevenoaks town; just E of A225 [188: TQ532543] *Bus:* From surrounding areas to bus station, ¾m (tel. (0800) 696996) *Station:* Sevenoaks 1½m

KENT

OLD SOAR MANOR

Plaxtol, Borough Green TN15 0QX (0892) 890651

The solar block of a late 13th-century knight's dwelling, Old Soar is owned by the National Trust and managed and maintained by English Heritage

- 1 April to end Sept: daily 10–6.00
- Free. No WCs. Exhibition on Manor and surrounding areas
- 2m S of Borough Green (A25); approached via A227 and Plaxtol; narrow lane, unsuitable for coaches [188: TQ619541] *Bus:* Maidstone & District 222 BR Borough Green–BR Tunbridge Wells; Nu-Venture 404 Sevenoaks–Plaxtol (passing BR Sevenoaks); on both alight E end of Plaxtol, thence ¼m by footpath (tel. (0800) 696996) *Station:* Borough Green & Wrotham 2½m

OWLETTS

Cobham, Gravesend DA12 3AP (0892) 890651

A modest red brick Charles II house with contemporary staircase and plasterwork ceiling, and small pleasure and kitchen gardens. Former home of the architect, Sir Herbert Baker, the property is now administered and largely maintained on the Trust's behalf by the tenant

- The property is closed for 1994

QUEBEC HOUSE

Westerham TN16 1TD (0959) 562206

General Wolfe spent his early years in this gabled, red brick 17th-century house. Four rooms containing portraits, prints and memorabilia relating to Wolfe's family and career are on view. In the Tudor stable block is an exhibition about the Battle of Quebec and the parts played by Wolfe and his adversary, the Marquis de Montcalm

- 1 April to end Oct: daily 2–6 but closed Thur & Sat. Last admissions 5.30. Parties only by prior arrangement with Custodian
- £2. Pre-booked parties £1.50, children 80p (prices include exhibition). Public car park E of house
- No picnicking. Refreshments in village, not NT
- At E end of village, on N side of A25, facing junction with B2026 Edenbridge road [187: TQ449541] *Bus:* All services quoted for Chartwell (p.138) passing close to the House *Station:* Sevenoaks 4m; Oxted 4m

REFER TO OPENING PAGES FOR GENERAL INFORMATION

KENT

ST JOHN'S JERUSALEM (GARDEN & CHAPEL)
Sutton-at-Hone, Dartford DA4 9HQ (0892) 890651

A large garden, moated by the River Darent. The house is the former chapel of a Knight's Hospitallers' Commandery, since converted into a private house. The east end of the chapel was retained for family worship, but was later converted into a billiard room

O   Please contact the regional office (tel. (0892) 890651) regarding opening arrangements for 1994

SCOTNEY CASTLE GARDEN
Lamberhurst, Tunbridge Wells TN3 8JN (0892) 890651

One of England's most romantic gardens, surrounding the ruins of a 14th-century moated castle. Rhododendrons, azaleas, water lines and wisteria flower in profusion

O   **Garden:** 2 April to end Oct: (Old Castle: May to 11 Sept) Wed to Fri 11–6; Sat & Sun 2–6, or sunset if earlier; BH Sun & Mon 12–6 (closed Good Fri). Last admissions 1hr before closing

£   £3.20. Pre-booked parties £2; (no party reduction on Sat, Sun or BH Mon)

      Shop open as garden

      Garden partly accessible to wheelchair users, but strong companion necessary; approach to garden and paths very steep in places. Wheelchairs available

      Herb garden for visually impaired visitors

      In Goudhurst & Lamberhurst villages (not NT). Picnicking in car park area only

E   Open Air Opera, July; for details contact NT Regional Box Office, (tel. (0892) 891001)

→   1m S of Lamberhurst on A21 [188: TQ688353] *Bus:* Warrens Coaches 256 Tunbridge Wells–Wadhurst (passing BR Tunbridge Wells), alight Lamberhurst Green, 1m (tel. (0800) 696996) *Station:* Wadhurst 5½m

143

KENT

SISSINGHURST GARDEN

Sissinghurst, nr Cranbrook TN17 2AB (0580) 712850

The 5½ acre famous connoisseurs' garden created by the late Vita Sackville-West and her husband, Sir Harold Nicolson, between the surviving parts of an Elizabethan mansion. A series of small, enclosed gardens, intimate in scale & romantic in atmosphere with much to see in all seasons. Also, the study where Vita Sackville-West worked, and the Long Library

Note: Due to the limited capacity of the garden, timed tickets are in operation and visitors will often have to wait before admission. The property is liable to be closed at short notice once it has reached its visitor capacity for the day; visitors may however, still visit the woodland walks, exhibition, restaurant and shop. No tripods or easels in the garden

- 1 April to 15 Oct: Tues to Fri 1–6.30; Sat, Sun & Good Fri 10–5.30. Closed all Mon, incl. BH. Last admissions ½hr before closing. Ticket office & exhibition open at 12 on weekdays

- £5. Coaches and parties by appointment only; no reduction. Tel. Bookings Secretary for details (0850) 715330

- Shop open same days as garden. Tues to Fri 12–5.30; Sat, Sun & Good Fri 10–5.30. Christmas shop, tel. (0580) 713090 for details

- Admission restricted to two chairs at any one time because of narrow and uneven paths; wheelchair available. (Not suitable for powered vehicle.) Disabled visitors may be set down at garden entrance. Plan of recommended wheelchair route available. No access for powered vehicles. WC

- Braille guide available on request; scented plants & flowers; herb garden

- Coffee, lunches, teas in Granary Restaurant (Licensed – no spirits) Tues to Fri 12–5.30, Sat, Sun & Good Fri 10–5.30. Christmas opening, tel. restaurant for details ((0580) 713097). Picnic area near car park and in grass field in front of castle.

- Not ideal for children. Baby back carriers available. No pushchairs admitted, as paths are narrow and uneven. No children's games in garden

- Not admitted to garden; welcome on leads in surrounding areas

- 2m NE of Cranbrook, 1m E of Sissinghurst village (A262) [188: TQ8138] *Bus:* Maidstone & District/Westbus 4/5 Maidstone–Hastings (passing BR Staplehurst), alight Sissinghurst, 1¼m (tel. (0800) 696996) *Station:* Staplehurst 5½m

SMALLHYTHE PLACE

Smallhythe, Tenterden TN30 7NG (0580) 7622334

The Ellen Terry memorial: an early 16th-century half-timbered house, home of Ellen Terry from 1899 to 1928. The house contains many personal and theatrical mementoes. The Barn Theatre also open most days by courtesy of the Barn Theatre Society. Charming cottage garden including Ellen Terry's rose garden

KENT

- ⭕ April to end Oct: daily except Thur & Fri (open Good Fri) 2-6, or dusk if earlier. Last admissions ½hr before closing. (The Barn Theatre may be closed some days at short notice)
- 💷 £2.50, children £1.30. Pre-booked parties Tues am only; no reduction. Max. 25 people in the house at any one time, garden has shelter for a further 25. No picnicking
- 👶 Children must be accompanied by an adult
- ➡️ 2m S of Tenterden, on E side of the Rye road (B2082) [189: TQ893300] *Bus:* Rye Coaches/Fuggles 312 BR Rye–Tenterden (tel. (0800) 696996) *Station:* Rye 8m; Appledore 8m; Headcorn 10m

SOUTH FORELAND LIGHTHOUSE
St Margaret's-at-Cliffe, Dover (0892) 890651

A distinctive landmark on the White Cliffs of Dover with views to France. The lighthouse was built in 1843 and used by Marconi for first radio communications as an aid to navigation in 1898. Tower & information room are open (the cottage is tenanted) & you can climb the spiral stairs to the balcony around the light

Note: There are no WCs or parking facilities at the lighthouse which can be reached on foot from NT car park at Langdon Cliffs (2 miles) or from St Margaret's village

- ⭕ April to end Oct: Sat, Sun & BH Mon 2-5.30. Last admissions 5
- 💷 £1, children 50p. No reduction for parties, must pre-book with Regional Office (see final page)
- ♿ Park at lighthouse
- 👶 Working model and exhibition
- ➡️ At St Margaret's-at-Cliffe [179: TR359433] *Bus:* East Kent 90 Folkestone–Deal (passing BR Dover Priory & Walmer) (tel. (0800) 696996) *Station:* Martin Mill 2½m

SPRIVERS GARDEN
Horsmonden TN12 8DR (0892) 723553

This garden includes flowering and foliage shrubs, herbaceous borders, old walls and spring and summer bedding. The garden is administered and largely maintained on the Trust's behalf by the tenant

- ⭕ Garden only May to 30 Sept: Wed only 2-5.30. Last admissions 5
- 💷 £1. No reduction for children or parties. Parking limited; space for one coach only. No WCs
- ➡️ 2m N of Lamberhurst on B2162 [188: TQ6940] *Bus:* Maidstone & District/Wealden Beeline/Fuggles 297 BR Tunbridge Wells–Tenterden (tel. (0800) 696996) *Station:* Paddock Wood 4m

145

KENT

STONEACRE
Otham, Maidstone ME15 8RS (0622) 862871

A half-timbered mainly late 15th-century manor house, with great hall and crownpost, and newly restored cottage-style garden. A tenanted property, administered and largely maintained on the Trust's behalf by the tenant

- **O** April to end Oct: Wed & Sat 2-6. Last admissions 5
- **£** £2. No reduction for parties. Car park 100yds; drive narrow, coach drivers please set passengers down at road junction
- Garden recommended to accompanied visually impaired visitors
- No dogs
- **→** At N end of Otham village, 3m SE of Maidstone, 1m S of A20 [188: TQ800535] *Bus:* Maidstone & District/Nu-Venture 12, 812 Maidstone–Tenterden (passing close BR Maidstone E & W), to within 1m (tel. (0800) 696996) *Station:* Bearsted 2m

TUDOR YEOMAN'S HOUSE
Sole Street, Cobham DA12 3AX (0892) 890651

A yeoman's house of timber construction. A tenanted property, administered and maintained on the Trust's behalf by the tenant

- **O** Main hall only, by written application to tenant
- **£** 50p. No reduction for children or parties. No WCs
- **→** 1m SW of Cobham, on W side of B2009, just N of Sole Street Station [177: TQ657677] *Station:* Sole Street, few yds

WOOL HOUSE
Wells Street, Loose, Maidstone ME15 0EH (0892) 890651

A 15th-century half-timbered house, thought to have been used for the cleaning of wool. The house is administered and largely maintained on the Trust's behalf by the tenant

- **O** April to end Sept by written application to tenant
- **£** 50p. No reduction for children or parties. No WCs
- **→** 3m SE of Maidstone, ¼m W of the Cranbrook Road (A229) [188: TQ755521] *Bus:* Maidstone & District/Westbus 4/5 Maidstone–Hastings (passing close BR Maidstone E & W) (tel. (0800) 696996) *Station:* Maidstone E 3m; Maidstone W 3m

REFER TO OPENING PAGES FOR GENERAL INFORMATION

Lancashire

COAST AND COUNTRY

The Trust owns nearly 200 acres of land at **Silverdale**, overlooking the saltmarshes of the Kent estuary just over the Cumbrian border. Silverdale village was once on the River Kent, but the river changed its course in the 1920s and now flows some 4 miles away. Fifty-seven acres of **Bank House Farm** [97: SD460752] on the northern fringe of the village are owned by the Trust with neat limestone walls enclosing a patchwork of small fields and spinneys. The shoreline is marked with low limestone cliffs and the fields are full of daffodils in the spring time. A coastal footpath crosses this property. **Jack Scout**, 16 acres of cliff and foreshore on the fringe of Morecambe Bay, was the first coastal property north of the River Ribble to be owned by the Trust [97: SD459737]. It was acquired in 1983, and has much to interest historians, scientists, botanists, bird-watchers and country-lovers. There are extensive views from the clifftops to the Lake District hills across the Kent estuary.

LANCASHIRE

More recently still the Trust acquired **George's Lot**, a 9-acre cliff field, to extend the length of foreshore open to the public [97: SD459750]. All this coastal limestone pasture and scrub is crossed by public footpaths, and a little further inland 106 acres of **Eaves and Waterslack Woods** present a fine variety of trees and other flora, with many woodland birds and animals and a 2-mile nature walk [97: SD465758]. **Burton Well Scar Wood** [97: SO470754] is 10½ acres of attractive woodland over limestone pavement. A public footpath passes right through the wood to **Lambert's Meadow** [97: SD471754], 4 acres of wet meadowland, with a great variety of trees, shrubs and wild flowers, making it an excellent site for invertebrates.

North of Bury, astride the B6214, is the **Stubbins Estate**, 436 acres of agricultural land with numerous public footpaths through fields and woodland full of interesting wildlife and flowers. The estate, given to the Trust in 1943, provides access from the industrial Rossendale Valley to Holcombe Moor, a bleak area of rough grassland and heath, notable especially for its numerous bird species [109: SD785177].

GAWTHORPE HALL

Padiham, nr Burnley BB12 8UA (0282) 778511

The house was built in 1600–1605, and restored by Sir Charles Barry in the 1850s; Barry's designs have been re-created in the principal rooms. Gawthorpe was the home of the Shuttleworth family, and the Rachel Kay-Shuttleworth textile collections are on display in the house; private study by arrangement. Also of interest is the collection of portraits on loan from the National Portrait Gallery. A recently restored 17th-century estate building houses a broad programme of art, craft and management courses

NT members please note: Gawthorpe Hall is financed and administered by Lancashire County Council

- **Hall:** 1 April to 30 Oct: daily except Mon & Fri, but open Good Fri & BH Mon, 1–5. Last admissions 4.15. **Garden:** all year: daily 10–6

- Hall: £2.30, children £1. Garden: free. Parties by prior arrangement. Free parking 150yds. We regret Hall is not suitable for baby back-packs or pushchairs

- Open 1 April to 30 Oct: daily except Mon & Fri 12–5

- Access by flagged walkway across cobbled yard to shop. WC in same area. Limited access to ground floor of hall, via ramps (prior warning of visit is essential). Some steps inside ground floor. Access to grounds and garden incl. rose garden and top terrace; some steps and gradients. Cars may bring passengers to front door of Hall, and to courtyard for shop. Tea-room upstairs

- Limited tea-room facilities; still to be determined at time of going to press

- Tapestry Exhibition 14 May to 6 Aug only: a celebration in tapestry of insights that have motivated the Quakers since 1652. Textile craft exhibitions during high season

- On E outskirts of Padiham; ¾m drive to house on N of A671 [103: SD806340] *Bus:* frequent services from Burnley. All pass close BR Burnley Barracks & Burnley Manchester Road. (tel. (0257) 241693) *Station:* Rose Grove (U) 2m

REFER TO OPENING PAGES FOR GENERAL INFORMATION

LANCASHIRE

RUFFORD OLD HALL
Rufford, nr Ormskirk L40 1SG (0704) 821254

One of the finest 16th-century buildings in Lancashire, the Tudor hall, timber framed in late medieval style, is remarkable for its ornate hammer beam roof and screen. Here, and in the Carolean Wing, altered in 1821, there are fine collections of 17th-century oak furniture, 16th-century arms, armour and tapestries

- **House:** 2 April to 31 Oct: Sat to Wed 1-5. Last admissions 4.30. **Garden:** same days 12-5.30; Sun 1-5.30
- Hall and garden £3. Garden only £1.60. Reduction for pre-booked parties (no parties Sun & BH Mon)
- Shop open as garden. Also 1 Nov to 18 Dec: daily except Mon & Fri 12-4.30 (Sun 2-5)
- Access to entrance hall, café & garden only, otherwise many steps & narrow passages; wheelchair available
- Braille guide
- Light lunches (licensed for cider & wine) and teas; available 12-5; Sun 2-5 (teas only). 1 Nov to 18 Dec, as shop, see above. Picnic site adjacent to car park
- House not suitable for baby back-packs or pushchairs
- Accompanied visit and teacher's pack
- Please send s.a.e. for details
- In grounds only, on leads
- 7m N of Ormskirk, in village of Rufford on E side of A59 [108: SD463160] *Bus:* Ribble/N Western 101 Ormskirk–Preston; ABC 754/8 Liverpool–Blackpool (tel. (0257) 241693) *Station:* Rufford (U), not Sun, ½m; Burscough Bridge 2½m

149

Leicestershire

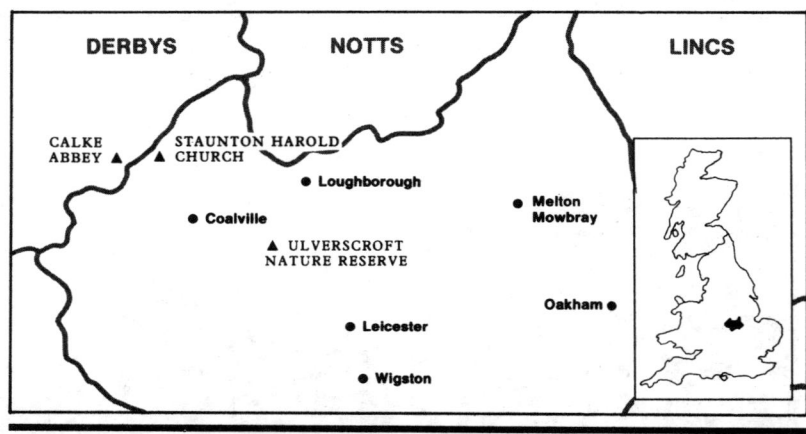

STAUNTON HAROLD CHURCH ✝ ♣

Staunton Harold, Ashby de la Zouch (0332) 863822

One of the very few churches to be built during the Commonwealth, erected by Sir Robert Shirley, an ardent Royalist. The interior retains its original 17th-century cushions and hangings, and includes fine panelling and painted ceilings. The wrought iron screen was designed by Robert Bakewell. The church is in an attractive parkland setting, with Staunton Harold Hall (not NT) nearby

- 30 March to end Oct: Sat to Wed & BH Mon (closed Good Fri) 1–5 or sunset if earlier
- £ Donations of £1 requested – collection box. No WCs
- Church and park largely accessible; no wheelchair available
- Light refreshments available at Hall (Sue Ryder Foundation)
- → 5m NE of Ashby-de-la-Zouch, W of B587 [128: SK379208] *Bus:* Trent 68/9 Derby Integrated 69A Derby–Melbourne (passing close BR Derby) thence 3m (tel. (0332) 292200)

ULVERSCROFT NATURE RESERVE

nr Loughborough (0909) 486411

Part of the ancient Charnwood forest, now a nature reserve. The area is especially fine in spring during bluebell time

- Access by permit only from the Secretary, Leicestershire & Rutland Trust for Nature Conservation, 1 West Street, Leicester LE1 6UU

Lincolnshire

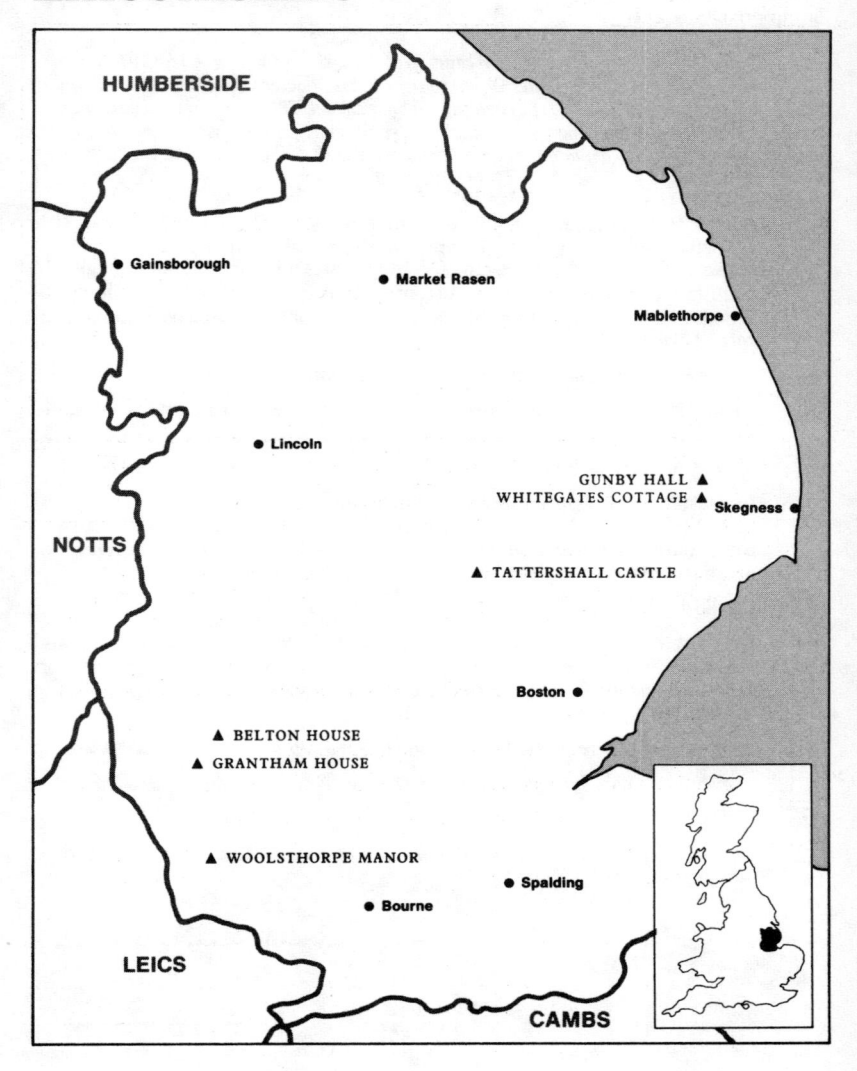

REFER TO OPENING PAGES FOR GENERAL INFORMATION

LINCOLNSHIRE

BELTON HOUSE
Grantham NG32 2LS (0476) 66116

The crowning achievement of Restoration country house architecture, built 1685–88 for Sir John Brownlow, and altered by James Wyatt in the 1770s. Plasterwork ceilings by Edward Goudge and fine wood carvings of the Grinling Gibbons school. The rooms contain portraits, furniture, tapestries, oriental porcelain, family silver gilt and Speaker Cust's silver. Formal gardens, an orangery and a magnificent landscaped park with a lakeside walk & the Bellmount Tower. There is also a fine church (not NT) with family monuments

- **House:** 30 March to end Oct: Wed to Sun & BH Mon (closed Good Fri) 1–5.30. **Garden & Park:** 11–5.30. Last admissions to House, Garden & Park 5. Free access to Park on foot only from Lion Lodge gates all year (this does not give admittance to house, garden or Adventure Playground). Access to Bellmount Woods and Tower from separate car park. Park may be closed occasionally for special events
- House & garden £4.30, children £2.10. Discount for parties
- Available outside normal hours only. Fee £10 per person (minimum charge £250)
- Shop same days as house 12–5.30. Also Nov to 18 Dec: Sat & Sun 12–4
- House difficult; please arrange with Administrator to visit Wed to Fri when less busy. Park, garden, restaurant, shop and refreshment kiosk accessible, but rough paths to playground, difficult in wet weather; car parking by prior arrangement; WC; wheelchair available for use in house
- Braille guide
- Licensed restaurant open as shop serving wide variety of home cooked hot and cold lunches 12–2, teas 2–5 (seats 96, children's portions available). Open for functions and pre-booked parties throughout year; details by written application (s.a.e. please) to Administrator

LINCOLNSHIRE

- [playground icon] Extensive Adventure Playground, incl. under 6 'corral'; miniature train rides in summer. Children's guide; parent and baby facilities; front baby slings available on loan
- [school icon] Educational visits from school parties welcomed (Education Liaison Officer, schoolrooms and teacher's pack available); also 'grounds only' arrangements available for school parties; contact Administrator for details
- [E] Belton Horse Trials (April); concerts in summer including Open Air concert 25 June; occasional events in the Park; special exhibitions; details from Administrator; (s.a.e. please)
- [dog icon] In parkland only, on leads
- [→] 3m NE of Grantham on the A607 Grantham–Lincoln road, easily reached, and signposted from the A1 [130: SK929395] *Bus:* Road Car 601 Grantham–Lincoln; 609 Grantham–Sleaford (both pass close BR Grantham) (tel. (0522) 553135) *Station:* Grantham 3m

GRANTHAM HOUSE
Castlegate, Grantham NG31 6SS (0909) 486411

The house dates from 1380, but has been extensively altered and added to throughout the centuries, resulting in a pleasant mixture of architectural styles. The walled gardens run down to the river, and on the opposite bank Sedgwick Meadows, also NT, form an open space in the centre of the town

- [O] Ground floor only 30 March to end Sept: Wed 2–5 by written appointment only with the tenant, Major-General Sir Brian Wyldbore-Smith
- [£] £1.50. Due to size of the rooms, numbers in parties should not exceed seven. No WCs
- [→] Immediately E of Grantham Church [130: SK916362] *Bus:* Road Car 601 Grantham–Lincoln, to within ¼m (tel. (0522) 553135) *Station:* Grantham 1m

GUNBY HALL
Gunby, nr Spilsby PE23 5SS (0909) 486411

A red brick house with stone dressings, built in 1700 and extended in 1870s. Within the house, there is good early 18th-century wainscoting and a fine oak staircase, also English furniture and portraits by Reynolds. Also of interest is the contemporary stable block, a walled kitchen and flower garden, sweeping lawns and borders. Gunby was reputedly Tennyson's 'haunt of ancient peace'

- [O] Ground floor of house & garden: 30 March to end Sept: Wed 2–6. Last admissions 5.30. Closed public holidays. Garden also open Thur 2–6. House & garden also open Tues, Thur and Fri by written appointment only with J. D. Wrisdale at above address
- [£] House & garden £3.00. Garden only £1.80. No reduction for parties. Access roads unsuitable for coaches which must park in layby at gates ½m from Hall

continued

LINCOLNSHIRE

- ♿ Access to garden only. Rose & herb garden suitable for visually impaired visitors. No wheelchairs available
- 🇪 Occasional concerts
- 🐕 In garden only, on leads
- ➜ 2½m NW of Burgh le Marsh, 7m W of Skegness on S side of A158 (access off roundabout) [122: TF467668] *Bus:* Road Car 6 Skegness–Lincoln (passing close BR Skegness) (tel. (0522) 553135) *Station:* Skegness 7m

GUNBY HALL ESTATE

Whitegates Cottage, Mill Lane, Bratoft, nr Spilsby (0909) 486411

A small cottage on the Gunby Hall Estate, built c.1770 to provide accommodation for workers next to land which lay some distance from the main body of the farm. Constructed in the once common, now extremely rare, Lincolnshire vernacular tradition of mud and stud walling under a long-straw thatch roof, the cottage was recently restored using traditional methods and materials

- 🕐 30 March to end Sept: Wed 2–6 by written appointment only with the tenant, Mr J. Zaremba
- £ £1.50. Numbers in parties visiting the property should not exceed six at any one time, due to the small size of rooms. WCs at Gunby Hall
- ➜ 2m W of Burgh le Marsh, 8m W of Skegness. Approached by Gunby Lane off A158 just W of the roundabout N of Gunby Hall. Public transport: as for Gunby Hall (see above)

TATTERSHALL CASTLE

Tattershall, Lincoln LN4 4LR (0526) 342543

A vast fortified tower built c.1440 for Ralph Cromwell, Lord Treasurer of England. The castle is an important example of an early brick building, with a tower containing state apartments, rescued from dereliction and restored by Lord Curzon 1911–14. Four great chambers, with ancillary rooms, contain late Gothic fireplaces and brick vaulting. There are tapestries and information displays in turret rooms. Lincoln Cathedral and Boston Stump are visible from the 100ft-high battlements on clear days

- 🕐 30 March to end Oct: Sat to Wed & BH Mon (closed Good Fri) 10.30–5.30. Nov to 18 Dec: Sat & Sun only 12–4. Last admissions ½hr before closing
- £ £2.20, children £1.10. Discount for parties; contact Custodian. Advance booking essential for coach parties. Limited number of floodlit evening visits available for organised parties £2.50, children £1.20 (incl. NT members). Min charge £100
- 🛍 Shop open same times as castle
- ♿ Access to ground floor of castle, shop and grounds. WC. No wheelchairs available

LINCOLNSHIRE

- 🍴 Limited service of drinks & ice creams available from shop. Picnicking welcome in grounds
- 🚼 WC with nappy changing facility; child back-packs allowed; children's guide
- 🏫 Castle is particularly suitable for school groups
- E Contact Custodian for details of events programme
- 🐕 In car park only on leads. Please note there will be a new car park for 1994 but with no shade
- ➡ On S side of A153, 15m NE of Sleaford; 10m SW of Horncastle [122: TF209575] *Bus:* Brylaine Boston–Woodhall Spa (passing close BR Boston) - (tel. (0522) 553135) *Station:* Ruskington (U) 10m

WOOLSTHORPE MANOR 🏠

23 Newton Way, Woolsthorpe-by-Colsterworth, nr Grantham NG33 5NR
(0476) 860338

This small 17th-century farmhouse was the birthplace and family home of Sir Isaac Newton. Some of his major work was formulated here, during the Plague years (1665–66) 'in the prime of my age for invention'; an early edition of his Principia Mathematica, *pub. 1687, is on display. The orchard includes a descendant of the famous apple tree*

- 🅾 30 March to end Oct: Wed to Sun incl. BH Mon (closed Good Fri) 1–5.30. Last admissions 5

  Note: In the interests of preservation, numbers of visitors admitted to rooms at any one time may be limited; particularly at peak weekends and Bank Holidays
- £ £2.30, children £1.10. No reduction for parties – must book in advance with Custodian as parking for coaches limited to one at a time. Picnicking in car park only
- 🚼 For all parties
- ♿ Limited access to ground floor only (assistance required). No wheelchairs available
- 🐕 In car park only, on leads
- ➡ 7m S of Grantham, ½m NW of Colsterworth, 1m W of A1 (not to be confused with Woolsthorpe near Belvoir) [130: SK924244] *Bus:* Road Car 606–8 Grantham–South Witham (passing close BR Grantham) (tel. (0522) 553135) *Station:* Grantham 7m

London

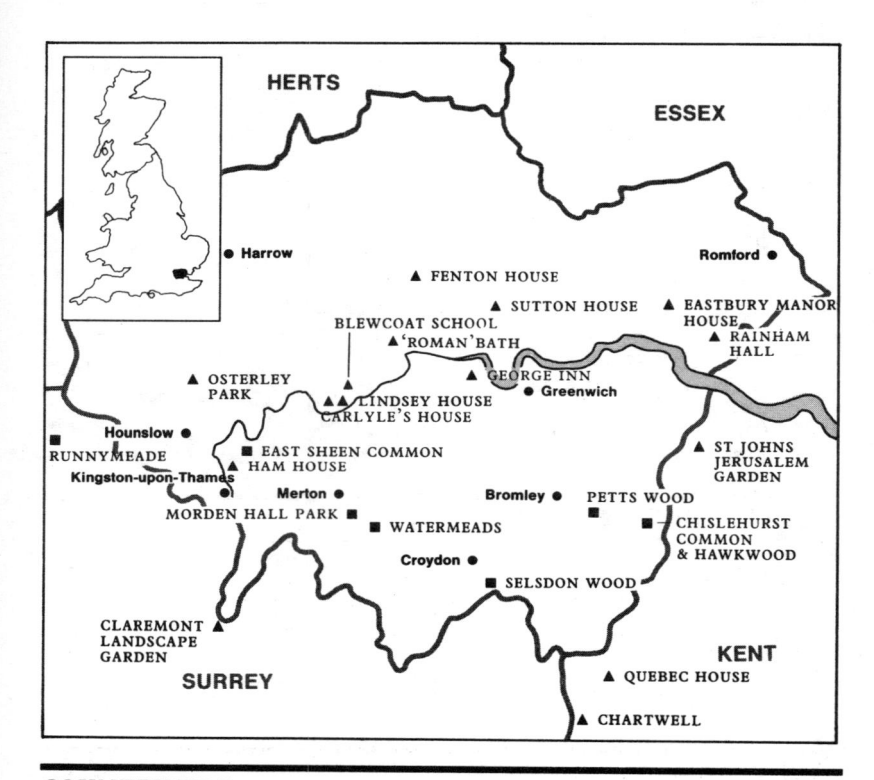

COUNTRYSIDE

Kent Border: The Trust owns two small strips of **Chislehurst Common**, acquired as part of a scheme for preserving the Common. It also has 88 acres of wood and heathland at neighbouring **Petts Wood** [177: TQ450681] which was bought by public subscription in 1927 as a memorial to the founder of British Summer Time, William Willett. Adjoining this land, at **Hawkwood**, is a further 245 acres of farm and woodland.

Surrey Border: Adjoining Richmond Park, 53 acres of **East Sheen Common** [176: TQ197746] are managed for the Trust by the London Borough of Richmond-upon-Thames. There are nature reserves at **Selsdon Wood** south-east of Croydon [177: TQ357615], and at **Watermeads** on the River Wandle in Mitcham where a key may be obtained from the Warden for a small deposit and annual subscription.

REFER TO OPENING PAGES FOR GENERAL INFORMATION

LONDON

BLEWCOAT SCHOOL
23 Caxton Street, Westminster SW1H 0PY 071-222 2877

Built in 1709 at the expense of William Green, a local brewer, to provide an education for poor children. The building was in use as a school until 1926, bought by the Trust in 1954 and restored in 1975. It is now the NT London Information Centre and Shop

- All year: Mon to Fri 10-5.30; late night shopping Thur until 7; also Sat 3, 10, & 17 Dec 11-4.30. Closed BH Mon, 25-31 Dec, 2 Jan & Good Fri
- Free
- Must be on leads
- *Bus:* Frequent local services (tel. 071-222 1234) *Station:* Victoria ¼m. *Underground:* St James's Park, few yds

CARLYLE'S HOUSE
24 Cheyne Row, Chelsea SW3 5HL 071-352 7087

This 18th-century town house was the home of Thomas and Jane Carlyle from 1834 until their deaths. It contains furniture, books, personal relics and portraits
Note: Certain rooms have no electric light. Visitors wishing to make close study of interior of the house should avoid dull days early and late in the season

- 30 March to end Oct: Wed to Sun & BH Mon 11-5. Closed Good Fri
- £2.80. No reduction for students or parties, which should not number more than 20. All parties must book in advance with Custodian
- Off Cheyne Walk, between Battersea and Albert Bridges on Chelsea Embankment, or off Oakley Street [176: TQ272777 *Bus:* frequent local services (tel. 071-222 1234) *Station:* Victoria 1½m *Underground:* Sloane Sq 1m

EASTBURY MANOR HOUSE
Barking, Essex IG11 9SN 081-507 0119

An important example of a medium-sized Elizabethan manor house
Eastbury Manor House is let to the London Borough of Barking and Dagenham for use as an Arts & Cultural Centre

- By appointment with Administrator only; tel. 081-507 0119
- £2.50; OAPs & students £1. School parties 50p. Limited street parking
- Very limited access to ground floor
- In garden only
- In Eastbury Square, 10 min walk S from Upney station [177: TQ457838] *Bus:* LT 287, 368 BR Barking-Rainham/Chadwell Heath (tel. 071-222 1234) *Station:* Barking, thence one stop on Underground District line to Upney ¼m

LONDON

FENTON HOUSE

Windmill Hill, Hampstead NW3 6RT 071-435 3471

A late 17th-century house with an outstanding collection of porcelain and early keyboard instruments. The large walled garden is sometimes used for open-air plays. Opening of the house may be delayed due to building work

Note: For permission to use the early keyboard instruments, please apply in writing one month in advance to the Keeper of Instruments, c/o Fenton House

- March: Sat & Sun only 2-5; April to end Oct: Sat, Sun & BH Mon 11-5.30; Mon, Tues & Wed 1-5.30; last admissions ½hr before closing. Parties received at other times by appointment
- £3. Family ticket £9. No reduction for pre-booked parties. No parking facilities
- Access to ground floor only
- Events & concert series: please send s.a.e. for details
- Visitors' entrance on W side of Hampstead Grove *Bus:* frequent local services (tel. 071-222 1234) *Station:* Hampstead Heath 1m *Underground:* Hampstead 300yds

GEORGE INN

The George Inn Yard, 77 Borough High St, Southwark SE1 071-407 2056

The only remaining galleried inn in London, famous as a coaching inn in the 18th and 19th centuries, and mentioned by Dickens in Little Dorrit. *Leased to & run by Whitbread Plc as a public house*

- During licensing hours
- Bar food daily; à la carte restaurant Mon to Fri & Sat evening
- Allowed subject to normal licensing regulations
- On E side of Borough High Street, near London Bridge stn *Bus:* Frequent local services (tel. 071-222 1234) *Station & Underground:* London Bridge, BR and Underground, few min. walk

HAM HOUSE

Ham, Richmond, Surrey TW10 7RS 081-940 1950

Outstanding Stuart house, built about 1610; enlarged, redecorated and furnished in the 1670s in the most up-to-date style of the time by the Duke and Duchess of Lauderdale, much of which survives

Note: 17th-century garden in process of restoration

- **House:** 30 March to end Oct: Mon to Wed 1-5, Sat 1-5.30, Sun 11.30-5.30, (open Good Fri 1-5, but closed Tues following) Nov to 18 Dec: Sat & Sun 1-4.

LONDON

[£] House: £4, children £2. Pre-booked parties 15+ (rates on application). Garden free. Parking 400yds

Last admission ½hr before closing. **Garden:** open daily except Fri (open Good Fri) 10.30-6 (or dusk if earlier). Closed 25/26 Dec & 1 Jan

[i] Guided tours, including 'Focus' tours, mornings of normal opening days (not BH Mon) by prior arrangement

[◉] April to end Oct: daily except Fri (open Good Fri. but closed Tues following) 1-5.30, Nov-18 Dec 1-4. Tel. 081-940 2035

[♿] Parking near house for drivers with disabilities; disabled and elderly visitors may be set down and collected near house. Access to house by steep ramps; lift access to 1st floor by request. Grounds include some deep gravel paths. Staff trained in sympathetic hearing.WC

[👁] Braille guide

[🍽] Orangery restaurant (licensed) open same days as house; waitress service, lunches 12-2, teas 3-5.30. Self-service refreshments and tea-garden, open April to end Oct same days as garden; 11-5.30. Picnics in Rose Garden only

[👶] Nappy changing facility in WCs. House unsuitable for back-packs or pushchairs. Highchairs in restaurant

[🐕] No dogs

[→] On S bank of Thames, W of A307, at Petersham [176: TQ172732] *Bus:* LT 65 Ealing Broadway–Kingston; 371 Richmond–Kingston; London & Country 415 Victoria–Guildford; London & Country 427 Richmond–Addlestone (all passing BR Richmond & Kingston) (tel. 071-222 1234) *Station:* Richmond BR & Underground 1½m by footpath, 2m by road; Kingston 2m

LINDSEY HOUSE 🏠

99/100 Cheyne Walk SW10

Part of Lindsey House was built in 1674 on the site of Sir Thomas More's garden, overlooking the River Thames. It has one of the finest 17th-century exteriors in London

[O] Ground floor entrance hall and garden room; main staircase to first floor and front and rear gardens open by written appointment only with the tenant. Please write to Alana Lacy, 6 Burnsall Street, London SW3 3ST

[£] Free. No parking (nearest car park Battersea Park)

[♿] Inaccessible

[🐕] No dogs

[→] On Cheyne Walk, W of Battersea Bridge near junction with Milman's Street on Chelsea Embankment [176: TQ268775] *Bus:* Frequent local service (tel. 071-222 1234) *Stations:* Clapham Junction 1½m, Victoria 1¾m *Underground:* South Kensington 1¼m

REFER TO OPENING PAGES FOR GENERAL INFORMATION

LONDON

MORDEN HALL PARK ●

Morden Hall Road, Morden SM4 5JD 081-648 1845

A green oasis in the heart of SW London, this former deer park has waterways, a tree-lined avenue, Elizabethan hay meadows and an interesting collection of vernacular buildings. A series of craft workshops house local artists

- **O** Park only, open all daylight hours

  Note: car park by the café/shop and Garden Centre closes at 6

- **£** Free

- Daily throughout the year: 10–5. Closed 25 & 26 Dec and 1 Jan 1995 (tel. 081-687 0881)

- Restaurant, shop & Garden Centre fully accessible. WC. Access available from car park through Garden Centre to Riverside walkways. New wheelchair path through rose garden and beside river

- Licensed riverside café serving coffee, lunches and teas daily throughout the year: 10–5. Closed 25 & 26 Dec and 1 Jan (tel. as shop). Garden Centre independently run by Capital Gardens Plc as National Trust tenants (tel. 081-646 3002)

- **E** Craft Fair: tel. Four Seasons Events (0344) 874787 for information

- Please keep dogs under control at all times and on leads around buildings, paths & picnic area

- Off A24, S of Wimbledon, N of Sutton [176: TQ259687] *Bus:* frequent from surrounding areas (tel. 071-222 1234) *Station:* Morden Road, not Sun, ½m *Underground:* Morden 500yds

OSTERLEY PARK ●

Isleworth, Middlesex TW7 4RB 081-560 3918

Set in 140 acres of landscaped park with ornamental lakes, Osterley is one of the last great houses with an intact estate in Greater London. Completed in 1575 for Sir Thomas Gresham, founder of the Royal Exchange, the mansion was transformed into an 18th-century villa with neo-classical interior decoration by Robert Adam between 1760–80 for the banker, Robert Child

- **O** **House:** 30 March to end Oct: Wed to Sat 1–5; Sun & BH Mon 11–5. Closed Good Fri. Last admissions 4.30. **Park and pleasure grounds:** all year 9–7.30 or sunset if earlier. Park will close early during major events (see p.161). Car park closed 25 & 26 Dec

- **£** £3.50. Family ticket £9. Parties Wed to Sat £3 – must book. Park and pleasure grounds free. Car park £1

- Pre-booked guided 'Private View' Wed–Sat mornings £5 per person (including NT members). Minimum charge £100. 1 hour guided Estate walk may be pre-booked for parties £1 per person

LONDON

[♿] Car park is 250 yards from house and tea-room. Courtesy vehicle available to ferry less mobile visitors during house and tea-room opening hours. WC in park. Park is level and accessible to wheelchairs. Self drive battery-powered vehicles available Wed, Thur, Sun 2-5 in summer. Indoor & outdoor wheelchairs available. Stairclimber gives wheelchair access to principal floor of house but must be pre-booked. Self-drive battery-powered vehicles available Wed, Thur & Sun 2-5 in summer

[👁] Braille guide

[☕] Coffee, light lunches & teas in stables, same days as house 11.30-5; open Good Fri

[🏫] Pre-booked school groups welcome. Education room available for pre-booked parties (max. 30 children). Children's guide

[E] Annual Summer Band Concert and other events. Please send s.a.e. to 'Events', Osterley Park House

[🐕] In park only (guide dogs excepted). Must be on leads unless indicated

[➔] Access via Thornbury Road on N side of A4 between Gillette Corner and Osterley underground station; M4, Jn 3 [176: TQ146780] *Bus:* LT H91 Hounslow–Hammersmith, to within ½m (tel. 071-222 1234) *Station:* Syon Lane, 1½m *Underground:* Osterley ¾m

RAINHAM HALL 🏛

The Broadway, Rainham, Essex RM13 9YN

An attractive red brick house, with stone dressing on a symmetrical plan, built in 1729. There are fine contemporary wrought iron gates in front of the house and original panelling inside

[O] April to end Oct: Wed & BH Mon 2-6; also Sat by written application to tenant

[£] £2. No reduction for parties. Parking limited. No WCs

[👁] Guide dogs by special arrangement with tenant

[➔] Just S of the church, 5m E of Barking [177: TQ521821] *Bus:* Frequent local services (tel. 071-222 1234) *Station:* Rainham, few yds

161

LONDON

ROMAN BATH 🏛

5 Strand Lane WC2 071-798 2064 – answerphone

The remains of a bath, restored in the 17th century, believed by some to be Roman

The 'Roman' Bath is administered and maintained by Westminster City Council

- 🅾 Bath visible through window from pathway all year. Otherwise May to end Sept: every Wed 1–5 by appointment only (24 hours notice) during office hours
- 💷 50p. Children under 16 and OAPs 25p. No WCs
- ➡ Just W of Aldwych (Piccadilly Line) station, approach via Surrey Street [176: TQ309809] *Bus:* Frequent local service (tel. 071-222 1234) *Station:* Blackfriars or Charing Cross, both ½m *Underground:* Temple, not Sun, few yds; Embankment ½m

SUTTON HOUSE 🏛

2 & 4 Homerton High Street, Hackney E9 6JQ 081-986 2264

In London's East End; a rare example of a Tudor red brick house, built in 1535 by Sir Rafe Sadleir, Principal Secretary of State for Henry VIII, with 18th-century alterations and later additions. The house contains the original linenfold panelling, decorated stone fireplaces and 17th-century painted staircase. Recently restored and opened to visitors

Note: The restoration of Sutton House is now complete and rooms now on show include a mid-18th-century parlour, 19th-century study, tudor kitchen and craft workshop and Edwardian chapel.

- 🅾 2 Feb to 30 Nov & 1 Feb 1995 onwards: Wed, Sun & BH Mon 11.30–5.30 (closed Good Fri). Last admissions 5
- 💷 £1.50. Group visits by prior arrangement. Rates on application. Public car park in Morning Lane and St John's Churchyard, ¼m
- 🚶 Guided tours available. Rates on application
- 🛍 Open as house
- ♿ Ground floor only accessible to wheelchairs. No lift. WC
- 👁 Braille guide
- 🍴 Café bar all year except 24 Dec to 17 Jan, Wed to Sun 11.30–5.30
- 🚼 Baby changing facilities in WC. Family trails
- 📚 Teacher's resource book. School visits by prior arrangement. Rates on application
- 🇪 For full programme of concerts, exhibitions, fairs, lectures and other events, please contact Project Manager on above number
- ➡ At the corner of Isabella Road and Homerton High Street [176: TQ352851] *Bus:* frequent local services *Station:* Homerton ¼m; Hackney Downs ½m

Merseyside

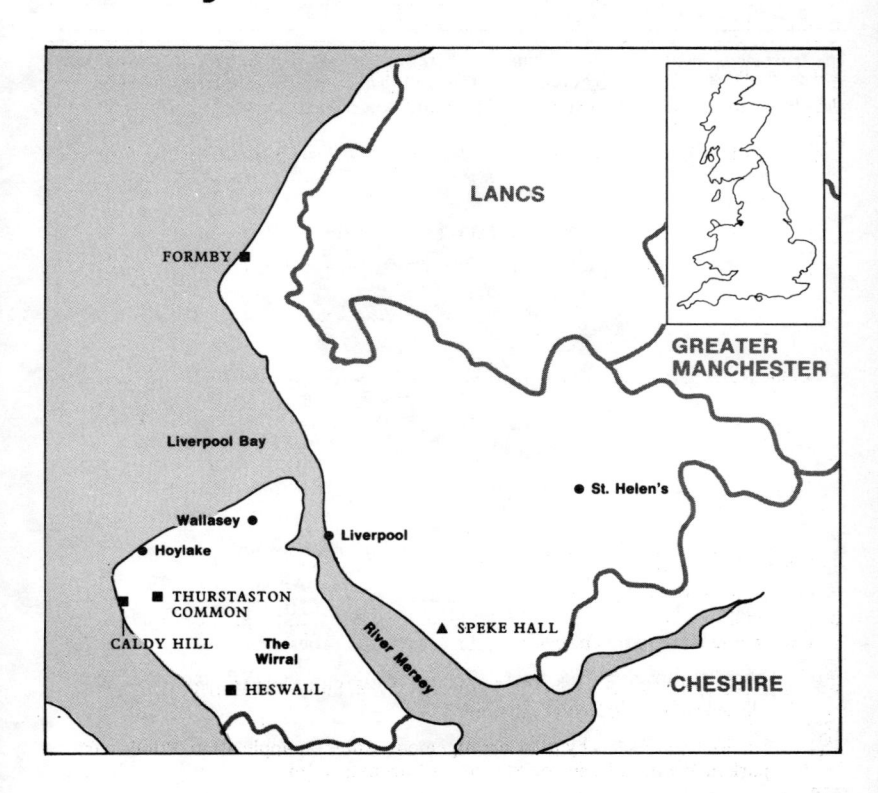

COAST AND COUNTRY

Formby: see entry on p.164

On the north bank of the Mersey at **Speke Hall** (see p.164), the Trust now owns the remainder of the historic landscape surrounding the Hall, consisting of farmland and **Stocktons Wood** [108: SJ423826]. Research indicates that this wood has never been cultivated, which accounts for its rich variety of insects.

The Wirral Peninsula has a 12-mile long Country Park, several parts of which are owned by the Trust. **Caldy Hill** [108: SJ224855] gives views across the mouth of the River Dee where bird-watchers will find many varieties of duck and waders in large numbers. It has been estimated that over 20,000 oystercatchers roost here. At **Heswall** [108: SJ246825] are 40 acres of meadow and farmland on the Dee Estuary with fine views to Wales.

The acid heathland of **Thurstaston Common** [108: SJ244853] is rich in insect life.

MERSEYSIDE

FORMBY

Victoria Road, Freshfield, Formby L37 1LJ (0704) 878591

The Trust owns about 500 acres of dune, foreshore and pinewood between the sea and the town of Formby, 2 miles inland. Red squirrels can frequently be seen in the pine trees and the shoreline attracts waders such as oystercatchers and sanderlings

RED SQUIRREL

- All year during daylight hours. Country walk around squirrel reserve
- Entrance per car: 1 April to end Oct: £1.70; 1 Nov to end March 1995: weekdays £1.20, Sat, Sun & BHs £1.70. Coaches £10 all year
- Hard surface paths to red squirrel reserve and Cornerstone Walk
- School groups should contact Sefton Coast Management Scheme Education Officer for information tel. 051-934 2940
- Details from Head Warden, s.a.e. please
- On leads around squirrel reserve
- 15m N of Liverpool, 2m W of Formby, 2m off A565 [108: SD275080] *Bus:* Merseytravel 4/A, 161/4/5 BR Formby–BR Freshfield, to within ½m (tel. 051-236 7676) *Station:* Freshfield 1m

SPEKE HALL

The Walk, Liverpool L24 1XD 051-427 7231

One of the most famous half-timbered houses in the country. The Great Hall evokes the communal living of Tudor times while the small rooms, some with William Morris wallpapers, show the Victorian preference for privacy and comfort. Fine plasterwork and priestholes, plus a fully equipped Victorian Kitchen and Servants' Hall. The restored garden has spring bulbs, bluebell walks in the woodland area, rhododendrons, rose garden, summer border and stream garden. Speke Hall is administered and financed by the National Trust with the help of a grant from the National Museums & Galleries on Merseyside

MERSEYSIDE

- **House:** 26 March to 30 Oct: daily except Mon (open BH Mon but closed Good Fri) 1–5.30. 5 Nov to 18 Dec: Sat & Sun 1–4.30. **Garden:** 26 March to 30 Oct: open as house; Nov to March 1995: daily except Mon 12–4 (closed Good Fri, 24, 25, 26, 31 Dec & 1 Jan)
- House & Garden £3.40. Family £8.50 Garden only £1. Reduction for pre-booked parties. Car park 200yds
- Guided tours and evening tours by prior arrangement with the Administrator
- Shop open as house
- Access to ground floor (includes most principal rooms) and tea-room; special car parking by arrangement; WC
- Braille & large print guides
- Refreshments and teas; tea-room open same days as house from noon; light lunches 12–2; parties should book. Also open Sundays in March 1–4.30 for drinks; seating capacity 40. Picnics in orchard
- High chairs in tea-room
- Pre-booked school visits; details from Administrator
- Details from Administrator: please send s.a.e.
- On leads in Stocktons Wood only. No dogs in garden
- On N bank of the Mersey, 1m off A561 on W side of Liverpool airport. Follow airport signs from M62; M56 Jn 12 [108: SJ419825] *Bus:* Merseybus 80, 80A, 81; Liverpool Lime St–Liverpool Airport (passing BR Garston) thence ½m (tel. 051-236 7676) *Station:* Garston 2m; Hunt's Cross 2m

Norfolk

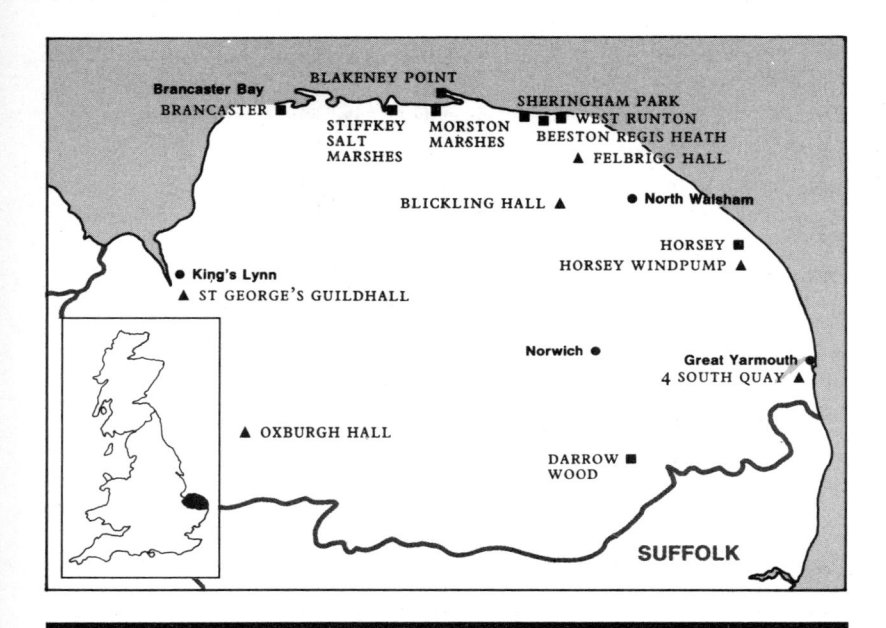

COAST

There are entries in the following pages for the major coastal estates belonging to the Trust: **Blakeney Point**, p.167, and **Brancaster**, p.168.

COUNTRYSIDE

The Trust owns more than 2000 acres at **Horsey**, including **Horsey Windpump** (see p.171), marshland, marrams, farmland and the Mere. There is restricted access to the Mere, part of the Norfolk Broads, with brackish water because of seepage from the nearby sea, although it is separated from it by sand dunes. Car park and WCs.

At **West Runton** between Sheringham and Cromer the Trust owns about 70 acres, known locally as the Roman Camp and including the highest point in the county [133: TG184414]. Adjoining **Beeston Regis Heath** is about 30 acres of heathland and woodland giving fine views of the coastline. There is access to the long distance coastal footpath. Car parking for both properties at West Runton ('Roman Camp'). (See also **Sheringham Park**, p.172.) **Darrow Wood** near Harleston is the site of a small motte and Bailey Castle [TM265894].

REFER TO OPENING PAGES FOR GENERAL INFORMATION

NORFOLK

BLAKENEY POINT

Warden's address: 35 The Cornfield, Langham, Holt, Norfolk NR25 7DQ (tel. April to Sept: (0263) 740480; Oct to March: (0328) 830401)

A 3½ mile long sand and shingle spit, summer home for over eleven species of seabird, including common and sandwich tern, oystercatcher and ringed plover; winter visitors include large flocks of brent geese. Common seals breed off the point of the spit. Information Centre at Morston Quay

Note: Adjoining properties at Morston and Stiffkey comprise 1,000 acres of saltmarsh and intertidal mudflats. In July the marshes are coloured purple with sea lavender; breeding ground for waders in the summer and visited by brent geese in the winter

- All year
- No landing fee. Access on foot from Cley Beach (3½m) or by ferry from Morston and Blakeney (tidal). Restricted access to certain areas of the Point during the main bird breeding season (May to July). Car park at Blakeney Quay and Morston Quay £1, NT members free
- For pre-booked school parties and special interest groups (small charge)
- A 400ft long wheelchair walkway leads to the bird hide on the Point; local boatmen will help disabled visitors with wheelchairs; please give advance warning of a visit to Warden (address above). WC
- Light refreshments and exhibition in the Old Boathouse (April–Sept)
- Resource book available from Warden; price £1.50 plus postage
- Must be on leads. No dogs west of old Lifeboat House on Blakeney Point April to Sept
- Morston Quay, Blakeney [133: TG0046] and Cley are all off A149 Cromer–Hunstanton road *Bus:* Sanders Coaches, Eastern Counties Coastliner, from BR Sheringham (tel. (0603) 613613) *Station:* Sheringham 8m

BLICKLING HALL

Blickling, Norwich NR11 6NF (0263) 733084)

One of the greatest houses in East Anglia, Blickling dates from the early 17th-century. Its collections include fine furniture, pictures and tapestries. A spectacular Jacobean plaster ceiling in the 123ft long gallery is particularly impressive. The gardens are renowned for massive yew hedges, magnificent herbaceous borders and contain a late 18th-century orangery; the parkland has a lake, and good walks

- **House:** 26 March to 30 Oct: Tues, Wed, Fri, Sat, Sun & BH Mon (closed Good Fri) 1–5. **Garden:** as house (daily July & Aug) 12–5. Park: daily all year
- House & garden £4.50 (Sun & BH Mon £5.50). Garden only £2.50. Parties £3.50 (Sun & BH Mon £4.50) please book with s.a.e. to Administrator. Coarse fishing in lake; permits available from Warden at 1 Park Gates (tel. (0263) 734181). Free access to South Front, shop and restaurant on open days

continued

NORFOLK

- 🕊 Private and school party guided tours available outside normal opening hours. Details from Administrator
- 🛍 Shop open as garden 12-5.30. Also 3 Nov to 18 Dec: Thur to Sun 11-4; Jan to end March 1995: Sat & Sun 11-4. Plant Centre in orchard open 26 March to 30 Oct: daily 10-5.30; also 1 Nov to end March 1995: daily 10-4 (closed 25 & 26 Dec, 1 Jan & Good Fri)
- ♿ Reserved parking area: obtain tickets from Visitor Reception in main car park and proceed as directed by Visitor Reception staff. Entrance gate ramped; entrance to House ramped; ground floor on one level; lift to upper floor. Ramp to Shop and Restaurant. WCs
- 👁 Braille guide
- 🍴 Lunches & teas in restaurant (capacity 110) all season when house and garden open 11-5 (3 Nov to 18 Dec & Jan to end March 1995: Sat & Sun 11-4); table licence (parties by arrangement). Picnic area in orchard. Buckinghamshire Arms Inn open all year (except 25 & 26 Dec), normal pub hours, for bar lunches, evening bar & restaurant meals, and B & B accommodation (tel. (0263) 732133)
- 👶 Children's guide. Baby slings available. Nappy changing facilities. Restaurant: children's menu, baby food, high chairs, scribble sheets
- 🏫 School visits welcome. Details from Administrator
- E Full list available from Administrator
- 🐕 In park and picnic area only, on leads
- ➡ On N side of B1354, 1½m NW of Aylsham on A140, 15m N of Norwich, 10m S of Cromer [133: TG178286] *Bus:* Eastern Counties 751/8/9, 761 Norwich–Sheringham ; sets down at Blickling during main season (passing close BR Norwich), alight Aylsham, 1¼m (tel. (0603) 613613) *Station:* Aylsham (Bure Valley Railway from BR Hoveton & Wroxham) 1¾m, North Walsham (U) 8m

---

BRANCASTER 🚤 🏞 🏛 👶 🕊

Warden's address: Dial House, Brancaster Staithe, Kings Lynn PE31 8BW (0485) 210719

2,000 acres of beach with 4½ miles of tidal foreshore, sand dunes, and saltmarsh, including the site of the Roman Fort of Branodunum

Note: A boat can be hired at Brancaster Staithe (weather permitting) to take visitors to the National Nature Reserve on Scolt Head Island. It is managed by English Nature (EN Warden: tel. (0485) 210330). The Island is an important breeding site for four species of tern, oystercatcher and ringed plover. Nature Trail. It is inadvisable to walk at low tide over the saltmarshes and sand flats. Dial House Basecamp available for hire, sleeps 20, contact NT Warden for further details

- 🅾 All year. Information Centre and cycle hire at Brancaster Staithe Harbour, April to end June: Sat & Sun 10-6; July & Aug: daily 10-6. Golf club car park at Brancaster Beach, parking charge (incl. NT members)
- ♿ Access to Information Centre only

168

NORFOLK

- Near the Harbour (not NT)
- Guided walks programme; leaflet from Warden
- Under control at all times on the beach and not on Scolt Head Island from mid April to mid Aug. Dog-free area on Brancaster Beach, W of golf club house May–Sept
- Brancaster Staithe is halfway between Wells and Hunstanton on A149 coast road [132: TF800450] *Bus:* Sanders/Dunthorne/Eastern Counties Coastliner Hunstanton–Wells, with connections from King's Lynn (passing close BR King's Lynn) (tel. (0603) 613613)

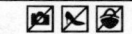

FELBRIGG HALL
Felbrigg, Norwich NR11 8PR (0263) 837444

One of the finest 17th-century houses in Norfolk, with its original 18th-century furniture and pictures, and an outstanding library. The Walled Garden has been restored, complete with dovecote, greenhouses and the traditional layout of herbaceous plants and fruit trees, including the national collection of colchicums. There are extensive walks in the Park, woods and around the lake

Note: New for 1994 are 11 rooms, including Domestic Wing and Morning Room

- **House:** 26 March to 30 Oct: Mon, Wed, Thur, Sat & Sun 1–5; BH Mon & Sun preceding BH Mon 11–5. **Garden:** same days 11–5. Woodland, lakeside walks and parkland all year (except Christmas Day): daily, dawn to dusk
- House & garden £4.60. Garden only £1.80. Parties £3.40, Mon, Wed, Thur & Sat only, please book with s.a.e. to Administrator. Garden tours available for parties
- Guided tours of Hall outside normal opening hours available for pre-booked parties.
- Shop same days as house. Also 3 Nov–18 Dec, Thur–Sun 11–4 & Jan–March, Sat & Sun 11–4. Tel. (0263) 838237
- Parking spaces allocated in main car park by information board. Wheelchairs available from Visitor Reception building 100yds; 2 self-drive scooters available. Access to ground floor only, shop, restaurant and Turret tea-room. WC. Woodland, lakeside and parkland walks
- Braille guides to house and walks
- Park Restaurant (waitress service) and Turret tea-room (counter service; both licensed) 26 March to 30 Oct: same days as house 11–5.15 (occasionally only one of these facilities available). Booking advisable for Park Restaurant and Sun lunches. Private functions catered for (tel. (0263) 838237. Also 3 Nov to end March 1995: same days as shop 11–3.30. Picnic area ½m beyond Hall
- Baby slings available. Parent & baby room. High chairs in restaurant. Children's menu. Scribble sheets. Free Family Woodland Trail
- Teacher's resource book and young person's guide. Hostel accommodation, all facilities, sleeps 33. s.a.e. to Administrator for details   *continued*

NORFOLK

- **E** 10-12 June, mid summer festival; 8-10 July, opera/concert weekend. £6.50 per person (minimum charge £2) 28-30 May, Felbrigg Coast and Country Fair; box office (0263) 838297. For details of these and other events please send s.a.e to Administrator
- In woods under close control; in parkland and lakeside walk on leads only
- Nr Felbrigg village, 2m SW of Cromer; entrance off B1436, signposted from A148 and A140 [133: TG193394] *Station:* Cromer (U) or Roughton Road (U), both 2¼m

---

4 SOUTH QUAY, GREAT YARMOUTH

Great Yarmouth NR30 2SH (0493) 855746

A 16th-century building with panelled rooms and 19th-century frontage, leased to the Norfolk Museums Service as a museum of domestic life

- All year: Mon to Fri (& Sun June to end Sept) 10-1 & 2-5.30. Opening times subject to review. Closed 11 April-29 May
- **£** Adults 60p; children 30p; students, registered unemployed & OAPs 40p
- [134: TG523073] *Bus:* Local services (tel. (0493) 844928); also from surrounding areas (tel. (0493) 842341) *Station:* Great Yarmouth ½m

NORFOLK

HORSEY WINDPUMP 🗷
Horsey, Great Yarmouth NR29 4EF (Regional Office (0263) 733471)

A drainage windmill that was working until 1943 when lightning severely damaged it. Acquired by the Trust in 1948 and restored

- 🅾 26 March to 30 Sept: daily 11–5 (July & Aug 11–6)
- 💷 £1. No reduction for parties. Car parking charge for non-members
- ♿ Unsuitable for disabled or visually impaired visitors; difficult staircase. WC
- ☕ Light refreshments and small shop
- 🐕 On leads only
- ➡ 2½m NE of Potter Heigham, 11m N of Yarmouth near B1159 [134: TG457223] *Bus:* Eastern Counties 623/6 Great Yarmouth–Martham (passing close BR Yarmouth), alight W Somerton School, 1¼m (tel. (0493) 842341) *Station:* Acle (U) 10m

OXBURGH HALL 🏛 ✝ ❋ 👤   📷 🚫 ✉
Oxborough, King's Lynn PE33 9PS (0366) 328258

This moated house was built in 1482 by the Bedingfeld family, who still live here. The rooms show the development from medieval austerity to Victorian comfort, with embroidery worked by Mary Queen of Scots, during her captivity, on display. The magnificent Tudor gatehouse rises 80 feet above the moat, and the garden includes lawns, fine trees, colourful borders and a French parterre. There are also delightful woodland walks, including a new two mile walk through Home Covert

- 🅾 **House:** 26 March to 30 Oct: daily except Thur & Fri 1–5; BH Mon 11–5; **Garden:** same days as house 12–5.30
- 💷 House, Garden & Estate £3.80. Pre-arranged parties £3, please book with s.a.e. to Administrator. Garden & Estate only £2
- 📷 As house
- ♿ Access to house 200yds; shallow ramp to 4 ground floor rooms; difficult stairs to upper floors. WC in west wing of house. Easy access to tea-room and shop. 2 shallow steps to Chapel, 100yds from Hall. 4 wheelchairs available
- 👁 Braille guide
- ☕ Light lunches and teas in Old Kitchen 12–5 on open days. Table licence. Capacity: 100
- 👶 Baby slings available. Children's guide. Restaurant: children's menu, baby foods, high chairs, scribble sheets
- 🇪 s.a.e. to Administrator for details
- ➡ At Oxborough, 7m SW of Swaffham on S side of Stoke Ferry road [143: TF742012] *Station:* Downham Market 10m

171

NORFOLK

SHERINGHAM PARK 🅿️ ♿ 📷 🚶

Warden: Gardener's Cottage, Sheringham Park, Upper Sheringham NR26 8TB
Warden: tel. (0263) 823778

This 770-acre property includes the outstanding landscaped park by Humphry Repton, with fine, mature, mixed woodland, plus large area of species rhododendrons and azaleas, which flower in late May/June. Spectacular views of coast and countryside may be enjoyed from the viewing towers. Wonderful walks all year round

- 🅾️ Park open all year round, dawn to dusk. Numerous waymarked walks through woodland, parkland and to the coast; leaflet on sale in car park. Sheringham Hall is privately occupied. Limited access is available to selected rooms only, April to Sept, by written appointment with the leaseholder
- 💷 £2.30 per car, incl. all passengers. Coaches £6.90; please book in advance with Warden. Pay and display car park. Coaches display 3 vaild tickets. Members display membership card or pass (available when staff on duty)
- ♿ Raised walkway from car park to park viewpoints. Batricar & wheelchair available on request when car park attendant present, Easter to end Sept. WC
- 🍴 Refreshments and shop at nearby Felbrigg Hall during open hours
- 🐕 On leads in park
- ➡️ 2m SW of Sheringham, access for cars off A148 Cromer–Holt road; 5m W of Cromer; 6m E of Holt [133: TG135420] *Station:* Sheringham (U) 2m

ST GEORGE'S GUILDHALL 🏛️

27 King Street, King's Lynn PE30 1HA (0553) 774725

The largest surviving English medieval guildhall, with an adjoining medieval warehouse now in use as an Arts Centre

- 🅾️ The Guildhall is not usually open on the days when performances are taking place in the theatre (please refer to current King's Lynn Arts Centre brochure for details). Open all year Mon to Fri (closed Good Fri & Aug BH Mon) 10–5; Sat 10–12.30 & 2–3.30 (25 June–9 July limited to 10–12.30). Sun 2–4 (29 May–25 Sept but closed 17, 24, 31 July). Closed 25, 26, 27 Dec & 1 Jan
- 💷 50p
- 🛍️ Crafts. Christmas shop (open from mid-Nov)
- ♿ Access to Galleries
- 🍴 Light lunches & teas from Crofters Coffee Bar. Also, restaurant open for lunch and dinner Mon to Sat
- 🇪 King's Lynn Festival in late July. Performances, workshops and art exhibitions throughout the year; for details write to address above or tel. (0553) 773578
- ➡️ On W side of King Street close to the Tuesday Market Place [132: TF616202] *Bus:* from surrounding areas (tel. (0603) 613613) *Station:* King's Lynn ½m

172

Northamptonshire

CANONS ASHBY HOUSE
Canons Ashby, Daventry NN11 6SD (0327) 860044

Home of the Dryden family since the 16th century, this manor house was built c.1550, added to in the 1590s, and altered in the 1630s and c.1710; largely unaltered since. Within the house, Elizabethan wall paintings and outstanding Jacobean plasterwork are of particular interest. A formal garden includes terraces, walls and gate piers of 1710. There is also a medieval priory church and a 70-acre park

NORTHAMPTONSHIRE

House: 30 March to end Oct: Wed to Sun & BH Mon (closed Good Fri) 1–5.30 or dusk if earlier. Last admissions 5. **Park:** open as house, access through garden

£3.20; children £1.60. Discount for parties; contact Administrator. Donation box for church. Parking 200yds; coaches and parties should pre-book in writing with the Administrator. Conducted tours in French by prior arrangement

Shop open as house

Access to garden and ground floor via 3 steps. House difficult but please telephone Administrator for special arrangements. WC

Taped guide for visually impaired and guidebook for deaf visitors

Light lunches 12–2 and afternoon tea 2–5 in Brewhouse; same days as house. Party bookings by prior arrangement. 36 seats

Teacher's pack available; contact Administrator

Occasional outdoor events; details from Administrator; please send s.a.e.

On leads, in Home Paddock only

Easy access from either M40, junction 11 or M1, junction 16. From M1, signposted from A5 2m S of Weedon crossroads, along unclassified road (3m) to Banbury. From M40 at Banbury take A422 exit, then left along B4525 and after 3m turn left up unclassified road (signed). [152: SP577506]
Bus: Geoff Amos from BR Banbury to house; also Saunterbus from Northampton some Sundays (tel. (0604) 236712) *Station:* Banbury 10m

NORTHAMPTONSHIRE

LYVEDEN NEW BIELD 🏠 ✝

nr Oundle, Peterborough PE8 5AT (083 25) 358

The shell of an uncompleted 'lodge' or garden house, begun c.1595 by Sir Thomas Tresham, and designed in the shape of a cross. The exterior incorporates friezes inscribed with religious quotations and signs of the Passion. Sir Thomas died before the building was completed, and his son, Francis Tresham, was then imprisoned in connection with the Gunpowder Plot. Viewing platform at the south window

- **O** All year: daily. Parties by arrangement with the Custodian, Lyveden New Bield Cottage, Oundle, Peterborough PE8 5AT
- **£** £1.20. Limited roadside parking; access on foot ½m along farm track; no parking for coaches which may drop and return to pick up passengers. No WCs
- **K** Tours of the remains of the late Elizabethan Water Gardens by prior arrangement with the Custodian
- **E** National Music Day 26 June
- 🐕 On leads only
- ➔ 4m SW of Oundle via A427, 3m E of Brigstock, just off Harley Way [141: SP983853] *Bus:* United Counties X65 Northampton–Peterborough (passing close BR Peterborough); alight Lower Benefield, 2m by bridlepath; United Counties/Blands 8 Kettering Corby, alight Brigstock, 2½m. Both pass close BR Kettering (tel. (0536) 512411) *Station:* Kettering 10m

PRIEST'S HOUSE 🏠

Easton on the Hill, nr Stamford, Lincolnshire

Pre-Reformation priest's lodge, of specialist architectural interest. There is a small museum of village bygones upstairs

- **O** By appointment only with Mr R. Chapman, Glebe Cottage, 45 West Street, Easton on the Hill, Stamford PE9 3LS (tel. (0780) 62506)
- **£** Free. Unsuitable for coaches
- ♿ Ground floor room only
- ➔ Approx. 2m SW of Stamford off A43 [141: TF011045] *Bus:* Road Car 180, Blands from Stamford (passing close BR Stamford), alight Easton, ½m (tel. (0604) 236712) *Station:* Stamford 2m

Northumberland

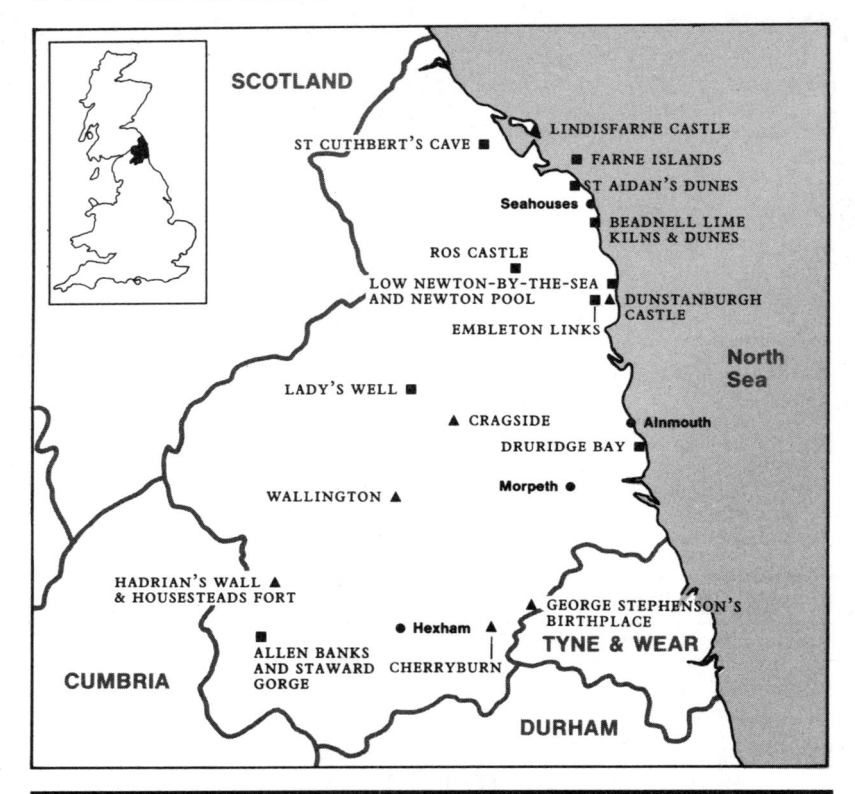

COAST

Here is one of the most beautiful stretches of English coastline, with its castles – some ruined, some in splendid repair – its miles of sandy beaches, links, and sand dunes, and its nature reserves and rocky offshore islands.

If you are visting Northumbria or Scotland by car, the A189 from the A1 north of Newcastle will take you within easy reach of **Druridge Bay** [81: NZ2896]; here the Trust owns a mile of coastline with 99 acres of golden sand dunes and grassland, and further north there are dunes at **Alnmouth**. The A189 road rejoins the A1 at Alnwick, but B roads lead to the starkly dramatic ruin of **Dunstanburgh Castle** (see p.180). From Craster the Trust owns a 5-mile stretch of coastline, including **Embleton Links** [75: NU243235] and **Low Newton-by-the-Sea** [75: NU241246]. Almost the whole of the square at Low Newton is owned by the Trust as well as **Newton Pool** [75: NU243240], a freshwater lake behind the dunes. This nature reserve is home to breeding birds such as blackheaded gull, teal, mute swan, dabchick, sedge warbler and reed bunting and in

176

NORTHUMBERLAND

winter goldeneye and pochard. Two hides are provided for birdwatchers, one adapted for disabled visitors with a wheelchair pathway. There are parking bays for disabled visitors at Low Newton. From Craster to Low Newton there is a beautiful 2½-mile walk along the rocky coastline and the dunes. Information boards have been placed at the access points to help introduce this coastline to visitors.

The road leads on to **Beadnell Harbour** where the Trust owns the 18th-century sandstone **Lime Kilns** and just to the north, a ½ mile of sand dunes [75: NU237286]. From Beadnell the B1340 hugs the coast for about 6 miles to Bamburgh, passing **St Aidan's Dunes** [75: NU211327] with spectacular views of the **Farne Islands** (see p.180) on clear days. On the way, at Seahouses, is a Trust Information Centre and Shop – and access to the Farnes. The Trust's coastal holdings in Northumberland culminate at **Lindisfarne Castle** on Holy Island (see p.182) from where there are views not only seawards, but inland to the Cheviot Hills. On all properties dogs must be kept under control at all times.

COUNTRYSIDE

The Allen and Tyne rivers meet 3 miles west of Haydon Bridge off the A69 where nearby the Trust owns **Allen Banks** [86/87: NY799630] and **Staward Gorge**, over 500 acres of hillside, woodland and riverside walks along the steep banks of the Allen; there is a picnic site in the car park, which is accessible to wheelchair users. **Bellister Pele Tower** [86: NY699631], surrounded by 1,120 acres of Trust land, can be visited by written appointment with the tenant. Across the Tyne valley, four miles north on the B6318, is access to the Trust's **Hadrian's Wall Estate** (see p.181). More than 2,700 acres of farmland, about 5 miles of the course of the Hadrian's Wall, Vallum etc, including stretches of the stone wall and ditch, **Housesteads Fort**, several milecastles and, at Shield on the Wall, one of the best preserved sections of the Vallum, form one of the Trust's most fascinating and breath-taking antiquities. There is an adapted WC for wheelchair users at **Housesteads** car park; dogs on leads only.

Seven miles west of Rothbury at Holystone on the edge of the Cheviots is **Lady's Well** which has probable associations with St Ninian [81: NT953029]. Views of the Cheviots, Lindisfarne, Chillingham Park (not NT) and Bamburgh Castle (not NT) can be seen from the hilltop of **Ros Castle** [75: NU081253] near Wooler between the A1 and the A697. North-east of Wooler near Holburn Grange is a natural stone cave in the Kyloe Hills – **St Cuthbert's Cave**, where the saint's body is said to have rested on its journey from Lindisfarne to Durham [75: NU059352].

At Wallington (see p.183), the Trust owns 13,000 acres of beautiful countryside. The land is farmed, but with the agreement of the farmers, circular walks are open during the summer months for visitors to the Estate. Walks leaflets are available at Wallington and they introduce the walker to the geology, history, flora and fauna of the area. The 1,000-acre **Cragside House, Garden and Grounds** (see p.178) is a must for walkers: 40 miles of footpaths and carriage drives are available. The Power Circuit, a 1½-mile circular walk, highlights the industrial archaeology of Cragside. It includes the restored hydraulic and hydro-electric machinery at the Ram and Power Houses and the Iron Bridge, one of the first steel bridges in the world. Walks leaflets are available at the Visitor Centre. During June, the Grounds come alive with a superb display of rhododendrons and azaleas and in the autumn the colours are quite breathtaking. There is also the Armstrong Energy Centre, an exhibition of energy technology over the past 100 years, and into the future. The latest acquisition is Cragside Garden, the formal gardens originally part of the Lord Armstrong's estate.

REFER TO OPENING PAGES FOR GENERAL INFORMATION

NORTHUMBERLAND

CHERRYBURN

Station Bank, Mickley, Stocksfield NE43 7DB (0661) 843276

The birthplace of Thomas Bewick, Northumbria's greatest artist, wood engraver and naturalist (b.1753). The 19th-century farmhouse, home of the Bewick family, houses a small exhibition on Bewick's life and works. Also birthplace cottage, farmyard animals and garden for picnics. There are beautiful views of Tyne Valley and short walk from the south bank of the River Tyne

- **O** 1 April to 30 Oct: daily except Tues 1–5.30. Last admissions 5
- **£** £2.50. No reduction for parties, which must be pre-booked (s.a.e. to Custodian)
- Small shop open as house, selling prints, books & mementoes
- Some gravel paths; few steps; cobbled farmyard, some help needed; ramped entrance to house; WC
- Braille booklet 'Discover Thomas Bewick at Cherryburn' available from reception
- Farmyard animals usually include donkeys, pigs, poultry, lambs
- **E** Occasional wood engraving demonstrations; printing most days; evening opening for pre-booked parties (min. charge £80) incl. sherry reception & printing demonstration (s.a.e. to Custodian)
- No dogs
- 11m W of Newcastle, 11m E of Hexham; ¼m N of Mickley Square (leave A695 at Mickley and follow signposts). Cherryburn situated close to S bank of River Tyne [88: NZ075627] *Bus*: Northumbria 602 Newcastle–Hexham (passes BR Newcastle) (tel. 091-232 4211) *Station*: Stocksfield 1½m

CRAGSIDE HOUSE, GARDEN AND GROUNDS

Rothbury, Morpeth NE65 7PX (0669) 20333/20266

A Victorian mansion, mainly designed by R. Norman Shaw, in 1,000 acres of grounds created by the 1st Lord Armstrong. It was the first house in the world to be lit by hydro-electricity; the system was developed by Armstrong with man-made lakes and underground piping. He also planted millions of trees and shrubs and built 40 miles of drives and footpaths. 'The Power Circuit', a 1½ mile circular walk, includes the restored Ram and Power Houses with their hydraulic and hydro-electric machinery, and in the Visitor Centre, the Armstrong Energy Centre. In 1991 the Trust acquired Cragside Garden, the original formal pleasure garden for the house. The remarkable Orchard House, ferneries, rose loggia and Italian garden were opened in 1992 and are undergoing restoration work. The restored 19th-century clock tower can be seen by visitors to the garden from April 1994

- **O** **House:** 1 April to 30 Oct: daily except Mon but open BH Mon, 1–5.30. Last admissions 4.45. **Grounds:** as house 10.30–7; also 1 Nov to 18 Dec: Tues, Sat & Sun 10.30–4. **Garden:** 1 April to 30 Oct; as House 10.30–5.30

178

NORTHUMBERLAND

[£] House, Garden, Grounds & Visitor Centre £5.50; pre-booked parties £5.10. Garden, Grounds & Visitor Centre only £3.40; pre-booked parties £3.10. Family (House, Garden & Grounds) 2 adults & 2 children £14. Car park 100yds from house (7 car parks in Grounds). Coach park 350yds (advance booking essential). Please note coaches cannot tour grounds as drive is too narrow in places. Free access to Grounds and Visitor Centre, Shop and Restaurant from 1 Nov to 18 Dec; Tues, Sat & Sun

Visitor Centre (including Shop, Vickers Rooms Restaurant, Information Centre & Armstrong Energy Centre): same days as house: 10.30–5.30; 1 Nov to 18 Dec: Tues, Sat & Sun 12–4. Tel. (0669) 20448

Access to house (lift to first floor) & Visitor Centre. WC at Visitor Centre & by house and Crozier Drive car park; wheelchair path, adapted picnic tables & parking at Nelly's Moss Upper Lake; adapted fishing pier at Tumbleton Lake; for details tel. (0669) 20266 (Estate office)

Braille guide

Morning coffee, lunches and teas in Vickers Rooms Restaurant in Visitor Centre. Tel. (0669) 20134. Picnicking in all car parks and around Nelly's Moss Lakes

No back-packs in house; front sling baby carriers available; facilities for mothers and babies, including use of private room for nursing mothers. Adventure playground at Dunkirk car park. Children's guide. Family Fun Day July 9

Education Room/School party base. School parties may visit all attractions with a guide. Need to book with Education Officer tel. (0669) 21145

[E] For list of events and guided walks send s.a.e. to Administrator

Note: Trout fishing from boats on Tumbleton Lake; bird hides at Blackburn Lake; for fishing bookings tel. (0669) 21051 (answerphone)

In Grounds only (not in formal garden)

13m SW of Alnwick (B6341) and 15m NW of Morpeth–Wooler road turn left onto B6341 at Moorhouse Crossroads, entrance at Debdon Gate, 1m N of Rothbury, public transport passengers enter by Reivers Well Gate from Morpeth Road (B6344) [81: NU073022]
Bus: Northumbria 516 Morpeth–Thropton, Postbus 817 (both passing BR Morpeth) with connections from Newcastle (passing Tyne & Wear Metro Haymarket), alight Reivers Well Gate, ¾m (tel. 091-232 4211)

NORTHUMBERLAND

DUNSTANBURGH CASTLE 🏰 📷 🚶

Craster, Alnwick (0665) 576231

The castle was built in 1316 by Thomas Earl of Lancaster and enlarged later by John of Gaunt. The dramatic ruin encloses 11 acres of dolerite promontory with sea cliffs to the north

Dunstanburgh Castle is owned by the National Trust, and maintained and managed by English Heritage

- 🅾 1 April to 31 Oct: daily 10–6. 1 Nov to 31 March: Wed to Sun 10–4. Closed 24–26 Dec and 1 Jan
- 💷 Adults £1.25. OAP/UB40/students, 95p. Children 60p. Free admission to English Heritage members. Car parks at Craster & Embleton, 1½m (no coaches at Embleton)
- ♿ Castle unsuitable for wheelchairs. WC at Craster car park
- 🍴 In Craster (not NT)
- 🐕 Must be kept on leads
- ➡ 9m NE of Alnwick, approached from Craster on S and Embleton on N (pedestrians only) [75: NU258220] *Bus:* Northumbria 501 Alnwick–Berwick upon Tweed (passing close BR Berwick upon Tweed) with connections from Newcastle (passing Tyne & Wear Metro Haymarket), alight Craster, 1¼m (tel. 091-232 4211) *Station:* Chathill (U), not Sun, 5m from Embleton, 7m from Castle; Alnmouth, 7m from Craster, 8¼m from Castle

FARNE ISLANDS ✝ 📷 🐦 🚶   🍴

Information Centre tel. (0665) 721099 Warden (0665) 720651

The islands provide a summer home for over 17 different species of seabirds, including puffin, kittiwake, eider duck, guillemot, fulmar, tern; they also provide a base for a large colony of grey seals. St Cuthbert died on Inner Farne in 687 and there is a chapel built to his memory in 14th century and restored 1845

Note: Public car park in Seahouses opposite harbour. NT Information Centre & Shop at 16 Main Street, Seahouses. WC on Inner Farne. Visitors to the islands are particularly asked to keep to the rules which have been made to preserve these islands as a bird sanctuary

- 🅾 Inner Farne and Staple Islands only are open to visitors. 1–30 April & 1 Aug to 30 Sept: daily 10.30–6. During breeding season (1 May to 31 July) access is restricted: Staple 10.30–1.30, Inner Farne 1.30–5. Visitors are advised to wear hats!
- 💷 May to end July £3.50; pre-booked school parties £1.60. At other times £2.70; pre-booked school parties £1.30. Admission fees do not include boatmen's charges. Tickets may be bought from Warden on landing and boat tickets from boatmen in Seahouses Harbour. No landing in bad weather. Enquiries about landing answered by Warden, tel. (0665) 720651; The Sheiling, 8 St Aidan's, Seahouses, Northumberland NE68 7SR

NORTHUMBERLAND

- Refreshments in Seahouses (not on islands), not NT. NT Information Centre and shop tel. (0665) 721099
- Nature walks on Inner Farne & Staple Island. Islands are difficult for disabled or visually impaired visitors and unsuitable for wheelchairs; some wheelchair access, but please tel. Warden before attempting this. WC on Inner Farne
- Teacher's resource book
- 2-5m off the Northumberland coast, opposite Bamburgh: trips every day from Seahouses Harbour, weather permitting [75: NU2337] *Bus:* as for Dunstanburgh Castle (see p.180) but alight Seahouses *Station:* Chathill (U), not Sun, 4m

GEORGE STEPHENSON'S BIRTHPLACE

Wylam NE41 8BP (0661) 853457

A small stone tenement built c.1760 to accommodate four pitmen's families. The furnishings reflect the age of George Stephenson's birth here in 1781; one room only open to public

- 1 April to 30 Oct: Thur, Sat & Sun, BH Mon & Good Fri 1-5.30. Last admissions 5
- 70p. Access by foot and bicycle through Country Park. No parties. No WCs. Parking by War Memorial in Wylam village, ½m
- 8m W of Newcastle, 1½m S of A69 at Wylam. Access on foot and bicycle through Country Park, ½m E of Wylam [88: NZ126650] *Bus:* OK Travel 684 Newcastle-Ovington, alight Wylam, 1m (tel. (0388) 450000) *Station:* Wylam (U) ½m

HADRIAN'S WALL & HOUSESTEADS FORT

Bardon Mill, Hexham NE47 6NN English Heritage Custodian, tel. (0434) 344363
NT Warden, tel.(0434) 344314

The Trust owns approx. 5 miles of the Wall running west from Housesteads Fort (including the Fort itself) and 2750 acres of farmland. Access to the Wall and the public rights of way from car parks at Housesteads, Steel Rigg and Cawfields Quarry

Housesteads Fort owned by the National Trust, and maintained and managed by English Heritage

- Housesteads Fort and Museum: 1 April to 31 Oct: daily, 10-6. 1 Nov to 31 March: daily 10-4 (closed 24-26 Dec, 1 Jan)
- Hadrian's Wall, Information Centre and shop free. Housesteads Museum & Fort prices: Adults £2.20. OAP/UB40/students £1.65. Free admission to English Heritage members. Car & coach parks at Housesteads, ½m, 40p, at the western end at Steel Rigg and Cawfields Quarry, managed by the National Park Authority. No access for vehicles to Housesteads Fort
- For details of guided walks send s.a.e. to Information Centre and Shop

continued

NORTHUMBERLAND

- 🛍 Shop & Information Centre at Housesteads car park: March: Sat & Sun 11–5; April & Oct: daily 11–5, May to end Sept: daily 10–5, Nov: Sat & Sun 11–dusk. Tel. (0434) 344525
- ♿ Access to Information Centre and shop only; parking available near Housesteads Fort; ask Information Centre and shop Manager for details. WC at Information Centre and shop. Housesteads Fort not suitable for wheelchairs
- ☕ Hot and cold drinks, sandwiches and ice cream at Information Centre and shop. Picnicking
- 👶 Children's guide
- 📕 Education Room. School party base. Book through English Heritage tel. 091-261 1585
- 🐕 Must be kept on leads
- ➡ 6m NE of Haltwhistle, 3m N of Bardon Mill railway station; ½m N of B6318; best access from car parks at Housesteads and Steel Rigg [87: NY790688]
  Bus: Rochester & Marshall 890 Hadrian's Wall summer service BR Hexham–BR Haltwhistle (tel. (0434) 600263) *Station:* Bardon Mill (U) 4m

LINDISFARNE CASTLE

Holy Island, Berwick-upon-Tweed TD15 2SH (0289) 89244

Built in 1550 to protect Holy Island Harbour from attack, the castle was restored and converted into a private house by Sir Edwin Lutyens in 1903. The small walled garden was designed by Gertrude Jekyll. 19th-century lime kilns in field by the castle

- 🕐 1 April to 30 Oct: daily except Fri (but open Good Fri) 1–5.30. Last admissions 5. Admission to garden only when gardener is in attendance (usually Tues afternoons & Fri but please check with Administrator
- £ £3.40. No party rate. Parties of 15 or more must pre-book. No WCs. Main public car park approx. 1 mile away, & further parking off approach road to Castle £1, incl. NT members (NB 1993 prices). No large camera cases or boxes
- 🛍 NT shop in Main Street, Holy Island Village; tel. (0289) 89253
- Braille guide
- ☕ In Holy Island Village (not NT)
- 👶 No back-packs in Castle (including framed baby carriers); front sling baby carriers available
- ℹ *Note:* It is impossible to cross the island between the 2 hours before high tide and the 3½ hours following. Tide tables are printed in local newspapers, and displayed at the causeway
- 🐕 On leads as far as Lower Battery only
- ➡ On Holy Island, 6m E of A1 across causeway [75: NU136417]
  Bus: Northumbria 477 from Berwick-upon-Tweed (passing close BR Berwick-upon-Tweed). Times vary with tides: tel. (0670) 533998
  Station: Berwick-upon-Tweed 10m from causeway

NORTHUMBERLAND

WALLINGTON
Cambo, Morpeth NE61 4AR (067 074) 283

Built on the site of a medieval castle in 1688 and altered in the 1740s. Rooms range from elegant mid-Georgian to a Victorian nursery with fine furniture and china, and a collection of dolls' houses. The plasterwork and porcelain is exceptional, and the 19th-century Central Hall contains paintings by William Bell Scott. There is a terraced walled garden and conservatory, an Estate Room with exhibition, and coaches displayed in the West Coach House

House: 1 April to 30 Oct: daily except Tues 1-5.30. Last admissions 5. **Walled Garden:** 1 April to 30 Sept: daily 10.30-7; Oct: 10.30-6; Nov to March 1995: 10.30-4 (or dusk if earlier). **Grounds:** all year during daylight hours

House, walled garden & grounds £4.40. Parties £3.90. Walled garden & grounds £2.20; parties £1.70. Parties must book in advance

Shop open 1 April to 30 Oct: daily except Tues 10.30-5.30; 2 Nov to 18 Dec: Wed to Sun 12.30-4.30. Tel. (067 074) 249. Plant centre: 1 April-31 Aug: 1-5.30 except Tues. Sept & Oct: Sat & Sun only, 1-5.30

Access to ground floor of house only; wheelchairs available. Apply to parking attendant for reserved bays; most of grounds, conservatory and Walled Garden terrace accessible, but no wheelchair access to rest of Walled Garden; powered scooters for hire (contact Administrator for details). WC in courtyard and restaurant

Braille guide; scented roses in garden

Coffee, lunches & teas in Clock Tower Restaurant same times as shop, see above. Tel. (067 074) 274. Picnics in car park and West Woods. Access to shop and restaurant is free from 2 Nov-18 Dec, Wed to Sun

No back-packs or pushchairs in house; front sling baby carriers available; please enquire about other facilities for mothers and babies. Dolls' houses and toy soldier collections. Children's guide. Family Fun Day 21 Aug

Send s.a.e. to Administrator for details of walks and events

Note: New circular walks open on the Wallington Estate; leaflets available at the shop. Open air Shakespeare 21-25 June

In walled garden on leads, and in grounds only

12m W of Morpeth (B6343), 6m NW of Belsay (A696), take B6342 to Cambo [81: NZ030843] *Bus:* Northumbria/Vasey 419 from Morpeth (Wed, Fri, Sat only) (passing close BR Morpeth); otherwise National Express 375, 394 from Newcastle (passing close BR Newcastle), alight Capheaton Road End, 2m (tel. (0670) 533998)

REFER TO OPENING PAGES FOR GENERAL INFORMATION

Nottinghamshire

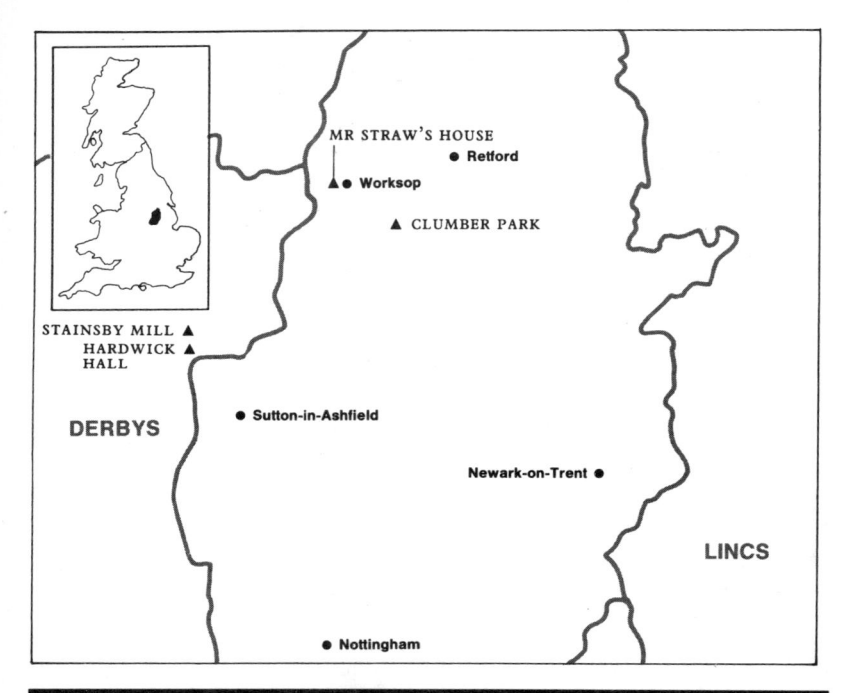

CLUMBER PARK 🏠✝✿🌳🚶 ❌
The Estate Office, Clumber Park, Worksop S80 3AZ (0909) 476592

3,800 acres of parkland, farmland, lake and woodlands. The mansion was demolished in 1938, but the fine Gothic Revival Chapel, built 1886–89 for the 7th Duke of Newcastle, survives. Park includes the longest double lime avenue in Europe and a superb 80-acre lake. Also, Classical bridge, temples, lawned Lincoln Terrace, pleasure grounds and the stable block with restaurant, shop and information point. Vineries & Garden Tools Exhibition, Clumber Conservation Centre with large scale models of park and former Clumber House

- **○** **Park:** open all year during daylight hours. **Vineries & Garden Tools Exhibition:** 2 April to end Sept: Sat, Sun & BH Mon 10-5. Last admissions 4.30. **Conservation centre:** 2 April to 25 Sept: Sat, Sun & BH Mon 1-5

    Note: Chapel will be closed throughout 1994 for essential conservation work

- **£** Pedestrians free. Cars, motorbikes & caravanettes £2.50 (exemption for NT members only); cars with caravans & mini coaches £3.70; coaches midweek £6, weekends and BH £12. Parking 100yds from visitor facilities. Bicycle hire

NOTTINGHAMSHIRE

(identification essential) including cycles with child carriers £2.50 for 2hrs; (midweek party bookings for min. 20 cycles) book through Visitor Liaison Officer. Orienteering by arrangement (orienteering packs £1.20). Horse riding by permit. Coarse fishing: 16 June to 14 March; 7am to dusk; day ticket £2.50; season ticket £40. Day tickets available on the bank from fishing bailiff. Vineries & Garden Tools Exhibition 60p. Boat trips on lake: £1.50 adults, £1 children under 14; under 5's free

Guided walks may be booked for parties throughout the summer

Clock Tower Shop (tel. (0909) 474468) open all year daily: Jan to 26 March 10.30-5; 27 March to 22 Oct 10.30-6; 23 Oct to 24 Dec 10.30-5; 27 Dec to end March 1995 10.30-5. Plant Sales Centre: open daily 27 March to 22 Oct 10.30-6

13 miles of tarmac roads; most areas accessible; Vineries & Garden Tools Exhibition fully accessible. Restaurant & shop accessible. Wheelchairs (incl. child size) available (identification required) from NT shop and cycle hire. Access across grass for special events (see below). WCs. Visitors with special needs please contact Visitor Liaison Officer. Batricar and scooter also available free of charge weekdays (except Thur) – booking essential from Estate Office (positive identification is required)

Self-service cafeteria: daily Jan to 26 March: 10.30-5; 27 March to 22 Oct: 10.30-6; 23 Oct to 24 Dec: 10.30-5 closed 25 & 26 Dec; 27 Dec to end March 1995 10.30-5. Restaurant open at same times as cafeteria. Open for functions and booked parties throughout the year. Bookings and enquiries: tel. (0909) 484122. Seats 150; children's portions available

Parent and baby facilities; high chairs in restaurant; cycles with child carriers or buggies; open parkland ideal for family activities

Conservation Centre available for school parties; educational exhibitions; please contact Warden, Estate Office

Full programme of events, including Clumber Park Horse Trials, 7/8 May; Clumber Park Show, Sun 19 June; Open Air Concerts with fireworks – Herb Miller Orchestra & the Pasadena Roof Orchestra, Sat 9 July and Kenny Ball, 'The Best of British' and the Temperence Seven, Sat 6 August. Credit card line for outdoor concerts: 0909 476592

Note: All enquiries to Visitor Liaison Officer (tel. (0909) 476592). Guided walks may be booked for parties throughout the summer. Information point open April to Oct afternoons (tel. (0909) 484977). 150-berth caravan site run by Caravan Club; open to non-members. NT & Caravan Club members have priority (tel. (0909) 484758). Camp site run by Camping & Caravanning Club of Great Britain (booking advisable due to limited spaces): April to end Sept (tel. (0909) 482303). Clumber Conservation Centre for school and other groups (book with Head Warden): open weekends April to end Oct and other times by arrangement

$4\frac{1}{2}$m SE of Worksop, $6\frac{1}{2}$m SW of Retford, 1m from A1/A57, 11m from M1 Jn 30. [120: SK645774 or 120: SK626746] *Bus:* Notts CC summer network services from Worksop and other towns to Park; E Midland 33 Worksop–Nottingham (passing close BR Worksop), alight Carburton, $1\frac{1}{4}$m (tel. (0602) 240000) *Station:* Worksop $4\frac{1}{2}$m; Retford $6\frac{1}{2}$m

NOTTINGHAMSHIRE

MR STRAW'S HOUSE 🏠
7 Blyth Grove, Worksop, Nottinghamshire S81 0JG (0909) 482380

A semi-detached house built at the turn of the century, belonging to William Straw and his brother, Walter. The interior has been preserved since the death of their parents in the 1930s with 1920s' wallpaper, furnishings and local furniture. Museum room contains displays of family memorabelia, and there is a suburban garden

- 🅾 30 March to end Oct: Tues to Sat (closed Good Fri)1–5.30. Last admissions 5. Admission for all visitors (incl. NT members) by pre-booked timed ticket only. All bookings by telephone (see above) or letter (s.a.e. please) to Custodian

  Note: Blyth Grove is a private road; there is no access without booking in advance

- £ £2.50, children £1.20. Parties (max. 16) on Wed & Fri mornings only; one party per day to be guided (£10 extra per party, incl. NT members) 10.30–12

- ♿ Wheelchair access not possible

- ➔ In Worksop, follow signs to Bassetlaw General Hospital. House signed from Blyth Road B6045 [120: SK590802] *Bus:* from surrounding areas (tel. (0602) 240000) *Station:* Worksop ½m

Oxfordshire

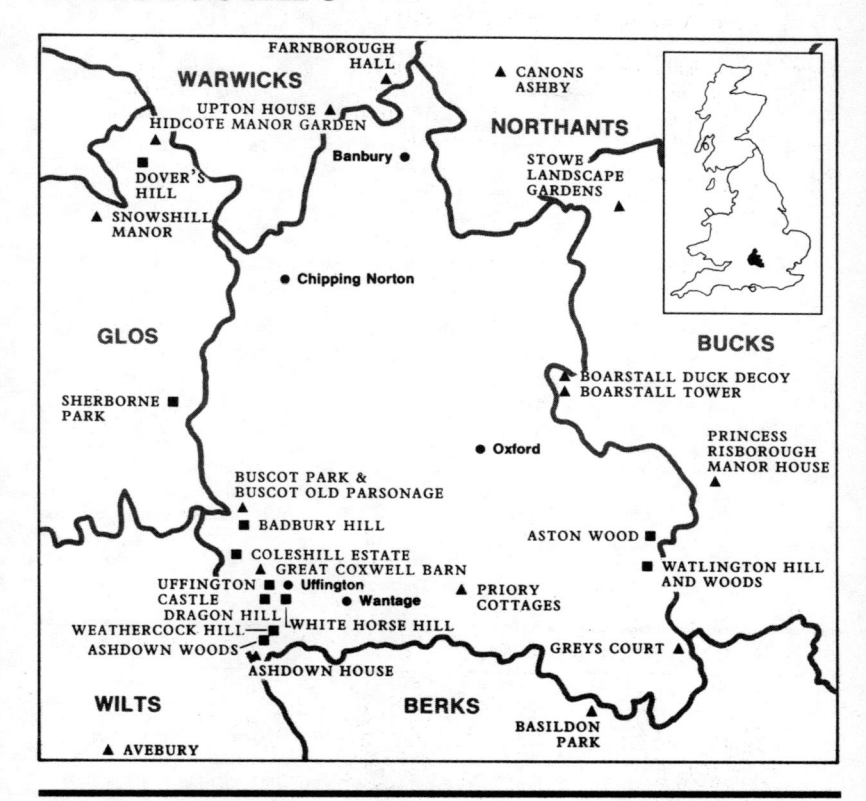

COUNTRYSIDE

The **Buscot and Coleshill** estates extend to about 7,500 acres of farmland and woodland [163: SU2694]. This beautiful, rural area includes **Badbury Hill**, at which there is a car park. An Iron Age hill-fort gives fine views over the upper Thames Valley and south to the Berkshire Downs on which is **White Horse Hill**. Buscot is an attractive stone village close to the Thames, with a popular picnic area at Buscot Weir. You may park in the village a short walk away. There is also a picnic site and small car park by the Thames to the west of Buscot on the road to Lechlade. Coleshill village is a typical estate village of Cotswold stone-and-tile houses and cottages. Box hedges are an attractive feature of the village.

A mile south-east of Watlington, on an escarpment of the Chilterns, **Watlington Hill** [175: SU702935] rises to 700ft and gives splendid views over much of Oxfordshire. The scenery alone is rewarding, and for the naturalist the area offers much fascination. This chalk and flint hill is overlaid with clay and flints, so the vegetation includes both clay

OXFORDSHIRE

and chalk loving plants. There is a fine yew forest, and whitebeam, dogwood, hawthorn and the wayfaring tree grow in profusion. The hill is skirted by the Upper Icknield Way. It is an ideal spot for picnics or simply enjoying the view.

An interesting feature to look out for on the side of the hill is the White Mark, a triangle cut out of the chalk and kept free of vegetation. Just south of the hill lie **Watlington Woods**, which are especially attractive at bluebell time. There is a small car park for both the hill and woods off the Watlington to Northend road.

Aston Wood [165: SU740973], to the west of Stokenchurch, is a pleasant pocket of Chiltern woodland. An area rich in wildlife, it adjoins the Nature Conservancy Council's National Nature Reserve at Aston Rowant. There is parking in a layby beside the A40.

There are some excellent archaeological monuments in the open countryside south of Uffington, south-west Oxfordshire. The famous landmark of **White Horse Hill** has a 360ft long figure of a horse cut in the chalk. At the foot of the hill is a sheltered grassy area known as 'The Manger', where traditionally the horse comes to feed! The origin of the White Horse is unknown, but it is probably early Iron Age and is certainly one of the oldest such figures in Britain. Above it is an ancient barrow. The hill is crowned by the Iron Age hill-fort of **Uffington Castle**, which dates from the 1st century BC and is surrounded by a strong defensive bank and ditch. The smaller, flat-topped **Dragon Hill** is nearby. It is traditionally the site where St George slew the dragon, and legend has it that the distinctive bare patch is where the dragon's blood was spilled on the earth.

All three monuments [174: SU301869] belong to the Trust but are in the care of English Heritage. This fascinating area may be approached on foot from the Ridgeway path or by car from the B4507. Large car park 500 yards away from monuments.

South of White Horse Hill, there is much pleasant countryside to be explored at **Ashdown Woods** [174: SU283824], adjoining the 17th-century **Ashdown House** (see below), and **Weathercock Hill** on the opposite side of the B4000. There is a car park 250 yards from the house. Please note that the estate and car park are closed to the public for estate management purposes on Fridays throughout the year.

ASHDOWN HOUSE

Lambourn, Newbury, Berkshire RG16 7RE (Regional Office (0494) 528051)

A 17th-century house built by 1st Lord Craven and by him 'consecrated' to Elizabeth, Queen of Bohemia. The great staircase, rising from hall to attic, is impressive, and the house contains portraits of the Winter Queen's family. There are fine views from the roof; also, a box parterre, lawns, avenues and woodland walks

- **Hall, stairway, roof and grounds only:** April to end Oct: Wed & Sat 2–6. Closed Easter & every BH. **Woodlands:** all year: Sat to Thur dawn to dusk

- Grounds, hall, stairway & roof £2. No reduction for parties, which should book **in writing**. Woodland free. Car park 250yds. No WCs or refreshments available. No picnicking

- Guided tours only; at 2.15, 3.15, 4.15 & 5.15 from front door

- Access to grounds only; house not accessible to wheelchair users

- Dogs in woodland only (not in house or grounds)

- 2½m S of Ashbury, 3½m N of Lambourn, on W side of B4000 [174: SU282820] *Bus:* Thamesdown 47/8 Swindon–Lambourn, with connections from Newbury (passing close BR Swindon & Newbury) (tel. (0345) 090899)

OXFORDSHIRE

BUSCOT OLD PARSONAGE 🏠 ❖   🚫 ✈ ✗

Buscot, Faringdon SN7 8DQ (Regional Office (0494) 528051)

An early 18th-century house of Cotswold stone on the bank of Thames; small garden

- **O**   April to end Oct: Wed only 2–6 by appointment in writing with tenant
- **£**   £1. Not suitable for parties. No WCs
- **→**   2m from Lechlade, 4m from Faringdon on A417 [163: SU231973]
  Bus: Carterton 64, X64 Swindon–Carterton, or Thamesdown 77 Swindon–Cirencester (both passing close BR Swindon). On both, alight Lechlade, 1½m (tel. 0345 090 899)

BUSCOT PARK 🏠 ❖ ♣   🚫 ✈ ✗ ⛵

Faringdon SN7 8BU (0367) 242094

A late 18th-century house set in parkland, with pleasure grounds that include water gardens (Harold Peto), avenues and a lake. The contents of the house are owned by the Faringdon Collection Trustees. 2 holiday cottages

Buscot Park, with access to *piano nobile* and pleasure grounds, is administered for the National Trust by Lord Faringdon

- **O**   April to end Sept (including Good Fri, Easter Sat & Sun): Wed, Thur, Fri 2–6. Also open every 2nd & 4th weekend 2–6 (i.e. 9 & 10, 23 & 24 April; 14 & 15, 28 & 29 May; 11 & 12, 25 & 26 June; 9 & 10, 23 & 24 July; 13 & 14, 27 & 28 Aug; 10 & 11, 24 & 25 Sept). Timed entry to house may be imposed if crowding occurs. Last admissions 5.30
- **£**   House & grounds £4. Grounds only £3. No reduction for parties which must book in writing to the Housekeeper; please advise numbers and time of arrival. Unsuitable for wheelchair users due to gradients, gravel paths throughout grounds and steep flight of steps to house
- **🍽**   Afternoon teas in tea-room; lunches available for groups by prior arrangement with Housekeeper. Self-pick fruit available when advertised
- **→**   Between Lechlade and Faringdon, on A417 [163: SU239973]
  Bus: Thamesdown 67 Swindon–Faringdon (Fri only); otherwise as for Buscot Old Parsonage, (see above) but 2¾m walk from Lechlade (tel. (0345) 090899)

GREAT COXWELL BARN 🏠

Great Coxwell, Faringdon (Regional Office (0494) 528051)

A 13th-century monastic barn, stone-built with stone-tiled roof, which has interesting timber construction

- **O**   All year: daily at reasonable hours
- **£**   50p. No WCs

continued

OXFORDSHIRE

- On leads only
- 2m SW of Faringdon between A420 and B4019 [163: SU269940]
  Bus: Swindon & District 66/B Swindon–Oxford (passing close BR Swindon & passing BR Oxford), alight Great Coxwell Turn, ¼m (tel. 0345 090 899)
  Station: Swindon 10m

GREYS COURT

Rotherfield Greys, Henley-on-Thames RG9 4PG (0491) 628529

Rebuilt in the 16th century and added to in the 17th, 18th and 19th centuries, the house is set amid the remains of the courtyard walls and towers of a 14th-century fortified house. A Tudor donkey wheel well-house and an ice house are still intact, and the garden contains Archbishop's Maze, inspired by Archbishop Runcie's enthronement speech in 1980

- April to end Sept: House (part of ground floor only): Mon, Wed & Fri: 2–6 (closed Good Fri); Garden: daily except Thur & Sun 2–6 (closed Good Fri). Last admissions 5.30
- House & garden £3.80. Family ticket £9.50. Garden only £2.80. No reduction for pre-booked parties. Parking 220yds. No picnicking in grounds
- Teas in Cromwellian stables: April to end Sept: Mon, Wed, Fri & Sat 2.30–5.15
- In car park only
- 3m W of Henley-on-Thames, east of B481 [175: SU725834] *Bus:* Oxford Tube 390 Victoria/Heathrow Airport–Oxford, alight Bix, 1¼m (tel. (0865) 727000); Reading Buses 136/7 from Reading (passing close BR Reading), alight Peppard Common, 2m (tel. (0734) 509509) *Station:* Henley-on-Thames 3m

PRIORY COTTAGES

1 Mill Street, Steventon, Abingdon OX13 6SP (Regional Office (0494) 528051)

Former monastic buildings, converted into two houses. South Cottage contains the Great Hall of the original priory

Note: Property may be closed during 1994 for building works

- The Great Hall in South Cottage only, April to end Sept: Wed 2–6; by written appointment with tenant
- £1. No reduction for parties. No WCs

  Note: very small house, unsuitable for coach parties

- 4m S of Abingdon, on B4017 off A34 at Abingdon West or Milton interchange on corner of The Causeway and Mill Street, entrance in Mill Street [164: SU466914] *Bus:* Thames Transit 32/A, Oxford 37 Oxford–BR Didcot Parkway (passing close BR Oxford) (tel. (0865) 727000 & 711312) *Station:* Didcot Parkway 5m

Shropshire

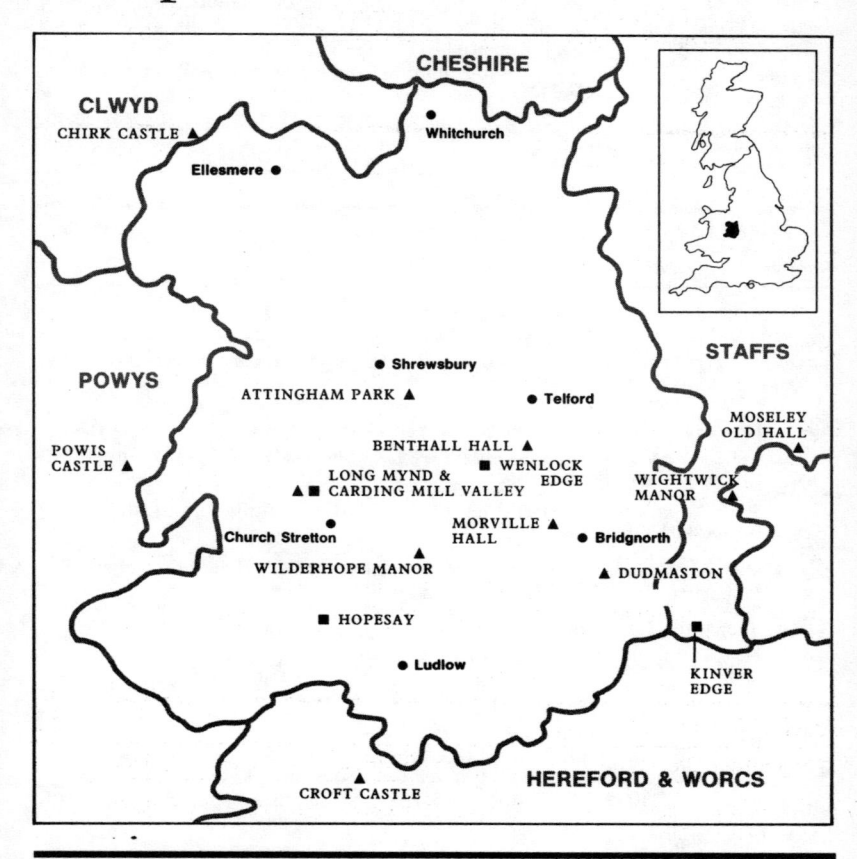

COUNTRYSIDE

Perhaps one of the most famous landmarks in this border county is the Long Mynd [137: SO430940] a heather-covered upland, of which the Trust owns some 5,850 acres. A good starting point is the **Carding Mill Valley** (see p.193) from which paths lead to the high moorland and its prehistoric remains which include burial mounds, hill-forts and the ancient Port Way track which traverses the hill. Vehicle access is by a steep road which is liable to congestion in summer. On fine days there are views from the summit to Snowdonia, the **Brecon Beacons** (see p.284), the **Clent Hills** and the Cotswolds. Wheelchair users may reach some viewpoints on the Long Mynd, and visit the shop and restaurant at Carding Mill Valley.

The patchwork of heather provides a home for the red grouse and for a variety of other

SHROPSHIRE

upland birds, including raven, buzzard and dipper, which are joined by wheatear and ring ouzel in the summer months.

Since 1981 the Trust has acquired about 550 acres of **Wenlock Edge** including **Easthope Wood** [138: SO570965], **Harley Bank** [127: SO605002], **Blakeway Coppice** [138: SO595988] and **Longville Coppice** [137: SO54899400]. This wooded limestone escarpment runs from Craven Arms to Ironbridge and is internationally famous for its geology, in particular its coral reef exposures. A rich limestone flora includes the wild service tree and nine species of orchid. Public and permitted paths traverse the Edge; the road along the escarpment gives extensive views and passes close by the Elizabethan Wilderhope Manor (see p.195). Exhibition in Much Wenlock Museum.

ATTINGHAM PARK

Shrewsbury SY4 4TP (0743) 709203

An elegant neo-Classical mansion of the late 18th century with magnificent state rooms, Italian furniture, Regency silver and impressive picture collection. The deer park was landscaped by Humphry Repton; there are good walks along the river and through the park all year

- **House:** 26 March to 28 Sept: Sat to Wed 1.30–5; BH Mon 11–5; also Oct: Sat & Sun 1.30–5. Last admissions to house 4.30. **Deer park & grounds:** daily (except Christmas Day) dawn to dusk

- House & Park £3.30. Family ticket £8.25. Park & grounds only £1.30. Parties by arrangement.

- Morning & evening opening for pre-booked parties; £100 minimum charge for party of 20 (£5 per person) incl. guided tour

- Shop same days as house 1.30–5

- Prior notice of visit appreciated; disabled visitors may be driven to entrance. Electric mobility vehicle available for use in grounds. Tea-room access difficult. WC at brewhouse. Lift available

- Braille and large print guides

- Light lunches and refreshments in tea-room same days as house 12.30–5, lunches 12.30–2.30. BH Mon 11–5. Licensed. Lunches & suppers at other times for pre-booked parties. Separate tea-room available. Picnic sites along Mile Walk

- Mother & baby room

- Education room available for pre-booked parties (max. 30 children); contact Education Assistant for details (0743) 709483. Park activity pack; park exhibition in bothy

- Details from Administrator; send s.a.e.

- No dogs in deer park, on leads in immediate vicinity of house

- 4m SE of Shrewsbury, on N side of the Telford road (B4380, formerly A5; from M54 B5061, then B4380) [126: SJ550099] *Bus:* Williamsons X96, Midland Red North 81/2 Shrewsbury–Telford/Wellington (all passing close BR Shrewsbury & Telford Central (tel. (0345 056) 785) *Station:* Shrewsbury 5m

SHROPSHIRE

BENTHALL HALL 🏠 ✝ ❁   ▨ ✖ ✉ ✦

Broseley TF12 5RX (0952) 882159

A 16th-century stone house with mullioned windows and moulded brick chimneys. The interior includes intricately carved oak staircase, decorated plaster ceilings and oak panelling; also family collections of furniture, ceramics and paintings. Plantsman's garden with additional areas now open. Tenants: Mr and Mrs J. Benthall. Restoration church

🅾	3 April to 28 Sept: Wed, Sun & BH Mon 1.30–5.30. Last admissions 5. House and/or garden for parties at other times by arrangement: Tues & Wed am
£	£3. Reduced rates for booked parties. Garden £2. Parking 150yds. Coaches by appointment
♿	Access to ground floor and parts of garden. WC. No wheelchairs available
👁	Braille guide; large print guide
🍽	Catering for groups by arrangement at Dudmaston (Wed only). No picnics in garden
E	Church services most Suns 3.15. Visitors welcome
🚫	No dogs
→	1m NW of Broseley (B4375), 4m NE of Much Wenlock, 6m S of Wellington [127: SJ658025] *Bus:* Midland Red North 39 Telford–Much Wenlock, to within ½m; 9 Telford–Bridgnorth, alight Broseley, 1m (both pass close BR Telford Central) (tel. (0345) 056 785) *Station:* Telford Central 7½m

CARDING MILL VALLEY & LONG MYND 🏞

Chalet Pavilion, Carding Mill Valley, Church Stretton SY6 6JG (0694) 722631

5,850 acres of historic moorland, part of the Long Mynd, extending for 4 miles, and including the Carding Mill Valley where the Trust has a café, shop & Information Centre in the Chalet Pavilion. The land rises to 1,700ft, providing magnificent views of the Shropshire and Cheshire plains and the Black Mountains

🅾	**Moorland: all year. Chalet Pavilion (café, shop & information centre):** 26 March to end June, & Sept: Tues to Sun & BH Mon 11–5 (shop 12–5); July to end Aug: daily 11–5 (shop 12–5); Oct: Sat & Sun 12–4 (shop 1–4). Booked parties at other times by arrangement
£	£1.50 per vehicle. (including coaches)
🚶	Guided walks in summer
🛍	See above for opening times
♿	Café, shop & information centre accessible. Parking immediately outside building
🍽	Light lunches & teas at the Chalet Pavilion. Seating capacity 80
👶	High chairs available

193

SHROPSHIRE

- Environmental education resource book available
- Must be kept under control on moorland; not admitted to the Chalet Pavilion
- 15m S of Shrewsbury, W of Church Stretton valley and A49; approached from Church Stretton and, on W side, from Ratlinghope or Asterton [137: SO443945] *Bus:* Midland Red West 435 Shrewsbury–Ludlow, alight Church Stretton, ½m (tel. (0345) 212 555) *Station:* Church Stretton (U) 1m

DUDMASTON

Quatt, nr Bridgnorth WV15 6QN (0746) 780866

Late 17th-century house with fine furniture; Dutch flower paintings, modern pictures, watercolours and botanical art, modern sculpture, family and natural history; lakeside garden and walk through the Dingle

- 27 March to 28 Sept: Wed & Sun only 2–5.30. Last admissions 5. Special opening for pre-booked parties only, Thur 2–5.30
- House & garden £3.50. Family £8. Garden only £2.50. Parking 100yds
- For pre-booked parties
- Shop open as house
- Ramp to entrance; access to main and inner halls, Library, Oak Room, No 1 & Darby galleries and Old Kitchen. Tea-room accessible. Special access arrangements; apply to Administrator; WC by car park

- Braille & large print guides for house and woodland; taped guide for house with cassette players
- Home made teas 2–5. Light lunches Sundays only 1–2. Light lunches for booked parties by arrangement on Wed and Thur
- High chair in tea-room. Baby slings available
- S.a.e. from administrator
- In Dingle and park only, on leads

SHROPSHIRE

→ 4m SE of Bridgnorth on A442 [138: SO746887] *Bus:* Midland Red West 297 Kidderminster–Bridgnorth (passing close BR Kidderminster) (tel. 0345 212 555) *Station:* Bridgnorth (Severn Valley Rly) 4m; Kidderminster 10m

MORVILLE HALL

nr Bridgnorth WV16 5BN

An Elizabethan house of mellow stone, converted in the 18th century. Attractive gardens

- By written appointment only with the tenant, Mrs J. K. Norbury
- For pre-booked parties
- Ground floor and most of garden accessible. No wheelchairs available
- [138: SO668940] *Bus:* Midland Red West 436/7 Shrewsbury, Bridgnorth (passing close BR Shrewsbury & Severn Valley Rly Bridgnorth) (tel. (0345) 212 555) *Station:* Bridgnorth (Severn Valley Rly) 3½m

TOWN WALLS TOWER

Shrewsbury, Shropshire SY1 1TN (Regional Office (074 377) 343)

The last remaining watchtower, built in the 14th century and overlooking the River Severn

- By written appointment only with the tenant, Mr A. Hector, 26a Town Walls, Shrewsbury
- A few minutes walk from town centre, on S of Town Walls *Bus:* from surrounding areas (tel. (0345) 056 785) *Station:* Shrewsbury ½m

WILDERHOPE MANOR

Longville, Much Wenlock TF13 6EG (0694) 771363

This limestone house stands on southern slope of Wenlock Edge in remote country with views down to Corvedale. Dating from 1586, it is unaltered but unfurnished; features include remarkable wooden spiral stairs, unique bow rack and fine plaster ceilings. Let to the Youth Hostels Association. Circular walk through farmland and woods

- April to end Sept: Wed & Sat 2–4.30. Oct to end March 1995: Sat only 2–4.30
- £1. No reduction for parties
- Access to house difficult
- Longville Arms, Longville (not NT); home cooked food
- Field Study Centre run by YHA
- On leads in area around Manor
- 7m SW of Much Wenlock, 7m E of Church Stretton, ½m S of B4371 [138: SO545929] *Station:* Church Stretton (U) 8m

195

Somerset

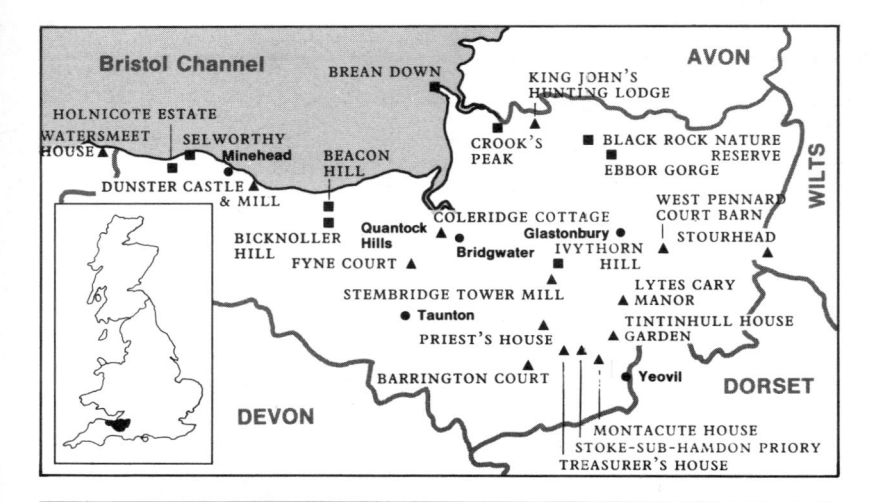

COAST AND COUNTRY

Just over the Somerset/Avon border, south-west of Weston-super-Mare, **Brean Down** forms the southern arm of Weston Bay, jutting out into the Bristol Channel [182: ST2959]. A steep path with steps cut into the hillside leads to the top of this limestone headland, once the site of a Roman temple. The ruins of a large 19th-century fort remain at the seaward end, built when it was feared that the French might sail up the Bristol Channel to attack the mainland. There is a bird sanctuary here, and good sea fishing from the rocks.

Further to the south-west on the southern edge of Bridgwater Bay the beautiful range of the Quantock Hills meets the sea at Quantoxhead. The Trust owns more than 1,100 acres of these hills; some of the more dramatic parts are **Beacon and Bicknoller Hills**, east of Williton – some 630 acres of moorland with the Iron Age fort of **Trendle Ring** which is an Ancient Monument. From these hills are magnificent views over the Bristol Channel, the Vale of Taunton Deane and Exmoor [181: ST125410/124397]. At **Fyne Court** (see p.200) there are three walks over the eastern Quantocks, taking in heathland, forest and farmland.

Inland to the east of the Quantocks the long low ridge of the Polden Hills overlooks Sedgemoor and Athelney – the large wetland area of Somerset once drained and used for agricultural purposes by the monks of Glastonbury Abbey. Glastonbury Tor dominates the area. At the summit (520ft) an excavation has recovered the plans of two superimposed churches of St Michael, of which only the 15th-century tower remains. One of the several small properties owned by the Trust in this area is **Ivythorn and Walton Hills**, 89 acres of high land and woodland on the A39 which runs along the crest of the Poldens [182: ST474348].

On Exmoor on the Somerset/Devon border the Trust owns the 12,400-acre **Holnicote Estate** [181: SS8844], including the high tors of Dunkery and Selworthy Beacons with breathtaking views in all directions, 15 farms and part or all of many small villages and hamlets, one of which is the beautiful model village of **Selworthy** with its cream cob walls, thatched roofs and lovely cottage gardens. There is a shop and information centre at Selworthy open 26 March to 30 Oct: Mon to Sat 10-5, Sun 2-5. Tel. (0643) 862745. The estate covers 4½ miles of coastline between Porlock Bay and Minehead. The South-West Peninsula Coastal Path which begins at Minehead curves inland to avoid the possibility of landslips in the Foreland sandstone which predominates at Hurlstone Point. The Trust has, however, made an alternative but tougher footpath on the cliff top which is recommended to more experienced walkers. There is a circular nature walk which begins and finishes at the car park at Webber's Post.

On the limestone Mendip Hills above Wells a smaller but no less interesting valley vies with the famous Cheddar Gorge (caves not NT). **Ebbor Gorge**, managed by English Nature, offers two nature walks, one takes ½ hour and is recommended to wheelchair users (strong pusher needed); the other takes 1½hrs and climbs to 800ft giving superb views. In this woodland badgers are plentiful and birds of prey such as buzzard and sparrowhawk may be seen. The caves are home to greater and lesser horseshoe bats [182: ST525485]. The Trust also owns the **Black Rock Nature Reserve**, managed by the Somerset Trust for Nature Conservation, at Cheddar and the northern slopes of Cheddar Gorge; a circular walk from the B3135 road at Black Rock Gate traverses plantations, natural woodland, limestone screen, rough downland and dramatic rock faces [182: ST468543].

Three miles west of Cheddar lies the only pointed hill in the Mendips, **Crook Peak**.

BARRINGTON COURT

Barrington, nr Ilminster TA19 0NQ (0460) 241938

The best example of Gertrude Jekyll garden within the National Trust's care. A beautiful garden laid out in a series of three rooms; the White Garden, the Iris Garden & the Lily Garden. The working kitchen garden has apple, pear & plum trees trained along high stone walls. The Tudor manor house was restored in the 1920s by the Lyle family. It is now let to Stuart Interiors

Note: The Iris garden will be fallowed during 1994

Barrington Court Garden: 26 March to 1 Oct: daily except Fri 11-5.30. Last admissions 5. **Court House:** 26 March to 1 Oct: Wed only 11-5.30 (last admission 5). Coach parties by appointment only – tel. (0985) 847777

continued

SOMERSET

£	£3.10, children £1.50. Parties £2.60, children £1.20. Court House: additional charge; adults £1, children 50p
♿	Garden & restaurant accessible, ideal for wheelchairs. Powered self-drive car available
👁	Braille guide
☕	Licensed restaurant facilities; fresh produce from kitchen garden. Lunches & cream teas: tel. (0460) 241244. Open as garden. Also available for functions and meetings
E	Outdoor theatre. For details ring the Events Organiser (0985) 847777
→	In Barrington village, 5m NE of Ilminster, on B3168. Visitors approaching from A303 follow signs for Ilminster town centre *Bus:* Southern National 32/3 Ilminster–South Petherton with connections from Taunton (passing close BR Taunton) (tel. (0823) 272033) *Station:* Crewkerne 7m

COLERIDGE COTTAGE

35 Lime Street, Nether Stowey, Bridgwater TA5 1NQ (0278) 732662

Coleridge's home for three years. It was here that he wrote The Rime of the Ancient Mariner, *part of* Christabel *and* Frost at Midnight

○	27 March to 2 Oct: Tues to Thur, & Sun 2–5 (parlour and reading room only shown). In winter by written application to the Custodian. Parties please book
£	£1.50, children 80p. No reduction for parties
☕	In village (not NT)
→	At W end of Nether Stowey, on S side of A39, 8m W of Bridgwater [181: ST191399] *Bus:* Southern National 15 Bridgwater–Nether Stowey/Minehead (passing close BR Bridgwater) (tel. (0823) 272033) *Station:* Bridgwater 8m

DUNSTER CASTLE

Dunster, nr Minehead TA24 6SL (0643) 821314

The fortified home of the Luttrell family for 600 years, with a 13th-century castle building below a Norman motte. The 17th-century mansion was remodelled by Salvin in 1870 but retains its fine staircase and plasterwork. There is a terraced garden of rare shrubs, and a 28-acre park

○	**Castle:** 26 March to 2 Oct: open daily except Thur & Fri (closed Good Fri) 11–5; also 3 Oct to 30 Oct: daily except Thur & Fri 11–4. **Garden and Park:** 1 Feb to 11 Dec daily: Feb, March, Oct, Nov, Dec 11–4; April to Sept 11–5; (open Good Fri). Last admissions in all cases $\frac{1}{2}$hr before closing
£	Castle, garden & park: £4.60, children (under 16) £2.30. Pre-booked parties £4.10. Garden & park only £2.50, children (under 16) £1.20. Family ticket to garden & park £6.50 (2 adults & up to 3 children); includes exploration trail. A 10 min. steep climb to Castle from car park, but electrically-powered vehicle available to give lifts when necessary

SOMERSET

- 🛍 Shop open daily 1 April to 2 Oct 11–5; 3 Oct to 18 Dec 11–4; 1 Jan to 31 Jan (weekends only) 11–4; 1 Feb to end March 11–4 weather permitting. Tel. (0643) 821626
- ♿ Castle & garden are situated on a steep hill and access is difficult, but not impossible with a strong companion. Volunteer-driven multi-seater and self-drive vehicle available from car park; close parking available by arrangement. Areas of the house can be visited via steps and assistance given if needed. WC near shop
- 👁 Braille guide. Guided tours by prior arrangement. Scented plants & flowers in conservatory & garden
- 🍴 In Dunster watermill and village (not NT). Picnic area in park, near car park
- 👶 Children's guidebook. Exploration trail in grounds
- 🏛 Study centre. Two outdoor trails
- **E** Civil War garrison weekend 4 & 5 June; no extra charge. For details of other outdoor events contact the Administrator
- 🐕 No dogs in garden. In park area on leads
- ➡ In Dunster, 3m SE of Minehead. NT car park approached direct from A39 [181: ST995435] *Bus:* Southern National 28 Taunton–Minehead (passing BR Taunton); 38/9 from Minehead. On all, alight Dunster Steep, ½m (tel. (0823) 272033) *Station:* Dunster (W Somerset Steam Rly) 1m

DUNSTER WORKING WATERMILL

Mill Lane, Dunster, nr Minehead TA24 6SW (0643) 821759

Built on the site of a mill mentioned in the Domesday Survey of 1086, the present mill dates from the 18th century and was restored to working order in 1979

- 🕐 April to end June: daily except Sat (open Easter Sat) 11–5. July & Aug: daily 11–5. Sept & Oct: daily except Sat 11–5
- £ £1.50, children 75p. Family tickets available; party rates by prior arrangement. The mill is run and maintained by private funding; NT members must pay normal admission charge. Parking, ¾m
- 👤 For groups by arrangement
- 🛍 Selling mill flour, museli & mill souvenirs
- ♿ Ground floor only at no charge
- 🍴 Tea-room and tea garden (not NT)
- **E** National Mills Day Sun 8 May: Mill in production. Opportunity to taste samples of products baked with mill flour. Normal admission charges apply
- ➡ On River Avill, beneath Castle Tor; approach via Mill Lane or Castle Gardens on foot; from car park in Dunster village or in old park [181: ST995435] *Bus/Rail:* as for Dunster Castle, above

REFER TO OPENING PAGES FOR GENERAL INFORMATION

SOMERSET

FYNE COURT

Broomfield, Bridgwater TA5 2EQ (0823) 451587

Headquarters of the Somerset Trust for Nature Conservation and visitor centre for the Quantocks. The former pleasure grounds of the now demolished home of the pioneer electrician, Andrew Crosse

- All year: daily 9–6 or sunset if earlier
- Free. Car park charge. Coach parking by prior arrangement only. Shop (not NT) open Easter to Christmas daily 2–5
- Trail for disabled visitors. Access to tea-room. WC
- Teas on Sun and Bank Holidays during summer (not NT). Picnic sites
- 6m N of Taunton at Broomfield; 6m SW of Bridgwater [182: ST222321] *Station:* Taunton 6m

KING JOHN'S HUNTING LODGE

The Square, Axbridge BS26 2AP (0934) 732012

An early Tudor merchant's house, extensively restored in 1971. The house is run as a museum by Sedgemoor District Council in co-operation with the Somerset County Museum and Axbridge Archaeological and Local History Society

- Easter to end Sept: daily 2–5
- £1, children 50p; school parties by arrangement. NT members free. Council car park, 2 min. walk
- In Axbridge (not NT)
- In the Square, on corner of High Street [182: ST431545] *Bus:* Badgerline 126, 826 Weston-super-Mare Wells (passing close BR Weston-super-Mare) (tel. (0934) 621201) *Station:* Worle 8m

LYTES CARY MANOR

Charlton Mackrell, Somerton TA11 7HU (Regional Office (0985) 847777)

A manor house with a 14th-century chapel, 15th-century hall and 16th-century great chamber. The home of Henry Lyte, translator of Niewe Herball *(1578). Hedged gardens with long herbaceous border*

- 26 March to 29 Oct: Mon, Wed & Sat 2–6 or dusk if earlier; last admissions 5.30
- £3.60, children £1.80. No reduction for parties. Unusual plants for sale

  Note: Large coaches cannot pass the gate piers so must stop in narrow road, ¼m walk. Coaches strictly by appointment only

SOMERSET

- ♿ Access to garden only. Scented plants in herbaceous borders; Braille guide. WC
- 🚸 Children's trail
- ➡ 1m N of Ilchester bypass A303; signposted from roundabout at junction of A303, A37 & A372 [183: ST529269] *Bus:* Badgerline 376 Bristol–Yeovil (passing BR Bristol Temple Meads) (tel. (0272) 553231); Southern National 54 Yeovil–Taunton (passing close BR Taunton) (tel. (0823) 272033). Both pass within ¾m BR Yeovil Pen Mill. On both, alight Kingsdon, 1m *Station:* Yeovil Pen Mill 8½m; Castle Cary 9m; Yeovil Junction 10m

MONTACUTE HOUSE 🏠 ❋ ♣
Montacute TA15 6XP (0935) 823289

A magnificent Elizabethan house, with an H-shaped ground plan and many Renaissance features, including contemporary plasterwork, chimneypieces and heraldic glass. The house contains fine 17th- and 18th-century furniture, an exhibition of samplers dating from the 17th century, and Elizabethan and Jacobean portraits from the National Portrait Gallery displayed in the Long Gallery and adjoining rooms. The formal garden includes mixed borders and old roses; also, a landscaped park

Note: For conservation reasons some rooms in the House do not have electric light. Visitors wishing to make close study of tapestries, textiles or paintings should avoid visiting on dull days

- ⭕ **House:** 26 March to 30 Oct: daily except Tues 12–5.30. Last admission 5. Closed Good Fri. **Garden and park:** 26 March to March 1995: daily except Tues 11.30–5.30 or dusk if earlier
- £ House, garden & park: £4.70, children £2.40. Parties £4.40, children £2.20. Garden and park only £2.60, children £1.20. No reduction for parties; from Nov to March 1995 £1.20; book in writing with s.a.e. to the Administrator
- 🛍 Open same days as house 11.30–5.30; closed Good Fri; also 2 Nov to 18 Dec, Wed to Sun 11.30–4.30; 1–31 March 1995, daily except Tues, 11.30–4.30. Tel. (0935) 824575. Plant centre (not NT) selling interesting and unusual locally grown plants: April to end Sept: daily except Tues 2–6
- ♿ Access to garden, restaurant & shop only; House difficult with many steps; WC; 2 wheelchairs; self-drive vehicle
- 👁 Braille guide; fragrant plants & shrubs
- 🍴 Licensed restaurant; light lunches and teas open as shop. Tel. (0935) 826294. Party organisers: please book lunches & teas in writing to the Administrator
- E For details of outdoor concerts & events write to the Administrator (with s.a.e.). Montacute Horse Trials 9 & 10 July. Enquiries tel. (0963) 32750
- 🐕 In park only, on leads
- ➡ In Montacute village, 4m W of Yeovil, on S side of A3088, 3m E of A303 [183 & 193: ST499172] *Bus:* Safeway/Stennings Yeovil–South Petherton (passing within¾m BR Yeovil Pen Mill) tel. (0823) 255696 *Station:* Yeovil Pen Mill 5½m; Yeovil Junction 7m; Crewkerne 7m

SOMERSET

PRIEST'S HOUSE 🏠 　　　　　　　　　　　　　　　　　🚫 ✖ ✖

Muchelney, Langport TA10 0DQ (0458) 252621

A late medieval hall house with large Gothic windows, originally the residence of priests serving the parish church across the road, recently refurbished

- 🅞　27 March to 1 Oct: Sun & Mon 2-5
- 💷　£1.30. No reductions for parties or children. No WCs
- ➡　1m S of Langport [193: ST429250] *Bus:* Southern National 54 Yeovil–Taunton (passing close BR Taunton & within ¼m Yeovil Pen Mill), alight Huish Episcopi, ¼m (tel. (0823) 272033)

STEMBRIDGE TOWER MILL ✖ 　　　　　　　　　　　🚫 ✖

High Ham TA10 9DJ (0458) 250818

The last thatched windmill in England, dating from 1822 and in use until 1910

- 🅞　27 March to 28 Sept: Sun, Mon & Wed 2-5; special arrangements may be made for coach and school parties
- 💷　£1.50, children 80p. Parties by prior appointment with the tenant; no reduction. Parking for coaches ¼m. No WCs
- ➡　2m N of Langport, ½m E of High Ham [182: ST432305] take the Somerton road from Langport and follow High Ham signs. *Bus:* Southern National 54 Yeovil–Taunton (passing close BR Taunton & within ¼m Yeovil Pen Mill), alight Langport, 2½m (tel. (0823) 272033) *Station:* Bridgwater 10m

STOKE-SUB-HAMDON PRIORY 🏠 　　　　　　　　　🚫 ✖

North Street, Stoke-sub-Hamdon TA4 6QP (Regional Office (0985) 847777)

A complex of buildings, begun in the 14th century for the priests of the chantry chapel of St Nicholas, which is now destroyed

- 🅞　All year, daily 10-6 or dusk if earlier. Great Hall only open
- 💷　Free
- ➡　Between A303 and A3088. 2m W of Montacute between Yeovil and Ilminster *Bus:* Safeway Yeovil–South Petherton (passing within ¼m BR Yeovil Pen Mill) (tel. (0460) 40309) *Station:* Crewkerne or Yeovil Pen Mill, both 7m

SOMERSET

TINTINHULL HOUSE GARDEN

Farm St, Tintinhull, Yeovil BA22 9PZ (0935) 822545

A 20th-century formal garden surrounding a 17th-century house. The garden layout, divided into areas by walls and hedges, has border colour, plant themes, and a kitchen garden

- 26 March to 29 Sept: Tues, Wed, Thur, Sat, Sun & BH Mon 2–6
- £3.30; children £1.60. No reduction for parties. Coach parties by arrangement in advance with the Gardener
- Parking in courtyard by arrangement.
- Roses, honeysuckles and other scented plants
- In courtyard, not NT
- 5m NW of Yeovil, ½m S of A303, on E outskirts of Tintinhull [183: ST503198] *Bus:* Southern National 52 from Yeovil (passing within ¼m BR Yeovil Pen Mill) (tel. (0935) 76233) *Station:* Yeovil Pen Mill 5½m; Yeovil Junction 7m

TREASURER'S HOUSE

Martock TA12 6JL (Regional Office (0985) 847777)

A small house dating from 13th and 14th centuries, with a medieval hall and kitchen, recently refurbished by the Trust

- By written appointment. Tel. Regional Office (0985) 847777
- Medieval hall and kitchen only £1.30. No reduction for children or parties. No WCs
- In Martock (not NT)
- Opposite church in middle of village; 1m NW of A303 between Ilminster and Ilchester [193: ST462191] *Bus:* Southern National 52 from Yeovil (passing within ¼m BR Yeovil Pen Mill) (tel. (0935) 76233) *Station:* Crewkerne 7½m; Yeovil Pen Mill 8m

WEST PENNARD COURT BARN

West Pennard, nr Glastonbury BA6 8NL (Regional Office (0935) 847777)

A 15th-century barn of five bays with a roof of interesting construction. Repaired and given by the Society for the Protection of Ancient Buildings 1938

- By written application to Mr P. H. Green, Court Barn Farm, West Bradley, Somerset
- Free
- 3m E of Glastonbury, 7m S of Wells, 1½m S of West Pennard (A361) [182/183: ST547370] *Bus:* Badgerline 378/9 Wells–Glastonbury, to within 1m (tel. (0934) 621201) *Station:* Castle Cary 8m

203

Staffordshire

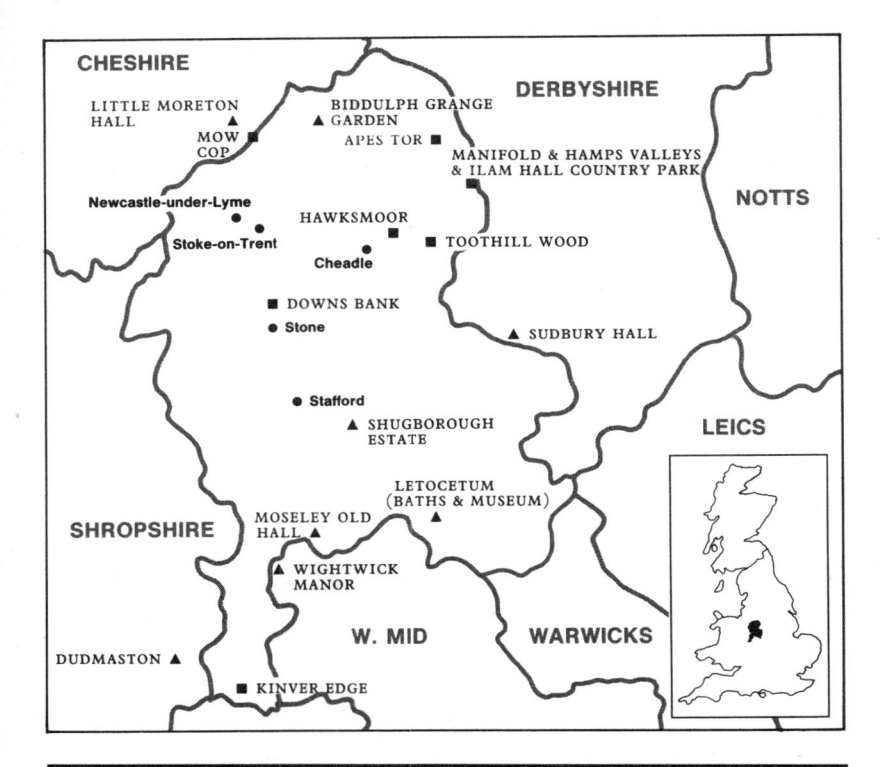

COUNTRYSIDE

On the Staffordshire/Derbyshire Peak District borders is **Apes Tor**, a rock face in the gorge of the River Manifold below Hulme End [119: SK100586]. It is of particular geological interest since it shows clearly the folding and faulting processes that have formed this part of the southern Peak District landscape.

The Trust owns over 1,000 acres of farmland and rock hills in the **Manifold** and **Hamps Valleys** (Staffordshire) and **Dovedale** (Staffordshire & Derbyshire see also p.81). The Manifold and Hamps are beautiful, but lesser known perhaps than their sister river, the Dove. In dry weather they vanish underground down 'swallet' holes in the limestone, leaving a dry watercourse for some miles until they reappear at Ilam. These river valleys support a wide range of limestone loving plants, and dippers and kingfisher haunt their waters. At Wetton Mill (NT) on the Manifold is a car park and refreshments (not NT). A well-surfaced, disused railway with adjacent car parks, gives good access to the Manifold and Hamps Valleys. The Manifold joins the Dove between Ilam and Thorpe, near **Ilam Hall** (see p.206).

STAFFORDSHIRE

A fourth river, the Churnet, flows through **Hawksmoor** [128: SK035445], an area of some 300 acres of woodlands and farmland. There are several walks through Hawksmoor, including a nature trail.

Further south near Alton Towers (not NT), a recent gift to the Trust was 10 acres of **Toothill Wood** [128: SK066425]. The property includes part of the Staffordshire Way long-distance footpath, and the viewpoint of Toothill Rock.

To the south-west and not far from the industrial landscape of Stoke-on-Trent is **Downs Banks** [127: SJ902370] just north of Stone – undulating moorland with a stream, given to the Trust as a war memorial in 1946.

BIDDULPH GRANGE GARDEN

Biddulph Grange, Biddulph, Stoke-on-Trent ST8 7SD (0782) 517999

An exciting and rare survival of a high Victorian garden, acquired by the Trust in 1988 and focus of an extensive restoration project. Conceived by James Bateman, the 15 acres are divided into a number of smaller gardens designed to house specimens from his extensive and wide-ranging plant collection. An Egyptian Court, Chinese Pagoda, Joss House, Bridge and Pinetum, together with many other settings, all combine to make the garden a miniature tour of the world

Note: at weekends and Bank Holidays in the high season, the garden and tea-room can be very crowded

- 30 March to 30 Oct: Wed to Fri 12-6, Sat, Sun & BH Mon 11-6 (closed Good Fri). Last admissions 5.30 or dusk if earlier. Also open 5 Nov to 18 Dec: Sat & Sun 12-4
- £3.90. Family ticket £9.75. Pre-booked guided tours £5 (NT members incl.). Free car park 50yds. Coach party organisers must book in advance
- Pre-booked guided tours in groups of 10 or more, at 10 on Wed, Thur & Fri
- Shop open as garden
- Access for disabled visitors extremely difficult; unsuitable for wheelchairs but access possible to tea-room & terrace with views over garden. Please contact Garden Office for details. WC
- Suitable for accompanied visually impaired visitors, with care. Braille & large print guides
- Tea-room serving coffee, teas and light refreshments open as garden. Light lunches 12-2. Seating for 50. Last admissions 5.30. Picnics in car park only
- 2 high chairs in tea-room
- School visits by arrangement
- No dogs in garden, car park only
- ½m N of Biddulph, 3½ SE of Congleton, 7m N of Stoke on Trent. Access from A527 (Tunstall/Congleton Road). Entrance on Grange Road [118: SJ895591]. *Bus:* PMT 6A/B from Hanley; C-Line 26, 86-8 from Congleton (passing BR Congleton) (tel. (0785) 223344) *Station:* Congleton 2½m

REFER TO OPENING PAGES FOR GENERAL INFORMATION

STAFFORDSHIRE

ILAM HALL COUNTRY PARK ✝ ● ♨ ⓘ

Ilam, Ashbourne, Derbyshire DE6 2AZ (033 529) 245

84 acres of attractive park and woodland on both banks of the river Manifold, in the South Peak Estate, with magnificent views towards Thorpe Cloud and the entrance to Dovedale

◯	**Grounds and Park:** all year, daily. Hall is let to YHA and is not open
£	Free. Car park £1 (NT members free); minibuses & coaches £1.50; no coaches Sun or BH Mon
ⓘ	Guided walks around the estate may be booked by groups; contact Head Warden, tel. (033 529) 503
⌂	Shop and Information Centre with an exhibition on Ilam and the South Peak Estate. 8 Jan to 26 March: Sat & Sun 11–4; 27 March to 22 Oct; daily 10.30–5.30; 23 Oct to 18 Dec: Sat & Sun 11–4; Jan to end March 1995: Sat & Sun 11–4
♿	Access to Information Centre. WC. No wheelchair available
☕	Manifold Tea-room open for selection of light refreshments & teas. Open 8 Jan to 26 March: Sat & Sun 11–4; 27 March to 22 Oct: Fri to Tues 10.30–5.30; 23 Oct to 18 Dec: Sat & Sun 11–4. Seats 60; children's portions available
▮	Day Visit room, resource material, illustrated talks and guided walks available for educational groups. Further details from the Educational Co-ordinator, South Peak Estate Office, Home Farm (tel. (033 529) 503)
E	*Note*: Small caravan site run by Caravan Club (no WCs), open to non-members of Caravan Club; Easter to mid Oct, tel. (033 529) 310. Lightweight camp site for back-packers (overnight stay only); no facilities; no groups. Book with Caravan Club site warden (see above)
🐕	On leads only
→	4½m NW of Ashbourne [119: SK132507] *Bus:* Warrington 443 from Ashbourne, Thur & Sat only, with connections from Derby; also various services from BR Buxton and Derby, summer Suns only; otherwise GM 201 Derby–Manchester (passing close BR Derby & Macclesfield), alight Ilam Cross Roads, 2m (tel. (0332) 292200)

KINVER EDGE ♨ ⓘ

The Warden's Lodge, The Compa, Kinver, nr Stourbridge DY7 6HU (0384) 872418

293 acres of wood and heath-covered sandstone ridge from which are views across Shropshire and the West Midlands. Rock houses, inhabited until 1950s: one rebuilt in 1993 for resident tenants (not open to public)

◯	Kinver Edge open all year. Rock house grounds open: April to Sept 9–7. Oct to March 9–4. Upper terrace open by prior appointment with the Custodian (tel. (0384) 872553)
£	Free

STAFFORDSHIRE

- ♿ Wheelchair access to a limited part of the Edge – restricted in the rock house area
- 🐕 On lead within grounds of rock house
- → 5m E of Stourbridge, 6m N of Kidderminster. 2½m off A458 [138: SO836836] *Bus*: West Midlands Travel/Midland Red West 242 BR Stourbridge–Kinver (tel. 021 200 2700) *Station*: Stourbridge Town 5m

MOSELEY OLD HALL

Moseley Old Hall Lane, Fordhouses, Wolverhampton WV10 7HY (0902) 782808

An Elizabethan house with later alterations. Charles II hid here after the battle of Worcester, and the bed in which he slept is on view, as well as the hiding place he used. The small garden has been reconstructed in 17th-century style with formal box parterre; 17th-century plants only are grown. The property is a Sandford Heritage Education Award winner

- ◯ 26 March to 30 Oct: Wed, Sat, Sun & BH Mon; also Tues in July & Aug 2–5.30 (BH Mon 11–5). Pre-booked parties at other times incl. evening tours
- £ £3.20. Family ticket £8. Reduced rate for booked parties
- 👤 Optional free guided tours
- 🛍 Shop open as house. Also 6 Nov to 18 Dec: Sun only 2–4.30
- ♿ Access to ground floor (3 rooms) and garden only. Two tables for wheelchair users on ground floor of tea-room. WC in garden. No wheelchairs available
- 👁 Braille & large print guides
- ☕ Tea-room in 18th-century barn. Teas, as house 2–5.30. Light lunches May to Sept: Sun & BH Mon only from 12.30. Christmas shop & tea-room open 6 Nov to 18 Dec: Sun 2–4.30. Other times for parties by prior arrangement (licensed). Seating for 40
- 🎭 Education programme includes living history
- E Programme available from Administrator: please send s.a.e.   *continued*

STAFFORDSHIRE

→ 4m N of Wolverhampton; S of M54 between A449 and A460; traffic from N on M6 leave motorway at Shareshill, then A460; 2½m S of Shareshill island; traffic from S on M6 & M54 take Jn. 1 to Wolverhampton; coaches must approach via A460 to avoid low bridge [127: SJ932044] *Bus:* Chaserider 870-2 Wolverhampton–Cannock, alight Bognop Road, ¼m; Stephensons 613 from Wolverhampton, thence ¼m (all pass close BR Wolverhampton) (tel. 021-200 2700) *Station:* Wolverhampton 4m

SHUGBOROUGH ESTATE
Milford, nr Stafford ST17 0XB (0889) 881388

The Shugborough Estate is being restored as a 19th-century working estate. Shugborough Hall is the magnificent 900-acre seat of the Earls of Lichfield. The house was enlarged c.1750, and altered by Samuel Wyatt 1790–1806, with collections of French and English china, silver, paintings and furniture, and rococo plasterwork by Vassalli. The Servants' Quarters in the stable block house the original kitchens and butlers pantry, laundry and restored working brew-house. In the parkland the Georgian farmstead built in 1805 for Thomas, Viscount Anson as home farm for the estate, is now a working farm museum with rare breeds, restored working corn mill and demonstrations of traditional farming methods. There are Victorian terraces, an Edwardian rose garden and extensive parkland, including neo Classical monuments

Shugborough is financed and administered by Staffordshire County Council. NT members are entitled to free entry to Mansion House, reduced rate to Servants' Quarters & Farm and must pay site admission charge per vehicle and any special event charge which may be in operation. Admission charges and opening arrangements may vary when special events are held. Tel. property for details of 1994 events programme

- **House, Servants' Quarters, Farm and Gardens:** 26 March to 28 Oct: daily 11–5. Open daily all year from 10.30 for booked parties, but not weekends from 31 Oct to 24 March 1995. (Servants' Quarters, Farm, Gardens and tours of house: tel. property for details)

- Parkland £1.50 per vehicle (NT members incl.), coaches free, giving access to parkland, gardens, picnic area and walks and trails. Free car park at Farm for Farm visitors. House £3.50 (NT members free), concessions £2; Farm £3.50 (NT members and concessions £2); Servants' Quarters £3 (NT members and concessions £2); All sites £7.50 (concessions £5). *Note:* concessions apply to children, OAPs, registered unemployed and parties. Guided walks and trails for booked parties throughout the year £3 per head. Evening visits for booked parties (min. 30) £4 per site plus cost of supper. Guided tours available for school parties at £1.50 per head per site (all 3 sites for £4); working demonstrations available from Oct to Easter; schools must book in advance

- Available throughout year; evening guided tours and garden tours also available. Range of connoisseur talks and tours designed for special-interest groups

- NT Shop at main site (tel. (0889) 882122). Open 26 March to 28 Oct: daily 11–5. NT shop also open 31 Oct to 16 Dec: Mon to Fri 11–4; also Sun 20 Nov to 18 Dec

STAFFORDSHIRE

- Servants' Quarters and Farm accessible (reduced charge); access can be arranged to ground floor of house for wheelchair by way of step-climber. WC. Staff trained in basic sign language. Tours can be adapted to your special needs. Self-drive cars and wheelchairs available
- Braille, taped & large print guides
- Lunches, high teas and snacks in café on main site; dinners available to pre-booked parties (min. 20). Tea-room at farm for light refreshments open as house. Picnic sites by main and farm car parks. Main site car park picnic area features special picnic tables for wheelchair users
- Farm gives children chance to see and touch domestic and rare breeds of animal and poultry. Games gallery in corn mill. Children's play area. Quiz books available from each site. Holiday Club programme
- Extensive schools and adult demonstration programme. Education rooms can be booked at each of the three sites. Holiday Club activities
- A wide range of events, incl. open-air concerts, and themed activities, Christmas evenings and Bank Holiday craft festivals available throughout the year
- On lead in parkland only. Guide dogs: House and Servants' Quarters
- Signed from M6; 6m E of Stafford on A513; entrance at Milford. Pedestrian access from E, from the canal/Little Haywood side of the Estate [127: SJ992225] *Bus:* Chaserider 5, 822/3/5 Stafford–Lichfield (passing close BR Lichfield City) (tel. (0785) 223344) *Station:* Stafford 6m

WALL ROMAN SITE (LETOCETUM)

Watling Street, Wall, nr Lichfield (0543) 480768

The excavated bath-house of a Roman posting station on Watling Street; the most complete example of its kind in Britain. Interesting museum

The wall is owned by the National Trust and managed and maintained by English Heritage

- 1 April to 31 Oct: daily 10–6
- Museum & site £1.25, children 60p. OAPs and UB40 holders 95p. Free admission to English Heritage members. Parties of 11 or more 15% discount. Schools free bookings (tel. (0604) 730332)
- *Note:* Informal talk given in museum for small parties only, on prior request
- Open same times as property
- Access to Museum only. Site on uneven ground
- Free entry for education groups who book in advance
- Details of events programme available from property (s.a.e. please)
- On leads only
- 2m SW of Lichfield, on N side of A5 [139: SK099066] *Station:* Shenstone 1½m

Suffolk

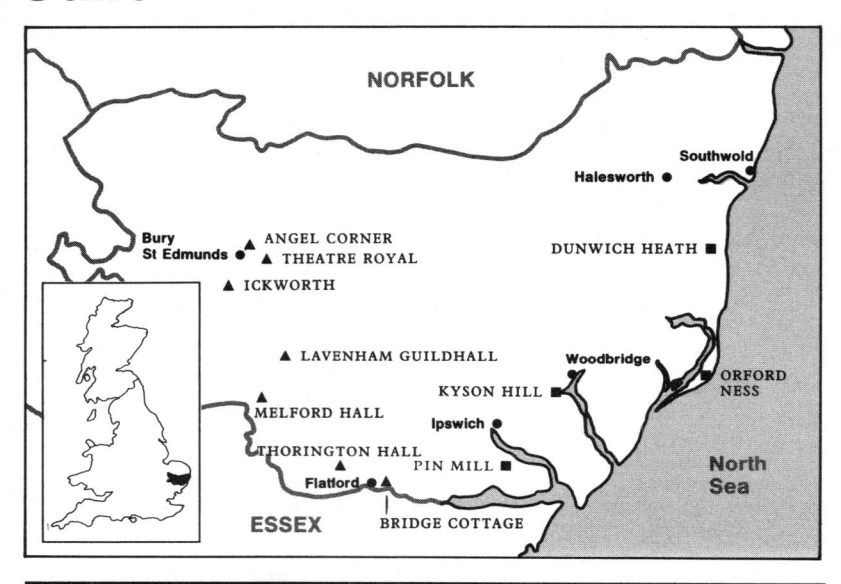

COAST AND COUNTRYSIDE

Dunwich Heath is described fully in the entry on p.211. At **Kyson Hill** just south of Woodbridge, there are lovely views of the winding River Deben from 4 acres of parkland, with fine walks [169: TM269477]. The Trust purchased 5 miles of **Orford Ness** (1550 acres) from the Ministry of Defence at the end of March 1993. There will be no public access on to the property until it has been cleared up and made safe for visitors. However there will be some special Members open days during 1994; contact the East Anglia Regional Office for details. It is hoped that regular access on foot (via ferry from Orford) will be opened during the summer of 1995.

Further south near Chelmondiston Village on the Orwell **Pin Mill**, a well-known beauty spot for visitors from Ipswich. This natural woodland is accessible on foot in any weather, and there are fine views of the river and an extremely varied collection of fishing boats, Thames barges and pleasure craft of all types are drawn up on the shore; waymarked walk [169: TM214380].

SMALL COPPER

SUFFOLK

ANGEL CORNER 🏛   🚫🚫

8 Angel Hill, Bury St Edmunds (Regional Office (0263) 733471)

A Queen Anne house leased to the Borough of St Edmundsbury

🅾	Open by appointment only. Further details from East Anglia Regional Office
£	Free. No WCs
➡	Directions needed [155: TL855643] *Bus:* From surrounding areas (tel. (0473) 265676) *Station:* Bury St Edmunds ½m

DUNWICH HEATH 🛏 🚗 🚶 🏃

Dunwich, Saxmundham IP17 3DJ From Aug 94: (0728) 648505

215 acres of Sandlings heathland with sandy cliffs and a mile of beach. One of Suffolk's most important conservation areas with good walks from the property and access to a public hide at the adjacent Minsmere Reserve. Information and observation room in the converted Coastgurard Cottages which also have a tea-room, shop and three holiday flats for rent

🅾	All year: dawn to dusk. Introductory talks available for group visits
£	Parking charge: coaches £6; season tickets £10; cars (pay & display) £1; July & Aug £1.50. Members should display membership card on dashboard or obtain pass from Coastguard Cottages
	Note: Day and season tickets for coarse fishing; sea angling
🏃	On request for groups
🛍	Shop: April, May, June, Sept & Oct: Wed to Sun 11–5; July & Aug: daily 11–5.30; Nov to end March: Sat & Sun only 11–4 (closed Christmas & New Year), open all BH Mons
♿	Car park viewing point and some footpaths accessible. Please contact the Warden for further information. Adapted WC at Coastguard Cottages; stairlift to viewing room. Self-drive powered car available. Holiday flat for disabled guests at the Coastguard Cottages
🍽	Tea-room in Coastguard Cottages, open as shop; also take away service June & Sept: Mon & Tues. Capacity 43 plus benches outside
👶	Tea-room: children's menu, baby food, high chairs, scribble boards
📚	Education Officer and Education Base
E	Send s.a.e. to Warden for list
🐕	Must be under tight control
➡	1m S of Dunwich, signposted off Dunwich to Westleton road [156: TM475683] *Bus:* Suffolk Bus 99A/B Ipswich–Lowestoft, summer Suns only (tel. (0473) 265676) *Station:* Darsham 6m

REFER TO OPENING PAGES FOR GENERAL INFORMATION

SUFFOLK

FLATFORD: BRIDGE COTTAGE

Flatford, East Bergholt, Colchester, Essex CO7 6OL (0206) 298260/298865

Just upstream from Flatford Mill, the restored thatched cottage houses a display about John Constable, several of whose paintings depict this property. Facilities include a tea garden, shop; boat hire and an Information Centre. Access by foot to Trust land in the Dedham Vale

Note: Flatford Mill, Valley Farm & Willy Lott's House are leased to the Field Studies Council which runs arts based courses for all age groups. For further information on courses tel. (0206) 298283. There is no general public access to the buildings, but the Field Studies Council will arrange tours for groups

- March to end May & Oct: Wed to Sun & BH Mon 11-5.30. June to end Sept: daily 10-5.30 (closed Good Fri). Nov: Wed to Sun 11-3.30
- Guided tours £1.50, accompanied children free. Parking 200yds; private car park, charge (NT members included). Free admission to Bridge Cottage
- Guided tours of the area: 2-4 April and every afternoon June to end Sept
- Shop open as cottage
- Close car parking; please ask for temporary permit. Access to tea garden and shop. Wheelchair and walking aid available at Bridge Cottage
- Teas & light lunches as cottage 10-5.30. Capacity 120
- Tea-room; children's menu, baby food, high chairs, scribble sheets
- No dogs in Bridge Cottage complex (guide dogs only)
- On N bank of Stour, 1m S of East Bergholt (B1070). [168: TM077332] *Bus:* Eastern Counties/Carters/Ipswich Buses 92-6 Ipswich–Colchester (passing BR Ipswich and close BR Colchester Town), alight E Bergholt, ¾m (tel. (0473) 265676) *Station:* Manningtree 1¾m by footpath, 3½m by road

ICKWORTH HOUSE, PARK & GARDEN

Ickworth, The Rotunda, Horringer, Bury St Edmunds IP29 5QE (0284) 735270

The eccentric Earl of Bristol (also Bishop of Derry) created this equally eccentric house, started in 1795 to display his collections. The paintings include works by Titian, Gainsborough and Velasquez and the magnificent Georgian Silver Collection is displayed in the oval Rotunda which is linked by curved corridors to flanking wings. The house is surrounded by an Italianate Garden and set in a Capability Brown Park with several waymarked woodland walks and a deer enclosure with hide

- **House:** 26 March to 30 Oct: Tues, Wed, Fri, Sat, Sun & BH Mon 1.30-5.30. **Park:** all year: daily 7-7. Closed Good Fri
- House, garden & park £4.30, children £2. Parties £3.50 (no party rate Sun & BH Mon). Access to park & garden £1.50, children 50p (access to shop & restaurant with park ticket)
- Shop same days as house 12-5.30. Also 5 Nov to 18 Dec: Sat & Sun 11-4

SUFFOLK

♿	Disabled visitors may be driven to the house. Access to house via 2 steps; then all ground floor rooms are level. Much of garden accessible, but gravel drive and paths. WC. Shop & restaurant in basement not accessible to wheelchair users
📖	Braille guide
☕	Lunches & teas; table licence, open as shop (Nov & Dec 11-4; Sat & Sun) Capacity: 60, plus overflow: 50
🚼	Children's playground next to car park. Children's guide. Baby slings available. Restaurant: children's menu, baby foods, high chairs, scribble books
🏫	School groups welcome & lecture room available
E	Events most weekends throughout the season. Contact the Property Manager's Office for details
🐕	In park only, on leads
→	In Horringer, 3m SW of Bury St Edmunds on W side of A143 [155: TL8161] *Bus:* Eastern Counties 141-4 Bury St Edmunds–Haverhill (passing close BR Bury St Edmunds) (tel. (0473) 265676) *Station:* Bury St Edmunds 3m

LAVENHAM: THE GUILDHALL OF CORPUS CHRISTI

Market Place, Lavenham, Sudbury CO10 9QZ (0787) 247646

This early 16th-century timber framed Tudor building, originally the hall of the Guild of Corpus Christi, overlooks and dominates the market place. Within the nine rooms of the Guildhall are displays of local history, farming, industry and the development of the railway, and a unique exhibition of 700 years of the medieval woollen cloth trade. There is a delightful walled garden with a 19th-century lock up and mortuary

🅾	26 March to 30 Oct: daily 11-5 (closed Good Fri). The building, or parts of it, may be closed occasionally for community purposes *continued*

SUFFOLK

- **£** £2.40. Children: first two free then 60p. Parties £2. School parties 50p by prior arrangement; all children free during school summer holidays
- 🛍 Shop open as Guildhall. Also 3 Nov to 18 Dec: Thur to Sun 11-4
- ♿ Access to shop & tea-room only
- ☕ Tea-room for coffee, light lunches & teas. April: Sat & Sun. May to Sept: Tues to Sun & BH Mon. Oct: Wed to Sun 11-5. Capacity: 43
- 👶 Children's guide. Tea-room: children's menu, baby foods, high chairs, scribble boards
- ➡ A1141 and B1071 [155: TL917494] *Bus:* Chambers Bury St Edmunds–Colchester (passing close BR Bury St Edmunds); Ipswich Buses 757 BR Colchester–Lavenham, Sun only. All pass close BR Sudbury (tel. (0473) 265676) *Station:* Sudbury (U) 7m

MELFORD HALL

Long Melford, Sudbury CO10 9AH (0787) 880286

A turreted brick Tudor mansion, little changed since 1578 with the original panelled banqueting hall, an 18th-century drawing room, a Regency library and a Victorian bedroom, showing fine furniture and Chinese porcelain. There is also a special Beatrix Potter display and a garden

- 🕐 April: Sat, Sun & BH Mon 2-5.30; May to end Sept: Wed, Thur, Sat, Sun & BH Mon 2-5.30; Oct: Sat & Sun 2-5.30
- **£** Principal rooms & garden £2.70. Pre-arranged parties £2.30 Wed & Thur only, please book with s.a.e. to Administrator
- ♿ Disabled visitors may be driven to the Hall. Ground floor rooms easily accessible; stairlift available to first floor. Some steps in garden. WC (by main entrance)
- ☕ In Long Melford
- 👶 Children's guide

SUFFOLK

→ In Long Melford on E side of A134, 14m S of Bury St Edmunds, 3m N of Sudbury [155: TL867462] *Bus:* Beestons/Chambers various services (but frequent) from Sudbury; Eastern National 601 Colchester–Saffron Walden & Ipswich Buses 757 BR Colchester–Lavenham (Sundays). All pass close BR Sudbury (tel. (0473) 265676) *Station:* Sudbury (U) 4m

THEATRE ROYAL
Westgate Street, Bury St Edmunds IP33 1QR (0284) 755127

Built in 1819 by William Wilkins, a rare example of a late Georgian playhouse with fine pit, boxes and gallery. Theatre Royal is a working theatre and presents a year-round programme of professional drama, comedy, dance music, mime, pantomime and amateur work. It boasts a national reputation and attracts the best touring companies in the country. For programme details ring (0284) 755469

- ○ All year: daily except Sun, 10–8 (closed every BH except for performances). No access to auditorium if theatrical activity is in progress
- £ Free. Ticket prices for performances in brochures. Limited parking in Westgate Street. No parking in front of the theatre
- 🎓 Organised guided tours and talks are available by prior arrangement. Ring (0284) 755127 to book (fee)
- 🛍 Wide selection of souvenirs available in Box Office
- ♿ Induction loop system available. Signed performances. Limited wheelchair access. Tel. (0284) 769505 for full details
- 🍽 Meals; licensed bar in theatre for all performances
- 📖 Tel. (0284) 755127 for details of education initiatives and teachers' magazine
- E For 1994 events programme please send s.a.e. to Administrator. Box Office (0284) 769505
- 🐕 No dogs
- → On Westgate Street on S side of A134 from Sudbury (one-way system) [155: TL855637] *Bus:* From surrounding areas (tel. (0473) 265676) *Station:* Bury St Edmunds ¾m

THORINGTON HALL
Stoke by Nayland, Colchester CO6 4SS (Regional Office (0263) 733471)

Oak framed, plastered, gabled house built in about 1600 and extended around 1700

- ○ By written appointment with the tenant
- 🐕 No dogs
- → 2m SE of Stoke by Nayland [155: TM013355] *Bus:* Hedingham 84, Carters 755 Colchester–Stoke by Nayland (passing BR Colchester), thence 1¼m (tel. (0473) 265676) *Station:* Colchester 7m

215

Surrey

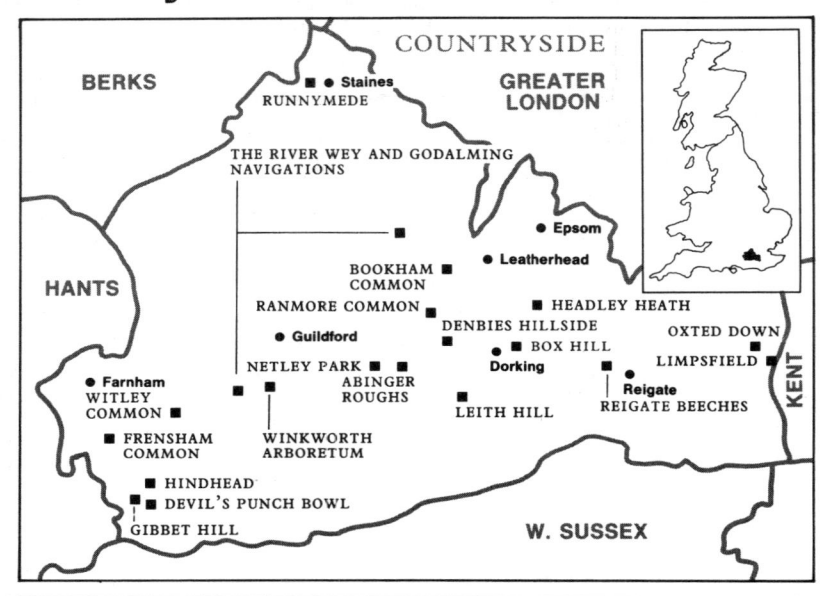

COUNTRYSIDE

The Trust owns a great deal of common land in Surrey and some famous viewpoints such as **Box Hill** (see p.217) and **Leith Hill, Coldharbour Common, Duke's Warren and the Rhododendron Wood** (see p.221). There are many lesser known properties, which are just as beautiful. **Bookham and Banks Commons** west of Leatherhead [187: TQ1256] are of particular interest for their rich bird life. The manor of Bocheham is known to have been owned by Chertsey Abbey as early as 666 AD, and in the Domesday Survey the commons are listed as providing pannage – the right to graze pigs on acorns – for the Abbey. Access is by footpaths and bridle ways and there are parking facilities. Not far away **Ranmore Common** [187: TQ1451] and **Denbies Hillside** [187: TQ145503] bound the southern edges of the Polesden Lacey estate (see p.222) and offer good walks on the south slopes of the North Downs. A car-parking fee is charged to non-members at Box Hill, Headley Heath, Leith Hill Rhododendron Woods, Ranmore Common and Abinger Roughs.

North of Abinger Hammer, and 4 miles west of Dorking there is a car park from which you can explore on foot the wooded ridge of **Abinger Roughs** and **Netley Park** [187: TQ111480]. Sadly, many of these areas were damaged in the great storms of October 1987 and January 1990 although trees are now growing back at a fast rate. **Holmwood Common** [187: TQ1746], 1 mile south of Dorking, offers many attractive walks through oak and birch woodland.

Nearer London, between **Reigate** and Banstead Heath [187: TQ250520] are 360 acres of open down, copse and beechwood on the North Downs with views towards the

SURREY

South Downs. This includes **Colley Hill**, **Reigate Fort**, **Reigate Hill**, a short strip of the **Pilgrim's Way**, **Margery Wood**, **Juniper Hill**, and wood and parkland at **Gatton**. On the eastern border of the county, almost in Kent, are Oxted Down on the chalk scarp with the North Downs way running through it and **Limpsfield**, a charming series of woodlands and small heaths on the greensand.

Four miles south of Epsom, near Box Hill, some 530 acres of **Headley Heath**, including the Lordship of Headley Manor [197: TQ2053] were originally grazed by sheep and other stock; continuing management by the Trust enables the various habitats to be maintained for the benefit of a great variety of plants, trees, birds and insects.

Much further south at **Hindhead** are more than 1,400 acres of heathland and woodland, covering valleys and sandstone ridges which radiate from Hindhead Village [186: SU890357]. There are nature walks through the **Devil's Punch Bowl**, one of the largest spring eroded valleys in Europe, and **Gibbet Hill**; from the latter are panoramic views to the Chilterns and over the Weald to the South Downs.

Astride the A287 Hindhead to Farnham road is **Frensham Common** [169: SU8540], now part of a country park managed by Waverley Borough Council in which the Trust owns about 1,000 acres, including Frensham Great and Little Ponds. There is a wide variety of wildlife, including wildfowl.

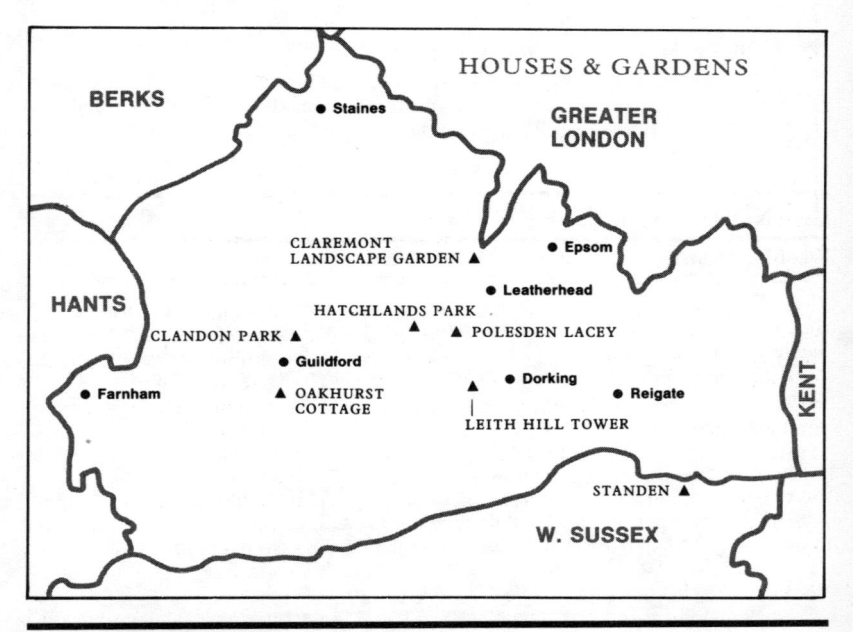

HOUSES & GARDENS

BERKS — Staines — GREATER LONDON

CLAREMONT LANDSCAPE GARDEN ▲ — ● Epsom — ● Leatherhead

HANTS — HATCHLANDS PARK ▲ — ▲ POLESDEN LACEY

CLANDON PARK ▲ — ● Guildford — ● Dorking — ● Reigate

● Farnham — ▲ OAKHURST COTTAGE — LEITH HILL TOWER — KENT

STANDEN ▲

W. SUSSEX

BOX HILL

General enquries: tel. (0306) 885502,

On the edge of the North Downs, rising 400ft from the River Mole, this Country Park consists of more than 1,000 acres of woods and chalk downland, with magnificent views to the South Downs. Summit buildings include an exhibition room and 1890s fort (not open to public)

SURREY

- **O** All year
- **£** Countryside free. Coaches must not use the zig-zag road from Burford Bridge on W side of the hill as a weight restriction applies, but must approach from E side of the hill B2032 or B2033; car/coach parks at top of hill; pay & display £1 (free to NT members displaying membership cards). Annual car park pass available
- Shop & Information Centre: March to Oct daily 10–5.30; Nov to Feb daily (weather permitting) 11–4, (closed 25/26 Dec) tel. (0306) 88793. Information Centre tel. (0306) 885502
- Access to summit area, including shop & take-away. Special parking behind take-away. Wheelchair path to viewpoint. WCs opposite main car park at summit
- Braille guides for short walk and nature walk
- Take-away, serving hot & cold snacks & drinks: open all year, daily. March to Sept 10–5.30; Oct to Feb 11–4 (except 25, 26 Dec). Tel. (0306) 888793
- **E** 26 June, Country Day (extra charge for cars, incl. NT members)
- Must be kept under control, sheep grazing
- 1m N of Dorking, 2½m S of Leatherhead on A24 [187: TQ171519] *Bus:* London & Country/Epsom Buses 516, 551 BR Leatherhead–Box Hill; London General 520 BR Sutton–Box Hill (Sat only) (tel. 081-668 7261) *Station:* Boxhill & West Humble ½m

CLANDON PARK
West Clandon, Guildford GU4 7RQ (0483) 222482

Clandon was built in the early 1730s for the 2nd Lord Onslow by the Venetian architect, Giacomo Leoni. This Palladian house with a two-storeyed Marble Hall, contains Onslow family pictures and furniture, the Gubbay collection of porcelain, furniture and needlework, and the Ivo Forde collection of Meissen Italian comedy figures. Also of interest are the old kitchens, the Queen's Royal Surrey Regiment Museum, and the garden with parterre, grotto and Maori House

SURREY

- ◯ 1 April to end Oct: daily except Thur & Fri (but open Good Fri) 1.30-5.30; BH Mon 11-5.30. Last admissions 5
- £ House, garden & museum £4. Parties, Mon to Wed only, £3.50; parties and guided tours by prior arrangement with Administrator. Parking 300yds
- 🛍 Shop open as house. Also open for Christmas shopping and some weekends in March. Tel. (0483) 211412
- ♿ Parking near front of house for disabled drivers only; disabled visitors may be set down at house; WC on lower ground floor difficult for wheelchairs; ramp to garden. House difficult as several steps to ground floor which is completely level. Restaurant accessible. Access limited to ground floor and basement only
- 👁 Braille guide
- 🍽 Licensed restaurant in house on days house is open. Lunches 12.30-2; teas 3.15-5.30. Also open some weekends in March and pre-Christmas. Prior booking for lunch advisable (tel. (0483) 222502). Picnic area
- 🚼 Nappy-changing table available
- E Concerts are held in the Marble Hall; please send s.a.e. or telephone for information

Note: The house is available for non-residential private and commercial functions; the Administrator welcomes enquiries. The park is not owned by the National Trust and is not open to the public. Garden Centre (not NT); tel. (0483) 222925 for opening times

- 🐕 No dogs except on leads in picnic area and car park only
- → At West Clandon on A247, 3m E of Guildford; if using A3 follow signposts to Ripley to join A247 via B2215 [186: TQ042512] *Bus:* London & Country 563 Guildford–Addlestone (passing BR Clandon); otherwise London & Country 408 Guildford–W Croydon, 479 Guildford–Kingston, 432 Guildford–Wisley Gardens, 433 Guildford–Dorking (all pass close BR Guildford), alight W Clandon Cross Roads, ¼m (tel. 081-668 7261) *Station:* Clandon 1m

CLAREMONT LANDSCAPE GARDEN

Portsmouth Road, Esher KT10 9JG (0372) 469421

One of the earliest surviving English landscape gardens, restored by NT to its former glory. Begun by Sir John Vanbrugh and Charles Bridgeman before 1720, the gardens were extended and naturalised by William Kent. Capability Brown also made improvements. Features include a lake, island with pavilion, grotto, turf amphitheatre, viewpoints and avenues. The house is not NT

- ◯ All year: Jan to end March daily (except Mon) 10-5 or sunset if earlier. April to end Oct: Mon to Fri 10-6; Sat, Sun & BH Mon 10-7. (13-17 July garden closes 4). Nov to end March 1995: daily (except Mon) 10-5 or sunset if earlier. Last admissions ½hr before closing. Closed 25 Dec & 1 Jan
- £ Sun & BH Mon £2.60, Mon to Sat £1.80; no reduction for parties. All coach parties must book; no coaches on Sun. Parking at entrance   *continued*

SURREY

- 🚶 Guided tours (min. 15 persons) £1.30 extra per person by prior booking: tel. (0372) 469421
- 🛍 Shop: 15 Jan to end March: Sat & Sun 11-4.30; April to end Oct: daily (except Mon) 11-5.30; Nov to 11 Dec; daily (except Mon) 11-4; 14 Jan to end March 1995: Sat & Sun 11-4.30. Open BH Mon
- ♿ Level pathway around lake, and level grassland. Wheelchairs available. Access to tea-room. WC in car park. Parking by entrance. Accessible events; for details see Events below
- 👁 Braille Guide
- ☕ Tea-room serving morning coffee, homemade lunches (12-2) and teas. Open as shop. Last orders ½hr before closing
- **E** 13-17 July, Fête Champêtre and Jazz Concert; send s.a.e. for booking form, to Claremont Box Office, c/o Southern Regional Office, or tel. (0372) 459950 for information. Telephone bookings taken from 31 May. Please note garden closes at 4 on 13-17 July
- 🐕 On leads Nov to end March but not admitted April to end Oct
- ➡ On S edge of Esher, on E side of A307 (no access from Esher bypass) [187: TQ128634] *Bus:* London & Country 415 Victoria–Guildford (passing close BR Esher) (tel. 081-668 7261) *Station:* Esher 2m; Hersham 2m; Claygate 2m

---

HATCHLANDS PARK 🏛 ✤
East Clandon, Guildford GU4 7RT (0483) 222482

A handsome brick house built in the 1750s by Stiff Leadbetter for Admiral Boscawen, hero of the Battle of Louisburg. The house has splendid interiors by Robert Adam and in 1988 the Cobbe collection of fine keyboard instruments, paintings and furniture was installed and the house was extensively redecorated. The garden, by Repton and Gertrude Jekyll, has been restored and new walks opened in the park

- 🕐 3 April to end Oct: Tues, Wed, Thur, Sun & BH Mon (and Fri in Aug) 2-5.30. Last admissions ½hr before closing. Grounds open 12.30-6
- £ £4. Parties £3.50, Tues, Wed & Thur only. Grounds £1 only. Parking 300yds
- 🛍 Shop open same days as house 1.30-5.30
- ♿ Access to ground floor, terrace and part of garden. WC. Wheelchair available. Alternative easier access to restaurant for wheelchair users. Special car parking for disabled drivers only, by prior arrangement with Administrator; batricar available for transport to house
- ☕ Licensed restaurant 12.30-2 and home made teas 3-5 same days as house tel. (0483) 211120
- 👶 Facilities in ladies' cloakroom for nursing mothers; nappy changing table. Back-packs not permitted
- **E** Concerts are held in the house and garden; please send s.a.e. for further information

SURREY

🐕 No dogs except on lead in car park only

➡️ E of East Clandon, N of A246 Guildford–Leatherhead road [187: TQ063518] *Bus:* London & Country 408 Guildford–W Croydon, 479 Guildford–Kingston, 432 Guildford–Wisley Gardens, 433 Guildford–Dorking (all pass close BR Guildford) tel. 081-668 7261 *Station:* Clandon 2½m, Horsley 3m

LEITH HILL TOWER 🏠 ☕

during opening hours: (0306) 712434

An 18th-century tower on the highest point in south-east England. The top of the tower is 1,029ft above sea level and provides magnificent views to the North and South Downs. The beautiful Rhododendron Wood is ¾m to the south west and at its best in April/May

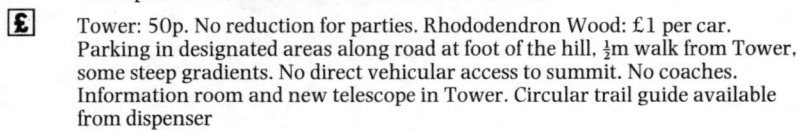

🕐 1 April to end Sept: Wed 2–5; Sat, Sun & BH 11–5. Last admissions 4.30. Also open fine weekends Oct to end March 11–3.30

£ Tower: 50p. No reduction for parties. Rhododendron Wood: £1 per car. Parking in designated areas along road at foot of the hill, ½m walk from Tower, some steep gradients. No direct vehicular access to summit. No coaches. Information room and new telescope in Tower. Circular trail guide available from dispenser

♿ Limited access to Rhododendron Wood. Access path to upper part of Wood

🍴 Light refreshments open same times as Tower

🐕 Dogs not allowed in Rhododendron Wood picnic area; elsewhere in Rhododendron Wood on leads. No dogs in Tower

➡️ On summit of Leith Hill, 1m SW of Coldharbour A29/B2126 [187: TQ139432]. Rhododendron Wood: [187: TQ131427] *Bus:* London & Country 433 from BR Guildford & BR Dorking, summer Suns only (tel. 081-668 7261); otherwise Tillingbourne 21 Guildford–Dorking (passing close BR Guildford and passing BR Chilworth and Dorking), alight Holmbury St Mary, 2½m (tel. (0483) 276880) *Station:* Holmwood (U), not Sun, 2½m: Dorking 5½m.

OAKHURST COTTAGE 🏠

Hambledon, nr Godalming (0428) 684733

A very small timber-framed cottage, restored and furnished as a cottager's dwelling, with a delightful cottage garden

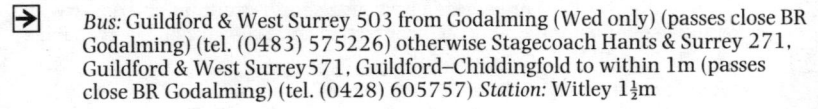

🕐 30 March to end Oct: Wed, Thur, Sat, Sun & BH Mon 2–5. Strictly appointment only with Mrs E. Hardy (tel. no. above)

£ £2.20, children £1.10 (incl. guided tour). No reduction for parties. Schools & groups by special arrangement. Parking 200yds. No WCs

➡️ *Bus:* Guildford & West Surrey 503 from Godalming (Wed only) (passes close BR Godalming) (tel. (0483) 575226) otherwise Stagecoach Hants & Surrey 271, Guildford & West Surrey 571, Guildford–Chiddingfold to within 1m (passes close BR Godalming) (tel. (0428) 605757) *Station:* Witley 1½m

221

SURREY

POLESDEN LACEY 🏛 ✤ ♣   📷 ✕ ▦

nr Dorking RH5 6BD House enquiries to Administrator: (0372) 458203 or 452048. General NT enquiries to Regional Office (0372) 453401

Originally an elegant 1820s Regency villa, the house was remodelled after 1906 by the Hon. Mrs Ronald Greville, a well-known Edwardian hostess. Her collection of fine paintings, furniture, porcelain and silver are still displayed in the reception rooms, plus photographs from Mrs Greville's albums. Extensive grounds, walled rose garden, lawns and tree-lined walks. King George VI and Queen Elizabeth (now the Queen Mother) spent part of their honeymoon here

- **House:** March only: Sat & Sun only 1.30–4.30; 30 March to end Oct: Wed to Sun (incl. Good Fri) 1.30–5.30; also open BH Mon & preceding Sun 11–5.30. **Grounds:** daily all year: 11–6 or dusk if earlier. Last admissions to house ½hr before closing

  Note: This property is very busy on summer weekends & BH. Access may be restricted at peak times for limited periods due to over-crowding. Members may prefer to avoid these times

- Garden and grounds open all year round: £2.50. House: £3 extra. Pre-booked parties £4.50 (house & garden) weekdays only. No prams, back-packs or pushchairs in house. Parking 150yds. Coaches approaching from Dorking should not turn off through Westhumble, but take A246 at Givons Grove roundabout before Leatherhead

  Note: The croquet lawn is available for use. Equipment for hire from the House

- Shop open from 15 Jan to end March: Sat & Sun only 11–4.30; April to end Oct: Wed to Sun & BH Mon 11–6; Nov to 18 Dec: Wed to Sun 11–4.30. Tel. (0372) 457230

- Access to all showrooms, restaurant and parts of garden; some fairly firm gravel paths. Disabled drivers may park near shop, restaurant and house with permission of Administrator; WC near restaurant. Self-drive buggy available by arrangement with Administrator

- Braille guide to house; rose and lavender garden

SURREY

- Coffee, lunches and home made teas in licensed restaurant in courtyard. 15 Jan to end March (light refreshments): Sat & Sun only 11-4.30. 30 March to end Oct: Wed to Sun & BH Mon 11-5. Nov to 18 Dec: Wed to Sun 11-4.30. Tel. (0372) 456190. Picnic site by main car park; no picnics on lawns
- Nappy changing table in ladies' WC. High chair available in restaurant
- **E** 22 June to 10 July, Open Air Theatre: send s.a.e. for booking form to Ploat Box Office, c/o Southern Regional Office or tel. (0372) 457223 for information. Tel. bookings taken from 31 May.10 July, Polesden Fair; extra charge, incl. NT members

  Note: Estate includes a YHA hostel.

- No dogs in formal gardens, on paths or on lawns. Allowed in rest of grounds on leads. Good walks on estate
- 5m NW of Dorking, 2m S of Great Bookham, off A246 Leatherhead–Guildford road [187: TQ136522] *Bus:* London & Country 433 from BR Guildford & BR Dorking, summer Suns; otherwise 408 Guildford–W Croydon, (passing close BR Guildford & Leatherhead), alight Great Bookham, 1½m (tel. 081-668 7261) *Station:* Boxhill & Westhumble 2m by scenic path through NT park

THE RIVER WEY & GODALMING NAVIGATIONS

Navigation Office, Dapdune Wharf, Wharf Road, Guildford GU1 4RR (0483) 61389

One of the earliest historic waterways, built in 1670. Extending from the River Thames at Weybridge to Godalming Wharf, a distance of 19½m, and presently the most southerly point of the inland waterway system, this tranquil river retains its old locks and weirs, supporting many species of water birds and a varied flora and fauna. Dapdune Wharf at Guildford has a large horse-drawn barge on display with associated buildings for public viewing

- **O** Towing path for walkers, free visitors' moorings on the 19½m waterway throughout the year, open during daylight hours, subject to stoppages for major maintenance purposes
- **£** Towing path; walkers and moorings for visiting boats: no charge. Navigation licences (including all lock tolls) are payable on all powered and non-powered craft issued for the year or for 7- or 21-day visits, with 10% reduction (7or 21 days only), for visiting NT members on production of current membership card. There are insurance requirements & restrictions on engine size to preserve the property. Please check with Navigation Office in advance of journey

  Note: Boat trips & boats available for hire: Horsedrawn boat trips on narrow boat Iona (tel. (0483) 414938); Rowboats, punts, canoes and narrowboats at Farncombe Boat House (tel. (0483) 421306); Restaurant boats, tripping boats, row boats & canoes at Guildford Boat House (tel. (0483) 504494)

- Must be kept under control. All dogs to be kept on leads within lock areas
- Access from A3 & M25. Visiting craft can enter from the Thames at Shepperton or slipways at Guildford or Pyrford *Station:* Addlestone, Byfleet & New Haw; Guildford, Farncombe & Godalming all nearby

SURREY

RUNNYMEDE 🏞

Egham (0784) 432891

188 acres of historic meadows where King John sealed the Magna Carta in 1215; 110 acres of wooded slopes of Cooper's Hill overlook the meadows, giving fine views of the surrounding countryside. Memorials dedicated to the Magna Carta, John F. Kennedy and the Air Forces

- 🅿 All year. Riverside grass car park open April to end Sept, daily when ground conditions allow, 9.30–7. Pay & Display machine in operation
- £ Fees payable for parking, fishing and mooring. Fishing: day permits only; all year except during closed season (mid March to mid June); tickets available from riverbank. Mooring available for 24 hrs only
- 🛍 Open April to end Sept: daily 10.30–5.30
- ♿ Limited access to tea-room and meads by prior arrangement. Good vehicle access to riverbank during summer months
- ☕ Open as shop. Hard surface tea-room car park open Oct to March 9–7 and in wet weather during summer months
- 🐕 On leads within S.S.S.I. areas
- ➡ On the Thames, ½m W of Runnymede Bridge, on S side of A308 (M25, Junction 13). *Bus:* From surrounding areas tel. 081-668 7261 *Station:* Egham, ½m

SHALFORD MILL

Shalford, nr Guildford

18th-century watermill on the Tillingbourne, given in 1932 by 'Ferguson's Gang'. Part-tenanted, part-open

- 🅿 Daily 10–5
- £ No parking at property. Children must be accompanied by an adult
- ➡ 1½m S of Guildford on A281 opposite Sea Horse Inn *Bus:* (tel. (0483) 575226) *Station:* Shalford (U), not Sun, 1½m; Guildford 1½m

WINKWORTH ARBORETUM 🌼 🏞

Hascombe Road, Godalming GU8 4AD (0483) 208477

Hillside woodland with two lakes, many rare trees and shrubs and fine views. The most impressive displays are in spring for bluebells and azaleas, autumn for colour and abundant wildlife

Note: due to limited parking space at peak spring & autumn weekends, would all walkers who are not visiting the Arboretum park in the lower car park. This avoids disappointment to those wishing to visit the Arboretum

- 🅿 All year: daily during daylight hours

SURREY

£   £2. No reduction for parties. Coach parties must book in writing with Head of Arboretum to ensure parking space

👤   All groups must book in writing to Head of Arboretum. £2 per person. NT members free, but donations welcome

🛍   Shop open 1 April to 14 Nov: daily 11–5.30 or dusk if earlier. Also open weekends in Nov to 24 Dec & weekends in March 11–5.30. Open BH Mon. Christmas shop

♿   Limited access; viewpoint and lake from lower entrance are accessible. Unadapted WC; tea-room accessible via step

☕   Tea-room for light refreshments near upper car park; open daily, April to 14 Nov 11–5.30 (weather permitting), for light lunches & teas. Also open weekends in March & mid Nov to Christmas. Booking with Concessionaire, Winkworth Arboretum, address above (tel. (0483) 208265 when tea-room open)

→   Near Hascombe, 2m SE of Godalming on E side of B2130 [169, 170 or 186: SU990412] *Bus:* Tillingbourne 42/4/6 Godalming–Cranleigh (passing close BR Godalming) (tel. (0483) 276880) *Station:* Godalming 2m

WITLEY COMMON INFORMATION CENTRE

Haslemere Road, Witley, Godalming GU8 5QA (0428) 683207

A purpose-built Nature Information Centre set in pinewoods on the edge of the common. An audio visual programme and exhibition explain the history, natural history and management of Witley Common. Nature walks with interesting and varied flora and fauna

ⓘ   **Information Centre:** 1 April to end Oct: Mon to Thur & BH Mon 11–1 & 2–4, also Sat & Sun 2–5, car park 9–6. **Common:** open at all times

£   Free to Centre. Guided parties £1.60, childen 80p (min. charge £10). Parking 100yds from Centre; all groups must pre-book

🛍   Small shop offering limited souvenirs and natural history items

♿   Ground floor of Centre and 2 nature trails accessible; strong pushers advisable. Self-drive powered buggy available. Unadapted WC

👁   Braille guides

👥   Arrangements for schools and parties, including visits in March, Nov & Dec; please book with s.a.e.

🐕   Must be kept on leads on trails; no dogs in Centre

→   7m SW of Guildford between London Portsmouth A3 and A286 roads, 1m SW of Milford [186: SU9341] *Bus:* Stagecoach Hants & Surrey/Coastline 260 Guildford–Bognor Regis (passing close BR Godalming & passing BR Haslemere) (tel. (0428) 605757) *Station:* Milford 2m

REFER TO OPENING PAGES FOR GENERAL INFORMATION

Sussex (East)

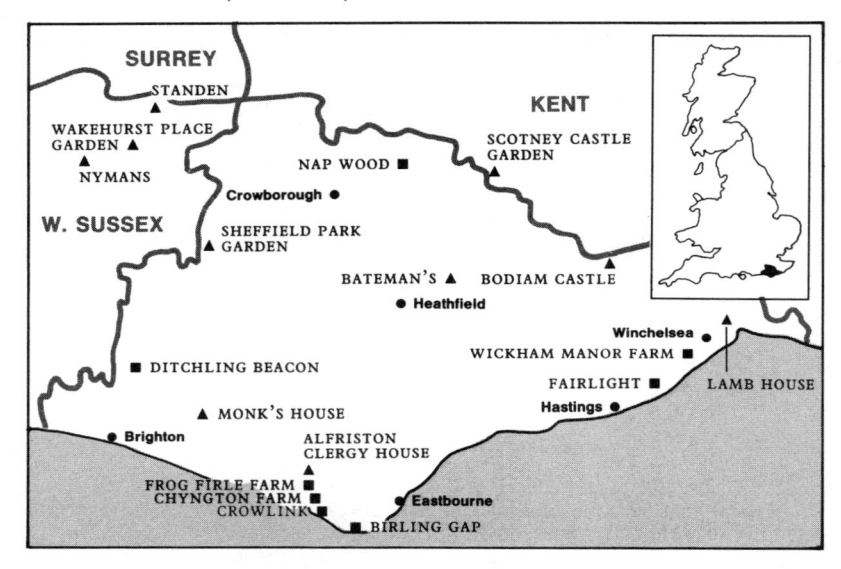

COAST

The South Downs meet the sea at the Seven Sisters, just west of Eastbourne, forming one of the best known and loved lengths of coast in England. At **Crowlink**, **Birling Gap** and **Chyngton Farm** [199: TV5497] the Trust owns some 1000 acres of chalk downland, cliff and river estuary. Here, and on the neighbouring downland, are some of the most delightful walks and unspoilt views. The downs at Crowlink have gradual slopes and short turf over which wheelchairs may be pushed; there are no designated wheelchair routes and visitors may wander where they wish. The beach at Birling Gap remains relatively uncrowded. There is access to the sea and fine views of the Seven Sisters from Chyngton Farm. The coastal strip is a Site of Special Scientific Interest [199: TV5497]. Car parking at both Crowlink and Birling Gap. To the east of Hastings, public footpaths give access to more Trust-owned cliffland at **Fairlight** [199: TQ884127].

COUNTRYSIDE

North of Brighton are the remains of **Ditchling Beacon** hill-fort [198: TQ332131], which lie across the South Downs Way; from the NT car park there is a splendid view across the Weald. On a clear day the North Downs can be seen, and nearer at hand Ashdown Forest and Crowborough Beacon.

Between Alfriston and Seaford lies **Frog Firle Farm** [TQ517012] 462 acres of unspoilt downland and river valley, with extensive footpath network car park (not NT) at High and Over.

SUSSEX (EAST)

Near Tunbridge Wells, the Sussex Wildlife Trust leases 107 acres of woodland from the Trust. **Nap Wood** [188: TQ585330] on the A267 is mostly oak woodland maintained as a nature reserve, with a footpath and limited parking.

ALFRISTON CLERGY HOUSE

The Tye, Alfriston, Polegate BN26 5TL (0323) 870001

This 14th-century Wealden hall house was the first building to be acquired by the Trust, in 1896. The building is half-timbered and thatched, and contains a medieval hall, exhibition room and two other rooms open to the public, plus a charming cottage garden

- April to end Oct: daily 10.30–5 or sunset if earlier. Last admissions ½hr before closing
- £2, children £1. Pre-booked parties £1.50. WCs and parking in car park at other end of village (not NT)
- Shop open as house. Also Christmas shop, tel. Custodian for details
- House unsuitable for wheelchair users
- In village (not NT)
- No dogs
- 4m NE of Seaford, just E of B2108, in Alfriston village, adjoining The Tye and St Andrews Church [189: TQ521029] *Bus:* Stagecoach South Coast726 Eastbourne–Brighton (passing close BR Polegate & Seaford); Autopoint 125 from Lewes (tel. (0273) 478007) *Station:* Berwick 2½m

BATEMAN'S

Burwash, Etchingham TN19 7DS (0435) 882302

Home of Rudyard Kipling from 1902–36, the house was built by a local ironmaster in 1634. Kipling's rooms and study are as they were during his lifetime. At the bottom of the garden, the watermill grinds corn for flour (Sat pm only). Alongside is one of the oldest working water-driven turbines in the world, installed by Kipling to generate electricity for the house. Kipling's 1928 Rolls Royce. Gardens maintained much as they were in Kipling's time

- **House, mill and garden:** April to end Oct: daily (except Thur & Fri) 11–5 (open Good Fri). Last admissions 4.30. The mill grinds corn every Sat at 2 in the open season
- £3.50, children £1.80. Pre-booked parties £3. Sun, BH Mon & Good Fri: £4 (no reduction for parties)
- Shop as house. Also Christmas shop, tel. Administrator for details
- The mill is not suitable for wheelchair users, but ground floor of house and garden are accessible; there are routes which avoid the steps. WC in car park
- Scented plants & flowers; watermill sounds (Sat only)
- Morning coffee, light lunches and teas in tea-room, open as house. Picnicking in copse adjacent to car park

SUSSEX (EAST)

- 👶 Baby-changing facilities. Children's guide
- 📖 Teacher's resource book
- 🇪 Concert with fireworks, 6 Aug; tel. Regional Box Office (tel. (0892) 891001)
- 🐕 On leads in car park only
- ➡️ ½m S of Burwash (A265); approached by road leading S from W end of village or N from Woods Corner (B2096) [199: TQ671238] *Bus:* RDH/Autopoint 318 Hurst Green–Heathfield (passing BR Etchingham) (tel. (0273) 478007) *Station:* Etchingham 3m

BODIAM CASTLE 📖 ⚔️

Bodiam, nr Robertsbridge TN32 5UA (0580) 830436

Bodiam Castle was built in 1385 against a French invasion which never came & as a comfortable dwelling for a rich nobleman. It has been voted one of the top six most popular castles for children. The virtual completeness of the exterior, the best example of its type in the country, makes it an exciting place for children to explore, with spiral staircases and battlements. Although a ruin, the floors have been replaced in some of the towers, and impressive views can be enjoyed from the battlements. There is an audio-visual presentation on life in a medieval castle, and small museum

- 🕐 All year. Jan to March: Tues to Sun 10–sunset. April to end Oct: daily 10–6 or sunset if earlier. Nov & Dec: Tues to Sun 10–sunset. Last admissions ½hr before closing
- £ £2.50, children £1.30. Parties £2. Car park ¼m 50p (NT members free)
- 🛍️ Shop open as Castle, but closes ½hr before Castle
- ♿ Access to car park, shop and restaurant/tea-room; WC in car park. Castle (but not its towers) is accessible to wheelchair users, but it is ½m from car park over uneven ground; for alternative access details please tel. Administrator before visiting
- 👁️ Braille guide available from ticket office

228

SUSSEX (EAST)

☕ Lunches, teas and snacks in car park tea-room, open April to 24 Dec: daily 10.30-½hr before Castle closes; Jan: Sun only; Feb: Sat & Sun; March: Wed, Sat & Sun 10.30-5.30 or sunset if earlier. Fast food kiosk open as tea-room. Picnicking in castle grounds

👶 Baby changing facilities. Children's guide

🎒 Teacher's resource book. Education rooms with hands-on resources; tel. Administrator for details

E Family Days, concerts & Medieval Fair; tel. Administrator for details

🐕 On leads in grounds only, not in Castle

➡ 3m S of Hawkhurst, 2m E of A21 Hurst Green [199: TQ782256] *Bus:* Stagecoach South Coast 349 from BR Hastings (tel. (0424) 433711) *Station:* Robertsbridge 5m

LAMB HOUSE 🏠 ❂

West Street, Rye TN31 7ES (0892) 890651

The home of the writer Henry James from 1898 to 1916 where he wrote the best novels of his later period. The walled garden, staircase, hall and three rooms on the ground floor containing some of James's personal possessions are on view. Also home to E. F. Benson. The house & gardens are administered and largely maintained on the Trust's behalf by the tenant

O April to end Oct: Wed & Sat only 2-6. Last admissions 5.30

£ £2. No reduction for parties or children. WCs and car park available in Rye

🐕 No dogs

➡ In West Street, facing W end of church [198: TQ920202] *Bus:* From surrounding areas to Rye (tel. (0424) 433711) *Station:* Rye ½m

MONK'S HOUSE 🏠 ❂

Rodmell, Lewes BN7 3HF (0892) 890651

A small village house and garden, and the home of Leonard and Virginia Woolf from 1919 until Leonard's death in 1969. The house and garden are administered and largely maintained by the tenant on the Trust's behalf

O April to end Oct: Wed & Sat 2-5.30. Last admissions 5

£ £2. No reduction for children or parties; max. 15 people in house at a time. Parties only by prior arrangement with the tenant. Car park 50yds; village street too narrow for coaches; drivers please set passengers down at main road junction, and park elsewhere

🐕 No dogs

➡ 4m SE of Lewes, off former A275 (now unclassified) in Rodmell village, near church (no access from A26) [198: TQ421064] *Bus:* Stagecoach South Coast123 Lewes-Newhaven (passing BR Lewes) (tel. (0273) 478007) *Station:* Southease (U) 1¼m

SUSSEX (EAST)

SHEFFIELD PARK GARDEN ✤
Uckfield TN22 3QX (0825) 790655

A magnificent 100-acre landscape garden, with 5 lakes linked by cascades and waterfalls, laid out in the 18th century by Capability Brown. Carpeted with daffodils and bluebells in spring, its rhododendrons, azaleas & stream garden are spectacular in early summer. In autumn the garden is ablaze with colour. Its collection of rare trees and shrubs makes the garden wonderful to visit at all time of year

- 🅾 March: Sat & Sun only 11-4. April to 6 Nov: Tues to Sun & BH Mon 11-6 or sunset if earlier. 9 Nov to 17 Dec: Wed to Sat 11-4. Last admissions 1 hr before closing

- 💷 March, April & June to end Sept, Nov & Dec 3.50, children £1.80; parties £2.50. May & Oct £4, parties £3. No reduction for parties on Sat, Sun & BH Mon

- 🛍 Shop as garden. Also Christmas shop, tel. Administrator for details

- ♿ Most parts of garden accessible; powered self-drive car and wheelchairs available. WC. Car parking near entrance; follow access sign at entrance

- 🍴 Restaurant (not NT) and picnic area adjoining car park

- ➡ Midway between East Grinstead and Lewes, 5m NW of Uckfield, on E side of A275, ½m from Sheffield Park station (Bluebell line) [198: TQ415240] *Bus:* Stagecoach South Coast 769 from BR Haywards Heath & Lewes (summer Sun); Autopoint 121 from Lewes (Sat only); Horsham Buses 189 from Haywards Heath (summer Wed only); RDH 246 from Uckfield (Mon, Fri only); otherwise Stagecoach South Coast 781 Eastbourne–Haywards Heath (passing BR Haywards Heath & Uckfield), alight Chailey Crossroads, 1¾m (tel. (0273) 478007) *Station:* Sheffield Park (Bluebell Rly) ¼m; Haywards Heath 7m; Buxted 7m

Sussex (West)

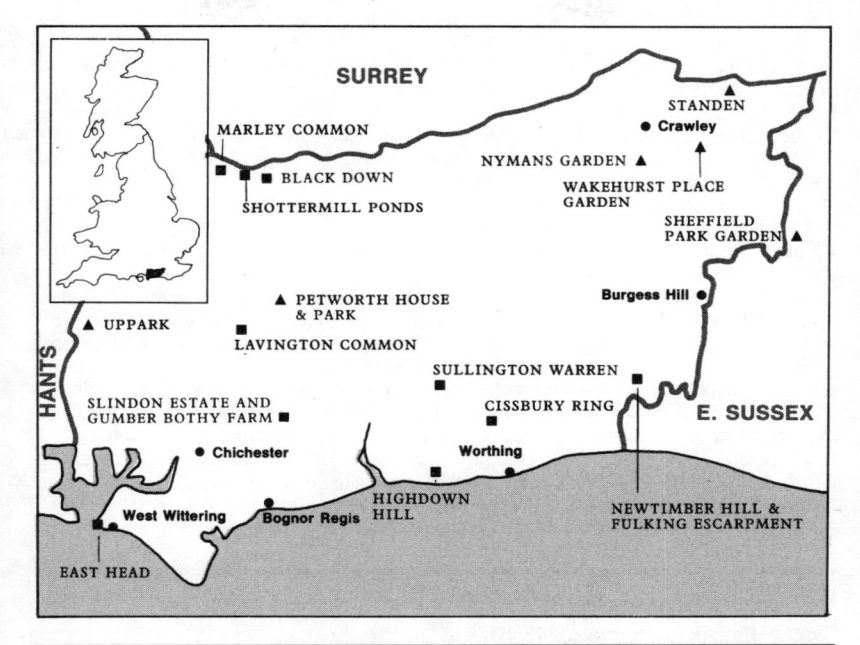

COAST

At West Wittering is the 110-acre sand and shingle spit of **East Head** east of the entrance to Chichester Harbour [181: SU766990]. Vulnerable to the constant battering it receives from the sea and, indeed, from the feet of visitors, East Head is important because it demonstrates how the sea has shaped this part of the coastline, and because it supports a variety of wildlife. The Trust has fenced off part of the spit, while marram grass has been introduced to 'bind' the dunes; naturalists come to see the waders, the plant and marine life, and the insect population.

COUNTRYSIDE

On the Surrey/Sussex borders a large acreage of sandstone moorland at **Black Down and Marley Common** gives fine views south to the South Downs and the English Channel. The highest point in Sussex providing commanding views across the Weald over the South Downs. Part of an area of outstanding natural beauty, the plateau was once an extensive heath created by common grazing, now woodland with small areas remaining. Magnificent views from the circular panoramic walk from the main car park. At the foot of Marley Lane are two hammer ponds: **Shottermill Ponds** [186: SU883324]. **Lavington Common** [197: SU950190], and **Sullington Warren**

SUSSEX (WEST)

[198: TQ096144] are heather-clad heathland properties, well supplied with footpaths and car parking areas. A famous landmark, **Cissbury Ring** [198: TQ140082] near Findon, gives views to Beachy Head and the Isle of Wight. There was a flint mining industry on the Ring in Neolithic times and its remains can still be seen at the western end of the hill. One of the largest Iron Age hill-forts in the country is on the summit. **Wolstonbury Hill**, **Newtimber Hill** [198: TQ2712] and the adjacent **Fulking Escarpment** are three downland properties providing spectacular views over the weald and to the sea. Rich in downland flora and fauna, these properties lavishly reward those who leave the beaten track to seek them out. **Harting Down**, near Petersfield [197: SU798184] is a 520-acre stretch of chalk downland. Magnificent views, good walks, traversed by South Downs Way, rich in downland flora and fauna.

Another archaeologically important site is **Highdown Hill** near Ferring [197/198: TQ092043]. This has a late Bronze Age settlement, and an Early Iron Age hill-fort with a pagan Saxon cemetery within its ramparts. Excavations were carried out in the summer of 1988.

The **Slindon Estate** north of Bognor Regis [197: SU9608] includes much of Slindon village with its 17th-century brick and flint cottages and links with Hillaire Belloc, who lived here. Within the Beech Wood, devastated by the Great Storm in 1987 and now re-planted with new beech trees, can be found a shingle beach, 130ft above sea level, which proves that the sea once reached here – it is now 5 miles away! Other archaeological sites on the estate include the Neolithic causewayed enclosure of Barkhale and the largest surviving section – 3½ miles – of Stane Street, which took the Roman legions to Chichester, past Bignor Hill. The park and Bignor Hill, spectacular views, and the South Downs Way car park are open daily and access to the remainder of the 3,520-acre estate is by public footpaths and bridleways.

GUMBER BOTHY, GUMBER FARM
Slindon Estate, nr Arundel (0243) 814484

A traditional farm building on a working downland sheep farm, newly converted to provide basic overnight accommodation for walkers, riders and cyclists 1m from the South Downs Way

- **O**   1 March to end Oct. Can be opened at other times by prior arrangement with warden. Accommodation consists of 27 sleeping platforms, showers, WCs, cookers, provision for camping and field for horses by arrangement with warden. Exhibition and information room

- **£**   £4 per person, per night. Reduction for parties of 12 or more. School parties: £2 per child per night

-   WC. Leaflet available describing facilities (please send s.a.e. to warden)

-   Children over the age of 5 welcome

-   Educational visits encouraged

- **E**   By arrangement with the Bothy warden

-   No dogs except guide dogs by arrangement

- **→**   Vehicular access by prior arrangement only. 1m to S of South Downs Way, [197: SU96119] *Bus:* Amberley 4m via South Downs Way

SUSSEX (WEST)

NYMANS GARDEN

Handcross, nr Haywards Heath RH17 6EB (0444) 400321 or 400002

One of the great gardens of the Sussex Weald, with rare and beautiful plants, shrubs and trees from all over the world, including azaleas, rhododendrons, eucryphias, hydrangeas, magnolias, camellias and roses. Also, a walled garden, hidden sunk garden, pinetum, laurel walk and romantic ruins

- March: Sat & Sun only. 30 March to end Oct: daily except Mon & Fri (but open BH Mon & Good Fri) 11–7 or sunset if earlier. Last admissions 1hr before closing
- £3.50. Parties £3. Car park at entrance; space limited so coaches must book
- Shop & exhibition
- Garden & tea-house accessible; wheelchair route indicated (map available); wheelchairs and powered self-drive buggy available on request. WC
- Braille guide. Old roses and other scented flowers and plants suitable for visually impaired visitors
- Light refreshments available
- Summer musical evening held in the garden; please send s.a.e. or tel.
- In car park only
- On B2114 at Handcross, 4½m S of Crawley, just off London–Brighton M23/A23 [187: TQ265294] *Bus:* Brighton & Hove/Lewes Coaches/London & Country 773 Brighton–Crawley, (tel. (0272) 821111); Brighton Buses 33 Haywards Heath–Crawley (tel. (0273) 674881), alight Handcross ¼m–¾m according to direction; all pass BR Crawley *Station:* Crawley 5½m or Balcomber 4½m

PETWORTH HOUSE

Petworth GU28 0AE (0798) 42207/as from mid 1994; 342207

More of a palace than a conventional country house, this magnificent late 17th-century mansion is set within a beautiful deer park (see following entry). Turner worked here for many years in the early 19th century, and many of his pictures are on display, plus other important pictures (several by Van Dyck), sculpture, furniture and carving by Grinling Gibbons. Recently restored North Gallery. Pleasure Grounds

Note: Visitors are advised that the interior is being restored and rooms are in the course of rearrangement

- **House:** 1 April to end Oct: daily except Mon & Fri (but open Good Fri & BH Mons, closed Tues following) 1–5.30. **Gardens and car park:** 12.30–6. Last admissions to house 5. Extra rooms shown Tues, Wed & Thur
- £4. Pre-booked parties of 15 or more, £3.50, children £2. Coach parties alight at Church Lodge entrance, coaches then park in NT car park
- Guided tours certain mornings by arrangement (additional charge)   *continued*

SUSSEX (WEST)

- 🛍 Shop open same days as house 1-5. Also open for Christmas shopping
- ♿ Car park is 800yds from house; volunteer driven vehicle available to take less able visitors to house; or disabled visitors may be set down at the Church Lodge entrance. Disabled drivers should make arrangements with the Administrator. All ground floor public rooms accessible except Chapel; wheelchairs available. WC in Servants' Block
- 👁 Braille guide
- 🍽 Light lunches in licensed restaurant 12.30-2.30; teas 3-5 same days as house
- 👶 Baby feeding/changing facilities; high chair. No prams in house; pushchairs admitted. Quiz sheet
- 🐕 No dogs
- ➡ In centre of Petworth (A272/A283) [197: SU976218]; Car park well signposted *Bus:* Stagecoach Coastline 1/A Worthing–Midhurst (passing BR Pulborough) (tel. (0903) 237661) *Station:* Pulborough 5¼m

PETWORTH PARK ♣

As Petworth House, above

Beautiful 700-acre deer park, with lakes, landscaped by Capability Brown and immortalised in Turner's paintings

- ⭕ All year: daily 8 to sunset. Closed 24-26 June from 12
- £ Free. Car park for park only on A283, 1½m N of Petworth. No vehicles in park. Height restriction of 6ft 9in in car park
- ♿ Car park and part of park accessible with care; some uneven paths
- E 24-26 June: Open Air Concerts. Send s.a.e. for booking form or tel. (0798) 43748 for information
- 🐕 Dogs must be kept under control
- ➡ Pedestrian access from Petworth town and on A272 & A283 *Bus:* as for Petworth House *Station:* Pulborough 5¼m

STANDEN

East Grinstead RH19 4NE (0342) 323029

A family house of the 1890s, designed by Philip Webb, friend of William Morris. The remarkably complete interior has been carefully restored, with many Morris textiles and wallpapers, plus good furniture, pottery and pictures of the period as well as the original electric light fittings. There is a billiard room, conservatory and beautiful hillside garden with fine views across the Medway valley. 2 holiday cottages

- ⭕ 1 April to end Oct: Wed to Sun & BH Mon. Weekends: March 1.30-4.30, last admission 4. **House:** 1.30-5.30; **Garden:** 12.30-5.30. Last admissions 5

  Note: Property may close at peak times for limited periods due to overcrowding

SUSSEX (WEST)

£ House & garden weekdays £4; Sat, Sun, Good Fri & BH Mon £4.80. Garden only £2.50 and £3 respectively, children half price. Parties £3.50 weekdays only, if booked in advance; other times by prior booking with Administrator. Parking 180yds

By special arrangement – mornings only; Wed, Thurs, Fri

Shop open as house. Also for Christmas shopping

Ground floor of house, restaurant and part of garden accessible; some steps in house; wheelchairs available. Disabled drivers only may park on forecourt of house. Steps and gravel paths in garden

Braille guide to garden; scented plants & flowers

Light lunches & afternoon teas. Open 12.30–5 (March12.30–4). Light lunches available for coach parties by prior arrangement with Administrator. Picnics in lower car park & woodland area only

Note: The Barn (Restaurant) is available for non-residential private and commercial functions with limited associated use of the house. The Administrator welcomes enquiries

2 reins, 2 baby carriers available; suitable for children aged up to 16 months; no back-packs; pushchairs not allowed in house

In lower car park and woodland walks only (via lower car park)

2m S of East Grinstead, signposted from B2110 (Turners Hill road) [187: TQ389356] *Bus:* London & Country 474 BR E Grinstead–Crawley (passing close BR Three Bridges), alight Saint Hill, ½m (tel. 081-668 7261) *Station:* E Grinstead 2m

UPPARK

South Harting, Petersfield, Hampshire GU31 5QR (0730) 825317

This late 17th-century house was partially destroyed by fire in 1989. The attic and first floor were gutted but the structure of the state rooms and basement survives largely intact. Most of the Trust's 18th-century contents were saved and are now in safe storage. Restoration work will be in progress throughout 1994. The garden was landscaped by Repton

3 April to end Sept: Grounds only, Sun 1.30–5.30. Last admissions 5. Small shop, temporary exhibition and video. House closed

£ £1. Children free

Note: Arrangements are temporary and liable to change. It is essential to telephone the property to check details

Small shop open as grounds

The garden is largely accessible and a wheelchair is available

5m SE of Petersfield on B2146, 1½m S of South Harting [197: SU775177] *Bus:* Hants & Sussex 61, 302, Stagecoach Hampshire Bus 216, Stagecoach Coastline 272 BR Petersfield–Midhurst, alight S Harting, 1½m (tel. (0243) 372045) *Station:* Petersfield 5½m

SUSSEX (WEST)

WAKEHURST PLACE ✤
Ardingly, nr Haywards Heath RH17 6TN (0444) 892701 or 081-332 5066

A superb collection of exotic trees, shrubs and other plants, many displayed in a geographic manner. Extensive water gardens, a Winter Garden, a Rock Walk and many other features including a fine Elizabethan mansion. The Loder Valley Nature Reserve can be visited by prior arrangement

Wakehurst Place is leased to the Ministry of Agriculture and is administered and maintained by the Royal Botanic Gardens, Kew. Prices and opening times may be subject to alteration; please tel. 081-332 5066 for up to date information

- All year: daily (except 25 Dec & 1 Jan). Nov to end Jan: 10–4; Feb & Oct: 10–5; March: 10–6; April to end Sept: 10–7. Last admissions ½hr before closing. Mansion closes 1 hr before gardens
- £3.50, children (16 and under) £1.20. Students, OAPs and unemployed £1.80; discount available for pre-booked & pre-paid parties (prices subject to review). Parking 400yds from Mansion. Exhibition in Mansion
- Guided tours available most Sat & Sun – please call 081-332 5585/5058 from Tues onwards for times & availability. To book groups please write to the Ranger
- Books & gifts are sold in the shop in the Mansion
- Most of upper garden accessible, but steep paths elsewhere. Wheelchair available. WC. Parking arrangements should be carefully checked before visiting, as it may be possible for people with disabilities to be set down by the house
- New self-service restaurant opening 1994 (not NT) – open all year
- Contact the Education Officer at the above address
- No dogs (except guide dogs)
- 1½m NW of Ardingly, on B2028 [187: TQ339314] *Bus:* Gem Fairtax 472 Haywards Heath–Crawley (passing BR Haywards Heath & 3 Bridges) (tel. (0293) 527104) *Station:* Balcombe 5m; E Grinstead 6½m; Horsted Keynes (Bluebell Rly) 3¾m

Tyne & Wear

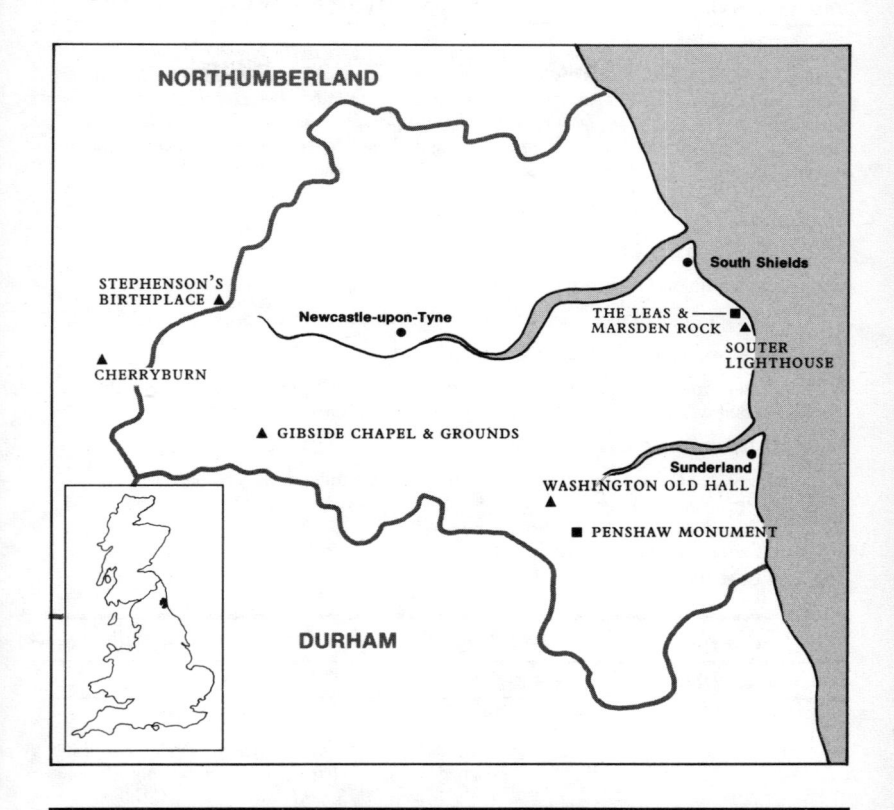

COAST AND COUNTRYSIDE

At South Shields, the Trust owns 2½ miles of spectacular coastline, from Trow Point to Lizard Point [88: NZ400650]. The property consists of **The Leas**, a large open area of grassland, bordered on the east by limestone cliffs, and **Marsden Rock**, with its famous bird colony of kittiwakes, cormorants and fulmars. Guided walks with the Warden take place on a regular basis during the season. At the southern end of this area is **Souter Lighthouse** (see p.238) with its complex of buildings [88:NZ641408].

Inland from The Leas can be found the well-known landmark of **Penshaw Monument** [88: NZ334544]. A Doric temple, built in 1844 to commemorate the first Earl of Durham, it can be seen from miles around. It is situated near the village of Penshaw and is just off the A183 Sunderland road; car parking in disused road at foot of monument. At **Gibside** (see p.238) new walks have been opened around the 18th-century landscaped park.

TYNE & WEAR

GIBSIDE

nr Rowlands Gill, Burnopfield, Newcastle-upon-Tyne NE16 6BG (0207) 542255

Gibside was one of the finest 18th-century designed landscapes in the North of England. In 1993 the Trust acquired 354 acres of the grounds and woodlands in addition to the beautiful Palladian Chapel and Grand Walk which it has owned since 1965. Long term restoration work is required to reunite the features of this landscape which includes the ruined Hall and Orangery, the Grand Walk, the Column of Liberty and the Chapel. New walks have been created along the River Derwent, to the Column of Liberty and through the woodlands

- 1 April to 30 Oct: daily except Mon but open BH Mon 11-5
- £2.50. No party rate
- Shop and tea-room run by the Friends of Gibside
- Contact Custodian for access details. Stairclimber for Chapel steps, WC
- Shop, tea-room and picnic area in car park
- Service in Chapel 1st Sunday each month. Programme of concerts, events and guided walks; apply to Custodian for further details, s.a.e. please
- In the grounds, on leads
- 6m SW of Gateshead, 20m W of Durham; entrance on B6314 between Burnopfield and Rowlands Gill [88: NZ172583] *Bus*: Go-Ahead Northern 601, M20/1 Newcastle/Gateshead–Rowland's Gill; 745 Newcastle–Consett (all passing close BR Newcastle). On all alight Rowlands Gill, ½m (tel. 091-232 5325) *Station*: Blaydon (U) 5m

SOUTER LIGHTHOUSE

Coast Road, Whitburn, Sunderland SR6 7NR 091-529 3161

This shore-based lighthouse was the first to be powered by alternating electric current. It was first opened in 1871. Visitors can view the Engine Room, Light Tower, Fog Signal Station and Lighthouse Keeper's cottage. Video, model and information displays

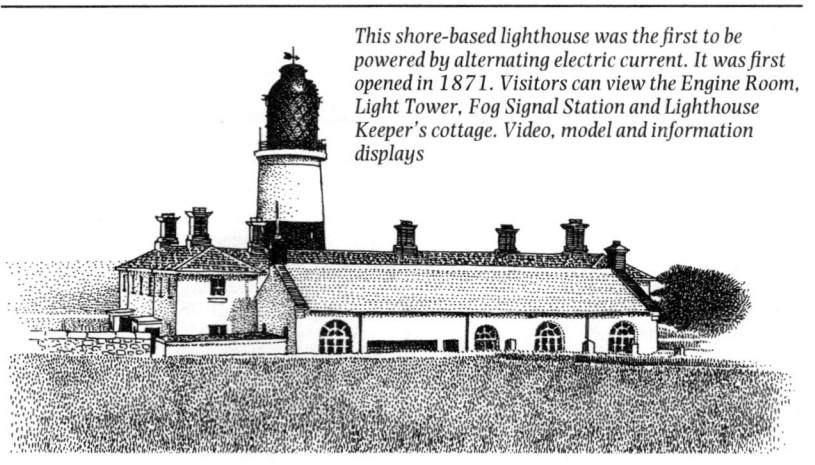

238

TYNE & WEAR

- ◯ 1 April to 30 Oct: daily except Mon (open BH Mon) 11–5. Last admissions 4.30
- £ £2.30. Pre-booked parties £1.70. Car and coach park 100yds
- 🎓 For pre-booked parties
- 🛍 Access to shop is free. Open as lighthouse
- ♿ Limited wheelchair access. WC. Light Tower not accessible for wheelchairs
- 🍴 Restaurant serving morning coffee, lunch and teas, open as lighthouse. Access is free. Picnicking in grounds
- 📖 Education Room; school base
- E Family Fun Day. For details send s.a.e. to Custodian
- → 2½m S of South Shields on A183, 5m N of Sunderland on A183 [88: NZ641408] *Bus:* tel. 091-232 5325 *Station:* East Boldon (U) 3m

WASHINGTON OLD HALL 🏛 ✺

The Avenue, Washington Village NE38 7LE 091-416 6879

The home of George Washington's direct ancestors from 1183–1288, remaining in the family until 1613. Substantially rebuilt in the 17th century

- ◯ 1 April to 30 Oct: closed Fri & Sat when the property is available for parties, weddings and meetings (but open Good Fri) 11–5. Last admissions 4.30
- £ £2.20. Parties £1.70 on application to Administrator. Coaches must park on the Avenue
- 🛍 Small shop in entrance hall, open as house
- ♿ Access to ground floor only. Please contact Administrator for access arrangements.
- 🍴 Tea, coffee and cake available during opening hours
- E Hall and garden available for weddings, parties & meetings; contact Administrator
- → 5m W of Sunderland, 2m E of A1, S of Tyne tunnel, follow signs, Washington New Town, District 4, then Washington village; situated on E side of Avenue [88: NZ312566] *Bus:* Go-Ahead Northern X85/9, 194, 293/4, Calvary 297 from Tyne & Wear Metro Heworth; also other services from surrounding areas (tel. 091-232 5325) *Station:* Heworth (Tyne & Wear Metro) 4m; E Boldon (U) 6m; Newcastle 7m

REFER TO OPENING PAGES FOR GENERAL INFORMATION

Warwickshire

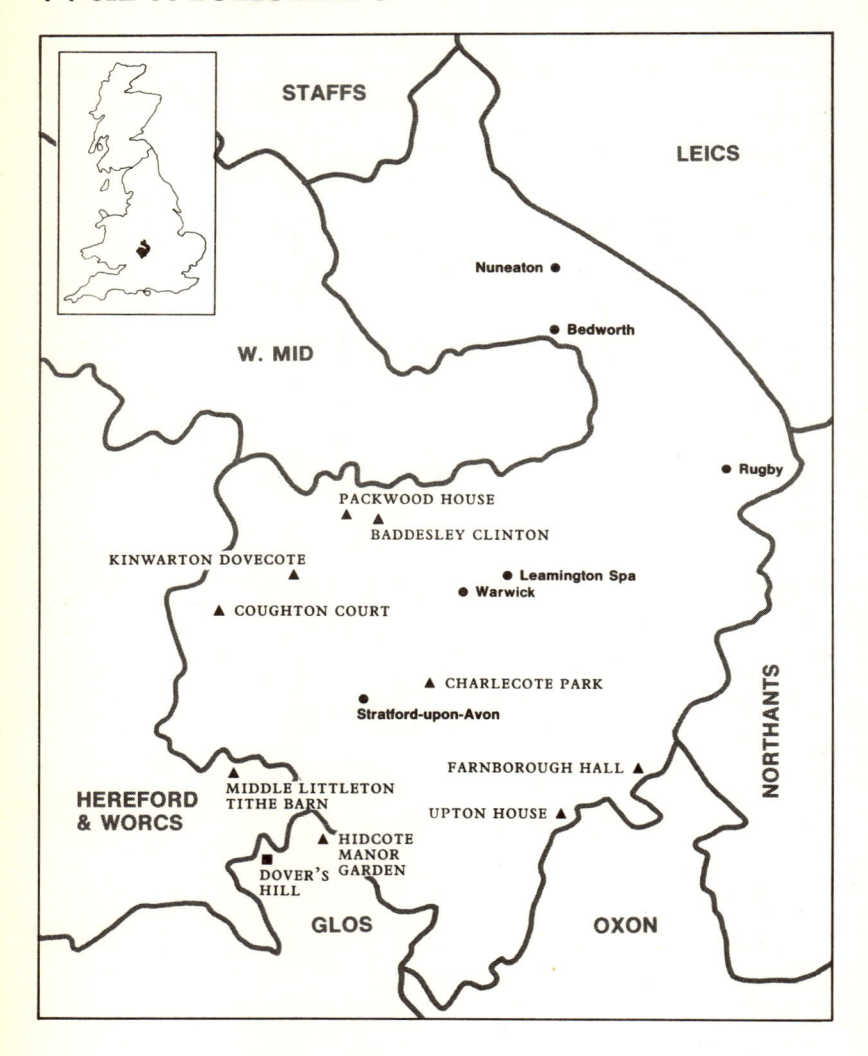

WARWICKSHIRE

BADDESLEY CLINTON

Rising Lane, Lapworth, Knowle, Solihull B93 0DQ (0564) 783294

A romantically sited medieval moated manor house, dating from the 14th century, and little changed since 1634. Contents include family portraits and priest holes. Also, a chapel, garden, ponds and lake walk

- 2 March to end Sept: Wed to Sun & BH Mon (closed Good Fri) 2-6 (grounds open from 12.30). Oct: Wed to Sun 12.30-4.30. March 1995: Wed to Sun 2-6. Last admissions to house, shop & restaurant ½hr before closing
- £4.00. Family ticket £11. Grounds, restaurant & shop only £2. Parties of 15 or more and coaches (not Suns) by prior written arrangement. Free parking. No perambulators, back-carriers or push-chairs in house. Timed tickets issued to control numbers in house
- Thur evenings by appointment. Supper can be included
- Shop open 12.30-5.30, Oct:12.30-4.30. Also 2 Nov to 18 Dec: Wed to Sun 12.30-4.30
- Access to ground floor and most of garden, restaurant & shop. Parking by visitor reception area. Wheelchairs available. WC near shop
- Available upon request
- Licensed restaurant, lunches & teas; same days as house 12.30-5.30. Closed 2-2.30. (Oct closes 4.30). Also Nov & Dec as shop. No picnicking in garden
- School parties by appointment: Wed, Thur & Fri mornings
- Please contact the Administrator for details
- ¾m W of A4141 Warwick/Birmingham road, at Chadwick End, 7½m NW of Warwick, 15m SE of central Birmingham [139: SP199715] *Station:* Lapworth (U), not Sun, 2m; Dorridge, not Sun except May to Sept, 4m; Birmingham International (BR & Airport) 9m

CHARLECOTE PARK

Warwick CV35 9ER (0789) 470277

Home of the Lucy family since 1247. The present house was built in 1550s and later visited by Queen Elizabeth I. Rich Victorian 'romantic' interiors were created from the 1820s onwards, and contain important objects from Willian Beckford's Fonthill Abbey. River Avon flows through park, landscaped by 'Capability' Brown, which supports herds of red and fallow deer, reputedly poached by Shakespeare, and a flock of Jacob sheep, introduced in 1756

- April to end Oct: Fri to Tues (closed Good Fri) 11-6. House closed 1-2, last admissions 5
- £4.00. Family ticket £11. Parties (max 60) by prior arrangement with Administrator. Car and coach park 300yds. Video film of life at Charlecote Park in the Victorian period

continued

WARWICKSHIRE

[figure] Evening guided tours for pre-booked parties May to Sept: Mon 7.30-9.30 (£4, incl. NT members; minimum charge £80 for party)

[figure] Shop & Victorian kitchens open as property 11-5.30. Also 5 Nov to 18 Dec: Sat & Sun open 1.30-4.30 for Christmas shopping

[figure] Access to all open rooms, except the Gatehouse Museum. Restaurant accessible. Shop & Victorian kitchens have alternative access avoiding steps. WCs behind Orangery and near Gatehouse. Arrangements can be made at the kiosk to drop off disabled visitors or park near house. The video can be viewed in the gatehouse. Wheelchairs available

[figure] Braille guide

[figure] Morning coffee, lunches, afternoon teas in the Orangery licensed Restaurant; open as property 11-5.30. Picnicking in Deer Park only

[figure] Baby changing facilities

[figure] School parties by prior arrangement with Administrator: schools base and resource pack available

[figure] 2 June: Family Day; 16-22 June: Midsummer Music Festival; 21 July: National Gardens Scheme; 4,11,18 & 24 Oct: Deer Park Tours. NT members are charged for events. Details from Administrator

[figure] In car park only. Reasonable walks outside park available

[figure] 1m W of Wellesbourne, 5m E of Stratford-upon-Avon, 6m S of Warwick on N side of B4086 [151: SP263564] *Bus:* Midland Red 18 Leamington Spa (Coventry Sun)–Stratford-upon-Avon (passing BR Leamington Spa) (tel. (0788) 535555) *Station:* Stratford-upon-Avon, not Sun, except May–Sept, $5\frac{1}{2}$m; Warwick, not Sun except May–Sept, 6m; Leamington Spa 8m

WARWICKSHIRE

COUGHTON COURT
nr Alcester B49 5JA (0789) 762435

An impressive central gatehouse dating from 1530 with Elizabethan half-timered courtyard. During the Civil War this mainly Elizabethan house was attacked by both Parliamentary and Royalist forces. It has important connections with the Gunpowder Plot and contains priests' hiding places. The contents of the Gatehouse and South Wing include some notable furniture, porcelain, portraits and memorabilia of Throckmorton family who have lived here since 1409. There are two churches, a tranquil lake, riverside walk and newly-created formal gardens

Coughton Court is managed by the Throckmorton family

- April: Sat & Sun 1.30-5.30 (BH Mon incl. Easter Mon 12.30-5.30); 5-6 April 1.30-5.30 (closed Good Fri). May to end Sept: daily except Thur & Fri 1.30-5.30. Oct: Sat & Sun 1.30-5. Grounds open 12-6 (Oct closes 5). Last admissions to house ½hr before closing
- £4.50. Family ticket £12. Parties of 15 or more (not BH) by prior arrangement. Grounds only £2.50
- Evening guided tours for pre-booked parties Mon to Wed. Garden tours by appointment. No party rate or membership concessions for out of hours visits
- Shop open as house (managed by family)
- Access to two rooms on ground floor, restaurant and shop. Wheelchairs available. WC with handrail, otherwise unadapted. Grounds, garden & riverside path suitable for wheelchairs
- Braille guide and audio cassette guide
- Restaurant managed by family, open for lunches & teas same days as house 12.30-5.45. Picnics in car park only
- Children play area and animal centre
- School visits by arrangement
- Concerts & other events; details from Administrator. Specail sealed knot event 18-19 June (NT members charged for admission)
- On leads in car park only
- 2m N of Alcester on A435 [150: SP080604] *Bus:* Midland Red West 146, Stratford Blue166 Redditch–Evesham (passing BR Redditch & close BR Evesham) (tel. (0905) 766800) *Station:* Redditch 6m

FARNBOROUGH HALL
Banbury, Oxfordshire OX17 1DU (0295 89) 202

A classical mid-18th century stone house, home of the Holbech family for 300 years. The entrance hall, staircase and 2 principal rooms are shown; the plasterwork is particularly notable. The grounds contain charming 18th-century temples, a ⅔ mile terrace walk and an obelisk

Farnborough Hall is occupied and administered by Mr & Mrs Holbech   *continued*

243

WARWICKSHIRE

- ⭕ **House, grounds & terrace walk:** April to end Sept: Wed & Sat 2–6, also 1 & 2 May 2–6. **Terrace walk only:** Thur & Fri 2–6. Last admissions 5.30
- 💷 House, grounds & terrace walk £2.60. Garden & terrace walk £1.50. Terrace walk only (Thur & Fri) £1. Parties by written arrangement only – no reduction. Coach and car park. Strong shoes advisable for terrace
- ♿ Ground floor of house and garden accessible (terrace walk is very steep)
- 🐕 Welcome, on leads in grounds only
- ➡️ 6m N of Banbury, ½m W of A423 [151: SP430490] *Bus:* Midland Red 509/10 from Banbury (passing close BR Banbury) (tel. (0788) 535555) *Station:* Banbury 6m

KINWARTON DOVECOTE

Kinwarton, nr Alcester Warwickshire (Regional Office (0684) 850051)

A circular 14th-century dovecote, with fine ogee doorway

- ⭕ April to end Oct: daily 9–6 or sunset if earlier. Closed Good Fri. Other times by prior appointment only with Severn Regional Office (see final page). Key obtainable from Glebe Farm next door
- 💷 60p
- ➡️ 1½m NE of Alcester, just S of B4089 [150: SP106585] *Bus:* As Coughton Court, but alight Alcester, 1½m; 228 passes close *Station:* Wilmcote (U), not Sun except May to Sept, 5m; Wootton Wawen (U), not Sun, 5m

PACKWOOD HOUSE

Lapworth, Solihull B94 6AT (0564) 782024

A fascinating timber-framed Tudor house containing a wealth of fine tapestries and furniture. The superb gardens are noted mainly for their yew topiary and Carolean Garden

WARWICKSHIRE

- ◯ April to end Sept: Wed to Sun & BH Mon 2–6. Closed Good Fri. Oct: Wed to Sun 12.30–4.30. Last admissions to house ½hr before closing
- £ £3.20. Family ticket £8.80. Garden only £2. Free car and coach park. Walks available through parkland and woodland
- 🛍 Shop open as house
- ♿ Access to ground floor (except Great Hall which can be seen from door) and part of garden. WC with handrails, otherwise unadapted
- ☕ Picnic site opposite main gates
- 🐕 No dogs
- ➡ 2m E of Hockley Heath (on A3400), 11m SE of central Birmingham [139: SP174722] *Bus:* Stratford Blue X20 Birmingham–Stratford-upon-Avon, alight Hockley Heath, 1¾m (tel. 021-200 2601) *Station:* Lapworth (U), not Sun, 1½m; Dorridge, not Sun except May–Sept, 2m; Birmingham International 8m

UPTON HOUSE 🏠 ❖
Banbury, Oxfordshire OX15 6HT (0295) 670266

The house, built of a mellow local stone, dates from 1695, but the outstanding collections it contains are the chief attraction. Assembled this century by the 2nd Lord Bearsted, they include paintings by English and Continental Old Masters, Brussels tapestries, Sèvres porcelain, Chelsea figures and 18th century furniture. The garden is also of great interest, with terraces descending into a deep valley from the main lawn; herbaceous borders, the national collection of Asters, over an acre of kitchen garden, a water garden laid out in the 1930s and pools stocked with ornamental fish

Note: Entry to house, tea-room and shop is by timed tickets at peak times on Sun in July, Aug & Bank Holidays, therefore delays are possible

- ◯ Due to works being carried out to improve environmental conditions, house, tea-room & shop will re-open 11 June to 31 Oct: Sat to Wed (incl BH Mon) 2–6. Last admissions 5.30. Garden only also open April: Sat, Sun & BH Mon 2–6; and 1 May to 8 June: Sat to Wed (inc BH Mon) 2–6 and there after as house
- £ £4.30. Family ticket £11.80. Garden only £2.15. Parties of 15 or more (no reduction) & evening guided tours by written arrangement (no reduction). Free parking
- 🛍 Shop open as house
- ♿ Access to ground floor rooms via ramped side door, tea-room and part of garden. Wheelchair available. WC. Special parking near house for disabled drivers. Motorised buggy with driver available for access to/from lower garden
- ☕ Tea-room in house
- 👶 Parent and baby room
- **E** Outdoor concert and play; also Fine Arts Study Afternoons: please send s.a.e. or tel. for information
- ➡ On A422, 7m NW of Banbury, 12m SE of Stratford-upon-Avon [151: SP371461] *Bus:* Banbury 7m

245

West Midlands

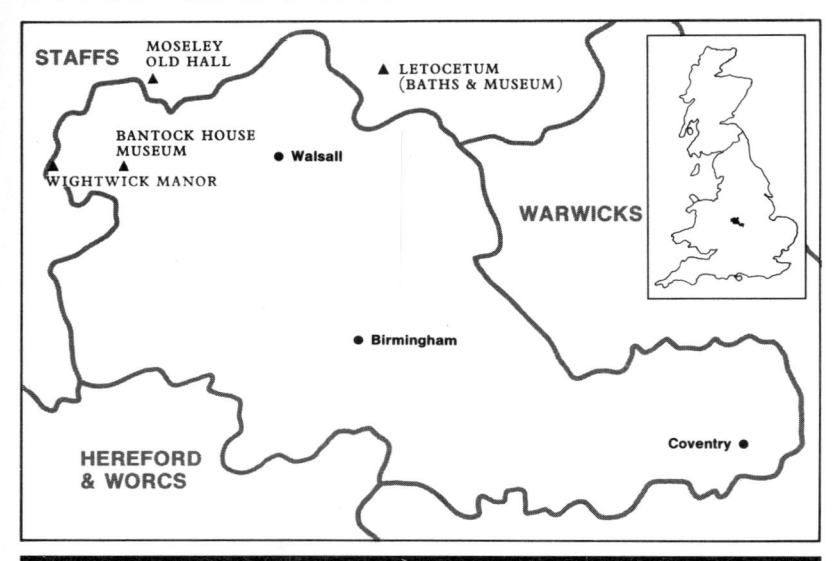

THE BALSTON COLLECTION, BANTOCK HOUSE MUSEUM

Bantock Park, Bradmore Road, Wolverhampton WV3 9LQ (0902) 312132

Thomas Balston's collection of Victorian Staffordshire portrait figures, which he presented to the Trust in 1960, is on permanent view at Bantock House Museum (not NT); also on view are the town's important collections of 18th-century English enamels; Georgian and Victorian japanned tin and papier mâché; good collections of Worcester porcelain, dolls and toys, and some local history. Located in public park with free access

- **O** All year: Mon & Thur 10-7; Tues, Wed, Fri & Sat 10-5; Sun 2-5. Closed Good Fri, Easter Sun, 1 Jan and 25 & 26 Dec; other days at Christmas, Bank & public holidays subject to arrangement. Tours by arrangement
- **£** Free. Parking outside museum for cars; 300yds for coaches, access via Finchfield Road
- **♿** Ground floor only, includes the Balston Collection; cars may draw up to the front door, access via Bradmore Road
- **👤** Children's holiday activities are arranged during each long holiday. Please enquire in advance
- **E** Contact Museum for details
- **→** SW of Wolverhampton town centre on B4161; access via Bradmore Road
  Bus: West Midlands Travel 513/4, Stephensons 585-8 from BR Wolverhampton (tel. 021-200 2700) *Station:* Wolverhampton 2m

WIGHTWICK MANOR

Wightwick Bank, Wolverhampton WV6 8EE (0902) 761108

Begun in 1887, the house is a notable example of the influence of William Morris, with many original Morris wallpapers and fabrics. Also of interest are pre-Raphaelite pictures, Kempe glass and de Morgan ware. The Victorian/Edwardian garden has yew hedges and topiary, terraces and two pools

- **House:** 30 April to 31 Dec and March 1995: Thur & Sat 2.30–5.30. Also open BH Sat, Sun & Mon 2.30–5.30 (ground floor only, no guided tours). Open for pre-booked parties Wed & Thur and special evening tours. Admission to house by timed ticket. Owing to the fragile nature of contents and the requirements of conservation, some rooms cannot always be shown; tours will therefore vary during the year. School visits on Wed & Thur, contact Administrator for details. **Garden:** same days as house 2–6; also open by appointment Mon to Fri
- £4.20. Students £2.10. Garden only £2. Parking: only room for one coach in layby outside main gate; car park (120yds) at bottom of Wightwick Bank. Pottery (not NT). Coffee and soft drinks available
- Except Bank Holidays
- Access to 5 rooms & garden (but site slopes). No wheelchairs available
- Braille guides
- Coffee and soft drinks available
- Pre-booked school visits; details from Administrator
- In garden only, on leads
- 3m W of Wolverhampton, up Wightwick Bank (A454), beside the Mermaid Inn [139: SO869985] *Bus:* Tellus/Midland Red West 890 Wolverhampton–Bridgnorth; 516 Wolverhampton–Pattingham (both pass close BR Wolverhampton) (tel. 021-200 2700) *Station:* Wolverhampton 3m

Wiltshire

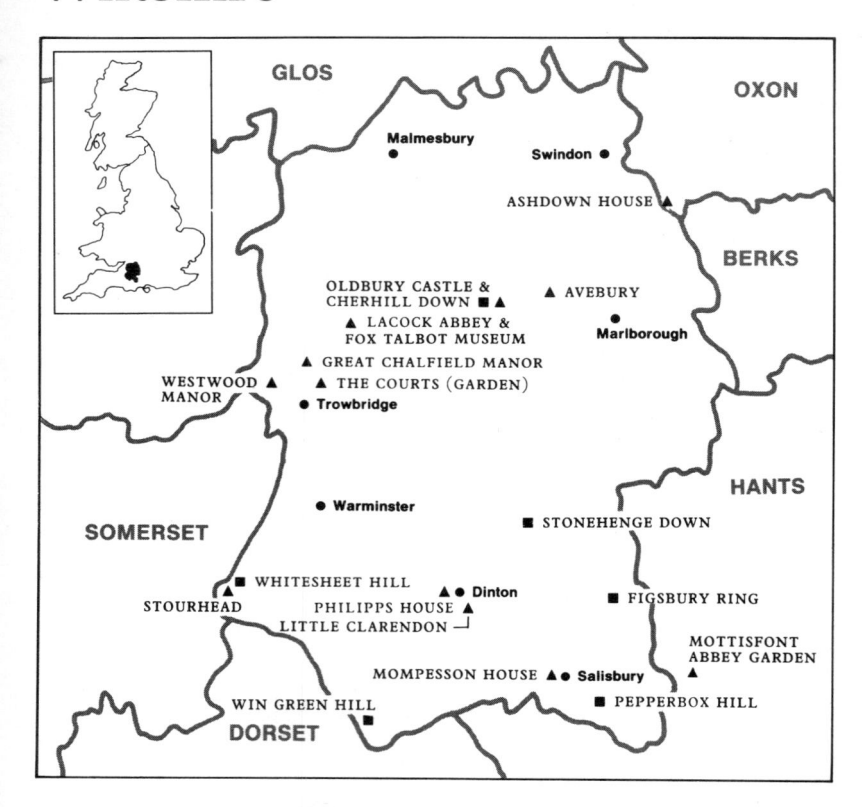

COUNTRYSIDE

As well as the important ancient monument of **Avebury** (see p.249) the Trust owns other notable antiquities in Wiltshire. **Figsbury Ring**, north-east of Salisbury and giving fine views over this city, is an Iron Age hill-fort [184: SU188338]. The Trust's land at Stonehenge is described in the entry on p.253.

West of Avebury, between Calne and Beckhampton, are **Cherhill Down** and **Oldbury Castle** [173: SU046694]. The Trust owns the earthwork of Oldbury Castle and the Landsdown Monument with about 500 acres of the unimproved downland. From the ridge are fine views over the Marlborough Downs to the east, south to Devizes and west to Chippenham. The Trust also owns **Whitesheet Hill** with its Iron Age hill-fort on the 2,400 acre Stourhead Estate.

In the extreme south of Wiltshire the highest point in Cranborne Chase is **Win Green Hill**, 911ft [184: ST925206], crowned with a clump of beech trees shielding a bowl

WILTSHIRE

barrow; from the summit are views south-east to the Isle of Wight and north-west to the Quantocks.

From **Pepperbox Hill** on the Southampton road (A36) [184: SU215248] there are spectacular views over Salisbury. The octagonal tower, which gives its name to these 72 acres is a 17th-century folly.

AVEBURY

nr Marlborough SN8 1RF (0672) 539250 – answerphone

One of the most important Megalithic monuments in Europe, this 28½-acre site with stone circles enclosed by a ditch and external bank is approached by an avenue of stones. The site also includes the Alexander Keiller Museum and the Wiltshire Life Society's display of Wiltshire rural life in the Great Barn. The NT also owns 1,400 acres, which provide the setting for the stone circle. The Museum collection is maintained and managed by English Heritage

- Stone Circle open daily. Museum open: 1 April to 31 Oct, daily 10–6. 1 Nov to 31 March: Wed to Sun 10–4 (closed 24–26 Dec, 1 Jan)

- Alexander Keiller Museum: Adult £1.35; Senior Citizens, UB40 holders, students, £1; children under 16, 65p. Free admission to NT members and English Heritage members. Great Barn: for admission charges and opening times tel. (0672) 539555. NT members free

- Open daily 26 March to 30 Oct: 11–5.30; 31 Oct to 11 Dec: Sat & Sun only 11.30–4. Tel. (0672) 539384

- Access to Museum, Barn and parts of Circle (access for disabled drivers to barn area). WC at Great Barn and in village High St

- Lunches & teas at licensed Stones Restaurant and Red Lion Inn (not NT)

- On leads in Stone Circle

- 6m W of Marlborough, 1m N of the Bath road (A4) on A4361 and B4003 [173: SU102699] *Bus:* Thamesdown/Fosseway 49, Wiltshire Downsman X49 Swindon–Devizes/Marlborough (passing close BR Swindon); Wilts & Dorset 5 Salisbury–Swindon (tel. 0345 090 899) *Station:* Pewsey, no practical Sun service, 10m; Swindon 11m

AVEBURY MANOR GARDEN

nr Marlborough, SN8 1RF (0672) 539388 answerphone

A regularly altered house of monastic origin, the present buildings date from the early 16th century, with notable Queen Anne alterations and Edwardian renovation by Colonel Jenner. The topiary and flower gardens contains medieval walls, ancient box and numerous compartments

Parts of the house may be open subject to restoration work; please telephone to check opening times

- **Garden:** 26 March to 30 Oct daily except Mon & Thur (open BH Mon) 11–5.30. Last admissions 5 or dusk if earlier

continued

249

WILTSHIRE

- £ Garden £2.10, children £1.30. Parties £1.90, children £1.10
- See Avebury
- Garden mostly level
- E Outdoor Theatre. For details ring the Events Organiser tel. (0985) 847777
- → *Bus/Rail:* as Avebury

THE COURTS (GARDEN)
Holt, nr Trowbridge BA14 6RR (0225) 782340

An 18th-century house (not open to the public), with an ornamental façade, flanked by a 7-acre garden of mystery

- **Garden only:** 27 March to 30 Oct: daily except Sat 2–5. Out of season by appointment
- £ £2.50, children £1.50. Parties by arrangement in advance with the Head Gardener. No WCs. NT shop in Melksham, 4m (tel. (0225) 706454)
- → 3m SW of Melksham, 3m N of Trowbridge, 2½m E of Bradford on Avon, on S side of B3107 [173: ST861618] *Bus:* Badgerline 237 Chippenham–Trowbridge (passing close BR Chippenham & Trowbridge) (tel. (0225) 464446) *Station:* Bradford-on-Avon 2½m; Trowbridge 3m

GREAT CHALFIELD MANOR
nr Melksham SN12 8NJ (0985) 847777

Dating from 1480, the manor house is set across a moat between parish church and stables. Restored early this century by Major R. Fuller, whose family still lives here

WILTSHIRE

- [O] 27 March to 27 Oct: Tues, Wed, Thur by guided tours only, starting 12.15, 2.15, 3, 3.45 & 4.30. Closed on public holidays

  Note: Members of historical and other societies wishing to visit the Manor in organised parties can usually be shown the church, house and garden on other weekdays, by written appointment with Mrs Robert Floyd

- [£] £3.50. No reduction for children or parties. No WCs
- [K] Guided tours of the manor take 45 minutes and numbers are limited to 25. It is suggested that visitors arriving when a tour is in progress visit the church and garden first
- [&] Limited access to garden only
- [→] 3m SW of Melksham via Broughton Gifford Common (sign for Atworth, drive on left) [166: ST860630] *Bus:* Badgerline 237 Chippenham–Trowbridge (passing close BR Chippenham & Trowbridge), alight Holt, 1m by footpath (tel. (0225) 464446) *Station:* Bradford on Avon, 3m

LACOCK ABBEY

Lacock, nr Chippenham SN15 2LG (0249) 730227

The Abbey was founded in 1232 and converted into a country house after 1539. There are medieval cloisters, sacristy and chapter house, a 16th-century stable court, and an 18th-century Gothick hall. 19th-century home of William Henry Fox Talbot, inventor of photography. Home of the Burnett-Brown family who are the direct descendants of the Talbot family who gave the Abbey and village to the Trust. Interesting features in grounds: unusual trees, 18th-century summer house, 19th-century rose garden

- [O] **House:** 26 March to 30 Oct: daily except Tues (closed Good Fri) 1–5.30. **Cloisters & grounds:** 26 March to 30 Oct: daily (closed Good Fri) 12–5.30. Last admissions 5
- [£] House, cloisters & grounds £4.10, children £2.10; parties £3.60, children £1.80. Cloisters & grounds £2.10, children £1
- [shop] Shop in village; 11 April to 30 Oct: daily 10–5.30; 31 Oct to 22 Dec: daily 11–4; 3 Jan 1995 to end March: Tues to Sat 11–4. Tel. (0249) 730302
- [&] Access to grounds and cloisters; house is more difficult with 4 sets of steps; car parking arrangements; wheelchairs available at Museum; WC at house.
- [braille] Braille guide and taped guides; pre-booked guided parties for visually impaired visitors
- [refreshments] In village (not NT)
- [school] Pre-booked school parties welcome. Tel. Administrator for details
- [E] For details of concerts and outdoor theatre events ring the Administrator
- [→] 3m S of Chippenham, just E of A350 [173: ST919684]; signposted to car park *Bus:* Badgerline 234/7 Chippenham–Trowbridge (passing close BR Chippenham & Trowbridge) (tel. (0225) 464446) *Station:* Chippenham 3½m

WILTSHIRE

LACOCK: FOX TALBOT MUSEUM
Lacock, nr Chippenham SN15 2LG (0249) 730459

A museum of photography commemorating the achievements of William Henry Fox Talbot (1800–77), the inventor of the modern photographic negative

- **O** 26 March to 30 Oct: daily (except Good Fri) 11–5.30. Last admissions 5. Visitors are advised to check opening times as some improvement work is being carried out
- **£** £2.30, children £1.10. Parties £2
- Shop selling photographic books, films, postcards. Open as museum
- All areas accessible (stair lift); and see Lacock Abbey, above; WC at Abbey & in Red Lion car park
- In village (not NT)
- **E** For special events, please check with the Curator
- **→** At entrance gates to Lacock Abbey (see above) *Bus:* as for Lacock Abbey

LITTLE CLARENDON
Dinton, Salisbury SP3 5OZ (0985) 847777

A Tudor house, but greatly altered in the 17th century

- **O** By prior written appointment with tenant
- **£** £1.50. No reduction for children or parties. House not suitable for pushchairs or prams. No coaches
- **→** ¼m E of Dinton Church [184: SU015316] *Bus:* as for Philipps House

MOMPESSON HOUSE
The Close, Salisbury SP1 2EL (0722) 335659

One of the finest 18th-century houses in the Cathedral Close, containing notable plasterwork, an elegant oak staircase, fine period furniture, the important Turnbull collection of 18th-century English drinking glasses and a china collection. The attractive walled garden is enclosed on one side by the great wall of the Cathedral Close

- **O** 26 March to 30 Oct: daily, except Thur & Fri 12–5.30. Last admissions 5
- **£** £3, children £1.50. Parties £2.70. Visitor sitting room. Parking in Cathedral Close (a charge is made by the Dean & Chapter). Coach parking in Central Car Park
- Shop at 41 High Street (tel. (0722) 331884)
- Access to ground floor, garden and tea-room only

WILTSHIRE

- 👁 Braille guide
- 🍽 Teas in Garden Room 12-5
- **E** Exhibition of paintings by Martin Yeoman throughout the season; for details ring Administrator
- ➡ On N side of Choristers' Green in the Cathedral Close, near High Street Gate [184: SU142295] *Bus:* From surrounding areas (tel. (0722) 336855) *Station:* Salisbury ½m

PHILIPPS HOUSE

Dinton, Salisbury SP3 5HJ (0722) 716208

A neo-Grecian house by Jeffry Wyattville, completed in 1816. It is let to, administered and maintained by, the Young Women's Christian Association for use as an art centre

- 🅞 On Sat only, by prior written arrangement only with the YWCA Warden. Ground floor only on view
- 💷 £1.50. No reduction for children or parties
- ♿ Access to grounds only
- 👁 Taped guide
- 🍽 Penruddocke Arms and Swordsman Inn, Dinton (not NT)
- ➡ 9m W of Salisbury, on N side of B3089 [184: SU009319] *Bus:* Wilts & Dorset 25-7 from Salisbury (passing BR Salisbury & Tisbury) (tel. (0722) 336855) *Station:* Tisbury 5m

STONEHENGE DOWN

Amesbury, nr Salisbury SP4 7DE English Heritage (0980) 623108

The Trust owns 1,450 acres of land surrounding the monument, including some fine Bronze Age barrow groups and the Cursus. There are recommended walks and an archaeological leaflet available at Stonehenge shop

The monument itself is owned, managed and maintained by English Heritage

- 🅞 1 April–31 Oct: daily 10–6. 1 Nov–31 March: daily 10–4 (closed 24–26 Dec, 1 Jan). NT land open at all times, but may be subject to closure at the Summer Solstice – 21 June for up to 2 days
- 💷 Adults £2.85. OAP/UB40/students £2.15. Children £1.40. Free admission to NT and English Heritage members
- 🛍 Shop run by EH adjacent to the monument
- ♿ Wheelchair access to the monument but not to land
- 🚫🐕 No dogs on archeological walks   *continued*

REFER TO OPENING PAGES FOR GENERAL INFORMATION

WILTSHIRE

→ Monument 2m W of Amesbury, at Jn of A303 & A344/A360 [184: SU1242]
Bus: Wilts & Dorset 3 BR Salisbury–Stonehenge (tel. (0722) 336855)
Station: Salisbury 9½m

STOURHEAD
Stourton, Warminster BA12 6QH House & Garden (0747) 840348
King Alfred's Tower (0985) 844785

Landscape garden laid out 1741–80, with lakes and temples, rare trees and plants. The house, begun in 1721 by Colen Campbell, contains furniture by the younger Chippendale, and fine paintings. King Alfred's Tower, a red brick folly built in 1772 by Flitcroft at the edge of the estate, is 160ft high giving fine views over neighbouring counties of Somerset, Dorset and Wiltshire

Garden: all year: daily 8–7 or sunset if earlier (except 20–23 July when garden will close at 5). **House:** 26 March to 30 Oct: daily except Thur & Fri 12–5.30 or dusk if earlier. Last admissions 5. Other times by written appointment with Administrator. **King Alfred's Tower:** 26 March to 30 Oct: daily except Fri & Mon (open Good Fri & BH Mon) 2–5.30 or dusk if earlier. Tower is 3½m by road from Stourhead House; parking 300yds. Dogs may be tied up outside, but are not allowed up the Tower. Tel. (0985) 844785

House: £4.10, children £2.10. Parties £3.50, children £1.60 by written appointment only. Garden: March to 30 Oct £4.10, children £2.10, parties £3.50; Nov to end Feb: £3.10, children £1.50; no reduction for parties. Parking ¼m from house, garden & facilities. King Alfred's Tower: £1.50, children (5–16) 70p

Exhibition about Stourhead Estate in new reception building in the main car park

Open daily 1 April to 29 Oct 11–6; 30 Oct to 18 Dec 11–4; Jan to end March 1995, 11–4. Tel. (0747) 840591

WILTSHIRE

- ♿ Garden largely accessible, but 13 steps up to house then ground floor rooms on one level; parking arrangements at house and garden; 1½m-long path round lake accessible to wheelchair users, but very steep in places. Battery-powered self-drive buggy. Please avoid congested times at weekends and in May & June; WC in Spread Eagle courtyard and in main car park. Scented azaleas in early summer. Alfred's Tower: level walk across grass – 300yds from car park. No wheelchairs at Tower

- ☕ Spread Eagle Inn (NT) at garden entrance (tel. (0747) 840587) open all year. Village hall restaurant: coffee, light lunches, teas, ice creams. Open daily 26 March to 30 Oct: 10.30-5.30 (tel. (0747) 840161). Picnicking in car park & garden

- 🚼 Parent's room next to reception building in main car park

- 🎦 Special events and projects can be organised by contacting the Administrator. History of Tower by arrangement

- **E** Fête Champêtre 20-23 July. Tickets (tel. (0747) 840142). Only ticket holders to the fête will be admitted to the garden after 5. For details of other outdoor theatre events ring the Administrator

- 🐕 No dogs in garden except Nov to end Feb; in woods throughout year. Special dog walks available

- ➡️ At Stourton, off B3092, 3m NW of Mere (A303) [183: ST7834] *Bus:* Leathers 20 BR Gillingham-Stourton (Wed & Sat only); Southern National 59 from BR Gillingham, alight Zeals, 1¼m (tel. (0345) 090899) *Station:* Gillingham 6½m; Bruton (U) 7m

WESTWOOD MANOR 🏛 ✱   🚫 🚷 ✖

Bradford on Avon BA15 2AF (0225) 863374

A 15th-century stone manor house, altered in the late 16th-century, with late Gothic and Jacobean windows and Jacobean plasterwork. There is a modern topiary garden
Westwood Manor is administered for the National Trust by the tenant

- **O** 27 March to 28 Sept: Sun, Tues & Wed 2-5. House unsuitable for children under 10. Other times parties of up to 20 by written application with s.a.e. to tenant

- **£** £3.30. No reduction for parties or children. No WCs

- ♿ No wheelchair access

- ➡️ 1½m SW of Bradford on Avon, in Westwood village, beside the church; village signposted off Bradford on Avon to Rode road (B3109) [173: ST812590] *Bus:* From surrounding areas to Bradford on Avon, thence 1½m (tel. (0225) 464446) *Station:* Avoncliff (U), 1m; Bradford on Avon 1½m

REFER TO OPENING PAGES FOR GENERAL INFORMATION

Yorkshire (North)

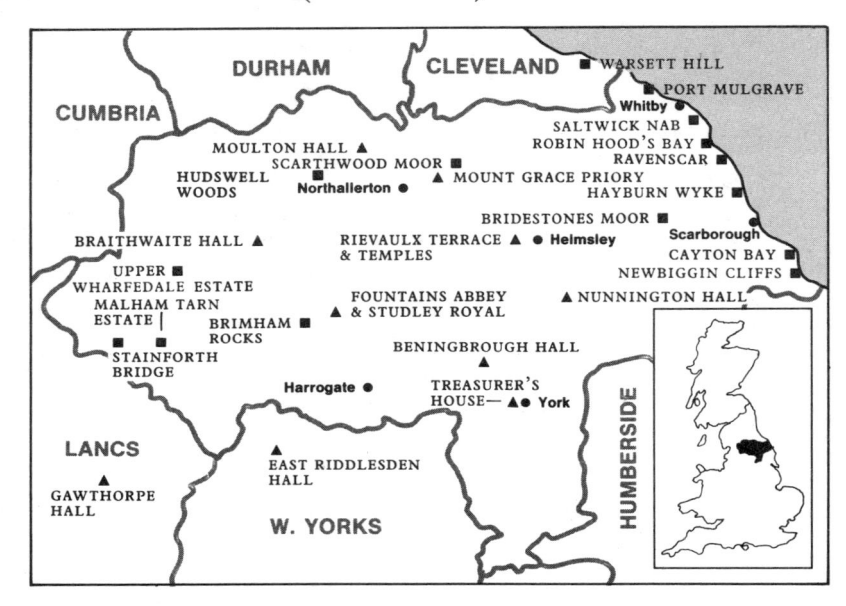

```
DURHAM        CLEVELAND    ■ WARSETT HILL
                                ▲ PORT MULGRAVE
CUMBRIA                      Whitby ●
                          SALTWICK NAB ■
           MOULTON HALL ▲   ROBIN HOOD'S BAY ■
             SCARTHWOOD MOOR ■    RAVENSCAR ●
           HUDSWELL          ▲ MOUNT GRACE PRIORY
           WOODS   Northallerton ●      HAYBURN WYKE ■
                            BRIDESTONES MOOR ■
BRAITHWAITE HALL ▲   RIEVAULX TERRACE ▲ ● Helmsley   Scarborough
                     & TEMPLES                       CAYTON BAY ■
    UPPER ■                              NEWBIGGIN CLIFFS ■
WHARFEDALE ESTATE
 MALHAM TARN      FOUNTAINS ABBEY  ▲ NUNNINGTON HALL
 ESTATE |         ▲ & STUDLEY ROYAL
    ■ ■   BRIMHAM ■
 STAINFORTH  ROCKS
 BRIDGE                  BENINGBROUGH HALL
                                ▲
              Harrogate ●    TREASURER'S
                             HOUSE— ▲● York
LANCS
    ▲            EAST RIDDLESDEN
 GAWTHORPE         HALL
 HALL
                W. YORKS
```

COAST

The Trust's many holdings on the North Yorkshire coast are crossed by the Cleveland Way long distance footpath. An alternative route for the Cleveland Way has now been completed via NT property at **Cayton Bay**, south of Scarborough [101: TA063850]. This provides an ideal opportunity to see the variety of habitats contained within its 90 acres. Extensive woodland and grassland management schemes are being undertaken to improve their nature conservation interest. [101: TA063850]. **Newbiggin Cliffs**, 25 acres on the Cleveland Way, 2 miles north-east of Filey [93: TA827105]; guillemot and razorbill nest here. Six miles north of Scarborough, at **Hayburn Wyke**, 65 acres of high cliffs overlook the Trust-owned bay and rocky beach. A stream provides a small waterfall to this attractive beach. **Robin Hood's Bay** is perhaps the best known feature of the North Yorkshire coast. Here the Trust's ownership is greatest with the whole of the headland north of the village of Robin Hood's Bay, **Boggle Hole** and most of the southern end and headland of the Bay including the clifftop south of **Ravenscar** above the magnificent and dramatic Beast Cliff. Steps have been built and experiments are being conducted to encourage vegetation to regrow on bare areas. The remains of the Peak Alum Works just north of Ravenscar have been investigated by an archaeologist and team of masons. A spur from the Cleveland Way gives access to information panels which explain the alum industry and the Trust's consolidation work on site [94: NZ973024]. A trail begins at the Trust's Coastal Centre at Ravenscar. Guided walks. Leaflet available. Coastal Centre and shop open: 1 April to 30 Sept. 1 April to 10 April,

YORKSHIRE (NORTH)

everyday. Weekends April–May and BH Mon & Tues. May 28–4 Sept everyday. Sept weekends 10.30–5.30 (under review). Refreshments available in village. [94: NZ980025]. Coastal Centre & shop open: 1 April to 30 September. 1 April to 10 April everyday. Weekends April–May & BH Mon & Tues. May 28–4 Sept everyday. Sept weekends 10.30–5.30 (under review).

Saltwick Nab, just south of Whitby is home to a wide variety of wild flowers and insects. **Port Mulgrave**, 5 miles north of Whitby: 38 acres of cliff and undercliff surrounding the harbour and the northern headland of the bay [94: NZ796175]. Recent acquisitions include 26 acres of cliff and farmland north of Runswick village, 57 acres at Hummersea, 140 acres at Boulby, together with 150 acres at Warsett Hill in Cleveland.

COUNTRYSIDE

The 4,200-acre **Malham Tarn Estate** between Ribblesdale and Wharfedale [98: SD8966] includes several farms and Ewe Moor, a dry valley of fissured limestone above Malham Cove. The Tarn and its wetlands are internationally important for wildlife and were given National Nature Reserve status by English Nature in 1992. The reserve is jointly managed by the National Trust and the Field Studies Council. Tarn House, overlooking the Tarn, was built in 1780 and is leased to the Field Studies Council who run it as a Field Centre. The area has a rich flora and has characteristic upland breeding birds such as wheatear, curlew, lapwing and redshank. Great crested grebes, coots and tufted ducks breed on the Tarn and can be seen from a bird hide situated at the north-west corner of the Tarn. The Pennine Way runs through the middle of the estate, skirting the eastern and northern shores of the Tarn. Access to the Tarn on foot only. The old drovers' road, Mastiles Lane, approaches the Tarn from Kilnsey, 5 miles away across the moors, and there were large gatherings of drovers at Great Close in the late 18th century. Towards Malham village, the Trust owns the popular waterfall at **Janet's Foss** and 93 acres of land surrounding Malham Cove; there is access for disabled people from the wooden pole barrier to the south-east of Malham Tarn, along the estate road for about 1½ miles, passing the Tarn shore.

To the north east of the Malham Tarn Estate is the recently acquired **Upper Wharfedale Estate**, amounting to some 5,200 acres with grazing rights over approximately a further 2,000 acres. This estate comprises the finest features of Dales landscape, including meadowland with over 100 field barns, mostly near the River Wharfe, limestone pasture and acid moorland stretching above the steep hillsides to over 2,000ft. The estate is criss-crossed with stone walls dividing eight farms, and also includes 400 acres of magnificent woodlands, waterfalls and a former deer park. Tel. (0729) 830416.

At **Stainforth**, the Trust owns a 17th-century single span packhorse bridge across the River Ribble; once part of the route from Ripon to Lancaster [98: SD818672].

Hudswell: 134 acres of semi-natural ancient woodland known as Calf Hall, Round Howe and Billy Bank Woods on the south bank of the River Swale between Richmond and Hudswell village [92: NZ158005]. The woodlands are rich in flora and fauna and there are fine views across the River Swale. Part of the property is within the Lower Swaledale Woods and Grasslands. Access from Richmondshire District Council car park off A6108, ¾m west of Richmond town centre. 40 acres of land at Hag Wood situated half a mile north west of Hudswell. Access from the A6108.

Near the Cleveland Hills to the north, **Scarthwood Moor** gives fine views of the Pennines [94 & 100: SE465995] from its moorland heights. It provides a popular picnic site beside the stream at its valley floor. Further east, the Trust owns 32 acres of mixed woodland known as **Farndale Woodlands** [94: SE654994]; Sonley, Sikehill & Hall woods in Upper Farndale lie 8 miles north of Kirkbymoorside, a valley famed for its wild

257

YORKSHIRE (NORTH)

daffodils. Access by foot from minor public highways running north from Church Houses.

Bridestones Moor [94: SE8791] lies within the North York Moors National Park on the edge of Dalby Forest, 12 miles south of Whitby, 7 miles north-east of Pickering and a mile east of the A169. Part of the property is a Nature Reserve which can be reached by taking the Forestry Commission's Dalby Forest Drive, for which a charge is made. A car park [94: SE879904] is situated 3 miles north-east of Low Dalby with WCs. The reserve contains a variety of plants and animals typical of the North York Moors, in addition to the Bridestones, which are impressive and oddly shaped sandstone outcrops. The Trust is currently carrying out important conservation work on this area of considerable natural history interest. Nature walk leaflet available.

Crosscliff and Blakey Topping. **Crosscliff** is an area of heather moorland ½ mile north of Bridestones Moor, situated approximately 1¼ miles east of Pickering–Whitby road, A169, 11 miles south of Whitby. At the northern end of the property lies **Blakey Topping**, a curiously shaped conical hill, rising to a height of 875ft above sea level. There are impressive all-round views from this point. The nearest car parking is either at the National Park car park at the Hole of Horcum on the A169 [101: SE852938] or the Forestry Commission's Crosscliff viewpoint car park, just off the Dalby Forest Drive [101: SE896915].

The strange and fantastic rock formations of **Brimham Rocks** [99: SE2165], 8 miles south-west of Ripon, off B6265, and 10 miles north-west of Harrogate off B6165, are set in open moorland overlooking Nidderdale. Information Centre, shop & refreshment kiosk open 26 March to 30 Oct: 26 March–10 April daily; 11 April–27 May Sat, Sun, BH only; 28 May–2 Oct daily; 3 Oct–21 Oct weekends only, 22–30 Oct daily. Parking (all day) cars £1.30; motorcycles 60p; minibuses £2.50; coaches £6. An adapted WC for wheelchair users, and special car parking by arrangement with warden; wheelchair available. Dogs must be on leads in April, May & June, and thereafter under strict control; grazing animals. Tel. (0423) 780688.

BENINGBROUGH HALL

Shipton-by-Beningbrough, York YO6 1DD (0904) 470666

John Bourchier built this imposing Georgian hall in 1716. This beautifully-restored house, set in 365 acres, contains exquisite carving, over 100 pictures on loan from the National Portrait Gallery, an impressive cantilevered staircase, furniture and porcelain. There is a servants exhibition and a well-equipped Victorian laundry, a potting shed and a 7-acre garden. Also, Pike Ponds walk, monthly exhibitions and croquet available for hire

Note: Certain rooms have no electric lights. Visitors wishing to make a close study of the interior and portraits should avoid dull days early and late in the season

- **O** 30 March to 30 Oct: Mon, Tues, Wed, Sat & Sun (open Good Fri). Also Fri in July & Aug. **House:** 11–5 (last admissions 4.30). **Grounds:** 11–5.30 (last admissions 5)

- **£** House, garden & exhibition: £4.50; children £2.30; family £11.30; parties £3.60, children £1.80. Garden & exhibition only: £3; children £1.50; family £7.50. School groups and parties by prior arrangement. For conservation reasons pushchairs are not allowed in the house

- **i** 3pm. Guided garden walks most weekends. 1.30 and 3pm

YORKSHIRE (NORTH)

- Open as grounds
- Access to ground floor only, by ramp; level garden paths (embedded gravel); parking spaces. Restaurant accessible; WC in stable block. Wheelchairs available. Self-drive scooter outdoor use only
- Homemade hot & cold lunches, coffee & teas in licenced restaurant, open as grounds. Kiosk open busy days. Special functions and pre-booked parties by arrangement. Picnic area in walled garden
- Baby changing and feeding room. Children's menu & high chairs in restaurant. Children's guide. Wilderness play area. Full programme of events for families
- Victorian 'Below stairs'; artwork with portraits; archive of materials
- Contact Administrator for full range of events
- 8m NW of York, 2m W of Shipton, 2m SE of Linton-on-Ouse (A19) [105: SE516586] *Bus:* Rider York 31 BR York–Newton-on-Ouse, thence 1m (tel. (0904) 624161) *Station:* York 8m

BRAITHWAITE HALL
East Witton, Leyburn DL8 4SY (0969) 40287

This 17th-century hall is now a working farmhouse with 748 acres of moor and farmland. It is a family home, furnished by the tenants, and contains oak panelling, staircase and fireplaces

- By arrangement with tenant, Mrs David Duffus
- 60p, incl. leaflet. No reduction for children. No access for coaches. No WCs
- 1½m SW of Middleham, 2m W of East Witton (A6108) [99: SE117857]

FOUNTAINS ABBEY & STUDLEY ROYAL
Fountains, Ripon HG4 3DY (0765) 608888/601005

YORKSHIRE (NORTH)

One of the most remarkable sites in Europe, sheltered in a secluded valley. Fountains Abbey and Studley Royal, a World Heritage Site, encompasses the spectacular ruin of a 12th-century Cistercian Abbey, a Jacobean Mansion, and one of the best surviving examples of a Georgian Green Water Garden. Lakes, avenues, temples and cascades provide a succession of unforgettable eye-catching vistas in an atmosphere of peace and tranquility. St Mary's Church, built by William Burges in the 19th century, provides a dramatic focal point to the 400-acre deer park

Audio visual and exhibition at Visitor Centre; small museum near to Abbey; exhibitions in Fountains Hall and Swanley Grange. 3 holiday cottages

Fountains Abbey is maintained by English Heritage. St Mary's Church is owned by English Heritage

- Fountains Abbey and Studley Royal Water Garden open all year daily except Fri in Nov, Dec and Jan and 24/5 Dec. April to Sept: 10-7 (closes at 5 on 10/11 June and 8/9 July); Oct to March 1995: 10-5 (or dusk if earlier). **Fountains Hall:** April to Sept 11-5; Oct to March 1995 11-4. **St Mary's Church:** May to Sept & Easter Week 1-5. **Deer Park:** open all year daily during daylight hours. **Floodlighting:** the Abbey is floodlit on Fri and Sat evenings until 10pm, 19 August to 15 Oct

- Fountains Abbey and Studley Royal Water Garden: April 1994 to March 1995 £4, children £2, family £10. Parties: over 15 £3.50, children £1.70; parties over 40 (pre-booked only): £3, children £1.50. Visitor Centre, Deer Park, St Mary's Church: free. Parking: visitor Centre: free; Studley Royal £2 (refundable on purchase of admission ticket)

- Free guided tours of Abbey, Water Garden and around estate April to Oct daily, afternoons and some mornings. Specialist guides for pre-booked parties (50p per person) and programme of discovery walks, tel. (0765) 609999

- Visitor Centre Shop: open all year except 24/25 Dec, April to Sept 10-6, Oct to March 10-5 (or dusk if earlier). Tel. (0765) 601004

- Minibus available from Visitor Centre; wheelchairs and self-drive buggies available by prior booking only tel. (0765) 601005; Sympathetic Hearing. WC's at Visitor Centre, Studley tea-room & nr Fountains Hall. Wheelchair access: most of the Estate accessible. Enquire for best route. Events: in Abbey grounds, water garden and visitor centre accessible

- Large print and Braille guide available from Visitor Centre

- Visitor Centre Restaurant: licensed, serving coffee, teas and a wide variety of home made lunches incl. children's menu and vegetarian; party bookings and functions welcome (tel. (0765) 601003); open daily, same times as Visitor Centre shop. Studley tea-room: light lunches, teas & refreshments (tel. (0765) 604246) open daily April to Sept, weekends Oct to March 1995,12-5 or dusk if earlier

- Baby rooms available at Visitor Centre, Fountains Hall (please ask). High chairs & children's menu in restaurant; children's guide and trail leaflets, programme of family and children's activities

- Special facilities linked to National Curriculum for pre-booked parties (Education Officer (0765) 608888), includes new study centre at Swanley Grange

YORKSHIRE (NORTH)

E Extensive programme of concerts, plays, walks & talks available all year, incl.: 10/11 June, Music in the Water Garden; 8/9 July, Music by Moonlight. Box Office, tel. (0765) 609999. Access over grass for all outside events.

On leads

4m W of Ripon off B6265 to Pateley Bridge, signposted from the A1, 10m N of Harrogate (A61) [99: SE271683] *Bus:* United 135, 145 from Ripon (with connections from BR Harrogate), Thurs, Sat, Sun only (tel. (0325) 468771)

MOULTON HALL
Moulton, Richmond (0325) 377227

Rebuilt about 1650, with fine carved wood staircase

O By arrangement with tenant, the Hon J. D. Eccles

£ 50p. Unsuitable for coaches. No WCs

Please enquire about access when arranging a visit

5m E of Richmond; turn off A1 ½m S of Scotch Corner [99: NZ235035] *Bus:* United 25 Darlington–Richmond (passing close BR Darlington), alight Moulton village, ½m (tel. (0325) 468771) *Station:* Darlington 9½m

MOUNT GRACE PRIORY
Osmotherley, Northallerton DL6 3JG (0609) 883494

The greater part of the remains of a 14th-century priory, this is the most important Carthusian ruin in England. There is a reconstructed and furnished cell on show, an exhibition on the Carthusians and NT/English Heritage information room

Mount Grace Priory is owned by the National Trust, and maintained and managed by English Heritage

O 1 April to 31 Oct: daily 10–6. 1 Nov to 31 March: Wed to Sun 10–4 (closed 24–26 Dec, 1 Jan)

£ £2; OAPs, students and UB40 holders £1.50; children (under 16) £1. Free admission to English Heritage members. Parties of 11 or more 15% discount. School visits Mon to Fri, free, but must be booked with English Heritage (tel. 091-261 1585). Bulky bags and pushchairs may be left in reception

Shop available

Access to grounds, shop and ground floor of reconstructed cell

Light refreshments available in shop. Picnics welcome

School visits free Mon–Fri. Must be booked in advance

E Events diary available in shop; free of charge

continued

YORKSHIRE (NORTH)

➡️ 6m NE of Northallerton, ½m E of A19 and ½m S of its junction with A172 [99: SE449985] *Bus:* United/Tees & District 90/A Northallerton–Middlesbrough (passing close BR Northallerton), alight Priory Road End, (½m) (tel. (0642) 210131) *Station:* Northallerton 6m

NUNNINGTON HALL
Nunnington, York YO6 5UY (0439) 748283

A manor house on the banks of the River Rye, partly 16th century, but mainly late 17th century; principal reception rooms include a magnificent panelled hall with a fine carved chimneypiece; also, panelled bedrooms, fine tapestries, china and the Carlisle Collection of Miniature Rooms, fully furnished in different periods; display of work by British Toymakers Guild; attractive walled garden

🅾️ 26 March to 30 Oct: Tues, Wed, Thur, Good Fri, Sat & Sun: 2–6. BH Mon: 12–6. Also Fri in July & Aug 2–6, Sat, Sun & BH Mon 12–6. Last admissions 5. School parties Tues & Wed 10–12 by appointment

£ House & garden £3.50, children £1.50. Parties £3; children £1.30. Garden only £2; children free. For conservation reasons pushchairs and prams are not allowed in the house. Car parking 50yds; unsuitable for trailer caravans

📷 Open as house

♿ Access to ground floor and tea-room only. Ramp to main garden; loose gravel paths; for special parking apply at Reception; WC

👁️ Braille guide

🍴 Tea-room and tea-garden serving home made teas, open as house; last admissions 5.30. Light lunches, BH Mon, Sat & Sun in July & Aug

👶 Collection of miniature rooms. Baby changing facilities. Children's menu in tea-room

E Varied programme of exhibitions through the year

🐕 In car park only

➡️ In Ryedale, 4½m SE of Helmsley (A170) Helmsley–Pickering road; 1½m N of B1257 Malton–Helmsley road [100: SE670795] *Bus:* Scarborough & District 128 Scarborough–Helmsley (passing close BR Scarborough & Seamer), alight Wombleton, 3m (tel. (0723) 375463)

RIEVAULX TERRACE & TEMPLES
Rievaulx, Helmsley, York YO6 5LJ (043 96) 340

A half-mile long grass-covered terrace and adjoining woodlands with vistas over Rievaulx Abbey (English Heritage) and Rye valley to Ryedale and the Hambleton Hills. There are two mid 18th-century temples: the Ionic Temple has elaborate ceiling paintings and fine 18th-century furniture. A permanent exhibition in the basement is on English landscape design in the 18th century

Note: No access to Abbey from Terrace. No access to property Nov to end March

YORKSHIRE (NORTH)

- ⊙ 26 March to 30 Oct: daily 10.30-6 (or dusk if earlier). Last admissions 5. Ionic Temple closed 1-2
- £ £2.50, children £1. Parties £1.70; children 80p. Parking at reception, but coach park 200yds; unsuitable for trailer caravans
- 🛍 Shop and Information Centre open same times
- ♿ Terrace recommended; access to Ionic temple not possible because of steps. Unadapted WCs. Powered buggy available
- ☕ Teas at Nunnington Hall, 7m (see entry, above)
- 🐕 On leads only
- → 2½m NW of Helmsley on B1257 [100: SE579848] *Bus:* Tees & District 294 from Middlesbrough (passing close BR Middlesbrough), Fri only (tel. (0642) 210131); or Scarborough & District 128 Scarborough–Helmsley or Moorsbus from BR Malton, summer Sun only (tel. (0723) 375463) or Yorkshire Coastliner 94 (tel. (0653) 692556). On both alight Helmsley, thence 2½m

TREASURER'S HOUSE 🏛 ❀

Chapter House Street, York YO1 2JD (0904) 624247

Standing in the shadow of York Minster, this elegant 17th/18th-century town house, the site of the former residence of the Treasurers of York Minster, is set in a peaceful garden. An exhibition and video film show the development of the house from Roman times. The rooms house the collection of the Yorkshire industrialist, Frank Green, who lived here from 1895 to 1930

- ⊙ 26 March to 30 Oct: daily 10.30-5. Last admissions 4.30
- £ House & garden: £3, children £1.50. Parties £2.50, children £1.20. No reduction on Sun or BH Mon. Guided tours by arrangement. Evening opening for pre-booked parties £3.50 (min. charge £75) incl. guided tour; contact Administrator. No parking facilities
- 🛍 NT shop at 32 Goodramgate open all year Mon to Sat 9-5.30
- ♿ Access to ground floor only; steps at back door to part of basement and tea-room very difficult; strong helpers needed. Access to outdoor events only. Cars may set down disabled passengers at door
- 👁 Braille guide
- ☕ Licensed tea-room open as house (tel. (0904) 646757); coffee, lunches & teas. Open for pre-booked parties during and outside normal opening hours and for private functions. NT tea-room at 32 Goodramgate open all year Mon–Sat
- 👶 Facilities for babies & nursing mothers; high chair. For conservation reasons pushchairs are not allowed in the house
- E Details of Coffee by Candlelight evenings and other events; apply to Administrator for details; s.a.e. please
- → In Minster Yard, on N side of Minster [105: SE604523] *Bus:* From surrounding areas (tel. (0904) 624161) *Station:* York ½m

263

Yorkshire (West)

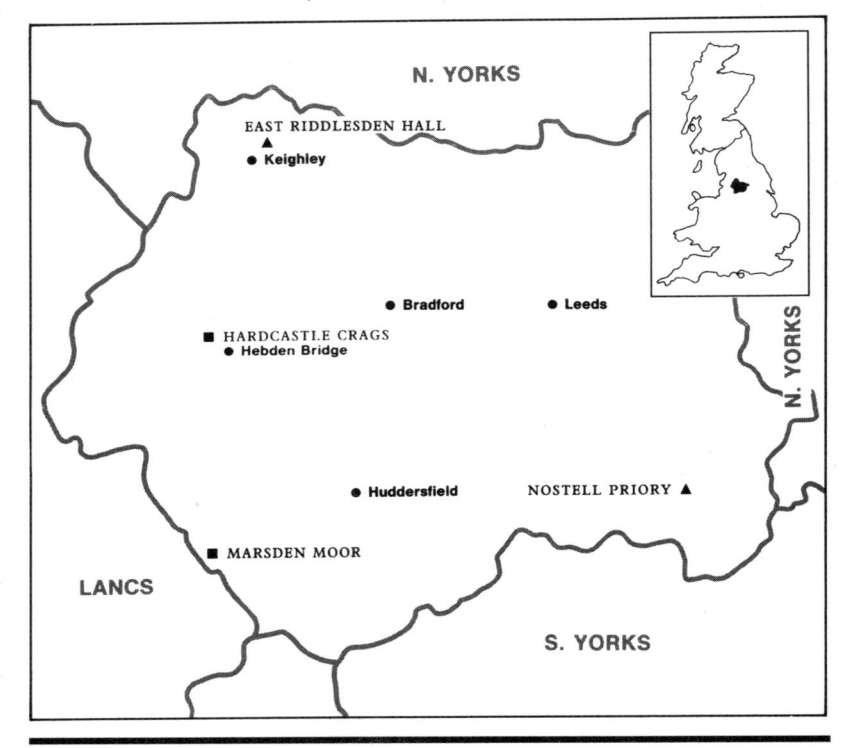

COUNTRYSIDE

Hardcastle Crags, 1½ miles north-west of Hebden Bridge, comprises two steep wooded valleys, each with a stream running through it. The woodland is predominantly broad-leaved, with areas of conifers. Rock outcrops (the Crags) and millponds are attractive features. A riverside walk beside Hebden Water takes you through the deciduous woodland and past a disused 19th-century cotton mill. The main track is accessible to wheelchair users, but most of the property is not negotiable; a Braille guide is available. There is a fine variety of wild flowers. The woodlands are inhabited by wood ants and red squirrels. The Slurring Rock at the highest point of one of the woodland walks, is so called because children once slid or 'slurred' down its slopes in wooden clogs, often carved from locally grown alder or 'clog wood'. Three self-guided walks enable the more adventurous walker to explore the woodlands in depth. A leaflet covering all three walks and the area in general, price 65p is available from the regional office (please send s.a.e.); a Braille guide, giving an introduction to the Crags, is available from the property. Always open. Guided walks available, please contact the Warden (tel. (0422) 844518). Parking at entrance: cars £1.50, motorcycles 60p, minibuses £3, coaches

YORKSHIRE (WEST)

£15; coaches by arrangement only; information caravan (Sundays; all year, weekends 26 March to 30 Oct, BH, Mon to Fri; July, Aug and Sept). Picnic sites. Public WCs available outside entrance to property. [103: SD988291].

Open moorland at **Marsden Moor** almost surrounding the town of Marsden, stretches from Buckstones Moor on the A640 to Wessenden Moor, north of the A635 [109: SE0210/0611]. This is wild, open moorland country, yet it has a surprising diversity of interest; valleys, reservoirs, peaks and crags and archaeological remains dating from pre-Roman settlements to the great engineering structures of the railway and canal developments. Guided walks are organised throughout the year. Details from the Warden at Marsden Moor Estate Office and Workshops, off Station Rd, Marsden, Huddersfield (please send s.a.e.) or tel. (0484) 847016, answerphone; information caravan (seasonal). Whilst at Marsden, also visit the Tunnel End Canal and Countryside Centre to find out more about this fascinating area.

EAST RIDDLESDEN HALL

Bradford Road, Keighley BD20 5EL (0535) 607075

A charming 17th-century West Yorkshire manor house with panelled rooms, fine plasterwork and mullioned windows, providing an ideal setting for embroideries, pewter, and Yorkshire oak furniture. A formal walled garden has now been restored to its original design. There is an impressive Great Barn with a collection of traditional agricultural machinery. Also, monastic fishponds and grounds running down to the River Aire

- 26 March to 30 Oct: Sat to Wed 12–5; also Good Fri and Thur in July & Aug. Last admissions 4.30

- £3, children £1.50, family ticket £8.50. Party rates on application. Parking 100yds; coaches must book as space limited. School groups and parties by arrangement. No large bags allowed in the house; pushchairs, rucksacks etc must be left at Reception. Open for pre-booked parties outside normal opening hours and for private functions

- Shop and information area in Bothy open as house. Also some Christmas openings

- Access to ground floor and garden; some uneven surfaces; loose gravel paths. Spaces reserved for disabled drivers in car park. Shop accessible via some steps. Tea-room on first floor of Bothy. Unadapted WC with access via some steps. Guided tours for groups of visually impaired people by arrangement

- Braille guide, large print guide

- Tea-room serving lunches and afternoon teas, open as property; also some Christmas openings. Open for pre-booked parties during and outside normal opening hours, and for private functions. Picnic area in field

- Baby changing facilities; high chairs in tea-room. Children's guide. Children's activity days & workshops. Children's menu in tea-room

- Living History for schools (details from Administrator)

- 1st Sunday of the month, Riddlesden Revels. For details of full programme send s.a.e. marked 'Events' to the Administrator

- In grounds only, on leads. Not permitted in walled garden

YORKSHIRE (WEST)

→ 1m NE of Keighley on S side of the Bradford Road in Riddlesden, close to Leeds & Liverpool Canal [104: SE079421] *Bus:* Frequent services from BR Bradford Interchange, Bingley & Keighley (tel. (0532) 457676) *Station:* Keighley 1m

NOSTELL PRIORY
Doncaster Road, Nostell, nr Wakefield WF4 1QE (0924) 863892

A fine Palladian house, built for the Winn family in 1733. An additional wing and many of the state rooms were designed by Adam. The Priory houses one of England's finest collections of Chippendale furniture, which was specially made for the house. There are delightful lakeside walks through the grounds

Nostell Priory is managed by Lord St Oswald

- 26 March to 30 Oct: March, April, May, June, Sept & Oct: Sat 12-5; Sun 11-5. July, Aug to 8 Sept: daily except Fri, 12-5, Sun 11-5. BH Mon (11-5) and Tues (12-5), not Good Fri
- House & grounds: £3.50, children £1.80. Parties of 30 or more: £3, children £1.50. Grounds only: £2.20, children £1.10. Pre-booked parties welcome outside published opening times (no reduction and charge made for NT members). Min. charge for parties of less than 30. Parking 350yds. NT members will be expected to pay additional charge for access to grounds during special events. For conservation reasons pushchairs must be left in reception
- Guided tours only on weekdays (last tour 4); free flow visiting at weekends
- 2 gift shops (not NT)
- Disabled visitors may usually be driven to front door. Level access to ground floor. Lift to first floor; grounds accessible; Batricar available; restaurant accessible; WC; wheelchairs available & self-drive buggy provided
- Braille guide, tactile books
- Light lunches and teas in Stable Block (not NT). Meals available to parties, by arrangement (tel. (0924) 862205 or 375910). Picnic site
- In grounds only on leads
- On the A638 out of Wakefield towards Doncaster [111: SE407172] *Bus:* W Riding 485/Yorkshire Traction 498 Wakefield–Doncaster; W Riding 122/3 from Wakefield; Yorkshire Traction 245 from Pontefract (tel. (0532) 457676) *Station:* Fitzwilliam 1½m

Wales: Clwyd

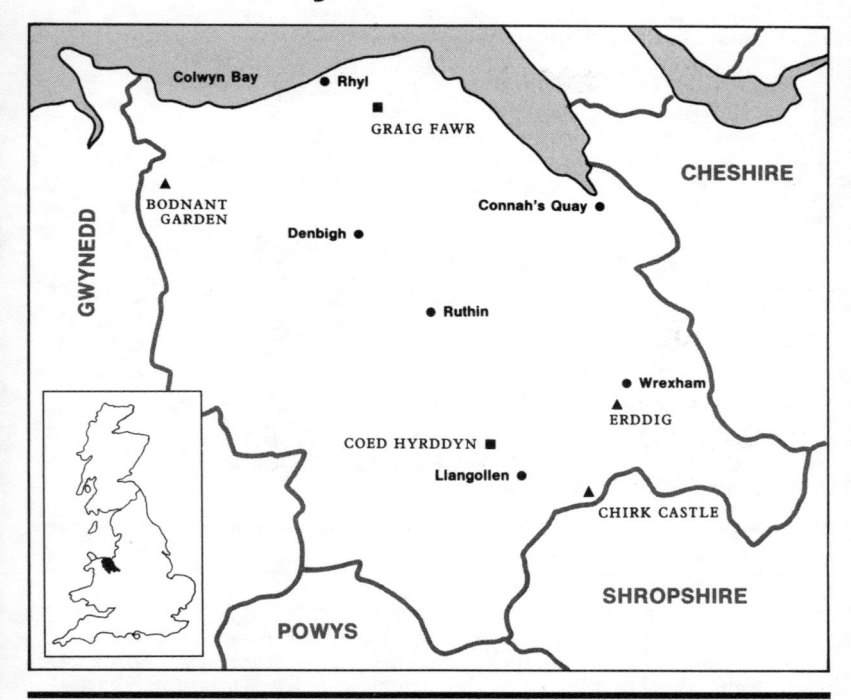

COUNTRYSIDE

Graig Fawr, a large limestone hill, south of Prestatyn [116: SJ060805] is a Site of Special Scientific Interest with many marine fossils and a treasure trove of lime-loving plants, such as harebells, small scabious, bird's-foot trefoil and hoary rock-rose. The common blue butterfly delights the visitors to this popular viewpoint. Leaflet from North Wales Regional Office (see final page); s.a.e. please.

Above the road from Llangollen to the Horseshoe Pass is **Coed Hyrddyn** (or Velvet Hill) [117 & 125: SJ200440], giving fine views.

CHIRK CASTLE
Chirk, Clwyd LL14 5AF (0691) 777701

A magnificent Marcher fortress, completed in 1310, commanding fine views over the surrounding countryside. Elegant state rooms with elaborate plasterwork, superb Adam style furniture, tapestries and portraits. In the formal gardens there are clipped yews, roses and a variety of flowering shrubs. Elaborate entrance gates were made in 1719 by the Davies brothers, and 18th-century parkland

CLWYD

🅾	1 April to 30 Sept: daily except Mon & Sat but open BH Mon; 1-30 Oct: Sat & Sun only. **Castle & Gardens:** 12-5 last admissions 4.30
£	£4, children £2. Pre-booked parties of 20 or more £3.20. Family ticket (max. 2 adults, 2 children) £10. Car park 200yds
🛈	Connoisseur's Tours, Tues am by prior arrangement; only for parties of min. 20
🛍	Shop open as Castle
♿	Very limited access to parts of castle; garden mostly accessible; gravel paths. Tea-room accessible. Special parking arrangements. WC. Room for CAPD
👁	Braille guide
☕	Licensed tea-room: light lunches and teas. Picnicking in car park only
👶	Baby facilities. Baby carriers for loan. Highchair in tea-room. Children's guide. Parent & baby room
🏫	Educational visits particularly welcome. Education officer and room available. School parties must be pre-booked
🐕	No dogs in Castle or Garden, dogs allowed in grounds & car park
➔	½m W of Chirk village off A5; 8m S of Wrexham, signposted off A483 *Bus:* Cambrian Midland Red/Crosville Wales 2/A Wrexham Oswestry (tel. (0352) 700250) *Station:* Chirk (U) 1½m

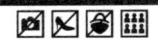

ERDDIG
nr Wrexham, Clwyd LL13 0YT (0978) 313333

This late 17th-century house, with 18th-century additions, is the most evocative upstairs-downstairs house in Britain. The range of outbuildings includes kitchen, laundry, bakehouse, stables, sawmill, smithy and joiners' shop, while the state rooms display most of the original furniture. A large walled garden restored to its 18th century formal design. Contains the National Ivy Collection. Surrounding parkland with extensive woods. There is a 10min video programme

🅾	1 April to 31 Aug: daily, except Thur & Fri (open Good Fri). **Garden:** 11-6. **House:** 12-5, last admissions 4
	Please note that Erddig will be closed for essential repairs during September & October
	Note: Due to the extreme fragility of their contents, the Tapestry and small Chinese Room are open on Wed & Sat only. Most rooms have no electric light; visitors wishing to make close study of pictures and textiles should avoid dull days
£	Family Rooms (incl. Belowstairs, outbuildings & garden) £5. Parties (20 or more) £4, children £2.50. Belowstairs (incl. outbuildings & garden) £3.20. Parties (20 or more) £2.50, children £1.60. Family ticket (max. 2 adults, 2 children) £8. Midweek discount: Mon, Tues, Wed (except July & Aug) Family Rooms: adult £4.50, Belowstairs: adult £2.70. All parties by prior arrangement please (send s.a.e. for details). Parking 200yds

CLWYD

- Meet the gardener Tours available by prior arrangement (20 or more)
- Shop and Plant Sales open as house. Also Christmas shop, tel. (0978) 311919 for details. Joiners shop manufacturing quality garden furniture; open same times as property; catalogue available
- Access to groundfloor, garden (ramps) and out-buildings only; not an easy property for wheelchairs, please discuss visits in advance with Administrator. WC in main yard, wheelchairs provided
- Braille guide
- Licensed restaurant: morning coffee, lunches and teas, open as property 1 April to 30 Oct, 11–5.15. Also open for pre-booked functions, incl. pre-booked Christmas lunches Administrator; tel. (0978) 311919. Picnicking in car park area
- Babyfeeding and changing facilities. Highchair in restaurant. Baby carriers on loan. Children's guide
- School and Youth Groups mornings only Mon, Tues & Wed by prior arrangement. Please send s.a.e. for details of Education Programme
- Programme of events; contact Administrator. Horse/pony rides available (not NT) tel. (0978) 310911
- In car park and Country Park only on lead
- 2m S of Wrexham, signposted A525 Whitchurch road, or A483/A5152 Oswestry Road [117: SJ326482] *Bus:* Crosville Bus Service 37, from Wrexham General BR Station, summer only tel. (0352) 700250 *Station:* Wrexham (U) 1m, Wrexham General $1\frac{1}{2}$m via Erddig Rd & footpath

Dyfed

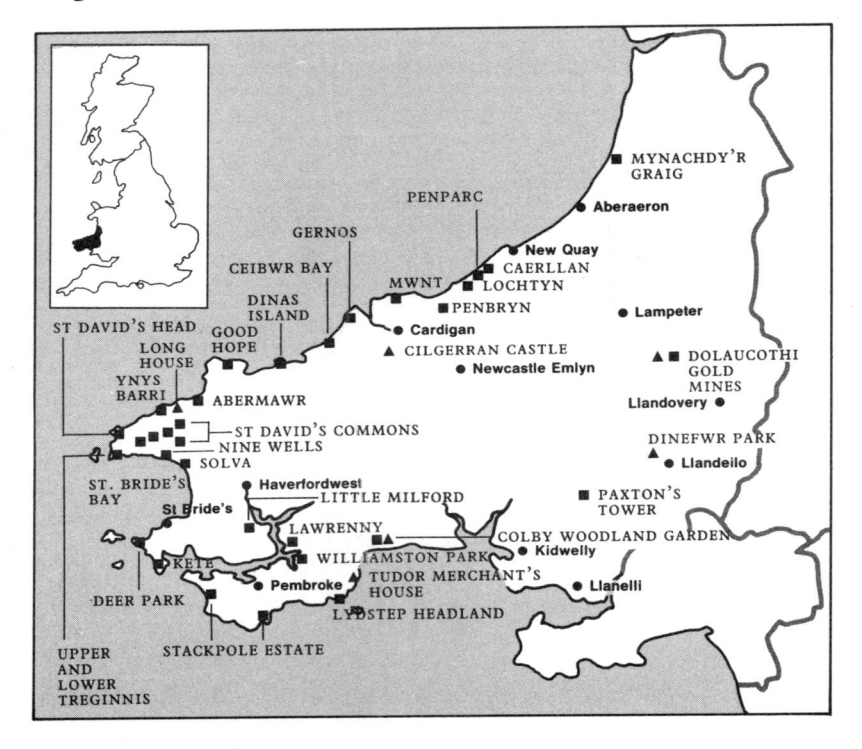

COAST

The 186-mile long Pembrokeshire Coast Path begins at Amroth on Carmarthen Bay and ends at St Dogmaels, a village on the outskirts of Cardigan. It traverses Trust property for much of its length, beginning with the 980-acre **Colby Estate** at Amroth, giving views of Somerset, Caldy and Gower. 1½ miles east of Manorbier is **Lydstep Headland** [158: SS090976] accessible by footpath from Lydstep village. NT shop in Pembroke.

The 2,000-acre **Stackpole Estate**, 6 miles south of Pembroke [158: SR977693] includes freshwater lakes at Bosherston, thick with waterlilies in summer; woods, 8 miles of cliffs, two beaches, farmland and sand dunes. From the tiny and beautiful Stackpole Quay where the Trust has several holiday cottages, you can walk over the headland to Barafundle Bay where there is a wide sweep of pale golden sand and good bathing. A recreation area near the Quay has been developed for able-bodied and disabled people (bookable through regional office, see p. 304). There are car parks at Stackpole Quay and Broadhaven – the second of the bathing beaches. About a mile from Broadhaven is St Govan's Chapel (not NT), a tiny 13th-century building clinging to a crevice half way

DYFED

down three steep cliffs and reached by a long flight of extremely uneven stone steps. The Ministry of Defence controls access and closes the road at certain times when the nearby firing ranges are in use. At Freshwater West, the Trust owns a farm and a large part of **Kilpaison Burrows**, one of the finest sand dune systems in Pembrokeshire

On the northern side of Milford Haven at **Kete**, west of Dale, the Trust owns 168 acres, giving views of Skomer and Skokholm Islands [157: SM800045]. From here is a good walk to the cliffs of St Anne's Head.

The Trust owns about 15½ miles of the coastline at **St Bride's Bay**, including the **Deer Park** at Marloes which is separated from the adjacent headland by a high stone wall built at the beginning of the 19th century, although deer were never introduced. It provides a suitable feeding habitat for certain coastal sea bird species, such as chough. There are marvellous views of Skomer and Skokholm to the south [157: SM78091]. Car park, information panel and WC at Martin's Haven.

Nearby at **Marloes Sands** [157: SM7707] a 2½-mile walk can be followed along the Pembrokeshire coastal path. It takes in the sandstone cliffs, an Iron Age fort and Marloes Mere; raven, chough and grey seal may be seen; the mere is an exciting place to watch birds. Leaflet from DWT, 7 Market Street, Haverfordwest, Dyfed SA61 1NF (45p by post). The area is also mentioned in National Park publications.

In the **St David's** area [145: SM740278] the National Trust owns land extending from west of Newgale Beach to St David's Head [145: SM721278], incorporating 1,309 acres of unspoilt coastline with four farms, and 2,150 acres of commons, all within the Pembrokeshire Coast National Park. The landscape is one of rocky outcrops, coastal plateau and spectacular coastline, important for geology and natural history. The views are extensive and beautiful along the coast to Marloes, west to Ramsey Island and north towards Strumble Head. NT shop at **Solva** (seasonal); visitor centre with shop at St David's.

Further acquisitions have added to the Trust's ownership on the North Pembrokeshire coastline. 200 acres of coastal farmland at **Ynys Barri**, Llanrhian [151(157): SM805328] includes 2 miles of coastland between Porthgain Harbour and Abereiddy. Near Abercastle, **Long House Farm** [157: SM853337] comprises 151 acres of farmland with 2½ miles of scenic rugged coastline. Two small islands are included with the land: Ynys-y-Castell and Ynys Deullyn. There is an Iron Age promontory fort on the property. **Dinas Island Farm** [157: SM0140] lies 5 miles east of Fishguard and 18 miles west of Cardigan; 414 acres of farmland with 2½ miles of coastline lying within the Pembrokeshire Coast National Park. Just to the east of Strumble Head, 3 miles north-west of Fishguard, on the Pembrokeshire coast is 97 acres of rugged coastal outcrop and largely unimproved pasture, known as **Good Hope** [157: SM912407]. 6½ acres are owned at **Ceibwr Bay**, Moylegrove [139(168): 109485]. **Abermawr**, [157: SN891347] is 10 miles from St Davids and a little to the south of Strumble Head; 268 acres comprising a shingle beach backed by a freshwater marsh lying in a wooded valley and forming about half a mile of coast. At **Gernos**, St Dogmaels, Cardigan [145: SM1340], the National Trust protects 2 more miles of the North Pembrokeshire coast; 106 acres to the west of Cemmaes Head, near St Dogmaels, including the promontory of Pen-yr-Afr.

Between Cardigan and Newquay the Trust owns **Mwnt** [145: SN1952], a family beach with parking, lavatories and a refreshment kiosk; **Penbryn** [145: SN295519], just north-east of Tresaith with extensive beaches, car parking, lavatories and café/refreshment facilities (no dogs at Mwnt and Penbryn beaches between 1 May and 30 Sept); **Caerllan** at Cwmtudu [145: SN355577], with 1½ miles of cliff walks to Newquay; and **Lochtyn** [145: SN315545], a rocky headland near the village of Llangranog; from the highest point, **Pen-y-Badell**, splendid views can be seen across Cardigan Bay to the Llyn Peninsula and Snowdonia. **Penparc Farm** consists of 120 acres south-west of Cwmtudu including one mile of coastline and ¾ mile of valley bluff.

DYFED

Between Aberaeron and Aberystwyth, the Trust has acquired **Mynachdy'r Graig** [135: SN563742], a 153-acre coastal firm with stunning views to the extremities of Cardigan Bay

Recent acquisitions on the Pembrokeshire coast include 4 farms, comprising over 800 acres of farmland, and further areas of coastal land, totalling some 10 miles of coastline.

COUNTRYSIDE

Two rivers, the Western and Eastern Cleddau, begin in the Preselli Hills and meet south-east of Haverfordwest, to form a fascinating 10-mile long estuary, finally reaching the sea beyond Milford Haven. The Trust owns two areas of woodland here; one at **Little Milford** on the Western Cleddau, south of Haverfordwest [158: SM967118] with public footpaths; the other a 71-acre hanging wood at **Lawrenny** on the east side of Castle Reach.

Two other rivers which enter this estuary are the Creswell and the Carew. **Williamston Park**, a promontory between these rivers south-east of Lawrenny, is one of the two deer parks of Carew Castle – now a dramatic ruin (not NT). The Park is a Nature Reserve, managed by the Dyfed Wildlife Trust; access is by footpath only [158: SN030057].

The Trust owns 15 acres at **Paxton's Tower**, 7 miles east of Carmarthen [159: SN541191]. This folly was once known as Nelson's Tower, and was built in the early 19th century on a hill giving fine views over the countryside.

CILGERRAN CASTLE

nr Cardigan, Cadw (0222) 465511

This 13th-century ruin has inspired many artists, including Turner

Cilgerran Castle is in the guardianship of Cadw (Welsh Historic Monuments)

£ Please telephone Cadw for opening times and admission prices

→ On rock above left bank of the Teifi, 3m SE of Cardigan, 1½m E of A478 [145: SN195431] *Bus:* Bws Dyfed 430 from Cardigan; otherwise Bws Dyfed 460/1 BR Carmarthen–Cardigan, alight Llechryd. 1¾m by footpath (tel. (0267) 231817)

DYFED

COLBY WOODLAND GARDEN

Colby Bothy, Amroth, Narberth SA67 8PP
(Enquiries: tel. (0834) 811885 or (0558) 822800)

An attractive woodland garden. The early 19th-century house is not open; (Mr & Mrs A. Scourfield Lewis kindly allow access to the walled garden during visiting hours). There are walks through secluded valleys along open and wooded pathways, one of which links the property with the nearby coastal resort of Amroth

- Weekends from 12 March 1994; 11-4. Full opening (7 days a week); 26 March to 30 Oct, daily 10-5. Walled garden 26 March to 30 Oct only, 11-5
- £2.50, children £1. Group adult £2, group child 80p. 1 child (16 and under) free entry per 1 paying adult from 25 July to 4 Sept. Coaches by prior arrangement (narrow approaches)
- Shop, gallery and plant sales, open as property
- Limited facilities, parts of garden accessible; disabled visitors may park closer to the garden on request
- Morning coffee, home-made light refreshments & tea; open as property
- Adjoining Amroth beside Carmarthen Bay [158: SN155080] *Bus:* Bws Dyfed 350/1 from Tenby (passing BR Kilgetty) (tel. (0267) 231817) *Station:* Kilgetty (U) 2½m

DINEFWR PARK

Llandeilo, Dyfed SA19 6RT (Estate Office: tel. (0558) 823902, or Regional Office (0558) 822800)

A Victorian-Gothic mansion within an 18th-century landscaped park. Parts of the ground floor are accessible (no contents inside house, which is under repair), and a minor exhibition explains the history of Dinefwr. There is a rear Victorian garden, and an ancient deer park with White Park cattle. Access to the outside of Dinefwr Castle and Llandyfeisant Church (owned by Dyfed Wildlife Trust). Also, footpaths through parts of 400 acre estate and outstanding views of Towy Valley

- 30 March to 30 Oct: daily 10-5. The park is open during the winter in daylight hours
- £1.60, children 80p. Parties £1.20, children/school groups 60p. 1 child (16 and under) free per 1 paying adult from 25 July to 4 Sept. Coaches by prior appointment only due to narrow access. WCs in car park
- Cafeteria open 11-4.30, 30 March to 30 Sept
- In outer park only on leads. No dogs in deer park
- On N outskirts of Llandeilo A40(T); from Swansea take M4 to Pont Abraham, thence A48(T) to Cross Hands and A476 to Llandeilo; entrance by police station [159: SN625225] *Bus:* From surrounding areas to Llandeilo, thence 1m (tel. (0267) 231817) *Station:* Llandeilo ½m

DYFED

DOLAUCOTHI GOLD MINES
Pumsaint, Llanwrda SA19 8RR (0558) 650359

These unique Roman Goldmines are set amid wooded hillsides overlooking the beautiful Cothi Valley on the Dolaucothi Estate. First exploited by the Romans some 2,000 years ago and last worked in 1938, the Trust's New Exhibition Centre vividly illustrates the ancient and modern mine workings. Guided tours with miners' helmets and lamps further provide the visitor with an authentic feeling to this exciting visit. Gold panning & displays of 1930s mining machinery in the Mine Yard

- **O** High Season: 21 May to 24 Sept (incl.) daily 10–6. Low Season: 30 March to 20 May and 25 Sept to 30 Oct; daily 11–5
- **£** High Season: adults £4.80, children £2.40, adult groups £3.80, child groups £1.80. NT members: adults £2, children £1. Low season: adults £3, children £1.50, adult groups £2.40, child groups £1.20. NT members: free. 1 child (16 and under) free per 1 paying adult during low season. Last admission 1 hr before closing
- Tours last about 1hr, involving rugged climbing; helmets with lights provided; stout footwear recommended. The underground tour is unsuitable for disabled or infirm visitors; the Trust regrets children under 5 are not admitted. Limited places are available on underground tours; tours are very busy during late July and Aug; please come early to avoid disappointment
- Shop and restaurant open daily 11–5, high season 11–6
- Light lunches and refreshments available
- On leads, but not underground
- → Between Lampeter and Llanwrda on A482 [146: SN6640] *Bus:* Bws Dyfed 284 from Llandeilo, Tues only (tel. (0267) 231817) *Station:* Llanwrda (U), not Sun, except May to Sept, 8m

TUDOR MERCHANT'S HOUSE
Quay Hill, Tenby SA70 7BX (0834) 842279

A late-15th century town house, characteristic of the building tradition of south-west Wales. The ground floor chimney at the rear of the house is a fine vernacular example, and the original scarffed roof trusses survive. The remains of early frescoes can be seen on three interior walls

- **O** 30 March to 30 Oct: Mon to Fri 11–6; Sun 2–6. Closed Sat. Last admissions 15 min. before closing
- **£** £1.60, children 80p. Groups £1.30, children 60p. 1 child (16 and under) free with 1 full paying adult between 25 July–4 September. No WCs. Car parking in town
- Not recommended for wheelchair users; difficult steps and stairs
- → [158: SN135004] *Bus:* From surrounding areas (tel. (0267) 231817). *Station:* Tenby 700yds

Gwent

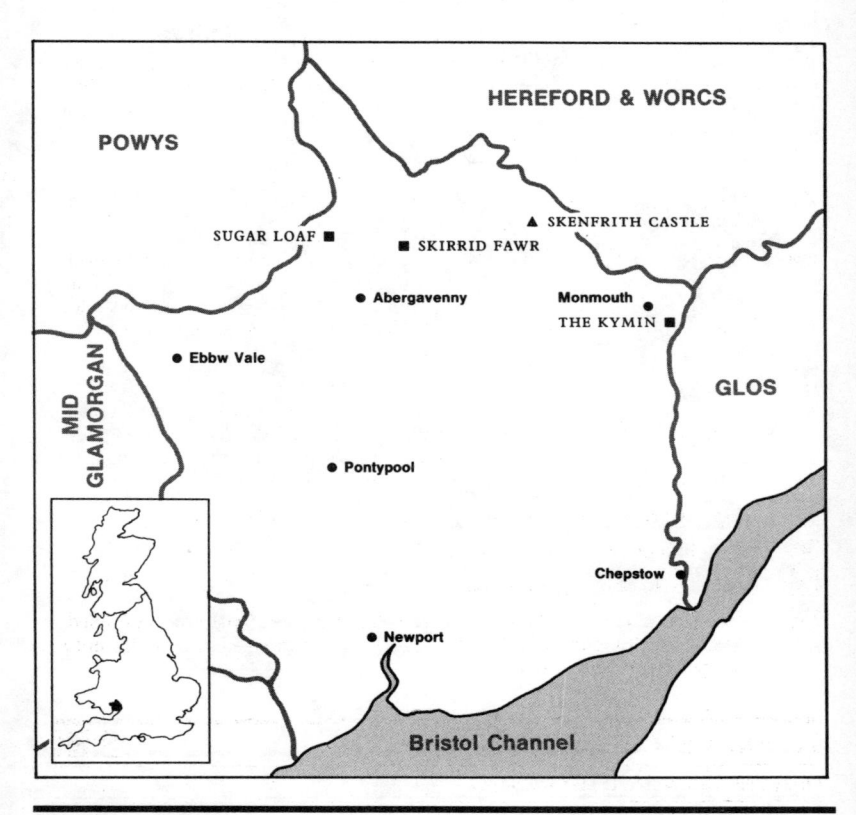

COUNTRYSIDE

A mile east of the border town of Monmouth is **The Kymin**, an 800ft high hill giving views over the valleys of the Wye and the Monnow. The 'first gentlemen in Monmouth' built a tower they called The Round House as a dining club on the summit, and also a bowling green and a Naval Temple which was visited by Nelson and Emma Hamilton in 1802 [162: SO02718]. Access from A4136.

The **Sugar Loaf** just west of Abergavenny [161: SO2718] is 2,000ft high and cone-shaped. There is access to the summit and footpaths across common land, open mountainside woodland and valleys. **Park Lodge Farm**, a 500-acre working hill farm crossed by many footpaths, lies beneath the Sugar Loaf. Another nearby viewpoint is **Skirrid Fawr** [161: SO330180], 1,600ft, giving views of the Sugar Loaf, the Usk valley and the Black Mountains.

GWENT

With the Usk Valley, **Coed y Bwnydd**, a well-preserved Iron Age hill-fort close to Bettws Newydd, has magnificent displays of bluebells in spring. The Trust also owns the attractive parkland of **Clytha**, on the banks of the River Usk, with distant views of the Black Mountains; there is a riverside picnic site here and walks along waymarked paths. Clytha Castle, the folly overlooking the estate, is leased to the Landmark Trust as holiday accommodation.

SKENFRITH CASTLE

Skenfrith, nr Abergavenny Regional Office

A Norman castle, built to command one of the main routes between England and Wales. A keep stands on the remains of the motte, and the 13th-century curtain wall with towers has also survived

Skenfrith Castle is in the guardianship of Cadw (Welsh Historic Monuments)

- ◻ All year: at any reasonable time
- £ Free
- ♿ Wheelchair access
- → 6m NW of Monmouth, 12m NE of Abergavenny, on N side of the Ross road (B4521) [161: SO456203]

Gwynedd

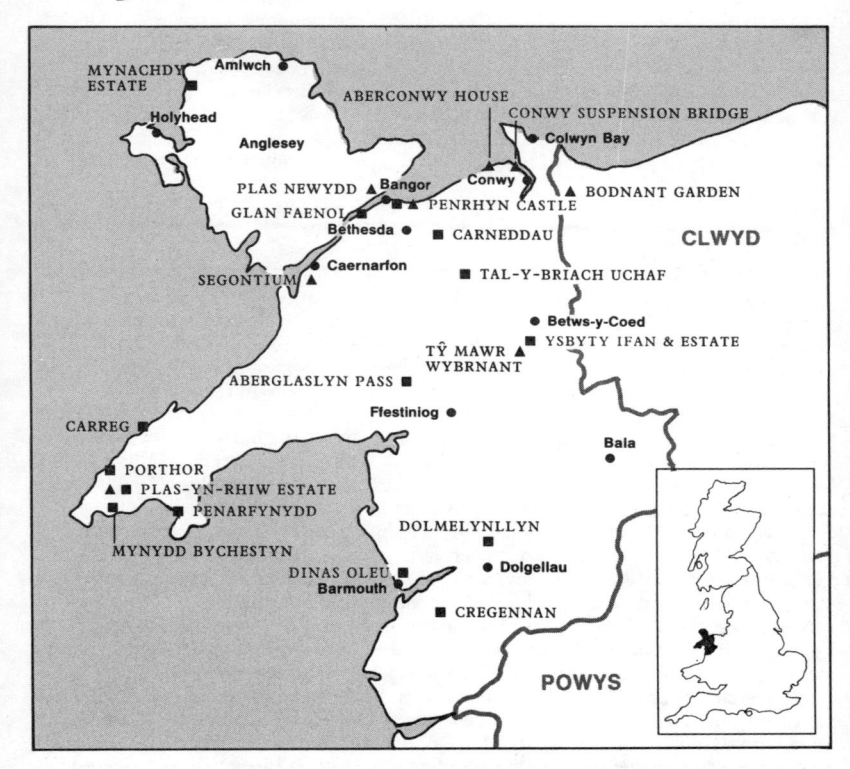

COAST

It is fascinating to think that with all its vast holdings the Trust can never forget a small 4½-acre field above Barmouth, overlooking the wide sweep of Cardigan Bay with views of the Llŷn Peninsula: **Dinas Oleu**. This was the first property ever to be owned by the National Trust, given in 1895 [124: SH615158]. Since then the Trust has added many miles to its coastal properties in Gwynedd, including the beautiful **Mynachdy Estate** on the north-western coast of the island of Anglesey. (*Note:* there is a covenanted area which is not Trust-owned; access to this area is totally banned between 15 Sept and 1 Feb). The Trust now owns 7½ miles of Anglesey's coastline including the section at **Plas Newydd**, the home of the Marquess of Anglesey (see p.281). Recently acquired to protect the view across the Menai Strait from Plas Newydd, is **Glan Faenol** – more than 300 acres of farm and woodland stretching from Faenol Wood to Y Felinheli [114: SH530695].

Probably the most spectacular coastal scenery in North Wales can be seen from the gentle green slopes of the beautiful Llŷn Peninsula. The Trust's benefactresses on the

GWYNEDD

Llŷn – the Misses Keatings, were three sisters who gave **Plas-yn-Rhiw** (see p.282), their lovely manor house and garden above Porth Neigwl. From 1950-66 they were tireless in their quest to rescue threatened land in the vicinity and present it to the Trust. The result is that the original estate of 416 acres has been reclaimed; 410 acres of which is coastal land. The Trust has kept up the Misses Keatings' good work by adding to the money they gave, a proportion of its Enterprise Neptune funds to acquiring more of the Llŷn coast – at **Penarfynydd**, **Mynydd Bychestyn**, **Porth Gwylan** and **Carreg**. The most recent acquisition of the Llŷn peninsula is **Porthor**, [123: SH166298] a delightful sandy cove protected by rocky promontories and backed by sand dunes. The beach is also known as 'Whistling Sands' owing to the whistling noise produced when the dry sand is walked on.

COUNTRYSIDE

The Trust owns well over 50,000 acres in this large county, dominated inland by the Snowdonia National Park. Many of its holdings are within the Park, the two largest properties being the **Ysbyty** and **Carneddau Estates** [115/116: SH8448 and 115: SH6760] of 20,000 acres and 18,000 acres respectively, both of which were transferred to the Trust with **Penrhyn Castle** through the National Land Fund in 1951.

Ysbyty has over 50 farms, and includes the upper valleys of the Conwy, Eidda and Machno rivers, whilst the **Carneddau Estate** has some of the most exciting scenery in Snowdonia. The Trust owns ten of the main mountain peaks over 3,000ft, including Tryfan, where the first successful Everest climbers trained, together with land through the Ogwen and Nant Ffrancon valleys between Capel Curig and Bethesda.

The **Cwm Idwal** Nature Reserve near Ogwen has a low level mountain walk around Llyn Idwal. The cwm or corrie has been famous since the 17th century for its rich variety of mountain flora. The reserve is in the care of the Countryside Council for Wales, Penrhos Road, Bangor, who can provide detailed information.

South west of Betws y Coed is **Tŷ Mawr** in the little valley of Wybrnant. The Wybrnant Trail is a short waymarked walk, a leaflet (s.a.e. please) is available from Tŷ Mawr (see p.283). Parts of Trail are accessible to wheelchair users from car park.

At **Cregennan** [124: SH6614] are two lakes, hill farms and mountain land giving fine views to Cadair Idris where two sheepwalks are owned on the north face – **Tan-y-Gadair** and **Llyn-y-Gadair** [124: SH7013/7115] – both with spectacular views.

North-west of Dolgellau the **Dolmelynllyn** estate of 1,250 acres includes one of Wales's most spectacular waterfalls, Rhaeadr Ddu on the Gamlan, reached by footpath from the village of Ganllwyd; also two sheepwalks on **Y Llethr** [124: SH7222]. To the south of Beddgelert lies the Aberglaslyn Pass, with the famous view north from the stone bridge, Pont Aberglaslyn [115: SH595463].

Details of guided walks programme from the Trust's North Wales office, (address on final page).

ABERCONWY HOUSE

Castle Street, Conwy LL32 8AY (0492) 592246

Dating from the 14th century, it is the only medieval merchant's house in Conwy to have survived the turbulent history of this walled town for nearly six centuries. Furnished rooms and an audio-visual presentation show daily life from different periods in its history

31 March to 31 Oct: daily except Tues 11-5.30. Last admissions 5

GWYNEDD

Note: the house is without electric lighting and therefore is dark on dull days

£ £1.80, children 90p. Pre-booked groups £1.60. Family (2 adults, 2 children) £4.50

Shop open all year, daily 9.30–5.30. Jan to March, Nov to Dec; Mon to Sat only

No WCs. Steps up to entrance

Educational visits welcome. Pre-booked groups only

At junction of Castle Street and High Street [115: SH781777] *Bus:* From surrounding areas (tel. (0492) 596969) *Station:* Conwy 300yds

BODNANT GARDEN

Tal-y-Cafn, Colwyn Bay, Clwyd LL28 5RE (0492) 650460

The 80-acre garden at Bodnant is one of the finest in the world, situated above the River Conwy and looking across the valley towards the Snowdon range. The garden is in two parts. The Upper part around the house (the private residence of Lord and Lady Aberconway) consists of the Terrace Gardens as well as informal lawns shaded by trees. The lower portion, known as 'The Dell', is formed by the valley of the River Hiraethlyn, a tributary of the Conwy, and contains the Pinetum and Wild Garden. In March and April masses of daffodils and other spring bulbs make a very colourful display. Pride of place amongst the shrubs is held by rhododendrons, magnolias and camellias, which flower from March until the end of June. The famous Laburnum Arch, Embothriums and many of the azaleas are at their best at the end of May/beginning June. In the summer months the Terrace Gardens are very colourful with herbaceous borders, roses, water lilies, clematis and many unusual wall shrubs and climbers. Eucryphias and hydrangeas are a special feature in late summer, whilst an October visit is very worthwhile to see the splendid autumn colours. Bodnant garden is managed by Lord Aberconway VMH

19 March to end Oct: daily 10–5. Last admissions 4.30

£ £3.60, children £1.80. Pre-booked parties of 20 or more £3.20. Car park 50yds from garden entrance

Plant Centre and Gift Shop, open as garden

The garden is steep in places, has many steps, and is not easy for wheelchairs. Two wheelchairs are available, but cannot be reserved

Braille guide. Scented roses and other plants

Refreshment pavilion serving light lunches and teas open April to end Sept daily 11–5. Picnicking in car park area only

8m S of Llandudno and Colwyn Bay off A470, entrance ½m along the Eglwysbach Road [115 & 116: SH801723]. Signposted from A55 North Wales coastal route *Bus:* Bws Gwynedd 25, 67 from Llandudno (passing close BR Llandudno Junction) tel. (0286) 679535 *Station:* Tal-y-Cafn, not Sun, except July–Sept, 1½m

REFER TO OPENING PAGES FOR GENERAL INFORMATION

GWYNEDD

CONWY SUSPENSION BRIDGE 🚶

Conwy, Gwynedd

Designed and built by Thomas Telford, the famous engineer, this elegant suspension bridge was completed in 1826, replacing the ferry, previously the only means of crossing the river

- ⓘ Note: Closed through 1994 season. Re-opens April 1995
- ➔ 100yds from Conwy town centre, adjacent to Conwy Castle [115: SH785775]
  Bus: from surrounding areas (tel. (0492) 596969) *Station:* Conwy ¼m; Llandudno Junction ½m

LLYWELYN COTTAGE 🏠 🎒

Llywelyn Cottage, Beddgelert LL55 4YA (0766) 86293

Situated in the picturesque village of Beddgelert in the Aberglaslyn Valley, within the Snowdonia National Park. Superb walks, including a stroll to the legendary Gelert's grave and a level path along the track of the former Welsh Highland Railway

- ⓘ Shop & Information Centre open daily; 1 April to 30 Oct 12-5
- 🛍 Open daily 12-5
- ♿ Accessible to wheelchairs
- ➔ A5 to Capel Curig, on A4086 join the A498 at Pen-y-Gwryd. Well signposted from A5 and A487 [115:SH590481] *Bus:* tel. (0286) 679535
  Station: Penrhyndeudraeth (U) or Porthmadog (U), both 6m

PENRHYN CASTLE 🏰 ❀ 🚶   📷 ✕ 🐕

Bangor, Gwynedd LL57 4HN (0248) 353084 Information line: (0248) 371337

A huge neo-Norman castle placed dramatically between Snowdonia and the Menai Strait. Built by Thomas Hopper between 1820 and 1845, the castle contains interesting 'Norman' furniture, panelling and plasterwork designed by Hopper, and houses the best private collection of paintings in North Wales. There is also an industrial railway, a doll museum, and a Victorian walled garden. Specialist Heritage tours and meet-the-gardener tours by arrangement

- ⓘ 30 March to 30 Oct: daily except Tues. **Castle:** 12-5 (July & Aug 11-5) daily except Tues, last admissions 4.30 (last audio tour 4). **Grounds:** 11-6. *Note:* doll museum may be closed in 1994
- £ £4.40, children £2.20. Booked parties of 20 or more £3.50. Family ticket £11 (max. 2 adults, 2 children). Garden only £2, children £1. Audio tour 50p for members, for adults and children in Welsh and English. School and youth groups by arrangement. Parking 200yds
- 🚶 Garden tours arranged throughout the season
- 🛍 Shop open as Castle

GWYNEDD

- ♿ Access to all ground floor rooms; access ramps and handrail (but no access to shop in basement). Wheelchair available. Castle is least congested on Sat. Park paths are firm. Parking and volunteer-driven golf buggy, seating 3, for garden and park by arrangement. WC
- Braille guide. Inductive loop audio tour for hard of hearing, sympathetic ear
- Licensed tea-room; light lunches and teas. Picnicking in grounds. Tea-room opens 1hr before the Castle
- Industrial railway and doll museum. Adventure playground. Young Adventurers' audio tour. Baby facilities; baby carriers on loan. High chairs in tea-room. Permanent orienteering course in grounds – maps and instructions available from shop
- Educational visits particularly welcome. Hands-on educational facilities. Permanent orienteering course
- **E** A programme of events is run throughout the season. Events information line tel. (0248) 371337
- In grounds only on lead
- → 1m E of Bangor, at Llandegai on A5122 [115: SH603720]. Signposted from junction of A55 and A5 North Wales coastal route *Bus:* Bws Gwynedd 5 Caernarfon–Llandudno; 6/7 Bangor–Bethesda; 66 Bangor–Gerlan. All pass close BR Bangor and end of drive to Castle (tel. (0286) 679535) *Station:* Bangor 3m

PLAS NEWYDD

Llanfairpwll, Anglesey LL61 6EQ (0248) 714795

An impressive 18th-century house by James Wyatt in unspoilt surroundings on the Menai Strait, with magnificent views of Snowdonia. The house contains Rex Whistler's largest wall painting and an exhibition about his work. In the military museum are campaign relics of the 1st Marquess of Anglesey and the Battle of Waterloo. There is a fine spring garden and parkland

- **O** 30 March to 30 Sept: daily except Sat 12–5 (garden 11–5 in July & Aug). 2–30 Oct: Fri & Sun only 12–5. Last admissions 4.30

  Note: The Rhododendron Garden is open from April to early June only
- **£** £3.80, children £1.90. Family ticket (max. 2 adults, 2 children) £9.50. Pre-booked parties of 20 or more £3. Parking ¼m
- Connoiseur's Tours by prior arrangement
- Shop open daily 12–5. July & Aug 11–5. Also Christmas shop; tel. Administrator for details
- ♿ Ground floor accessible; ramps. Close parking, enquire at reception desk; wheelchair available. Easy access to tea-room and shop. WC
- Braille guide
- Licensed tea-room: morning coffee, light lunches & teas; open 11–5   *continued*

GWYNEDD

- Baby facilities. Baby carriers available. High chairs in tea-room. Children's adventure playground
- Youth and school groups by arrangement
- No dogs
- 1m SW of Llanfairpwll and A5 on A4080 to Brynsiencyn; turn off A5 at W end of Britannia Bridge [114 & 115: SH521696] *Bus:* Bws Gwynedd 42, 43A from Bangor (passing BR Bangor & Llanfairpwll) (tel. (0286) 679535) *Station:* Llanfairpwll (U), no practical Sun service, except May to Sept, 1¾m

PLAS YN RHIW
Rhiw, Pwllheli LL53 8AB (075 888) 219

A small manor house, with garden and woodlands, overlooking the west shore of Porth Neigwl (Hell's Mouth Bay) on the Llŷn peninsula. The house is part medieval, with Tudor and Georgian additions, and the ornamental gardens have flowering trees and shrubs, divided by box hedges and grass paths, rising behind to the snowdrop wood

- 1 April to 25 Sept: daily (except Sat) 12–5; also 2–30 Oct: Sun only 12–4. Last admissions ½hr before closing

  Note: In the interests of preservation, numbers of visitors admitted to the house at any one time may be limited, particularly in July and Aug and BH Mon

- £2.30, children £1.15. Family ticket (max 2 adults, 2 children) £6. Pre-booked parties evenings only (incl. full guided tour) £3. Parking 80yds. No coaches
- Advanced notice is required; no tours during July & Aug
- Small shop open as house
- Access to ground floor rooms only; most of garden very difficult for wheelchairs. WC
- School visits are encouraged, but Custodian must be informed 2 weeks in advance
- On leads on the woodland walk only
- 12m from Pwllheli on S coast road to Aberdaron (drive gate at the bottom of Rhiw Hill [123: SH237282] *Bus:* Bws Gwynedd 17 Pwllheli–Aberdaron (passing BR Pwllheli), passes House Wed only, on other days alight Botwnnog, 3¾m (tel. (0248) 370295) *Station:* Pwllheli 10m

SEGONTIUM
Caernarfon (0286) 675625

The remains of a Roman fort, with a museum containing relics found on site. Segontium is in the guardianship of Cadw (Welsh Historic Monuments)

- All year. March, April & Oct: Mon to Sat 9.30–5.30, Sun 2–5. May to end Sept: Mon to Sat 9.30–6, Sun 2–6. Nov to end Feb: Mon to Sat 9.30–4, Sun 2–4. Closed 24–26 Dec, New Year's Day, Good Fri & May Day

282

GWYNEDD

- £ Free. Parking on main road nearby
- No dogs
- → On Llanbeblig road, A4085, on SE outskirts of Caernarfon, [115: SH485624] *Bus:* From surrounding areas to Caernarfon, Bws Gwynedd 11 passes Museum, on others alight Castle, ½m) (tel. (0286) 679535) *Station:* Bangor 9m

TŶ MAWR WYBRNANT
Penmachno, Betws y Coed LL25 0HJ (0690) 760213

Situated in the beautiful and secluded Wybrnant Valley, Tŷ Mawr was the birthplace of Bishop William Morgan, first translator of the entire Bible into Welsh. The house has recently been restored to its probable 16th–17th-century appearance, with a display of Welsh Bibles. The surrounding fields are traditionally managed and the Wybrnant Walkers' Guide covers approximately one mile from the house and back

- O April to Sept; details on request
- £ No access for coaches. £1.50, children 75p. Family (max 2 adults, 2 children) £3.75. Pre-booked parties (20 or more) £1.20
- Educational visits particularly welcome for house and nature trail tour. Pre-booked school parties only
- In countryside only
- → At the head of the Wybrnant valley. From A5 3m S of Betws-y-Coed, take B4406 to Penmachno. House is 2½m NW of Penmachno by forest road [115: SH770524] *Station:* Pont-y-pant (U) not Sun, except July to Sept 1½m

TY'N-Y-COED
Ty'n-y-Coed, Penmachno, Betws-y-Coed (0690) 760229

A small holding with 19th-century farmhouse and outbuildings which provide a record of the Welsh, traditional, way of life. The house is approached by an interesting walk along the River Machno through fields of nature and conservation interest

- O April to Oct. Thurs: Fri & Sun 12–5. Ty'n-y-Coed is occupied by a tenant family. Please observe the property opening times. Please keep dogs on a lead in the fields. Car park (NT) next to car park for Penmachno Woollen Mills
- £ £1.50, children 75p. Family ticket (max 2 adults, 2 children) £3.75. Pre-booked groups (20 or more) £1.20
- Educational groups are especially welcome. Pre-booked only
- No dogs in the house; must be kept on leads in the countryside
- → 1½m S of Betws-y-Coed on the A5. Turn right at the NT sign for Tŷ Mawr on to the B4406 for ½m [116: SH803521] *Bus:* Bws Gwynedd 49 Llandudno–Cum (passes close BR Betws-y-Coed) tel. (0492) 596969 *Station:* Betws-y-Coed 3m

Powys

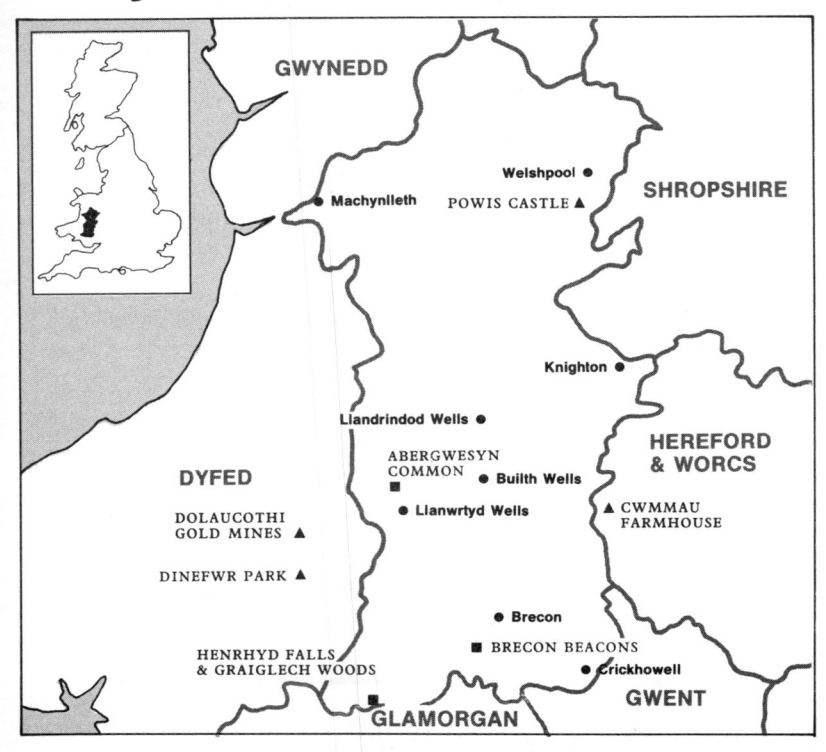

COUNTRYSIDE

The most famous mountains in Powys, the **Brecon Beacons** [160: SO010200] dominate the southern part of the county. The Trust was given over 8,000 acres of the main part of the range including the 2,900ft Penyfan, the highest peak in the Beacons by, aptly, Sir Brian Mountain, Chairman of the Eagle Star Insurance Company. **Cwm Oergwm**, 90 acres of fields and woods in a sheltered valley on the northern slopes of the Beacons, has recently been acquired. **Cwm Sere** is a small wood at the base of the Brecon Beacons, leased to the local wildlife trust who manage it as a local nature reserve, while **Blaenglyn Farm** and **Carno Wood**, a typical working Welsh hill farm at the head of the Tarrell Valley, is crossed by the Taff trail which is the new long-distance path from Cardiff to Brecon.

Henrhyd Falls, among the finest in the country, are in a beautiful spot near the edge of the South Wales coalfield, formed by the River Llech tumbling for 90ft through a deep wooded ravine; there is a car park and circular walk. **Graigllech Woods**, are also Trust-owned [160: SN850119].

POWYS

The Trust has more recently acquired 16,500 acres of **Abergwesyn Common** [127, 128 & 141: SN8359/9861]. This is a 12-mile stretch of high, beautiful, but wild and remote common land between Rhayader and the Irfon Gorge near Llanwrtyd Wells, accessible by public footpaths; but only recommended to the hardy hill walker! Dogs must be kept on a lead at all times.

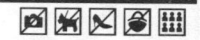

POWIS CASTLE
Welshpool SY21 8RF (0938) 554336

Perched on a rock above the late 17th-century garden terraces, this medieval castle contains the finest country house collection in Wales. It was built c.1200 by Welsh princes, and has been owned and altered by successive generations of Herberts and Clives for 400 years. The garden is of the highest horticultural and historical importance, and the Clive Museum displays treasures from India. 1 holiday cottage available

- 1 April to end June & Sept to 30 Oct: daily except Mon & Tues, July & Aug: daily except Mon, but open BH Mon. **Castle & Museum:** 12–5. Garden: 11–6. Last admissions $\frac{1}{2}$hr before closing

  Note: Castle open every Sun from April to Oct

- Garden £3.80, children £1.90. Family (max. 2 adults & 2 children) £9.50. Parties £3. All in ticket (incl. Castle, Museum & Garden) £5.80, children £2.90. Parties for Castle, Museum & Garden £5.40

- Tours, incl. dinner any evening by prior arrangement. Meet the Gardener tours available by prior arrangement

- Open as Castle; also Christmas shop open Sun 2–4 throughout the winter until Christmas (tel. Administrator for details)

- Castle not possible for wheelchair users; access to tea-room, shop and parts of garden only. Wheelchair available. No parking facilities near Castle & gardens entrances; elderly & disabled persons may be driven up to entrances but drivers should return car to car park; disabled drivers can use buggy provided (between 12 & 5) to travel between car park & entrances. WC. Buggy by arrangement only

- Braille guide; scented flowers

- Licensed restaurant: morning coffee, light lunches and teas. Open Sun 2–4 throughout the winter until Christmas

- Baby feeding and changing facilities. Baby carriers available on loan. High chairs in tea-room

- No dogs

- 1m S of Welshpool; pedestrian access from High Street (A490); cars turn right 1m along main road to Newtown (A483); enter by first drive gate on right [126: SJ216064] *Bus:* Cambrian Midland Red D71 Oswestry–Welshpool; D75 Shrewsbury–Welshpool, alight High Street, 1m (tel. 0345 056 785) *Station:* Welshpool 1$\frac{1}{4}$m via footpath in town

REFER TO OPENING PAGES FOR GENERAL INFORMATION

West Glamorgan

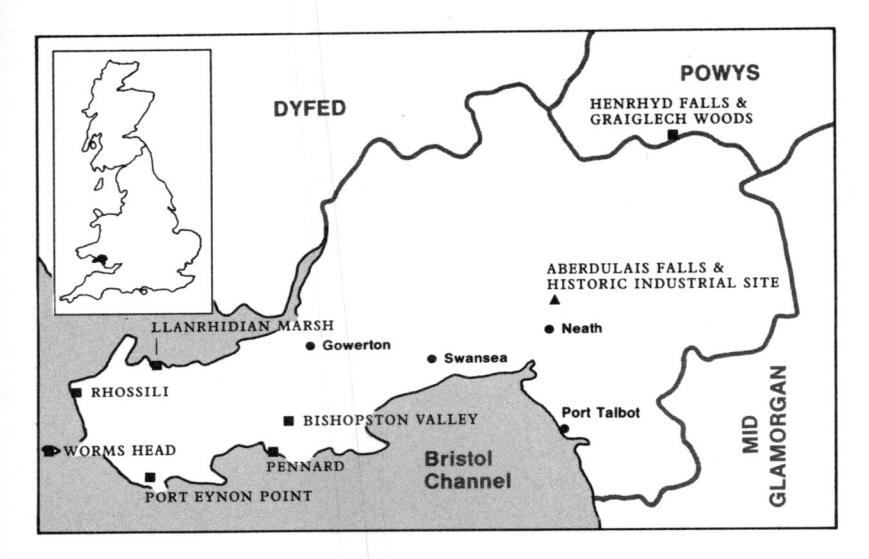

COAST

The lovely and varied scenery of the Gower peninsula, the first area to be designated an Area of Outstanding Natural Beauty, lies just west of the coastal city of Swansea. It is renowned for its wildlife, sandy beaches and magnificent coast – yet much of it is remote, wild and unpopulated save for vast colonies of seabirds and waders. The Trust owns about 5,000 acres in Gower, ranging from saltmarsh at **Llanrhidian** on the north coast [159: SS490932] to the limestone cliffs between **Port Eynon** [159: SS468845] and **Rhossili**, see Visitor Centre entry p.288, with prehistoric caves and a medieval dovecote known as the Culver Hole; the lovely wooded valley at Bishopston; and the elongated rocky headland of **Worms Head** [159: SS383878] at the extreme westernmost point of the peninsula which is a National Nature Reserve and is leased to the Countryside Council for Wales.

DUNLIN

WEST GLAMORGAN

ABERDULAIS FALLS 🐟 🆃
Aberdulais, nr Neath SA10 8EU (0639) 636674

For over 300 years this famous waterfall has provided the energy to drive the wheels of industry. Nestling amongst the site's historic remains, a unique hydro electric scheme has been developed to harness this great natural resource. The new Turbine House provides visitor access to the top of the falls, with views of power equipment, fish pass and displays. A special lift has been installed to allow disabled visitors access to roof level, with excellent views of the falls and new water wheel. Nearby, in the restored Victorian tinplate works' wheel pit, Britain's largest electricity generating water wheel makes Aberdulais Falls self sufficient in environmentally friendly energy. Situated in the historic village of Aberdulais, Aberdulais Falls is the ideal starting place for exploring the Vale of Neath

- ⭕ 1 Jan to 29 March: daily 11–4. 30 March to 30 Oct: Mon–Fri 10–5; Sat, Sun, Bank Hols 11–6. 31 Oct to 24 Dec: daily 11–4. Closed 25–31 Dec, re-opens 1 Jan 1995. Last admission 30 mins before closing
- £ Summer: adults £2.70, children £1.10, adult groups £2.10, child/school groups 90p. Winter: adults £2.40, children £1, adult groups £1.90, child/school groups 70p. 1 child (16 & under) free with each paying adult admission from Mon 25 July to Sun 4 Sept. NT members free. Parties (min15 people) by prior arrangement with the Warden. Children should be accompanied by an adult, or will be admitted at the discretion of the Administrator. Car and Coach Park 200 yds, signposted to Aberdulais Tourist Information Centre car-park. Availability subject to roadway construction
- 🚶 Guided tours every day during July and Aug, at other times by arrangement for pre-booked parties
- 🛍 Open during normal property opening times. Main shop opens from 1 April
- ♿ Much of the property is now accessible to disabled visitors. In the new Turbine House a special lift, capable of carrying two wheelchair visitors and their helpers, provides access to the roof level with excellent views of the falls and new water wheel. WC and wheelchair available
- 👁 Braille guide, tactile guide and taped guide
- 🍴 Light refreshments are served by Friends of Aberdulais Falls during summer weekends and public holidays
- 📷 Education facilities provided for pre-booked groups by arrangement with Education Officer. Teacher's resource pack available
- E Events held throughout the year, contact warden for full details
- 🐕 Must be kept on leads
- ➔ On A465, Heads of the Valleys road, 3m NE of Neath [170: SS772995]. Four miles from A48 (M) Junction 43 at Llandarcy, signposted Vale of Neath *Bus:* S Wales 158 Swansea–Banwen; 161, N10 from Neath (tel. (0792) 475511); Silverline Brecon–Swansea (tel. (0685) 382406). All pass close BR Neath *Station:* Neath 3m

REFER TO OPENING PAGES FOR GENERAL INFORMATION

WEST GLAMORGAN

RHOSSILI VISITOR CENTRE

Rhossili Visitor Centre, Coastguard Cottages, Rhossili, Gower SA3 1PR
(0792) 390707

Situated adjacent to extensive NT ownership of the Raised Terrace, the Down, the beach, coastal cliffs and the Worms Head

- 5 March to 3 Apr: Sat & Sun 11-4. 4 Apr to 23 Oct: daily 10.30-5.30. 24 Oct to 6 Nov: daily 11-4. 12 Nov to 18 Dec: Sat & Sun 11-4
- Free. No NT car park; public car park and WC nearby
- Visitor Centre ground floor accessible. No separate parking facilities
- Available nearby
- Guide dogs only in the Visitor Centre
- SW tip of Gower Peninsula approached from Swansea via A4118 and then B4247 *Bus:* South Wales 18/A/C from Swansea (passing close BR Swansea) (tel. (0792) 475511)

Northern Ireland

COAST

Most of the Trust's coastal holdings in Ulster are in Co. Down and Co. Antrim. The southernmost property in Co. Down is at the mouth of Carlingford Lough – **Blockhouse and Green Islands** [J254097]. These tiny islands total only 2 acres, but are important nesting sites for nesting terns, and are leased to the Royal Society for the Protection of Birds. To the north of Carlingford Lough are the Mourne Mountains, and here the Trust owns **Slieve Donard**, the highest mountain in the range, and two sections of the **Mourne Coastal Path** [J389269]. One runs south from Bloody Bridge at the foot of Slieve Donard, along the coast and past the site of St Mary's, Ballaghanary, an early Celtic church; the other leads up the valley of the Bloody River, giving access to the mountains. There is an adapted WC for wheelchair users at the car park, but the path is not recommended for wheelchairs.

On this same stretch of coast lies **Dundrum**, with the Widow's Row cottages and footpath along the old railway; also **Murlough National Nature Reserve**, near Newcastle,

NORTHERN IRELAND

Ireland's first such reserve. The oldest dunes here are at least 5,000 years old and the soil ranges from lime-rich to acid, supporting a wide variety of plants including pyramidal orchid, bell heather, primrose and dune burnet rose. In spring many birds nest in the sea buckthorn – reed bunting, stonechat, whitethroat; and in winter its orange berries attract thrushes and finches. Visitor facilities open June to mid Sept: daily 10-5, weather permitting; parking £1.50. There is a special slatted walkway across the dunes, suitable for wheelchair users. Holiday cottages now available on shores of Dundrum Inner Bay. Dogs on leads only.

Strangford Lough: the Trust's **Wildlife Scheme** here embraces the entire foreshore of Strangford Lough [J60615] and some 50 islands, totalling 5,400 acres. Vast flocks of wildfowl gather here, as well as nesting birds, seals and other marine animals. The wild flowers merit special attention. Bird hides and refuges are provided for study purposes. Birdwatching facilities, including those for disabled visitors, at Island Reagh, Castle Espie and Mount Stewart (tel. (0238) 510721 or (0396) 881411). The Quoile Estuary and two riverside areas forming part of the freshwater Quoile Pondage also comes under the Wildlife Scheme. Information at Strangford Lough Wildlife Centre, Castle Ward.

On the extreme easterly point of the Co. Down coastline is the former fishing village of **Kearney** [J650517] where the Trust owns 13 houses. **Ballymacormick Point** [J525837], is 1-3 miles north-east of Bangor on the south side of the entrance to Belfast Lough; there are 44 acres of rocky shore, and coastal heath of biological interest. **Orlock Point** [J559837] has wildfowl, wading birds and gulls. **Lighthouse Island** [J596858] is a 43-acre island with a bird observatory. Visits by arrangement with Mr Neville McKee, 67 Temple Rise, Templepatrick, Co. Down (tel. (084 94) 33068).

The North Antrim coastline is no less attractive, and is more dramatic than County Down. The Trust has a continuous series of coastal properties, beginning in the west with **Downhill** [C758363], (see p.294).

Portstewart Strand consists of 2 miles of duneland west of Portstewart [C720360]. Parking £2. Visitor facilities June to end Aug: daily 10-6, weather permitting. Beach accessible by car, but only suitable for wheelchair users at low tide when sand is hard. Dogs on leads only during summer months. **The Bar Mouth** and Grangemore Dunes 5 miles north-west of Coleraine at the mouth of the River Bann [C792355] is a wildlife sanctuary, with wheelchair access to observation hide – key available from Warden tel. (0265) 848728.

Between **Giant's Causeway** (see p.296) and the ruins of **Dunseverick Castle** [C987445] the Trust now owns 104 acres of the **North Antrim Cliff Path**. East of Dunseverick is the beautiful curve of **Whitepark Bay**, 180 acres of sand and white chalk cliff [D023440] with an information panel. Beyond this bay is the tiny stack of basalt connected in summer by a swinging rope bridge to the mainland; **Carrick-a-Rede**, the 'rock on the road'. This is the road the salmon take on their way to rivers in the north and there is a salmon fishery on the island [D062450]. Access to Carrick-a-Rede via cliff path from Larrybane where there is a car park, £1.50; coaches £6. Information Centre open April, May and Sept: weekends 11-6; June to Aug: daily 11-6, weather permitting; adapted WC for wheelchair users. Adjoining are 58 acres of coastline with a disused basalt quarry and lime-workings [D051449].

The headland of **Fair Head** rises 636ft above the sea, giving views over **Murlough Bay**. Dogs on leads only. Viewpoint car parks are accessible to wheelchair users. This is one of the most beautiful sections of the North Antrim coast [D185430/199418]. The Trust manages or owns 764 acres here, including woodlands of outstanding interest for the botanist. Turning south again, the lovely village of **Cushendun** at the foot of Glendun [D248327] contains cottages designed and built by the architect of Portmeirion in North Wales, the late Clough Williams-Ellis. The harbour is also owned by the Trust.

NORTHERN IRELAND

ARDRESS HOUSE
64 Ardress Road, Portadown, Co. Armagh BT62 1SQ (0762) 851236

Originally a 17th-century farmhouse, the main front and garden façades were added in the 18th century by the owner, architect George Ensor. The house contains some particularly fine neo-Classical plasterwork as well as good furniture and pictures. There is a display of farm implements and livestock in the farmyard, an attractive garden and woodland walks

- **House & Farmyard:** April: weekends & Easter (1-5 April) 2-6; May, June & Sept: Sat, Sun & BH 2-6; July to end Aug: daily except Tues 2-6. Farmyard also open weekdays (except Tues) May, June & Sept 12-4
- House and Farmyard £2.20, children £1.10, parties £1.60. Parties outside normal opening hours £2.80. Grounds and Farmyard only £1.60, children 80p, parties £1.40. Parties outside normal opening hours £2.40
- Guided tours in Spanish and French by arrangement
- Access to ground floor, picnic area and part of farmyard; WC in car park
- Picnics welcome. Picnic area opens at 12
- Play area with tree swings
- Pre-booked school groups welcome, especially those involved in the Cross Community Contact Scheme. Teacher's pack available
- Range of events and demonstrations during season. Tel. for details
- In garden only
- 7m from Portadown on Moy road (B28), 5m from Moy, 3m from Loughgall intersection 13 on M1, 9m from Armagh [H914559] *Bus:* Ulsterbus 67 Portadown–Kesquin Bridge (passing close NIR Portadown Stn) to within ¼m (tel. (0762) 342511) *Station:* Portadown 7m

THE ARGORY
(Co. Armagh) Moy, Dungannon, Co. Tyrone BT71 6NA (086 87) 84753

Set in over 300 acres of woodland overlooking the Blackwater river, the house dates from 1820 and was substantially changed in the 19th century. Fascinating furniture and contents, including an 1824 Bishop's barrel organ. There is an imposing stable yard with a coach house and carriages, harness room, laundry and acetylene gas plant. Also, an interesting sundial garden and extensive walks

- Easter (1-5 April): daily 2-6. April, May, June & Sept: Sat, Sun & BH 2-6; July to end Aug: daily except Thur 2-6. Open from 1-6 on all BH. Last tour 5.15
- £2.20, children £1.10. Parties £1.60. Parties outside normal opening hours £2.80. Car park 50p. Parking 100yds. Coaches must book with Administrator
- Shop open as house, but weekdays July & Aug 3-5, BH 1-6

continued

291

NORTHERN IRELAND

- ♿ Access to ground floor of house, all driveways, walks, tea-room and reception area; wheelchair available. Special car parking near east door of house (ramp); WC by reception area
- ☕ Light refreshments in tea-room, open as house except weekdays July & Aug 3-5. Picnics welcome
- 🧒 Adventure playground
- 🏫 Pre-booked school groups welcome, especially those in the Cross Community Contact Scheme. Study centre; teacher's pack and pupil worksheets; Key Stage 1 & 2 tours available
- E April 3/4, A Victorian Easter at the Argory; Vintage Vehicle Rally, April 30; Victorian Christmas Craft fair, Dec 3/4; please tel. for details of these and other events
- 🐕 In grounds and garden only, on leads
- ➡ 4m from Moy, 3m from M1, exit 13 or 14, NB coaches must use exit 13; weight restrictions at Bonds Bridge [H872580] *Bus:* Ulsterbus 67, 75 Portadown–Dungannon (both pass close NIR Portadown Stn), alight Charlemont on 67, Verner's Inn on 75, 2½m from both (tel. (0762) 342511)

CASTLE COOLE

Enniskillen, Co. Fermanagh BT74 6JX (0365) 322690

This very fine neo Classical late 18th-century house, with wings connected by colonnades, was designed by James Wyatt. It contains original decoration and furniture dating from before 1830, and is set in a landscaped parkland with mature oak woodland. State Bedroom prepared for Georger IV in 1821 is now re-opened after restoration work. Exterior attractions include servants' tunnel and stables

- ⭕ Easter (1-5 April): daily 2-6. April, May & Sept: Sat, Sun & BH only, 2-6; June to end Aug: daily except Thur 2-6. Last tour begins 5.15. Grounds open to pedestrians during daylight hours
- £ £2.40, children £1.20, parties £1.80. Parties outside normal opening hours £3. Estate £1 per car
- 🛍 Shop in reception area open as house
- ♿ Access to ground floor of house; disabled visitors may be driven to the house. WC in reception centre
- ☕ Picnics welcome. Tea-room in reception area open as house
- 🏫 Pre-booked school groups welcome especially those involved in the Cross Community Contact Scheme
- 🐕 In grounds on leads only
- ➡ 1½m SE of Enniskillen on main Belfast–Enniskillen road (A4) [H260430] *Bus:* Ulsterbus 95, Enniskillen Clones (tel. (0365) 322633)

292

CASTLE WARD

Strangford, Downpatrick, Co. Down BT30 7LS (0396) 881204

Castle Ward is set in a 700-acre country estate on the shores of Strangford Lough. This unique 18th-century mansion has opposing façades in different styles: the west front is Classical, and the east front Gothick. In the stable yard there is a Victorian laundry and theatre for visiting companies. Also, a formal and landscape gardens with specimen shrubs and trees, fortified towers, a sawmill and working cornmill and a wildfowl collection. Strangford Lough Wildlife Centre, located on the waters edge, has audio-visual shows. Caravan park, holiday cottages, and basecamp for young people

- **House:** Easter (1–10 April): daily 1–6. April, Sept & Oct: Sat & Sun 1–6; May to end Aug: daily except Thur 1–6. Last tour 5.10. **Estate & grounds:** open all year dawn to dusk (charge for car park only). **Strangford Lough Wildlife Centre:** open as house 2–6, except May & June when open Sat, Sun & BH only 2–6

- £2.50, children £1.25. Parties £2. Parties outside normal opening hours £3. Three car parks; parking £3.50 (£1.75 when house and other facilities are closed). Coaches; booked parties to house, free; others £15. Horses (using bridlepath) £5 per single horsebox

- Shop open same days as house: weekdays 1–5; Sat, Sun & BH Mon 1–6

- Access to formal garden, house and restaurant; and interpretation centre; wheelchair available. Disabled visitors may be set down at house; car park for disabled drivers behind stables; WC in stable yard

- Braille guide available

- Light refreshments, lunches and teas, open as shop. Party organisers should book visits and arrange teas in advance with Receptionist. Picnics welcome

- Changing facilities in WC. Adventure playground. Victorian Pastimes Centre; toys & dressing up

- Pre-booked school groups welcome especially those involved in the Cross Community Contact Scheme. Teacher's pack available and pupil worksheet. Nature trails. Key stage 2 tour available based on 'life in the big house'

- Craft fairs, guided walks, concerts opera season and other events. Tel. for details

- In grounds only, on leads

- 7m NE of Downpatrick, 1½m W of Strangford village on A25, on S shore of Strangford Lough, entrance by Ballyculter Lodge [J752494] *Bus:* Ulsterbus 16E Downpatrick–Strangford, with connections from Belfast (passing close NIR Belfast Central Stn); alight Ballyculter crossroads, 1m (tel. (0396) 612384)

NORTHERN IRELAND

CROM ESTATE 🏛️ 🌳 ♿

Newtownbutler, Co. Fermanagh (03657) 38174

1,350 acres of woodland, parkland and wetland on the shores of Upper Lough Erne. This is one of Northern Ireland's most important nature conservation areas, of international significance. Buildings include Crom Old Castle and Crichton Tower. New from 1993: visitor information centre on Lough shore. 7 holiday cottages

- 🕐 1 April to end Sept: daily 2-6
- £ Parking £2.50. Guided walks by arrangement
- ♿ Property partially accessible. WCs in Visitor Centre & next to Warden's office
- 🧺 Picnics welcome
- 🧒 Children's area in information centre
- 🏫 Pre-booked school groups welcome, especially those involved in the Cross Community Contact Scheme
- 🐕 On lead only
- ➡️ 3m W of Newtownbutler, on Newtownbutler–Crom road [J363245] *Bus:* Ulsterbus 95 Enniskillen–Clones (with connections from Belfast), alight Newtownbutler 3m (tel. (0365) 322633)

CROWN LIQUOR SALOON 🏛️

Gt Victoria Street, Belfast BT2 (0232) 325368

A magnificent High Victorian public house with rich ornamentation and fine woodwork, glass and tiles, built at the end of the 19th century; managed by Bass Ireland

- 🕐 Daily, during licensed hours 11.30am-11pm; Sun 12.30pm-2.30pm & 7pm-10pm
- 🧺 Full bar facilities, snack lunches
- ➡️ [J738332] *Bus:* From surrounding areas (tel. (0232) 246485 (Citybus) or 333000/320574 (Ulsterbus)) *Station:* Belfast Central ¼m

DOWNHILL CASTLE, MUSSENDEN TEMPLE, BISHOP'S GATE & BLACK GLEN 🏛️🏛️✣🧺🅿️🧒

Bishop's Gate, 42 Mussenden Road, Castlerock, Coleraine, Co. Londonderry BT51 4RP (Regional Office (0238) 510721)

A landscaped estate, laid out in the late 18th century by the energetic Earl Bishop, Frederick Hervey, Earl of Bristol and Bishop of Derry. The estate includes Mussenden Temple perched on the cliff, ruins of his palatial house, family memorials, gardens, fish pond, woodland and cliff walks, as well as panoramic views of Ireland's north coast. Modest camping facities in Walled Garden

NORTHERN IRELAND

- **Temple:** Easter (1-5 April); daily 12-6. April, May, June & Sept: Sat, Sun & BH 12-6; July & Aug: daily 12-6. **Grounds** open all year: dawn to dusk. Open for groups at other times by arrangement (tel. (0265) 848728)
- Free. Limited access for coaches. No WCs
- Paths through garden; cars may be taken to Bishop's Gate
- Picnics welcome
- Must be kept on leads
- 1m W of Castlerock and 5M W of Coleraine on the Coleraine–Downhill coast road (A2) [J757357] *Bus:* Ulsterbus 134 Coleraine–Limavady (tel. (0265) 43334) *Station:* Castlerock ½m

FLORENCE COURT

Enniskillen, Co. Fermanagh BT92 1DB (0365) 348249, shop 348788

One of the most important houses in Ulster, built in mid 18th century by John Cole, father of 1st Earl of Enniskillen. Contents include fine rococo plasterwork and good examples of 18th-century furniture. There are pleasure grounds with an ice house and water powered sawmill, plus a walled garden, and fine views over surrounding mountains

- Easter (1-5 April): daily 1-6. April, May & Sept: Sat, Sun & BH only 1-6; June to end Aug: daily except Tues 1-6. Last admissions 5.15. Grounds open all year 10-7. Closed Christmas Day
- House: £2.40, children £1.20. Parties £1.80. Parties outside normal opening hours £3. Estate: £1.50. Parking 50yds. Information room
- Shop as house but July & Aug open from 12
- Access to garden & ground floor only. North Pavilion restaurant accessible. WC and parking. Self-drive electric buggy available
- Teas & lunches downstairs in North Pavilion; open as shop. Picnics welcome
- Play area opening 1994
- Pre-booked school groups welcome, especially those involved in the Cross Community Contact Scheme. Teacher's pack and pupil worksheets available. Key Stage 1 & 2 tours available
- Country fairs, craft fairs and other events. Tel. for details
- In grounds and garden on leads
- 8m SW of Enniskillen via A4 Sligo Road and A32 Swanlinbar Road [H175344] 4m from Marble Arch Caves *Bus:* Ulsterbus 192 Enniskillen–Swanlinbar (tel. (0365) 322633)

REFER TO OPENING PAGES FOR GENERAL INFORMATION

NORTHERN IRELAND

GIANT'S CAUSEWAY 🏛️ 🚶

44a Causeway Rd, Bushmills, Co. Antrim BT57 8SU (026 57) 31582

The unusual basalt and volcanic rock formations harbour a wealth of local and natural history, which can be enjoyed from the coast and cliff paths. The wreck site of Armada treasure ship Girona (1588) is at Port-na-Spaniagh. The Visitor Centre, with interpretative displays, audio visual theatre and tourist information is owned by Moyle District Council

- 🅾 Giant's Causeway: all year. NT shop & tea-room in **Visitor Centre:** 14 March to end May: daily 11–5. June: daily 11–5.30. July & Aug: daily 10–7 (closing times may vary according to demand on Sun). Sept & Oct: Mon to Fri 11–5, Sat & Sun 10.30–5.30
- £ Free. Parking £2, incl. NT members (Moyle District Council car park)
- 🛍 Open as Visitor Centre
- ♿ Parking access close to buildings; mini bus with hoist for transport to Giant's Causeway during season; ramps to tea-room & Visitor Centre; WC
- ☕ Lunch, tea, snacks in tea-room at Visitor Centre (closes 6.15 in July & Aug)
- 🏫 Pre-booked school visits welcome especially those involved in the Cross-Community Contact Scheme. Activity trail. Coastal Guardians Scheme
- 🐕 On leads only, outdoors
- ➡ On B146 Causeway–Dunseverick road [C945438] *Bus:* Ulsterbus 138 from Coleraine (passing NIR Coleraine Stn & connecting with trains from Belfast Central Stn); 172 Ballycastle–Portrush (tel. (0265) 43334) *Station:* Portrush 8m

GRAY'S PRINTING PRESS 🏠 🅻ᴛ ❌

49 Main Street, Strabane, Co. Tyrone BT82 8AU (0504) 884094

An 18th-century printing press, shop and stationers. It may have been here that John Dunlap, the printer of the American Declaration of Independence and James Wilson, grandfather of President Woodrow Wilson, learned their trade. There is a collection of 19th-century hand printing machines, NT information in the stationer's shop and 'Power of Print' audio visual display

- 🅾 **Press:** April to end Sept: daily except Thur, Sun & BH 2–5.30. At other times by prior arrangement
- £ £1.40, children 70p. Parties £1. Public car park 100yds. Guided tours by arrangement
- 🛍 Shop (not NT) open all year same days as Press 9–1 & 2–5.30
- ♿ Access to shop and audio visual display only
- ☕ In town, not NT
- 🏫 Pre-booked school visits welcome, especially those involved in the Cross-Community Contact Scheme

NORTHERN IRELAND

→ [H345977] *Bus:* Ulsterbus Express 273 Belfast–Londonderry (passing close NIR Londonderry Stn), alight Strabane town centre; few min. walk (tel. (0504) 382393)

HEZLETT HOUSE

107 Sea Road, Castlerock, Coleraine, Co. Londonderry BT51 4TW (0265) 848567

A 17th-century thatched house, with an interesting cruck truss roof construction. Furnished in late Victorian style. Small museum of farm implements

- Easter (1–5 April): daily 1–5. April, May, June & Sept: Sat, Sun & BH only 1–5. July & Aug: daily, except Tues 1–5. Guided tours. Parties must book in advance (max. number in house 15 at any one time)

- £1.40, children 70p. Parties £1. Parties outside normal opening hours £1.80. Cycles can be parked at side of house

  Note: Hezlett now has WCs

- Access to ground floor only
- Pre-booked school groups welcome
- In garden only, on leads

→ 5m W of Coleraine on Coleraine–Downhill coast road A2 [C772349] *Bus:* Ulsterbus 134 Coleraine–Limavady, alight Liffock crossroads few minutes walk (tel. (0265) 43334) *Station:* Castlerock ¾m

MOUNT STEWART HOUSE, GARDEN & TEMPLE OF THE WINDS

Newtownards, Co. Down BT22 2AD (02477) 88387 or 88487

A fascinating 18th-century house with 19th-century additions, where Lord Castlereagh grew up. The gardens were largely created by Edith, wife of the 7th Marquess of Londonderry, with an unrivalled collection of plants, colourful parterres and magnificent vistas. The Temple of the Winds, James 'Athenian' Stuart's banqueting hall of 1785, overlooks Strangford Lough

- **House:** Easter (1–10 April): daily 1–6. April & Oct: Sat & Sun 1–6; May to end Sept: daily except Tues 1–6. Last tour 5. **Garden:** April to end Sept: daily 10.30–6; Oct: Sat & Sun only 10.30–6. **Temple:** As house but open 2–5

- House, Garden and Temple £3.30, children £1.65. Parties £2.60. Parties outside normal opening hours £4.30. Garden (incl. Temple when open) £2.70, children £1.35. Parties £2. Parties outside normal opening hours £3.70. Temple only 90p. Parking 300yds

- Open 1.30–5.30 same days as house and Sun until until 6. BH open 1–6
- Access to ground floor of house and large parts of garden; restaurant accessible; wheelchairs available. Disabled people may be set down at house; WCs. Powered buggy available

297

NORTHERN IRELAND

- Scented plants
- Light refreshments and teas same times as shop
- Baby changing facilities
- Pre-booked school groups welcome, especially those involved in the Cross Community Contact Scheme. Teacher's pack
- Seasonal guided walks, craft fairs & band concerts. Tel. for details
- On leads only
- 15m E of Belfast A20 Newtownards–Portaferry road, 5m SE of Newtownards [J553695] *Bus:* Ulsterbus 9, 10 Belfast–Portaferry (passing close Belfast Central Stn) to within ¼m (tel. (0247) 812391/2) *Station:* Bangor 10m

PATTERSON'S SPADE MILL

Antrim Rd, Templepatrick, Co. Antrim BT39 0AP (0238) 510721

The last surviving water driven spade mill in Ireland. Spades were made here until 1990 and all the original equipment has been fully restored. There are demonstrations of spade making during normal opening hours

- Easter (1–5 April): daily 2–6pm, April, May & Sept: Sat, Sun & BHs only, 2–6; June, end of Aug: daily except Tues 2–6
- £2.50; children £1.25; groups £1.75. Parties outside normal opening hours £3
- Ramp gives access to viewing platform. WC in reception area
- [J263/856] 2 miles south of Templepatrick on Antrim to Belfast Rd (A6) *Bus:* Ulsterbus 120 Belfast to Ballymena (passing close to NIR Belfast Cental & Antrim stations): alight Templepatrick (tel. (0232) 333000/320574) *Station:* Antrim 8m

ROWALLANE GARDEN

Saintfield, Ballynahinch, Co. Down BT24 7LH (0238) 510131

A 52-acre garden, with daffodils and rhododendrons in spring, summer flowering trees and shrubs and herbaceous plants, fuchsias and shrub roses in the Wall Garden. The garden also includes a national collection of Penstemons, and the rock garden with primula, meconopsis, heathers and dwarf shrubs is interesting throughout the year. There are several areas of natural wild flowers to attract butterflies

- 1 April to end Oct: daily (weekdays 10.30–6; weekends 2–6); Nov to end March 1994: daily except Sat & Sun 10.30–5. Closed 25, 26 Dec & 1 Jan
- Easter to end Oct £2.30, children £1.15. Parties £1.60; outside normal opening hours £2.80. Nov to end March 1994 £1.20, children 60p, parties 80p. Parking on N side of garden

NORTHERN IRELAND

- Easter (1–5 April): daily 2–6. April & Sept: Sat & Sun only 2–6. May to end Aug: daily 2–6
- Majority of garden accessible; wheelchair available
- Light refreshments, open as shop, above
- **E** Seasonal guided walks; midsummer concert; Yuletide Market. Tel. for details
- Must be kept on leads
- 11m SE of Belfast, 1m S of Saintfield, W of the Downpatrick road (A7) [J412581] *Bus:* Ulsterbus 15 Belfast–Downpatrick (passing close NIR Belfast Central Stn) (tel. (0396) 612384)

SPRINGHILL

20 Springhill Road, Moneymore, Magherafelt, Co. Londonderry BT45 7NQ
(064 87) 48210

A 17th-century 'Planter' house with 18th- and 19th-century additions. Springhill was the home of ten generations of a family which arrived from Ayrshire in the 17th century, and the house contains family furniture, a refurbished nursery, paintings, ornaments, curios and 18th-century hand blocked wallpaper. Outbuildings house an extensive costume collection, and there are walled gardens and woodland walks

- Easter (1–5 April): daily 2–6; April, May, June & Sept: Sat, Sun & BH 2–6; July & Aug: daily except Thur 2–6
- **£** £2.20, children £1.10. Parties £1.60. Parties outside normal opening hours £2.80. Parking 40yds
- Shop open as house
- Access to all ground floor rooms; special car parking at rear of house and adjacent to costume museum; access to small sales point by arrangement with guiding staff; picnic area accessible; WC.
- Herb garden
- Light refreshments in Servants' Hall, open as house. Picnic areas in garden and woodland
- Changing facilities toy collection; children's costumes and activities. Play area
- Pre-booked school groups welcome, especially those involved in the Cross-Community Contact Scheme. Study centre; teacher's pack and pupil worksheets. Key Stage 1 & 2 tours available
- **E** Children's & family events during the season. Tel. for details
- In grounds on leads
- 1m from Moneymore on Moneymore–Coagh road (B18) [H866828] *Bus:* Ulsterbus 110/20 Belfast–Cookstown (passing close NIR Antrim Stn), alight Moneymore Village, ¾m (tel. (0648) 32218)

REFER TO OPENING PAGES FOR GENERAL INFORMATION

NORTHERN IRELAND

TEMPLETOWN MAUSOLEUM

Templepatrick, Ballyclare, Co. Antrim (Regional Office (0238) 510721)

Built in 1783 by Robert Adam in memory of the Hon. Arthur Upton

- All year during daylight hours
- Free. No WCs
- Must be kept on lead
- In Castle Upton graveyard at Templepatrick on Belfast–Antrim road (A6) [J228859] *Bus:* Ulsterbus 120 Belfast–Ballymena (passing close NIR Belfast Central & Antrim Stns); alight Templepatrick village, few min. walk (tel. (0232) 333000 or 320574) *Station:* Antrim 6m

WELLBROOK BEETLING MILL

20 Wellbrook Road, Corkhill, Cookstown, Co. Tyrone BT80 9RY
(064 87) 51735/51715

A hammer mill powered by water for beetling – the final process in linen manufacture. Original machinery is in working order. The mill is situated in attractive glen, with wooded walks along the Ballinderry river and by the mill race

- Easter (1–5 April): daily 2–6. April, May, June & Sept: Sat, Sun & BH only 2–6. July & Aug: daily, except Tues 2–6
- £1.40, children 70p. Parties £1. Pre-booked parties outside normal opening hours £1.80. Parking. For information contact the Custodian (see tel. above)
- Shop open as Mill
- 'Touch and Sound' tour can be provided for visually handicapped visitors
- Pre-booked school visits welcome, especially those involved in the Cross-Community Contact Scheme. Key Stage 2 tour available based on technology & change in Victorian times
- In grounds only, on leads
- 4m W of Cookstown, ½m off Cookstown Omagh road (A505), from Cookstown turn right at Kildress Parish Church [H750792] or follow Orritor Road (A53) to avoid town centre *Bus:* Ulsterbus 90 from Cookstown, with connections from Belfast (passing close NIR Antrim Stn) (tel. (0648) 32218)

REFER TO OPENING PAGES FOR GENERAL INFORMATION

Index

(Properties only mentioned in the general Coast and Countryside sections are not included)

A la Ronde 91
Aberconwy House 278–9
Aberdulais Falls 287
Acorn Bank Garden 73
Alfriston Clergy House 227
Angel Corner 211
Anglesey Abbey 40–1
Antony 61
Ardress House 291
The Argory 291–2
Arlington Court 92
Ascott 32
Ashdown House 188
Ashleworth Tithe Barn 116
Ashridge Estate 131–2
Attingham Park 192
Avebury 249
Avebury Manor 249–50

Baddesley Clinton 241
Balston Collection 246
Barrington Court 197–8
Basildon Park 30
Bateman's 227–8
Bath Assembly Rooms 24
Beatrix Potter Gallery 73
Beatrix Potter's Lake District 74
Belton House 152
Bembridge Windmill 135
Beningbrough Hall 258–9
Benthall Hall 193
Berrington Hall 126
Biddulph Grange Garden 205
Bishop's Gate 294–5
Black Glen 294–5
Blakeney Point 167
Blewcoat School 157
Blickling Hall 167–8
Boarstall Duck Decoy 32–3
Boarstall Tower 33
Bodiam Castle 228–9

Bodnant Garden 279
Bourne Mill 112
Box Hill 217–8
Bradley 92–3
Braithwaite Hall 259
Brancaster 168–9
Bredon Barn 126
Brownsea Island 105–6
Buckingham Chantry Chapel 33
Buckland Abbey 93–4
Buscot Old Parsonage 189
Buscot Park 189

Calke Abbey 82–3
Canons Ashby House 173–4
Carding Mill Valley 193–4
Carlyle's House 157
Cartmel Priory Gatehouse 74
Castle Coole 292
Castle Drogo 94
Castle Ward 293
Charlecote Park 241–2
Chartwell 138–9
Chedworth Roman Villa 116
Cherryburn 178
Chirk Castle 267–8
The Church House 95
Cilgerran Castle 272
Clandon Park 218–9
Claremont Landscape Garden 219–20
Claydon House 33–4
Clevedon Court 24–5
Cliveden 34–5
Clouds Hill 106
Clumber Park 184–5
Coggeshall Grange Barn 113
Colby Woodland Garden 273

Coleridge Cottage 198
Coleton Fishacre Garden 95
Compton Castle 95–6
Conwy Suspension Bridge 280
Corfe Castle 106–7
Cornish Engines 62
Cotehele 63–4
Coughton Court 243
The Courts (Garden) 250
Cragside House, Garden & Grounds 178–9
Croft Castle 127
Crom Estate 294
Crown Liquor Saloon 294
Cwmmau Farmhouse 127

Dalton Castle 75
Dinefwr Park 273
Dolaucothi Gold Mines 274
Dorneywood Garden 35
Downhill Castle 294–5
Dudmaston 194–5
Dunham Massey 47–8
Dunstanburgh Castle 180
Dunster Castle 198–9
Dunster Watermill 199
Dunwich Heath 211
Dyrham Park 25

East Riddlesden Hall 265–6
Eastbury Manor House 157
Emmetts Garden 139–40
Erddig 268–9

Farnborough Hall 243–4
Farne Islands 180–1
Felbrigg Hall 169–70
Fell Foot Park 75
Fenton House 158
Flatford: Bridge Cottage 212
The Fleece Inn 128
Florence Court 295
Formby 164
Fountains Abbey 259–61
Fox Talbot Museum 252

INDEX

Fyne Court 200

Gawthorpe Hall 148
George Inn 158
Giant's Causeway 296
Gibside 238
Glendurgan Garden 64
Godalming Navigation 223
Grantham House 153
Gray's Printing Press 296-7
Great Chalfield Manor 250-1
Great Coxwell Barn 189-90
The Greyfriars 128
Greys Court 190
Gumber Bothy, Gumber Farm 232
Gunby Hall 153-4

Hadrian's Wall 181-2
Hailes Abbey 117
Ham House 158-9
Hanbury Hall 128-9
Hardwick Hall 83-4
Hardy's Cottage 107-8
Hare Hill 48
Hatchlands Park 220-1
Hatfield Forest 113
Hawford Dovecote 129
Hawkshead Courthouse 75-6
Hezlett House 297
Hidcote Manor Garden 117-8
Hill Top 76
Hinton Ampner 121
Horsey Windpump 171
Horton Court 26
Houghton Mill 41-2
Housesteads Fort 181-2
Hughenden Manor 35-6

Ickworth 212-3
Ightham Mote 140-1
Ilam Hall Country Park 206

Kedleston Hall 84-5
Keld Chapel 76

Killerton 96-7
King Alfred's Tower 254-5
King John's Hunting Lodge 200
King's Head 36
Kingston Lacy 108
Kinwarton Dovecote 244
Kinver Edge 206-7
Knightshayes Court 97-8
Knole 141

Lacock Abbey 251
Lamb House 229
Lanhydrock 64-5
Lavenham Guildhall 213-4
Lawrence House 65
Leith Hill Tower 221
Letocetum (Wall Roman Site) 209
Levant Steam Engine 62-3
Lindisfarne Castle 182
Lindsey House 159
Little Clarendon 252
Little Fleece Bookshop 118
Little Moreton Hall 48-9
Llywelyn Cottage 280
Long Crendon Courthouse 36
Long Mynd 193-4
Longshaw Estate 85-6
Loughwood Meeting House 98
Lower Brockhampton 129
Lundy 98-9
Lydford Gorge 99
Lyme Park 49-50
Lytes Cary Manor 200-1
Lyveden New Bield 175

Maister House 133
Marker's Cottage 100
Max Gate 109
Melford Hall 214
Middle Littleton Tithe Barn 130
Mompesson House 252-3
Monk's House 229

Montacute House 201
Morden Hall Park 160
Morville Hall 195
Moseley Old Hall 207
Mottisfont Abbey Garden 121-2
Mottistone Manor Garden 135-6
Moulton Hall 261
Mount Grace Priory 261-2
Mount Stewart 297-8
Mussenden Temple 294-5

Needles Old Battery 136
Nether Alderley Mill 50
Newark Park 118
Nostell Priory 266
Nunnington Hall 262
Nymans Garden 233

Oakhurst Cottage 221
The Old Bakery 100
The Old Manor 86
The Old Mill 100
Old Soar Manor 142
Old Town Hall, Newtown 136
Ormesby Hall 55
Osterley Park 160-1
Overbecks Museum & Garden 101
Owletts 142
Oxburgh Hall 171

Packwood House 244-5
Parke 101-102
Patterson's Spade Mill 298
Paycocke's 114
Peckover House 42
Penrhyn Castle 280-1
Petworth House 233-4
Petworth Park 234
Philipps House 253
Pitstone Windmill 36
Plas Newydd 281-2
Plas-yn-Rhiw 282
Polesden Lacey 222-3
Powis Castle 285
Priest's House (Easton) 175

INDEX

Priest's House (Muchelney) 202
Princes Risborough Manor House 37
Priory Cottages 190

Quarry Bank Mill 51-2
Quebec House 142

Rainham Hall 161
Ramsey Abbey Gatehouse 43
Rayleigh Castle 114
Rhossili Visitor Centre 288
Rievaulx Terrace & Temples 262-3
River Wey Navigation 223
'Roman' Bath 162
Rowallane Garden 298-9
Rufford Old Hall 149
Runnymede 224

St George's Guildhall 172
St John's Jerusalem Garden 143
St Michael's Mount 65-66
Saltram 102
Sandham Memorial Chapel 122-3
Scotney Castle Garden 143
Segontium 282-3
Shalford Mill 224
Shaw's Corner 132
Sheffield Park Garden 230
Sheringham Park 172
Shugborough Estate 208-9
Shute Barton 103
Sissinghurst Garden 144
Sizergh Castle 77
Skenfrith Castle 276
Smallhythe Place 144-5
Snowshill Manor 118-9
Souter Lighthouse 238-9
South Foreland Lighthouse 145

South Quay, Great Yarmouth 170
Speke Hall 164-5
Springhill 299
Sprivers Garden 145
Stagshaw Garden 77
Stainsby Mill 83-4
Standen 234-5
Staunton Harold Church 150
Steam Yacht Gondola 78
Stembridge Tower Mill 202
Stephenson's Birthplace 181
Stoke-sub-Hamdon Priory 202
Stoneacre 146
Stonehenge Down 253-4
Stourhead 254-5
Stowe Landscape Gardens 37-8
Mr Straw's House 186
Studland Beach & Nature Reserve 109
Studley Royal 259-61
Styal Country Park 52
Sudbury Hall & Museum of Childhood 86-8
Sutton House 162

Tattershall Castle 154-5
Tatton Park 52-3
Temple of the Winds, Mount Stewart 297-8
Templetown Mausoleum 300
Theatre Royal 215
Thorington Hall 215
Tintagel Old Post Office 66
Tintinhull House Garden 203
Townend 79
Town Walls Tower 195
Treasurer's House (Martock) 203
Treasurer's House (York) 262-3
Trelissick Garden 67
Trengwainton Garden 67-8

Trerice 68
Tudor Merchant's House 274
Tudor Yeoman's House 146
Tye Mawr Wybrnant 283
Ty'n-y-coed 283

Ulverscroft Nature Reserve 150
Uppark 235
Upton House 245

The Vyne 123-4

Waddesdon Manor 38-9
Wakehurst Place 236
Wallington 183
Washington Old Hall 239
Watersmeet House 103
The Weir 130
Wellbrook Beetling Mill 300
Westbury College Gatehouse 26
Westbury Court Garden 119
West Green Garden 124
West Pennard Court Barn 203
Westwood Manor 255
West Wycombe Park 39
West Wycombe Village & Hill 39
Whitegates Cottage 154
Wichenford Dovecote 130
Wicken Fen 43
Wightwick Manor 247
Wilderhope Manor 195
Willington Dovecote & Stables 28
Wimpole Hall 44-5
Wimpole Home Farm 45
Winchester City Mill 124
Winkworth Arboretum 224-5
Winster Market House 88
Witley Common 225
Wool House 146
Woolsthorpe Manor 155
Wordsworth House 79

303

IMPORTANT NOTES FOR NATIONAL TRUST MEMBERS

Regional Offices

1. **Cornwall:** Lanhydrock, Bodmin PL30 4DE (tel. (0208) 74281-4)

2. **Devon:** Killerton House, Broadclyst, Exeter EX5 3LE (tel. (0392) 881691 Information Office: (0208) 74287

3. **Wessex** *(Avon, Dorset, Somerset, Wiltshire)* Eastleigh Court, Bishopstrow, Warminster, Wiltshire BA12 9HW (tel. (0985) 847777)

4. **Southern** *(includes Hampshire, the Isle of Wight, South-Western Greater London, Surrey and West Sussex)* Polesden Lacey, Dorking, Surrey RH5 6BD (tel. (0372) 53401)

5. **Kent & East Sussex** *(includes South-Eastern Greater London),* The Estate Office, Scotney Castle, Lamberhurst, Tunbridge Wells, Kent TN3 8JN (tel. (0892) 890651)

6. **East Anglia** *(Cambridgeshire, Essex, Norfolk, Suffolk)* Blickling, Norwich NR11 6NF (tel. (0263) 733471)

7. **Thames & Chilterns** *(Buckinghamshire, Bedfordshire, Berkshire, Hertfordshire, London north of the Thames, and Oxfordshire)* Hughenden Manor, High Wycombe, Bucks HP14 4LA (tel. (0494) 28051)

8. **Severn** *(Gloucestershire, Hereford & Worcester, Warwickshire, part of West Midlands)* Mythe End House, Tewkesbury, Glos GL20 6EB (tel. (0684) 850051)

9. **South Wales:** *(Dyfed, Gwent, West Glamorgan, southern part of Powys)* The King's Head, Bridge Street, Llandeilo, Dyfed SA19 6BN (tel. (0558) 822800)

10. **North Wales:** *(Clwyd, Gwynedd, northern part of Powys)* Trinity Square, Llandudno, Gwynedd LL30 2DE (tel. (0492) 860123)

11. **Mercia** *(Cheshire, Merseyside, Shropshire, Greater Manchester, most of Staffordshire, part of West Midlands)* Attingham Park, Shrewsbury, Shropshire SY4 4TP (tel. (074 377) 343)

12. **East Midlands** *(Derbyshire, Leicestershire, Lincolnshire, Northamptonshire, Nottinghamshire, South Humberside, parts of Cheshire, Greater Manchester, Staffordshire, South Yorkshire and West Yorkshire)* Clumber Park Stableyard, Worksop, Notts S80 3BE (tel. (0909) 486411)

13. **Yorkshire** *(includes North, South and West Yorkshire, Cleveland, and North Humberside)* Goddards, 27 Tadcaster Road, Dringhouses, York YO2 2QG (tel. (0904) 702021)

14. **North-West** *(Cumbria and Lancashire)* The Hollens, Grasmere, Ambleside, Cumbria LA22 9QZ (tel. (05394) 35599)

15. **Northumbria** *(Durham, Northumberland, and Tyne & Wear)* Scots' Gap, Morpeth, Northumberland NE61 4EG (tel. (067 074) 691)

16. **Northern Ireland:** Rowallane House, Saintfield, Ballynahinch, Co. Down BT24 7LH (tel. (0238) 510721)